ACCA
STUDY TEXT

Paper 1.3

Managing people

BPP's NEW STUDY TEXTS FOR ACCA's NEW SYLLABUS

- Targeted to the syllabus and **study guide**

- Quizzes and questions to check your understanding

- Clear layout and style designed to save you time

- Plenty of exam-style questions

- Chapter Roundups and summaries to help revision

- Mind Maps to integrate the key points

BPP Publishing
February 2001

First edition February 2001

ISBN 0 7517 0727 9

British Library Cataloguing-in-Publication Data
A catalogue record for this book
is available from the British Library

Published by

BPP Publishing Ltd
Aldine House, Aldine Place
London W12 8AW

www.bpp.com

Printed in Great Britain by Ashford Colour Press

We are grateful to the Association of Chartered Certified Accountants for permission to reproduce past examination questions and questions from the pilot paper. The answers have been prepared by BPP Publishing Limited.

THE BPP STUDY TEXT

Aims of this Study Text

To provide you with the knowledge and understanding, skills and application techniques that you need if you are to be successful in your exams

This Study Text has been written around the **Managing People** syllabus.

- It is **comprehensive**. It covers the syllabus content. No more, no less.

- It is written at the **right level**. Each chapter is written with the ACCA's **study guide** in mind.

- It is targeted to the **exam**. We have taken account of the **pilot paper**, questions put to the examiners at the recent ACCA conference and the assessment methodology.

To allow you to study in the way that best suits your learning style and the time you have available, by following your personal Study Plan (see page (ix))

You may be studying at home on your own until the date of the exam, or you may be attending a full-time course. You may like to (and have time to) read every word, or you may prefer to (or only have time to) skim-read and devote the remainder of your time to question practice. Wherever you fall in the spectrum, you will find the BPP Study Text meets your needs in designing and following your personal Study Plan.

To tie in with the other components of the BPP Effective Study Package to ensure you have the best possible chance of passing the exam (see page (vi))

BPP
PUBLISHING

Recommended period of use	Elements of the BPP Effective Study Package
Three to twelve months before the exam	**Study Text** Use the Study Text to acquire knowledge, understanding, skills and the ability to use application techniques.
One to six months before the exam	**Practice & Revision Kit** Attempt the tutorial questions which are provided for each topic area in the Kit. Then try the numerous examination questions, for which there are realistic suggested solutions prepared by BPP's own authors.
From three months before the exam until the last minute	**Passcards** Work through these short, memorable notes which are focused on what is most likely to come up in the exam you will be sitting.
One to six months before the exam	**Success Tapes** These cover the vital elements of your syllabus in less than 90 minutes per subject with these audio cassettes. Each tape also contains exam hints to help you fine tune your strategy.
Three to twelve months before the exam	**Breakthrough Videos** Use a Breakthrough Video to supplement your Study Text. They give you clear tuition on key exam subjects and allow you the luxury of being able to pause or repeat sections until you have fully grasped the topic.

HELP YOURSELF STUDY FOR YOUR ACCA EXAMS

Exams for professional bodies such as ACCA are very different from those you have taken at college or university. You will be under **greater time pressure before** the exam - as you may be combining your study with work as well as in the exam room. There are many different ways of learning and so the BPP Study Text offers you a number of different tools to help you through. Here are some hints and tips: they are not plucked out of the air, but **based on research and experience**. (You don't need to know that long-term memory is in the same part of the brain as emotions and feelings - but it's a fact anyway.)

The right approach

1   **The right attitude**

Believe in yourself	Yes, there is a lot to learn. Yes, it is a challenge. But thousands have succeeded before and you can too.
Remember why you're doing it	Studying might seem a grind at times, but you are doing it for a reason: to advance your career.

2   **The right focus**

Read through the Syllabus and Study guide	These tell you what you are expected to know and are supplemented by Exam Focus Points in the text.
Study the Exam Paper section	The pilot paper is likely to be a reasonable guide of what you should expect in the exam.

3   **The right method**

The big picture	You need to grasp the detail - but keeping in mind how everything fits into the big picture will help you understand better. • The **Introduction** of each chapter puts the material in context. • The **Syllabus content**, **Study guide** and **Exam focus points** show you what you need to **grasp**. • **Mind Maps** show the links and key issues in key topics.
In your own words	To absorb the information (and to practise your written communication skills), it helps **put it into your own words**. • **Take notes.** • Answer the **questions** in each chapter. As well as helping you absorb the information you will practise your written communication skills, which become increasingly important as you progress through your ACCA exams. • Draw **mind maps**. We have some examples. • Try 'teaching' to a colleague or friend.

BPP
PUBLISHING

Give yourself cues to jog your memory	The BPP Study Text uses **bold** to **highlight key points** and **icons** to identify key features, such as **Exam focus points** and **Key terms.** • Try **colour coding** with a highlighter pen. • Write **key points** on cards.

4   **The right review**

Review, review, review	It is a **fact** that regularly reviewing a topic in summary form can **fix it in your memory**. Because **review** is so important, the BPP Study Text helps you to do so in many ways. • **Chapter roundups** summarise the key points in each chapter. Use them to recap each study session. • The **Quick quiz** is another review technique to ensure that you have grasped the essentials. • Go through the **Examples** in each chapter a second or third time.

Suggested study sequence

Tackle the chapters in the order you find them in the Study Text. Taking into account your individual learning style, you could follow this sequence.

Key study steps	Activity
Step 1 **Topic list**	Each numbered topic is a numbered section in the chapter.
Step 2 **Introduction**	This gives you the **big picture** in terms of the **context** of the chapter. The content is referenced to the **Study Guide**, and **Exam Guidance** shows how the topic is likely to be examined. In other words, it sets your **objectives for study.**
Step 3 **Explanations**	Proceed methodically through the chapter, reading each section thoroughly and making sure you understand.
Step 4 **Key terms and Exam focus points**	• **Key terms** can often earn you *easy marks* if you state them clearly and correctly in an appropriate exam answer (and they are indexed at the back of the text). • **Exam focus points** give you a good idea of how we think the examiner intends to examine certain topics.
Step 5 **Note taking**	Take brief notes if you wish, avoiding the temptation to copy out too much.
Step 6 **Examples**	Follow each through to its solution very carefully.
Step 7 **Case examples**	Study each one, and try to add flesh to them from your own experience - they are designed to show how the topics you are studying come alive (and often come unstuck) in the real world.
Step 8 **Questions**	Make a very good attempt at each one.
Step 9 **Answers**	Check yours against ours, and make sure you understand any discrepancies.
Step 10 **Chapter roundup**	Work through it very carefully, to make sure you have grasped the major points it is highlighting.
Step 11 **Quick quiz**	When you are happy that you have covered the chapter, use the **Quick quiz** to check how much you have remembered of the topics covered.

Key study steps	Activity
Step 12 **Question(s) in the Question bank**	Either at this point, or later when you are thinking about revising, make a full attempt at the **Question(s)** suggested at the very end of the chapter. You can find these at the end of the Study Text, along with the **Answers** so you can see how you did. We highlight those that are introductory, and those which are of the standard you would expect to find in an exam.

Developing your personal Study Plan

Preparing a Study Plan (and sticking closely to it) is one of the key elements in learning success.

Step 1. How do you learn?

First you need to be aware of your style of learning. There are four typical learning styles. Consider yourself in the light of the following descriptions and work out which you fit most closely. You can then plan to follow the key study steps in the sequence suggested.

Learning styles	Characteristics	Sequence of key study steps in the BPP Study Text
Theorist	Seeks to understand principles before applying them in practice	1, 2, 3, 6, 7, 8, 6, 8/9, 10, 11, 12 (5 continuous)
Reflector	Seeks to observe phenomena, thinks about them and then chooses to act	
Activist	Prefers to deal with practical, active problems; does not have much patience with theory	1, 2, 8/9 (read through), 6, 7, 4, 10, 3, 8/9 (full attempt), 11, 12 (5 continuous)
Pragmatist	Prefers to study only if a direct link to practical problems can be seen; not interested in theory for its own sake	8/9 (read through), 2, 4, 6, 7, 10, 1, 3, 8/9 (full attempt), 11, 12 (5 continuous)

Step 2. How much time do you have?

Work out the time you have available per week, given the following.

- The standard you have set yourself
- The time you need to set aside later for work on the Practice & Revision Kit and Passcards
- The other exam(s) you are sitting
- Very importantly, practical matters such as work, travel, exercise, sleep and social life

Note your time available in box A.

A

Step 3. Allocate your time

- Take the time you have available per week for this Study Text shown in box A, multiply it by the number of weeks available and insert the result in box B.

B

- Divide the figure in Box B by the number of chapters in this text and insert the result in box C.

C

Step 4. Implement

Set about studying each chapter in the time shown in box C, following the key study steps in the order suggested by your particular learning style.

This is your personal **Study Plan**.

Short of time: *Skim study technique?*

You may find you simply do not have the time available to follow all the key study steps for each chapter, however you adapt them for your particular learning style. If this is the case, follow the **skim study** technique below (the icons in the Study Text will help you to do this).

- Study the chapters in the order you find them in the Study Text.

- For each chapter, follow the key study steps 1-2, and then skim-read through step 3. Jump to step 10, and then go back to step 4. Follow through steps 6 and 7, and prepare outline answers to questions (steps 8/9). Try the Quick quiz (step 11), following up any items you can't answer, then do a plan for the Question (step 12), comparing it against our answers. You should probably still follow step 5 (note-taking), although you may decide simply to rely on the BPP Passcards for this.

Moving on...

However you study, when you are ready to embark on the practice and revision phase of the BPP Effective Study Package, you should still refer back to this Study Text, both as a source of **reference** (you should find the list of key terms and the index particularly helpful for this) and as a **refresher** (the Chapter roundups and Quick quizzes help you here).

And remember to keep careful hold of this Study Text - you will find it invaluable in your work.

BPP PUBLISHING

SYLLABUS

To develop knowledge and understanding of the techniques, processes and procedures which hare required to ensure the efficient and effective use and deployment of human resources, and consequently to use the human resource to the fullest possible benefit of the organisation.

Objectives

On completion of this paper candidates should be able to:

- identify, understand and explain the complex interpersonal relationships that exist within organisations

- appreciate the relationship between theory and practice

- understand the nature, processes and procedures of people management

- explain the principles of successful team performance and the need to plan, monitor and evaluate team based work activities

- investigate future personnel requirements and describe recruitment and selection procedures

- understand and describe the principles of motivation

- understand and describe the role and process of employee development

- understand the need for clear and precise communication

- explain the principles of effective counselling

- describe the elements of disciplinary and grievance procedures

Position of the paper in the overall syllabus

The paper is concerned with an understanding of people management and the techniques involved. The paper is constructed in such a way that it provides a broad introduction to the problems and opportunities involved in managing people. It is intended to cultivate an understanding of the importance of good practice in human resource management.

The professional accountant is often in a management position and thus fulfils another role, that of the management of the human resource. It is important therefore that the professional accountant understands issues of management and human resources.

Whilst there are no pre-requisites for this paper, candidates will be expected to demonstrate an understanding of the theory and issues involved in human resource management and to display appropriate writing skills in answering the examination paper.

Managing People is a pre-requisite for paper **3.5 Strategic Business Planning and Development**, where many of the ideas introduced are developed further.

It should also be noted that although the course follows this structure, the nature of the syllabus means that there will often be overlap between the individual topics.

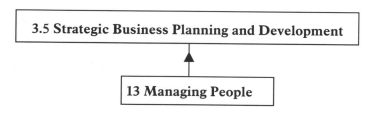

SYLLABUS

1 Management and team development

(a) The organisation of work

    (i) The need for formal organisations
    (ii) Organisational types and differences

(b) The role of management

    (i) Modern management writers
    (ii) Classical theories of management

(c) The role of the manager

    (i) The role of the manager in the organisation of work
    (ii) The responsibilities of the manager

(d) Individual and group behaviour

    (i) Organisational culture
    (ii) Groups and teams
    (iii) Perception and role theory

(e) Team management

    (i) The need for teams
    (ii) Team construction
    (iii) Team and group differences

(f) Objective setting

    (i) The need for objectives
    (ii) Profit and other objectives

(g) Authority, responsibility and delegation

    (i) Organisational structure
    (ii) Classical and modern approaches to structure
    (iii) Authority, responsibility and delegation

(h) Standard setting and performance management

    (i) Work standards and indicators
    (ii) Performance related pay

2 Recruitment and selection

(a) The recruitment and selection process

    (i) Process, roles and responsibilities
    (ii) Assessment criteria

(b) Effective recruitment

    (i) Recruitment and selection plan
    (ii) Process of recruitment
    (iii) Use of media

(c)   The job description and personnel specification

    (i)   Job description
    (ii)   Personnel specification

(d)   Job analysis

    (i)   Purpose of analysis
    (ii)   methods of analysis

(e)   Selection methods

    (i)   appropriate methods
    (ii)   usefulness of methods

(f)   The selection interview
    (i)   purpose
    (ii)   skills involved
    (iii)   importance of the selection process

(g)   Equal opportunities and the management of diversity

    (i)   Equal opportunity issues
    (ii)   Managing diversity

3   Training and development

(a)   The learning process

    (i)   The learning process
    (ii)   The role of management

(b)   Training and development

    (i)   Duties of the training manager
    (ii)   Methods for individual development

(c)   Effective training and development

    (i)   Benefits of training
    (ii)   Training needs analysis
    (iii)   Staff evaluation methods
    (iv)   Management development
    (v)   In-house and external training

(d)   Competence assessment

    (i)   Process and barriers
    (ii)   Staff appraisal
    (iii)   Measures of effectiveness

(e)   Conducting the appraisal interview

    (i)   Management skills involved
    (ii)   Key communication skills

(f)   Individual development

    (i)   Appraisal process and employee development

(g)   Skills development

    (i)   The role of management
    (ii)   The skills development programme

(iii) The mentoring process

(h) The management of health and safety

    (i) Health and safety awareness

4   Motivation and leadership

(a) Motivation, concepts, models and practices

    (i) The key theories of motivation
    (ii) Classical theories
    (iii) Modern theories
    (iv) Reward schemes

(b) Effective leadership

    (i) The nature and importance of leadership
    (ii) Classical theories
    (iii) Modern theories

5   Effective communication practices

(a) Working with people - interpersonal skills

    (i) Interpersonal skills
    (ii) Effective management practice
    (iii) Verbal and non verbal communication

(b) Communication

    (i) The need for communication
    (ii) Communication patterns

(c) the role of counselling

    (i) The role of management
    (ii) Skills of effective counselling

(d) Controlling conflict, grievance and discipline

    (i) Causes of conflict
    (ii) Managing conflict
    (iii) Appropriate procedures
    (iv) Process understanding
    (v) The role of management
    (iv) Appeals

Excluded topics

The syllabus content outlines the area for assessment. No areas of knowledge are specifically excluded from the syllabus.

Key areas of the syllabus

The key topic areas are as follows:

- an understanding of the theory, techniques, processes, procedures and practice of people management and team development

- differentiation of rules, procedures and processes of people management

- training and development, the trained workforce, employee assessment

- the theories of motivation and leadership and their application

- effective communication practices.

Paper 1.3(U)

Managing People
Study Guide

MANAGEMENT AND TEAM DEVELOPMENT

1a The organisation of work

(i) Explain the need for formal organisations.

(ii) Identify organisational types and differences.

2b The role of management

(i) Identify and explain the contribution made by modern writers on management: Drucker, Kanter, Mintzberg, Ouchi, Peters.

(ii) Identify and explain the contribution made by classical writers on management: Fayol, Steward, Taylor, Mayo, Weber.

(iii) Identify the difference between classical and modern theories of management.

(iv) Identify the difference between individual and group contribution to work performance: Schein.

(v) Outline areas of management authority and responsibility.

(vi) List the systems of performance reward for individual and group contribution.

3c The role of the manager

(i) Explain the role of the manager in the organisation of work.

(ii) List the management tasks involved in organising the work of others.

(iii) Illustrate the role of the manager in achieving tasks.

(iv) The responsibilities of the supervisor.

4d Individual and group behaviour

(i) Explain the concept of organisational culture: Anthony, Handy.

(ii) Discuss the differences between individual and group behaviour.

(iii) Outline the contribution of individuals and teams to organisational success.

(iv) Identify individual and team approaches to work.

(v) Understand perception and role theory.

5e Team management

(i) explain the role of the manager in building the team and developing individuals.

(ii) define the purpose of a team.

(iii) outline the composition of successful teams: Beblin, Peters and Waterman.

(iv) Explain the development of a team: Tuckman.

(v) List team buildings tools.

(vi) Examine ways of rewarding a team.

(vii) Identify methods to evaluate team performance.

6f Objective setting

(i) Explain the importance of objective setting.

(ii) Compare and contrast profit and other objectives: Drucker, Cyert and March, Marginalist Theories, Simon.

(iii) Explain the behavioural theories of objective setting.

(iv) Explain the importance of understanding ethics and social responsibility.

(v) Compare and contrast the difference between corporate objectives and personal objectives.

(vi) Illustrate the difference between quantitative and qualitative target setting.

(vii) Outline the management role in identifying performance standards and accountability.

(viii) Identify methods to measure achievement of objectives.

7g Authority, responsibility and delegation

(i) Describe, recognise and understand the importance of organisational structure.

(ii) Classical and modern approaches to organisational structure: Burns and Stalker, Contingency Theory, Fayol, Mintzberg, Trist and Bamforth, Urwick, Weber, Woodwasrd.

(iii) Define the terms authority, responsibility and delegation.

(iv) Explain the term legitimised power: Weber.

(v) Describe the process of determining authority and responsibility.

(vi) Examine the case of responsibility without authority.

8h Standard setting and performance management

(i) Define the term performance management.

(ii) Identify a process for establishing work standards and performance management.

(iii) Outline a method to establish performance indicators.

(iv) Illustrate ways of applying performance management.

(v) Describe management contribution to personal development planning.

(vi) Explain the term performance related pay.

RECRUITMENT AND SELECTION

9a The recruitment and selection process

(i) Explain the importance of effective recruitment and selection to the organisation.

(ii) Define the recruitment and selection process.

(iii) Outline the roles and responsibilities of those involved in the process.

(iv) List the most common reasons for ineffective recruitment and selection.

(v) List and describe criteria against which to assess successful recruitment and selection practices.

10b Effective recruitment

(i) Outline a plan for an effective recruitment process.

(ii) Identify the stages in the recruitment process.

(iii) Compare and contrast the choice of media for job advertising.

(iv) Analyse the purpose and effectiveness of the job application form.

(v) Explain the purpose and usefulness of applicant references.

11c The job description and personnel specification

(i) Outline the purpose and use of a job description and person specification.

(ii) Explain how to devise a job description and personnel specification: Rodgers, Fraser.

(iii) Compare and contrast the purpose of the job description and the person specification.

12d Job analysis

(i) Define the purpose of job analysis.

(ii) Identify methods of job analysis.

(iii) Outline the skills involved in carrying out job analysis.

(iv) Justify the sue of job analysis.

13e Selection methods

(i) List alternative methods of selection.

(ii) Evaluation the usefulness of selection methods.

(iii) Identify those involved in the process of selection.

(iv) Establish the skills involved in successful decision making.

(v) Explain the importance to the organisation of good selection decisions.

14f The selection interview

(i) Outline the purpose of the selection interview.

(ii) Identify who should be involved in selection interviewing.

(iii) Identify the key skills required for selection interviewing.

(iv) List the most common reasons for ineffective interviewing.

(v) Explain the importance of the selection interview in the selection process.

15g Equal opportunities and the management of diversity

(i) Understanding equal opportunities.

(ii) Measuring equal value.

(iii) The legal position.

(iv) The appropriateness of managing diversity in the workplace.

(v) Understanding individual circumstances.

TRAINING AND DEVELOPMENT

16a The learning process

(i) Explain the process of learning in the workplace.

(ii) Describe the ways in which individuals learn: Honey and Momford, Kolb.

(iii) Explain the effect on learning of individual differences.

(iv) Outline the barriers to learning.

(v) Describe the role of management and the organisation in the learning process.

17b Retention, training and development

(i) Explain the importance of training and development to the organisation and the individual.

(ii) Explain the roles and responsibilities of a training manager.

(iii) Compare and contrast the various methods used in developing individuals in the workplace.

18c Effective training and development

(i) List the benefits to the organisation and the individual of effective training and development.

(ii) Explain the methods used to analyse training needs.

(iii) Suggest ways in which training needs can be met.

(iv) Describe methods of staff evaluation and follow-up.

(v) Describe the skills involved in developing staff.

(vi) Explain the development methods available to management.

(vii) Evaluate the effectiveness of in-house and external training courses.

19d Competence assessment

(i) Explain the process of competence assessment.

(ii) Outline the purposes and benefits of staff appraisal in the process.

(iii) Describe the barriers to effective staff appraisal.

(iv) Suggest ways to measure the effectiveness of staff appraisal and the process of assessment.

20e Conducting the appraisal process

(i) Identify the benefits of the appraisal process.

(ii) Identify the management skills involved in the appraisal process.

(iii) Describe the process of preparation of an appraisal interview, including location of interview and pre interview correspondence.

(iv) Identify the key communication skills required to conduct an effective appraisal interview.

(v) Explain the importance of feedback from the appraisal interview.

21f Individual skills and development

(i) Explain the link between the appraisal process and effective employee development.

(ii) Describe the role of the appraisee in the process.

(iii) Suggest ways in which self-development can be part of the process.

(iv) Describe the role of the manager in work based skills development.

(v) Identify the methods used to develop skills.

(vi) Outline how to plan a skills development programme.

(vii) Explain the role of mentoring in the process of skills development.

22g The management of health and safety

(i) Preventative and protective.

(ii) Safety awareness and training.

(iii) Working conditions and hazards.

(iv) The legal context and the obligation of management.

MOTIVATION AND LEADERSHIP

23a Motivation, concepts, models and practices

(i) Outline the key theories of motivation.

(ii) Outline classical and modern theories of motivation: Argyris, Equity theory, Handy, Herzberg, Maslow, McClelland, McGregor, Vroom.

BPP PUBLISHING

(iii) Outline the difference between content and process theories of motivation.

(iv) Describe ways in which management can motivate staff.

(v) Explain the importance of the reward system in the process of motivation.

(vii) Explain the importance of constructive feedback in motivation.

24b Effective leadership

(i) Define the term 'leadership'.

(ii) Define the term 'leadership'.

(iii) Describe the nature and importance of leadership.

(iv) Outline classical and modern theories of leadership: Blake and Mouton, Contingency Theory, Fiedler, Handy, Hersey and Blanchard, Likert, Tannenbaum, Trait Theory, White and Lippit.

(v) Compare and contrast the terms 'leadership' and 'management'.

(vi) Identify the skills of a leader.

EFFECTIVE COMMUNICATION PRACTICES

25a Working with people - interpersonal skills

(i) Define the term 'interpersonal skills'.

(ii) Explain the importance of developing effective working relationships.

(iii) distinguish between verbal and non-verbal forms of communication.

(iv) Compare and contrast the difference between aggressive and assertive behaviour.

(v) Illustrate the link between interpersonal skills and effective management practice.

26b Communication

(i) Explain the importance of formal and informal communication in the workplace.

(ii) Explain communication models.

(iii) Outline the importance to the manager of effective communication.

(iv) Describe the effects of poor communication.

(v) List and describe the attributes of effective communication.

(vi) List the main methods and patterns of communication.

(vii) explain the importance of the process of consultation.

27c The role of counselling

(i) Define counselling in the management context.

(ii) Outline the role of the manager when counselling staff.

(iii) Explain the importance of effective counselling.

(iv) Identify the skills used in the process of effective counselling.

(v) Suggest reasons why the need to counsel a member of staff may arise.

28d Controlling conflict, grievance and discipline

(i) Identify the main causes of conflict within an organisation.

(ii) Outline procedures for managing conflict.

(iii) Outline a suitable framework (both internal and external to the organisation) for dealing with grievance and disciplinary matters.

(iv) Explain the need for effective organisational procedures.

(v) Explain the role of management in respect of disciplinary matters.

(vi) Suggest ways in which the outcome of the disciplinary process should be communicated to the individual concerned.

(vii) Outline the features of an appeals procedure.

THE EXAM PAPER

Approach to examining the syllabus

The examination is a three hour paper constructed in two sections.

Section A consists of a brief scenario with a number of questions totalling 40 marks. Each question carries two marks and all questions must be attempted. Section A is compulsory.

Section B consists of five essay type questions, with one question taken from each of the five topics in the syllabus. Each question carries 15 marks and all candidates must attempt four questions.

There are no calculations involved, and candidates should note that the answers in Section B **must be presented in essay form** (BPP emphasis). Candidates need to show an understanding of the detail of the topic. Candidates should be aware that although the course is made up of a number of discrete topics, examination questions may well require a knowledge of more than one of these topics.

		Number of Marks
Section A	Compulsory scenario question	40
Section B	Choice of 4 out of 5 essay questions (15 marks each)	60
		100

Additional information

The Study Guide provides more detailed guidance on the syllabus.

Analysis of pilot paper

Section A

1   Case study based on recruitment of a new member of staff to an accounts department

Section B

2   Teams and informal groups
3   Job analysis
4   Learning styles
5   Rewards and motivation
6   Communication

BPP PUBLISHING

Part A

Management and team development

ORGANISATIONS

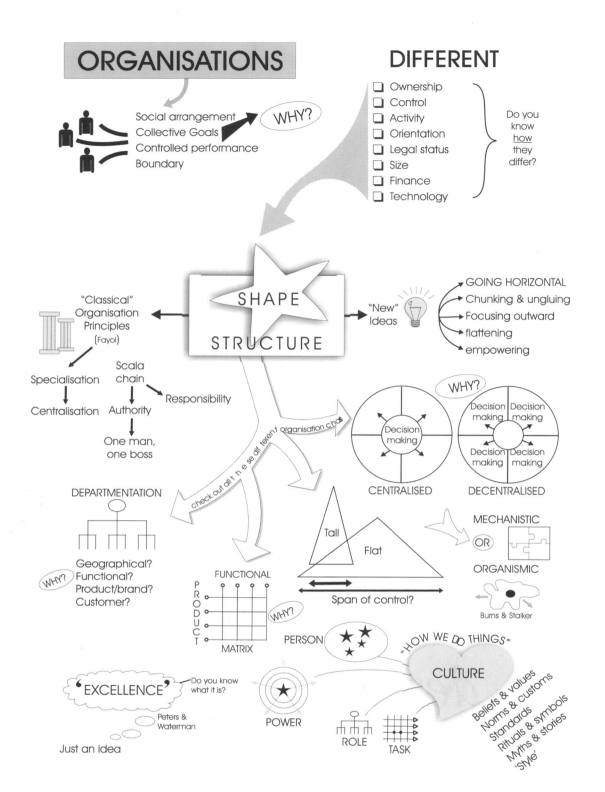

Social arrangement
Collective Goals
Controlled performance
Boundary

WHY?

DIFFERENT

- ☐ Ownership
- ☐ Control
- ☐ Activity
- ☐ Orientation
- ☐ Legal status
- ☐ Size
- ☐ Finance
- ☐ Technology

Do you know <u>how</u> they differ?

SHAPE STRUCTURE

"Classical" Organisation Principles (Fayol)

Specialisation → Centralisation

Scala chain → Authority → One man, one boss

Responsibility

"New" Ideas

→ GOING HORIZONTAL
→ Chunking & ungluing
→ Focusing outward
→ flattening
→ empowering

check out all t h e se dif ferent organisation cha

WHY?

Decision making

CENTRALISED

Decision making — Decision making — Decision making — Decision making — Decision making

DECENTRALISED

MECHANISTIC

OR

ORGANISMIC

Burns & Stalker

DEPARTMENTATION

WHY?
Geographical?
Functional?
Product/brand?
Customer?

FUNCTIONAL

P R O D U C T

MATRIX

WHY?

Tall / Flat

Span of control?

PERSON

"HOW WE DO THINGS"

CULTURE

Beliefs & values
Norms & customs
Standards
Rituals & symbols
Myths & stories
'Style'

'EXCELLENCE'
Do you know what it is?

Peters & Waterman

Just an idea

POWER

ROLE   TASK

Chapter 1

THE ORGANISATION OF WORK

Topic list	Syllabus reference
1 The organisation: types and differences	1(a), (f)
2 Formal organisation structures	1(a), (f)
3 Tall and flat organisations	1(a), (f)
4 Departmentation	1(a), (f)
5 Centralisation and decentralisation	1(a),(f)
6 Mechanistic and organic organisations	1(a), (f)
7 Technology and structure	1(a), (f)

Introduction

This chapter and the next cover largely background material that is essential to set your later studies in context. The management of people is a task which takes place largely within organisations. Organisation structure and culture (Chapter 3) are the background to all people management activities.

Study guide

Section 1(a) – The organisation of work

- Explain the need for formal organisations
- Identify organisational types and differences

Section 2(b) – The role of management

- Explain the need for formal organisations
- Identify organisational types and differences

Section 7(g) – Authority, responsibility and delegation

- Describe, recognise and understand the importance of organisational structure
- Classical and modern approaches to organisational structure: Burns and Stalker, contingency Theory, Fayol, Mintzberg, Trist and Bamforth, Urwick, Weber, Woodward

Exam guide

The material in this chapter could form the background to questions on most parts of the syllabus.

1 THE ORGANISATION: TYPES AND DIFFERENCES

1.1 Here are some examples of organisations.

- A multinational car manufacturer (eg Ford)
- An accountancy firm (eg Ernst and Young)
- A charity (eg Oxfam)
- A local authority
- A trade union (eg Unison)
- An army

What organisations have in common

1.2 The definition below states what all organisations have in common.

KEY TERM

An **organisation** is: 'a *social arrangement* which pursues collective *goals*, which *controls* its own performance and which has a *boundary* separating it from its environment'.

1.3 Here is how this definition applies to two of the organisations listed in paragraph 1.1.

Characteristic	Car manufacturer (eg Ford)	Army
Social arrangement: individuals gathered together for a purpose	People work in different divisions, making different cars	Soldiers are in different regiments, and there is a chain of command from the top to the bottom
Collective goals: the organisation has goals over and above the goals of the people within it	Sell cars, make money	Defend the country, defeat the enemy, international peace keeping
Controls performance: performance is monitored against the goals and adjusted if necessary to ensure the goals are accomplished	Costs and quality are reviewed and controlled. Standards are constantly improved	Strict disciplinary procedures, training
Boundary: the organisation is distinct from its environment	Physical: factory gates Social: employment status	Physical: barracks Social: different rules than for civilians

(a) Organisations are preoccupied with **performance**, and meeting or improving their standards.

(b) Organisations contain formal, documented **systems and procedures** which enable them to control what they do.

(c) Different people do different things, or **specialise** in one activity.

(d) Organisations pursue a **variety of objectives** and goals.

(e) Most organisations obtain **inputs** (eg materials), and **process** them into **outputs** (eg for others to buy).

Why do organisations exist?

1.4 Organisations achieve results which individuals cannot achieve by themselves. Organisations:

(a) **Overcome people's individual limitations**, whether physical or intellectual

(b) **Enable people to specialise** in what they do best

(c) **Save time**, because people can work together or do two aspects of a different task at the same time

(d) **Accumulate** and share **knowledge** (eg about how best to build cars)

(e) Enable people to **pool their expertise**

(f) Enable **synergy**: by bringing together two individuals their combined output will exceed their output if they continued working separately

In brief, organisations enable people to be **more productive**

How organisations differ

1.5 The enormous variety of organisations was suggested in paragraph 1.1, and organisations differ in many ways. Here are some possible differences.

Factor	Example
Ownership (public vs private)	Private sector: owned by private owners/shareholders. Public sector: owned by the government
Control	By the owners themselves, by people working on their behalf, or indirectly by government-sponsored regulators
Activity (ie what they do)	Manufacturing, healthcare
Profit or non-profit **orientation**	Business exists to make a profit. The army, on the other hand, is not profit orientated
Legal status size	Limited company or partnership
Sources of **finance**	Borrowing, government funding, share issues
Technology	High use of technology (eg computer firms) vs low use (eg corner shop)

Two key differences in the list above are what the organisation does and whether or not it is profit orientated.

What the organisation does

1.6 Organisations do many different types of work. Here are some examples.

BPP PUBLISHING

Industry	Activity
Agriculture	Producing and processing food
Manufacturing	Acquiring raw materials and, by the application of labour and technology, turning them into a product (eg a car)
Extractive/raw materials	Extracting and refining raw materials (eg mining)
Energy	Converting one resource (eg coal) into another (eg electricity)
Retailing/distribution	Delivering goods to the end consumer
Intellectual production	Producing **intellectual property** eg software, publishing, films, music etc
Service industries	These include retailing, distribution, transport, banking, various business services (eg accountancy, advertising) and public services such as education, medicine

1.7 The table below gives an idea of the relative importance of these sectors, by showing how many people are employed in them in the UK.

	1992	*1997*
	'000	'000
Agriculture	309	278
Manufacturing	4,083	4,106
Energy and water supply	341	250
Construction	952	885
Services	16,245	17,298
	21,930	22,817

(Adapted from the *Annual Abstract of Statistics* published by the Office for National Statistics.)

Profit vs non-profit orientation

1.8 An important difference in the list above is between profit orientated and non profit orientated organisations. The basic difference in outlook is expressed in the diagram below. Note the distinction between **primary** and **secondary** goals. A primary goal is the most important: the other goals support it.

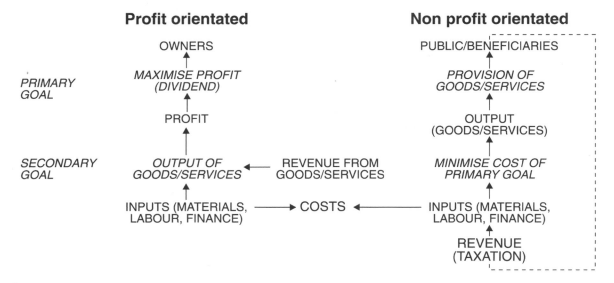

Profit maximisation and other objectives

1.9 **Profit maximisation** is assumed to be the goal of **business organisations**. Where the entrepreneur is in full managerial control of the firm, as in the case of a small owner-managed company or partnership, this assumption would seem to be very reasonable. Even in companies owned by shareholders but run by non-shareholding managers, we might expect that the profit maximisation assumption would be close to the truth. However, some writers have suggested that objectives other than profit maximisation might be pursued by firms.

1.10 **Managers will not necessarily make decisions that will maximise profits.**

(a) They may have **no personal interests** at stake in the size of profits earned, except in so far as they are accountable to shareholders for the profits they make; and

(b) There may be a **lack of competitive pressure** in the market to be efficient, minimise costs and maximise profits, for example where there are few firms in the market.

1.11 Price and output decisions might be taken by managers with **managerial objectives** in mind rather than the aim of profit maximisation. The profit level must be satisfactory and so acceptable to shareholders, and must provide enough retained profits for future investment in growth. But rather than seeking to **maximise** profits, managers may choose to achieve a **satisfactory** profit for a firm (this is called 'satisficing').

Baumol's sales maximisation model

1.12 One managerial model of the firm assumes that the firm acts to **maximise sales revenue** in order to maintain or increase its market share, ensure survival, and discourage competition. Managers benefit personally because of the **prestige** of running a large and successful company, and also because **salaries and other benefits are likely to be higher** in bigger companies than in smaller ones.

Drucker's multiple objectives

1.13 **Drucker** said:

'To manage a business is to balance a variety of needs and goals.... The very nature of business enterprise requires multiple objectives'. He proposed that objectives were needed in **eight key areas.**

(a) **Market standing**: this includes market share, customer satisfaction, size of product range and distribution resources

(b) **Innovation** in all major aspects of the organisation

(c) **Productivity**

(d) **Physical and financial resources**

(e) **Profitability**

(f) **Manager performance and development**

(g) **Worker performance and attitude**

(h) **Public responsibility**

Simon

1.14 *Simon* has pointed out that for many members of an organisation, decisions are taken without reference to the profit goal. This is not because they are ignoring profit, but because profit is not the most important constraint in their business. This is perhaps seen most clearly in areas where ethical constraints apply, such as staff relations.

Cyert and March's organisational coalition model

1.15 Cyert and March suggested that a firm is an **organisational coalition** of shareholders, managers, employees and customers, with each group having different goals, and so there is a need for 'political' compromise in establishing the goals of the firm. Each group must settle for less than it would ideally want to have. Shareholders must settle for less than maximum profits, managers for less than maximum utility, and so on.

2 FORMAL ORGANISATION STRUCTURES

> ### KEY TERM
>
> **Organisation structure** is the grouping of people into departments or section and the allocation of responsibility and authority.

2.1 Organisation structure implies a framework intended to:

(a) **Link individuals** in an established network of relationships so that authority, responsibility and communications can be controlled.

(b) **Allocate the tasks** required to fulfil the objective of the organisation to suitable individual or groups.

(c) Give each individual or group the **authority** required to perform the allocated tasks, while controlling their behaviour and use of resources in the interests of the organisation as a whole.

(d) **Co-ordinate** the objectives and activities of separate units, so that overall aims are achieved without gaps or overlaps in the flow of work.

(e) Facilitate the **flow of work**, information and other resources through the organisation.

Principles of organisation

2.2 Henry Fayol (1841-1925), an early management theorist, suggested that all organisations should follow the guiding principles outlined in the table below.

Principle	Comment
Division of work ie specialisation	The object of specialisation is to produce more and obtain better results.
Authority and **responsibility**	The holder of an office should have **enough authority** to carry out all the responsibilities assigned to him.
Discipline	A fair disciplinary system can be a strength of an organisation.

Principle	Comment
Unity of **command**	For any action, a subordinate should receive orders from one boss only. Fayol saw dual command as a disease, whether it is caused by imperfect demarcation between departments, or by a superior S2 giving orders to an employee, E, without going via the intermediate superior, S1.
Unity of **direction**	There should be one head and one plan for each activity. Unity of direction relates to the organisation itself, whereas unity of command relates to the personnel in the organisation.
Subordination of individual interests	The interest of one employee or group of employees should not prevail over that of the general interest of the organisation.
Remuneration	It should be 'fair', satisfying both employer and employee alike.
Scalar chain	The scalar chain is the term used to describe the chain of superiors from lowest to highest rank. (This is discussed in section 3 below.)

2.3　**Henry Mintzberg** took a slightly different approach, and said that an organisation can co-ordinate itself by various methods.

Method of co-ordination	Description
Mutual adjustment	Informal communication between people doing the work.
Direct supervision	One person supervises everybody and tells everybody what to do.
Standardisation of **work** processes	There is a uniform procedure for each task which is always adopted. For example, bank reconciliations in an accounts department must be done every week, no matter who does the work.
Standardisation of **outputs**	The results of work are specified, the means are not.
Standardisation of skills and knowledge	For example, all teachers have to be trained before being let loose in the classroom.

Components of the organisation

2.4　**Mintzberg** believes that *all* organisations can be analysed into five components, according to how they relate to the work of the organisation, and how they prefer to co-ordinate.

BPP PUBLISHING

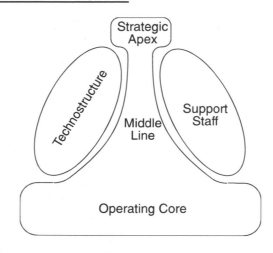

Component	Job	Preferred means of co-ordination
Strategic apex	Ensures the organisation follows its mission. Manages the organisation's relationship with the environment.	Direct supervision (especially in small businesses)?
Operating core	People **directly** involved in the process of obtaining inputs, and converting them into outputs	Mutual adjustment Standardisation of skills
Middle line	Converts the desires of the strategic apex into the work done by the operating core	Standardisation of outputs (Results)
Technostructure	• Analysers determine the best way of doing a job • Planners determine outputs (eg goods must achieve a specified level of quality) • Personnel analysts standardise skills (eg training programmes)	Standardisation of work processes or outputs
Support staff	Ancillary services such as public relations, legal counsel, the cafeteria. Support staff do not plan or standardise production. They function independ-ently of the operating core.	Mutual adjustment

2.5 Modern management theorists have moved away from 'classical' organisational principles such as those outlined by Fayol. They instead emphasise values such as the following.

(a) **Multi-skilling.** Contrary to the idea of specialisation, multi-skilled teams enable tasks to be performed more flexibly, using labour more efficiently.

(b) **Flexibility**. This is perhaps the major value of modern management theory. Arising from the competitive need to respond swiftly (and without organisational trauma) to rapidly-changing customer demands and technological changes, organisations and processes are being re-engineered. This has created the following.

    (i)   Smaller, multi skilled, temporary structures, such as project or task-force teams.

    (ii)   Multi-functional units, facilitating communication and co-ordination across departmental boundaries. This is called **matrix organisation**, and it blurs the principle of 'unity of command', since an employee may report both to his department superior **and** to a project or product manager whose job is to manage all areas of activity related to the product or project.

    (iii)   Flexible deployment of the labour resource, for example through part-time and temporary working, contracting out tasks, flexitime, annual (rather than daily) hours contracts and so on.

(c) **Empowerment**

    (i)   The purpose of empowerment is to free employees from rigorous control by instructions and orders, and give them freedom to take responsibility for their ideas and actions, and to release hidden resources, which would otherwise remain inaccessible.

    (ii)   People are asked to use their own judgement in the interests of the organisation and the customer, within a disciplined context.

2.6   **Contingency theory** holds that there is no universally best organisation structure, but that there could well be a best structure for each individual organisation, which will depend on **contingent** factors.

2.7   **Contingent factors influencing an organisation's structure**

(a) **Age.** The older the organisation, the more formalised its behaviour. Work is repeated, so is more easily formalised.

(b) **Size.** The larger the organisation; the more elaborate and bureaucratic its structure, the larger the average size of the units within it and the more formalised its behaviour .

(c) **Technology**

    •   The stronger the technical system, the more formalised the work, and the more bureaucratic the structure of the operating core.

    •   The more sophisticated the technology, the more elaborate and professional the support staff will be.

(d) **Geographical** dispersion. An organisation on one site will be organised differently to one which has several separately located units.

(e) **Personnel** employed. Bureaucracy might be needed for a large, low-skilled work-force.

(f) The **environment**

(g) The type of **activities** the organisation is involved in

(h) The business **strategy**

BPP PUBLISHING

3   TALL AND FLAT ORGANISATIONS

Span of control

> **KEY TERM**
>
> The **span of control** refers to the number of subordinates immediately reporting to a superior official.

3.1   Span of control or 'span of management', refers to the number of subordinates responsible to a superior. In other words, if a manager has five subordinates, the span of control is five.

3.2   Classical theorists such as **Urwick** and **Graicunas** suggest the following.

(a)   There are physical and mental **limitations** to any given manager's ability to control people, relationships and activities.

(b)   There needs to be **tight managerial control** from the top of an organisation downward. The span of control should therefore, they argued, be **restricted**, to allow maximum control consistent with the manager's capabilities: usually between three and six. If the span of control is too wide, too much of the manager's time will be taken up with **routine problems and supervision**, leaving less time for planning. Even so, subordinates may not get the supervision, control and communication that they require.

3.3   On the other hand, if the span is too **narrow**, the manager may **fail to delegate**, keeping too much routine work to himself and depriving subordinates of decision-making **authority** and **responsibility**. There may be a tendency to interfere in or over-supervise the work that is delegated to subordinates - and the relative costs of supervision will thus be unnecessarily high. Subordinates tend to be dissatisfied in such situations, having too little challenge and responsibility and perhaps feeling that the superior does not trust them.

3.4   **Influences on span of control**

(a)   A manager's **capabilities** limit the span of control. These are the physical and mental limitations to any single manager's ability to control people and activities.

(b)   The **nature of the manager's work load**

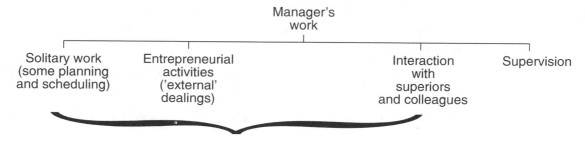

The more non-supervisory work in a manager's workload:

* The narrower the span of control
* The greater the delegation of authority to subordinates

(c)   The **geographical dispersion** of subordinates.

(d)   **Subordinates' work:** if all subordinates do similar tasks a wide span is possible

(e) The **nature of problems** that a supervisor might have to help subordinates with. Time consuming problems suggest a narrow span of control.

(f) The degree of **interaction between subordinates**. If subordinates can help each other, a wide span is possible.

(g) If **close group cohesion** is desirable, a narrow span of control might be needed.

(h) The amount of **help that supervisors receive** from other parts of the organisation.

Tall and flat organisations

3.5 The span of control concept has implications for the length of the **scalar chain**.

> ### KEY TERMS
>
> **Scalar chain**: the chain of command from the most senior to the most junior.
>
> A **tall organisation** is one which, in relation to its size, has a large number of levels of management hierarchy. This implies a **narrow** span of control.
>
> A **flat organisation** is one which, in relation to its size, has a small number of hierarchical levels. This implies a **wide** span of control.
>
> **Delayering** is the reduction of the number of management levels from bottom to top.

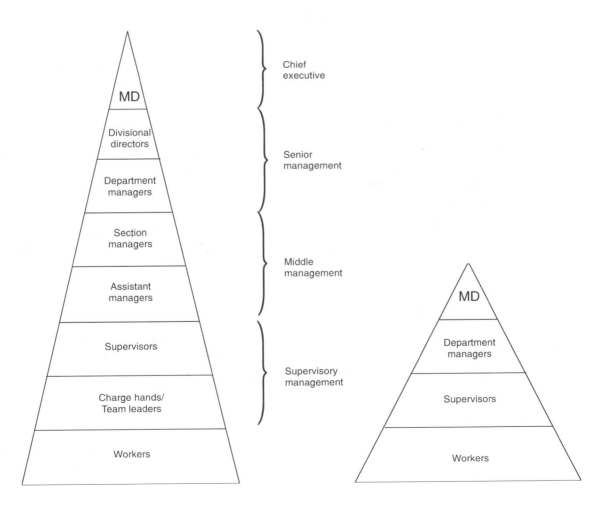

Tall organisation

For	Against
Narrow control spans	Inhibits delegation
Small groups enable team members to participate in decisions	Rigid supervision can be imposed, blocking initiative
A large number of steps on the promotional ladders - assists management training	The same work passes through too many hands
	Increases administration and overhead costs
	Extra communication problems, as the strategic apex is further away

Flat organisation

For	Against
More opportunity for delegation	Implies that jobs **can** be delegated. Managers may only get a superficial idea of what goes on. If they are overworked they are more likely to be involved in crisis management
Relatively cheap	Sacrifices control
In theory, speeds up communication between strategic apex and operating core	Middle managers are often necessary to convert the grand vision of the strategic apex into operational terms

3.6　Many organisations are delayering. Middle line jobs are vanishing. Organisations are increasing the average span of control, are reducing management levels and are becoming flatter. Why?

(a)　**Information technology** reduces the need for middle managers to process information.

(b)　**Empowerment.** Many organisations, especially service businesses, are keen to delegate authority down the line to the lowest possible level. Front-line workers in the operating core are allowed to take decisions. This is because it is often the best way to satisfy customers. This perhaps removes the needs for some middle management jobs.

(c)　**Fashion.** Delayering is fashionable, so if senior managers believe that tall structures are inherently inflexible they might cut the numbers of management levels.

4　DEPARTMENTATION

4.1　In most organisations, tasks and people are grouped together in some rational way: on the basis of specialisation, say, or shared technology or customer base. This is known as **departmentation**. Different patterns of departmentation are possible, and the pattern selected will depend on the individual circumstances of the organisation.

Geographic departmentation

4.2　**Geographic area.** Some authority is retained at Head Office but day to day operations are handled on a territorial basis. (eg Southern region, Western region). (Within many sales departments, the sales staff are organised territorially.)

14

(a) **Advantages**

    (i)   There is **local decision-making** at the point of contact between the organisation (eg a salesperson) and its customers suppliers or other stakeholders.

    (ii)   It may be **cheaper sometimes** to establish area factories/offices than to service markets from one location (eg costs of transportation and travelling may be reduced).

(b) **Disadvantages**

    (i)   **Duplication** and possible loss of economies of scale might arise. For example, a national organisation divided into ten regions might have a customer liaison department in each regional office. If the organisation did all customer liaison work from head office it might need fewer managerial staff.

    (ii)   **Inconsistency in standards** is likely to develop, ie there might be different standards adopted in different areas.

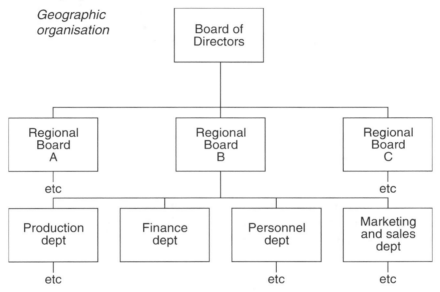

Geographic organisation

Function

4.3   **Functional organisation** involves setting up departments for people who do similar jobs. Primary functions in a manufacturing company might be production, sales, finance, and general administration. Sub-departments of marketing might be selling, distribution and warehousing.

(a) **Advantages**

    (i)   **Expertise is pooled** thanks to the division of work into specialist areas.

    (ii)   It **avoids duplication** (eg one management accounts department rather than several) and helps ensure economies of scale.

    (ii)   It makes **easier** the **recruitment**, training, and motivation of professional specialists.

    (iv)   It suits **centralised** businesses.

(b) **Disadvantages**

    (i)   It is organisation by **internal work**, rather than by **customer or product**, which are what ultimately drive a business. The customer is only interested in the product, and functional structure may not be the best at satisfying the customer.

(ii)   **Communication problems** may arise between different functions, who each have their own jargon.

(iii)   **Poor co-ordination**, especially if rooted in a **tall** organisation structure. Decisions by one function/department involving another might have to be referred upwards, and dealt with at a high level, thereby increasing the burdens on senior management.

Functional organisation

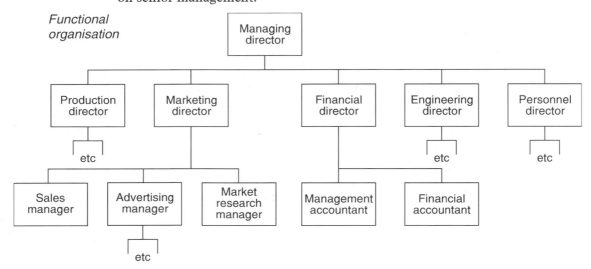

Product/brand departmentation

4.4   Some organisations group activities on the basis of **products** or product lines. Some functional departmentation remains (eg manufacturing, distribution, marketing and sales) but a divisional manager is given responsibility for the product or product line, with authority over personnel of different functions.

(a)   **Advantages**

(i)   **Accountability.** Individual managers can be held **accountable** for the **profitability** of individual products.

(ii)   **Specialisation.** For example, some salespeople will be trained to sell a specific product in which they may develop technical expertise and thereby offer a better sales service to customers.

(iii)   **Co-ordination.** The different functional activities and efforts required to make and sell each product can be co-ordinated and integrated by the divisional/product manager.

(b)   **Disadvantages**

(i)   It **increases the overhead costs** and managerial complexity of the organisation.

(ii)   Different product divisions may **fail to share resources** and customers.

4.5   **By brand.** A brand is the name (eg 'Persil') or design which identifies the products or services of a manufacturer or provider and distinguishes them from those of competitors. (Large organisations may produce a number of different brands of the same basic product, such as washing powder or toothpaste.) Branding brings the product to the attention of buyers and creates **brand loyalty** - often the customers do not realise that two 'rival' brands are in fact produced by the same manufacturer.

(a) Because **each brand is promoted and sold in its own way** it becomes necessary to have brand departmentation. As with product departmentation, some functional departmentation remains but brand managers have responsibility for the brand's marketing and this can affect every function.

(b) Brand departmentation has similar advantages and disadvantages to product departmentation.

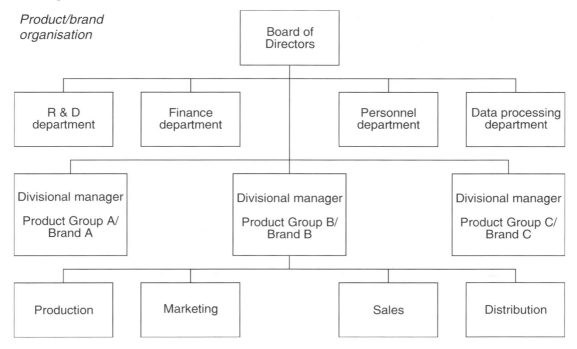

Product/brand organisation

Customer departmentation

4.6 An organisation may organise its activities on the basis of types of customer, or market segment.

(a) Departmentation by customer is commonly associated with **sales departments** and selling effort, but it might also be used by a jobbing or contracting firm where a team of managers may be given the responsibility of liaising with major customers (eg discussing specifications and completion dates, quality of work, progress chasing etc).

(b) Many businesses distinguish between **business** and **household** customers.

Divisionalisation

KEY TERM

Divisionalisation is the division of a business into **autonomous** regions or product businesses, each with its own revenues, expenditures and capital asset purchase programmes, and therefore each with its own profit and loss responsibility.

4.7 Each division of the organisation might be:

- Subsidiary companies under the holding company
- Profit centres or investment centres within a single company

BPP PUBLISHING

4.8 **Successful divisionalisation**

(a) Each division must have **properly delegated authority**, but must be held properly accountable to head office (eg for profits earned).

(b) Each unit must be **large enough** to support the quantity and quality of management it needs.

(c) It **must not rely on head office** for excessive management support.

(d) Each unit must have a **potential for growth** in its own area of operations.

(e) There should be scope and **challenge in the job for the management** of each unit.

(f) If units deal with each other, it should be as an **'arm's length' transaction**. There should be no insistence on preferential treatment to be given to a 'fellow unit' by another unit of the overall organisation.

4.9 **Advantages**

(a) It **focuses the attention of management** below 'top level' on business performance.

(b) It **reduces the likelihood of unprofitable products** and activities being continued.

(c) It encourages a **greater attention to efficiency**, lower costs and higher profits.

(d) **Knowledge.** The manager of the unit knows better than anyone else how he is doing, and needs no one to tell him. Senior managers need only set broad targets for achievement.

(e) It gives **more authority to junior managers**, and therefore provides them with work which grooms them for more senior positions in the future.

(f) It provides an organisation structure which **reduces the number of levels** of management. The top executives in each division should be able to report directly to the chief executive of the holding company.

4.10 **Disadvantages**

(a) It is **not always practical**. In some businesses, it is impossible to identify completely independent products or markets for which separate divisions can be set up.

(b) Divisionalisation is only possible at a fairly senior management level, because there is a **limit** to how much **independence** in the division of work can be arranged. For example, every product needs a manufacturing function and a selling function.

(c) There may be more **resource problems.** Many divisions get their resources from head office which chooses between other divisions. If it were an independent company, the division might find it easier to raise money.

Matrix and project organisation

Matrix

4.11 As discussed earlier, matrix organisation 'crosses' **functional** and **product/customer/project** organisation.

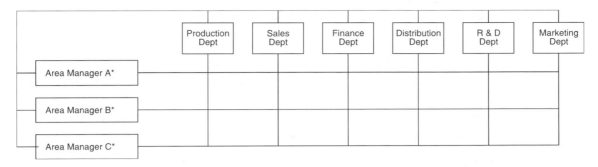

4.12 **Advantages**

(a) Greater **flexibility**

   (i) **People.** Employees develop an attitude geared to accepting change, and departmental monopolies are broken down.

   (ii) **Tasks and structure.** The matrix structure may be readily amended.

(c) **Better inter-disciplinary co-operation** and a mixing of skills and expertise.

(d) **Motivation by providing employees** with greater participation in planning and control decisions.

4.13 **Disadvantages**

(a) Dual authority threatens a **conflict** between functional managers and product/ project area managers.

(b) An individual with two or more bosses is more likely to suffer **stress** at work.

(c) Matrix management can be **more costly** - product management posts are added, meetings have to be held, and so on.

(d) **Slower decision making.**

The new organisation

4.14 **Some recent trends and ideas on organisation structure**

(a) **Flat structures.** The flattening of hierarchies does away with levels of organisation which lengthened lines of communication and decision-making and encouraged ever-increasing specialisation. Flat structures are more responsive, because there is a more direct relationship between the organisation's strategic centre and the operational units serving the customer.

(b) **'Horizontal structures'.** What Tom Peters (*Liberation Management*) calls 'going horizontal' is a recognition that functional versatility (through multi-functional project teams and multi-skilling, for example) is the key to flexibility. In the words (quoted by Peters) of a Motorola executive: 'The traditional job descriptions were barriers. We needed an organisation soft enough between the organisational disciplines so that ... people would run freely across functional barriers or organisational barriers with the common goal of getting the job done, rather than just making certain that their specific part of the job was completed.'

(c) **'Chunked' and 'unglued' structures.** So far, this has meant teamworking and decentralisation, or empowerment, creating smaller and more flexible units within the overall structure. Charles Handy's **'shamrock organisation'** (with its three-leafed structured of core, subcontractor and flexible part-time labour) is gaining ground as a workable model for a leaner and more flexible workforce, within a controlled framework.

(d) **Output-focused structures**. The key to all the above trends is the focus on results, and on the customer, instead of internal processes and functions for their own sake. A **project management** orientation and structure, for example, is being applied to the supply of services within the organisation (to internal customers) as well as to the external market, in order to facilitate listening and responding to customer demands.

(e) **'Jobless' structures**. Meanwhile, the employee becomes not a job-holder but the vendor of a portfolio of demonstrated outputs and competencies. However daunting, this is a concrete expression of the concept of **employability**, which says that a person needs to have a portfolio of skills which are valuable on the open labour market: employees need to be mobile, moving between organisations rather than settling in to a particular job.

Question 1

Why might a diversified conglomerate with lots of divisions have a small head office?

Answer

(a) The business may be so different that there is little point in integrating the functions.
(b) Head office management might be committed to delegation.

---

5 CENTRALISATION AND DECENTRALISATION

5.1 A centralised organisation is one in which authority is concentrated in one place. For example, if you meet a sales person who always says 'Sorry, I'll have to refer that to head office', this implies that the organisation is centralised.

5.2 We can look at centralisation in two ways.

(a) **Geography**. In some firms decision might have to be constantly referred to head office in a different country or region.

(b) **Authority**. Centralisation also refers to the extent to which people have to refer decisions upwards to their **superiors**.

5.3 The table following summarises some of the key issues.

Arguments in favour of centralisation and decentralisation	
Pro centralisation	*Pro decentralisation/delegation*
1 Decisions are made at one point and so are easier to co-ordinate.	1 Avoids overburdening top managers, in terms of workload and stress.
2 Senior managers in an organisation can take a wider view of problems and consequences.	2 Improves motivation of more junior managers who are given responsibility-important since job challenge and entrepreneurial skills are highly valued in today's work environment.
3 Senior management can keep a proper balance between different departments or functions - eg by deciding on the resources to allocate to each.	3 Greater awareness of local problems by decision makers. Geographically dispersed organisations should often be decentralised on a regional/area basis.
4 Quality of decisions is (theoretically) higher due to senior managers' skills and experience.	4 Greater speed of decision making, and response to changing events, since no need to refer decisions upwards. This is particularly important in rapidly changing markets.
5 Possibly cheaper, by reducing number of mangers needed and so lower costs of overheads.	5 Helps junior managers to develop and helps the process of transition from functional to general management.
6 Crisis decisions are taken more quickly at the centre, without need to refer back, get authority etc.	6 Separate spheres of responsibility can be identified: controls, performance measurement and accountability are better.
7 Policies, procedures and documentation can be standardised organisation-wide.	7 Communication technology allows decisions to be made locally, with information and input from head office if required.

6 MECHANISTIC AND ORGANIC ORGANISATIONS

Max Weber: bureaucracy

6.1 The German writer, *Max Weber* (1864-1920) was inclined to regard **bureaucracy** as the ideal form of organisation, because it is impersonal and rational, based on a set pattern of behaviour and work allocation, and not allowing personality conflicts to get in the way of achieving goals.

6.2 Weber regarded an organisation as an **authority structure**. He was interested in why individuals obeyed commands, and he identified three grounds on which **legitimate authority** could exist.

(a) **Charismatic leadership**: the leader is regarded as having some special power or attribute.

(b) **Traditional, or patriarchal leadership**: authority is bestowed by tradition or hereditary entitlement, as in the family firm. Decisions and actions are bound by precedent.

(c) **Bureaucracy**: authority is bestowed by dividing an organisation into jurisdictional areas (production, marketing, sales and so on) each with specified duties. Authority to carry them out is given to the **officials in charge**, and rules and regulations are established in order to ensure their achievement. Leadership is therefore of a '**rational-legal**' nature: managers get things done because **their orders are accepted as legitimate and justified.**

KEY TERMS

A **bureaucracy** is 'a continuous organisation of official functions bound by rules' (Weber).

- **Authority structure**. In a bureaucracy people obey instructions because their superiors have authority that is legitimate and rational.

- **Continuous organisation**. The organisation does not disappear if people leave: new people will fill their shoes.

- **Official functions**. The organisation is divided into areas (eg production, marketing) with specified duties. Authority to carry them out is given to the officials in charge.

- **Rules**. A rule defines and specifies a course of action that must be taken under given circumstances.

Characteristics of bureaucracy

6.3

Characteristic	Description
Hierarchy	An organisation exists even before it is filled with people. Each lower office is under the control and supervision of a higher one.
Specialisation and training	There is a high degree of specialisation of labour. Employment is based on ability, not personal loyalty.
Professional nature of employment	Officials are full-time employees; promotion is according to seniority and achievement; pay scales are prescribed according to the position or office held in the organisation structure.
Impersonal nature	Employees work full time within the impersonal rules and regulations and act according to formal, impersonal procedures.
Rationality	The jurisdictional areas of the organisation are determined rationally. The hierarchy of authority and office structure is clearly defined. Duties are established and measures of performance set.
Uniformity in the performance of tasks	Procedures ensure that, regardless of who carried out the tasks, tasks should be executed in the same way.
Technical competence	All officials are technically competent. Their competence within the area of their expertise is rarely questioned.
Stability	The organisation changes rarely.

6.4 **Benefits of bureaucracy**

    (a) Bureaucracies are **ideal for standardised, routine tasks**. For example, processing driving license applications is fairly routine, requiring systematic work.

    (b) Bureaucracies can be very **efficient**.

    (c) **Rigid adherence to procedures is necessary** for **fairness,** adherence to the **law, safety** and **security** (eg procedures over computer use).

    (d) **Some people like** the structured, predictable environment.

6.5 **Problems with bureaucracy**

    (a) It results in **slow decision-making,** because of the complexity of the organisation.

    (b) Uniformity creates **conformity**.

    (c) Bureaucracies can **inhibit people's personal growth**.

    (d) Bureaucracies are **bad at innovation**: they can repress creativity and initiative.

    (e) Bureaucracies find it **hard to learn from their mistakes**.

    (f) Bureaucracies are **slow to change.** *Crozier* stated that 'a system of organisation whose main characteristic is its rigidity will not adjust easily to change and will tend to resist change as much as possible'.

    (g) **Communication is restricted** to the established structures, and important information may avoid detection.

    (h) Bureaucracies find it **hard to deal with change in their environment**.

Question 2

Using Mintzberg's model, what component part of the organisation is responsible for designing rules and procedures?

Answer

The technostructure.

The organic organisation

6.6 A radical departure from the bureaucracy is the **organic organisation**. The term was coined by *Burns and Stalker,* who contrasted organic organisations with **mechanistic** organisations. 'Mechanistic organisation' is really another term for bureaucracy.

6.7 **Mechanistic and organic organisations**

Item	Mechanistic	Organic
The job	Tasks are specialised and broken down into subtasks	Specialist knowledge and expertise is **understood** to contribute to the common task of the concern
How the job fits in	People are concerned with completing the task **efficiently**, but are not concerned with how the task can be made to improve organisational **effectiveness**.	Each task is seen and understood to be set by the **total situation** of the firm: people are concerned with the task insofar as it contributes to **organisational effectiveness**
Co-ordination	**Managers** are responsible for co-ordinating tasks	People adjust and redefine their tasks through interaction with others. This is rather like co-ordination by **mutual adjustment**
Job description	There are **precise** job descriptions and delineations of responsibility	Job descriptions are **less precise:** it is harder to pass the buck
Commitment	**Doing the job** takes priority over serving the interests of the organisation	**Commitment to the organisation** concern spreads beyond any technical definition
Legal contract vs common interest	**Hierarchic** structure of control. An individual's performance assessment derives from a **contractual relationship** with an impersonal organisation	**Network structure** of control. An individual's job performance and conduct derive from a supposed **community of interest** between the individual and the organisation, and the individual's colleagues. (Loyalty to the team is an important control mechanism)
Decisions	Decisions are taken by senior managers who are assumed to know everything	Relevant technical and commercial knowledge can be located anywhere. 'Omniscience is no longer imputed to the head of the concern.'
Communication patterns	Communication is mainly **vertical** (up and down the scalar chain), and takes the form of **commands** and obedience.	Communication is **lateral** (eg along gangplanks) and communication between people of different rank represents **consultation**, rather than command
Content of communications	Operations and working behaviour are governed by **instructions** issued by superiors	Communication consists of **information and advice** rather than instructions and decisions
Mission	Insistence on **loyalty** to the concern and **obedience** to superiors.	Commitment to the organisation's **mission** is more highly valued than loyalty as such
Internal vs external expertise	**Internal knowledge** (eg of the organisation's specific activities) is more highly valued than general knowledge	'Importance and prestige attach to **affiliations and expertise valid** in the industrial, technical and commercial milieus **external to the firm'**

6.8   Organic organisations have their own structures and control mechanisms.

Feature	Description
Status	Although organic systems are not hierarchical in the way that bureaucracies are, there are **differences of status**, determined by people's greater expertise, experience and so forth.
Commitment	The degree of **commitment** employees have to the firm is more **extensive** in organic than in mechanistic systems. This is similar to the idea that an organisation's mission should motivate and inspire employees.
Shared values and culture	The reduced importance of hierarchy is replaced by 'the development of **shared beliefs and values**'. In other words, corporate **cultures** becomes very powerful.

6.9   The organic and mechanistic approaches represent **two ends of the spectrum**: there are intermediate stages between bureaucratic and organic organisations. Different departments of a business may be run on different lines.

7   **TECHNOLOGY AND STRUCTURE**

7.1   Two important research programmes took place in England in the 1950s. These programmes were concerned with the influence of production technology on the way work is organised.

Joan Woodward: type of production system

7.2   *Joan Woodward* investigated specific features of organisation structure, such as size of span of control and the extent of division of functions among specialists. She discovered considerable differences between firms in these matters and established that the differences were related to the type of production technology in use.

   (a) Production systems may be divided into three main categories, ranging from least to most complex.

   - Unit and small batch
   - Large batch and mass production
   - Process production

   These three categories were further subdivided into 9 sub-categories.

   (b) The main point of difference was the **degree of control possible over the output of the system**. In the case of one-off production to customers' requirements, it is very difficult to predict the results of development work, while in continuous flow production of chemicals, the equipment can be set for a given result.

7.3   Some aspects of the organisation vary directly as the technology varies. For instance, the length of the scalar chain increases as complexity increases. However, other variables, such as span of control, do not vary linearly. Woodward found that span of control was greatest in mass production systems, while small work groups with more personal relationships with their supervisors were typical of both unit and process systems.

BPP PUBLISHING

Socio-technical systems: Trist and Bamforth

7.4   *Trist and Bamforth* studied the effect of the introduction of new technology in coal mining.

Case example

The traditional method was based upon a small, integrated work group consisting of a skilled man, his mate and one or two labourers. There was a high degree of autonomy at the work group level and close working relationships. It was usual for the group to be paid for its work as a group. The work was hard, the conditions unpleasant and there was often conflict, and even violence between work groups. However, 'The system as a whole contained its bad in a way that did not destroy its good'.

The introduction of large-scale coal-cutting machinery created a need for larger, more specialised groups. A single cycle of mechanised production might extend over three 7 ½ shifts, each performing a separate process and made up of 10 to 20 men. The members of each shift would be spread over about 200 yards of coal face tunnel, which was typically 3 feet high and 6 feet wide. This physical dispersion and the spread of the work over three shifts destroyed the previous close working relationships. Many symptoms of social stress appeared, including scapegoating across shifts, formation of cliques and absenteeism.

Trist studied the new technology and found that it was possible to organise its use in such a way that some of the **social** characteristics of the traditional method were preserved. The use of this new method led to greater productivity, lower cost, considerably less absenteeism and accidents, and greater work satisfaction, since it was a **socio-technical system** which was better geared to the workers' social and psychological needs for job autonomy and close working relationships.

Chapter roundup

- An organisation is a **social arrangement** which pursues collective goals.

- Many organisations are based on the principle of **hierarchy**. There is a line of decision making power from the top of the organisation to the bottom. In general, no employee reports to two bosses, whereas the boss may manage a number of different employees. This **scalar chain** is intimately connected to the concept of **span of control**, which is the number of individuals under the direct supervision of any one person.

- Recent trends have been towards **delayering** organisations of levels of management. In other words, tall **organisations** (with many management levels, and narrow spans of control) are turning into **flat organisations** (with fewer management levels, wider spans of control) as a result of technological changes and the granting of more decision making power to front line employees.

- Organisations can be **departmentalised** on a **functional** basis (with separate departments for production, marketing, finance etc), a **geographical** basis (by region, or country), a **product** basis (eg world wide divisions for product X, Y etc), a **brand** basis, or a **matrix** basis (eg someone selling product X in country A would report to both a product X manager and a country A manager). Some organisations might feature a variety of these types.

- In a **divisional structure** some activities are **decentralised** to business units or regions. **Centralisation** offers control, but sacrifices local knowledge and flexibility.

- Modern management theory stresses **flexibility** as a key value, and organisational measures such as matrix and horizontal structures, multi-skilling, empowerment and flexible labour deployment are currently being explored.

Quick quiz

1 List the principles of organisation.

2 List the methods of co-ordination.

3 What is span of control? *Is either narrow or long depending on N° employees under supervision.*

4 What is delayering? *Reduction in the number of layers of management*

5 What is functional organisation?

6 What is a matrix organisation? *Where an employee reports to more than one boss*

7 What three types of legitimate authority did Max Weber identify?

Answers to quick quiz

1 Division of work; authority and responsibility; discipline; unity of command; unity of direction; subordination of individual interests; remuneration; scalar chain.

2 Mutual adjustment, direct supervision; standardisation (of work process, outputs, skills and knowledge).

3 The number of subordinates immediately reporting to a given official.

4 The reduction in the number of management levels.

5 People are grouped together as they do similar work.

6 A matrix organisation crosses functional boundaries and involves overlapping chains of command.

7 Charismatic, traditional and bureaucratic.

Now try the question below from the Exam Question Bank

Question to try	Level	Marks	Time
1	Exam	15	27

Chapter 2

THE ROLE OF MANAGEMENT AND SUPERVISION

Topic list	Syllabus reference
1 The purpose of management	1(c)
2 Classical writers on management	1(b)
3 Modern writers on management	1(b)
4 Modern writers: Mintzberg and the manager's task	2(c)
5 Management and supervision: achieving tasks	1(c)

Introduction

Management as a discipline has attracted increasing attention for over a century. In this chapter we look first at the overall organisational context of management and then at the work of some of the leading thinkers and experiments in the field. We also cover the nitty-gritty of the supervisor's role.

Study guide

Section 2(b) – The role of management

- Identify and explain the contribution made by modern writers on management: Drucker, Kanter, Mintzberg, Ouchi, Peters

- Identify and explain the contribution made by classical writers on management: Fayol, Stewart, Taylor, May, Weber

- Identify the differences between classical and modern theories of management

- Outline areas of management authority and responsibility

Section 3(c) – The role of management

- Explain the role of the manager in the organisation of work
- List the management tasks involved in organising the work of others
- Illustrate the role of the manager in achieving tasks
- The responsibilities of the supervisor

Exam guide

You need a thorough grasp of the work of the writers summarised in sections 3 and 4 of this chapter. Their ideas will be applicable to many questions on the nature of management. You may have to explain theory, or apply your knowledge in scenario format.

1 THE PURPOSE OF MANAGEMENT

1.1 Why is it that organisations have to be **managed,** and what is the purpose of management

> ## KEY TERM
>
> **Management: 'Getting things done through other people' (Stewart)**

1.2 An organisation has been defined as 'a social arrangement for the controlled performance of collective goals.' This definition leads us into why there is a need for management.

(a) **Objectives** have to be set for the organisation.

(b) Somebody has to ensure that objectives are met.

(c) Managers sustain **corporate values,** its ethics and operating principles.

(d) Somebody has to look after the interests of the **organisation's owners,** if the owners are not involved in the day to day running of the organisation.

(e) The interests of other **stakeholders** need to be looked after.

Question 1

John, Paul, George and Ringo set up in business together as repairers of musical instruments. Each has contributed £5,000 as capital for the business. They are a bit uncertain as to how they should run the business, and, when they discuss this in the pub, they decide that attention needs to be paid to planning what they do, reviewing what they do and controlling what they do.

Suggest two ways in which John, Paul, George and Ringo can manage the business assuming no other personnel are recruited.

Answer

The purpose of this exercise has been to get you to separate the issues of management functions from organisational structure and hierarchy. John, Paul, George and Ringo have a number of choices. Here are some extreme examples.

(a) All the management activities are the job of one person

Manager

Worker   Worker   Worker

In this case, Paul, for example, could plan direct and control the work and the other three would do the work.

(b) Division of management tasks between individuals (eg: repairing drums *and* ensuring plans are adhered to would be Ringo's job, and so on).

(c) Management by committee. All of them could sit down and work out the plan together etc. In a small business with equal partners this is likely to be the most effective.

1.3 In most Western companies, a separate group of people is responsible for carrying out **management functions**. Is this a good thing?

(a) **Specialisation.** Some organisations are so large and complex that if everybody participated in management nothing would get done.

(b) **Motivation.** Giving people more responsibility can be good for motivation and can lead to better decisions.

1.4 Different organisations have different structures for carrying out management functions. For example, some organisations have separate strategic planning departments. Others do not.

1.5 In a **private sector business,** managers act, ultimately, on behalf of shareholders. In practical terms, shareholders *rarely* interfere, as long as the business delivers profits year on year.

1.6 In a **public sector organisation,** management acts on behalf of the government. Politicians in a democracy are in turn accountable to the electorate. More of the objectives of a public sector organisation might be set by the 'owners' - ie the government - rather than by the management. The government might also tell senior management to carry out certain policies or plans, thereby restricting management's discretion.

2 CLASSICAL WRITERS ON MANAGEMENT

Henri Fayol

The classical school

2.1 Henri Fayol (1841-1925) was a French industrialist who put forward and popularised the concept of the '**universality of management principles**': in other words, the idea that all organisations could be structured and managed according to certain rational principles. Fayol himself recognised that applying such principles in practice was not simple: 'Seldom do we have to apply the same principles twice in identical conditions; allowance must be made for different changing circumstances.'

Henri Fayol: functions of management.

2.2 **Fayol** listed the **functions of management**. He suggested that they **apply to any organisation.**

Function	Comment
Planning	This involves selecting objectives, and the strategies, policies, programmes and procedures for achieving the objectives either for the organisation as a whole or for a part of it.
Organising	Establishing a structure of tasks which need to be performed to achieve the goals of the organisation, **grouping these tasks into jobs** for an individual, creating groups of jobs within sections and departments, **delegating** authority to carry out the jobs, and providing **systems of information** and communication, and for the co-ordination of activities.
Commanding	Giving **instructions** to subordinates to carry out tasks over which the manager has authority for decisions and responsibility for performance
Co-ordinating	**Harmonising** the activities of individuals and groups within the organisation, which will inevitably have different ideas about what their own goals should be. Management must reconcile differences in approach, effort, interest and timing of these separate individuals and groups.
Controlling	Measuring and correcting the activities of individuals and groups, to ensure that their performance is in accordance with plans. Deviations from plans are identified and corrected.

F W Taylor and scientific management

2.3 *Frederick W Taylor* pioneered the **scientific management** movement in the USA. He argued that management should be based on 'well-recognised, clearly defined and fixed principles, instead of depending on more or less hazy ideas.' Taylor was a very skilled engineer and he took an engineering efficiency approach to management.

2.4 **Principles of scientific management**

(a) **The development of a true science of work.** 'All knowledge which had hitherto been kept in the heads of workmen should be gathered and recorded by **management**. Every single subject, large and small, becomes the question for scientific investigation, for reduction to law.'

(b) **The scientific selection and progressive development of workers:** workers should be carefully trained and given jobs to which they are best suited.

(c) **The bringing together of the science and the scientifically selected and trained men.** The application of techniques to decide what should be done and how, using workers who are both properly trained and willing to maximise output, should result in maximum productivity.

(d) **The constant and intimate co-operation between management and workers:** 'the relations between employers and men form without question the most important part of this art.'

2.5 **Scientific management in practice**

(a) **Work study techniques** were used to analyse tasks and establish the most efficient methods to use, No variation was permitted in the way work was done, since the aim was to use the 'one best way'.

(b) **Planning the work and doing the work were separated.** It was assumed that the persons who were intellectually equipped to do a particular type of work were probably unlikely to be able to plan it to the best advantage. With a working population that had minimal education and included a high proportion of immigrants from non-anglophone countries, this was probably a reasonable approach.

(c) **Workers were paid incentives** on the basis of acceptance of the new methods and output norms; the new methods greatly increased productivity and profits. Pay was assumed to be the only important motivating force.

2.6 Scientific management as practised by Taylor and contemparies such as *Gilbreth* and *Gantt* was very much about **manual work**. However, the rational, efficiency oriented engineering approach of these pioneers is conceptually very close to the organisational ideas of *Weber* and *Fayol* discussed in Chapter 1.

2.7 Scientific management is still practised today, whenever there is a concern for productivity and efficiency.

Mayo: reaction to scientific management

2.8 It is clear to us today that treating work people as though they are machines is not a recipe for either harmony in the workplace or for high quality work. In the 1920s research began to show that managers needed to consider the complexity of **human behaviour**.

2.9   *Elton Mayo* was professor of industrial research at the Harvard Business School. He was involved in a series of large scale studies at the Western Electric Company's Hawthorne works in Chicago between 1924 and 1932. These studies were originally firmly set in the context of scientific management in that they began with a parochial experiment into the effect of levels of light upon output. However, it rapidly became apparent that first, **individual attitudes** and, second, **group relationships** were of great importance in determining the levels of production achieved.

2.10   An important element in the Hawthorne studies was the investigation of the **informal group structure** which grew up among the work people. It was found that the informal group was very effective in enforcing its behavioural norms in such matters as loyalty to colleagues and restricting output. It was concluded that people are strongly motivated by **social** or **'belonging' needs.**

An appraisal of the human relations approach

2.11   The human relations approaches contributed an important awareness of the influence of the human factor at work (and particularly in the work group) on organisational performance. Most of its theorists attempted to offer guidelines to enable practising managers to satisfy and motivate employees and so (theoretically) to obtain the benefits of improved productivity.

2.12   However, the approach tends to emphasise the importance of work to the workers without really addressing the economic issues: there is still no proven link between job satisfaction and motivation, or either of these and productivity or the achievement of organisational goals.

3   MODERN WRITERS ON MANAGEMENT

3.1   In the second half of the twentieth century, writing on management has become more diverse.

   (a) The early emphasis on the organisation of work and work people has been continued in the field of **supervisory studies** and the development of specific management techniques such as **project management.** The search for efficiency continues in the field of **work study** and **industrial engineering.**

   (b) Human relations theory has been enhanced by developments in the study of motivation, group and individual behaviour, leadership and other aspects of industrial psychology.

   (c) There has been much new writing on the nature of the **manager's task**: what it is to be a manager and what managers do.

3.2   This sector deals with the contributions of some more recent writers on the general nature of management.

Peter Drucker: the management process

3.3   Peter Drucker worked in the 1940s and 1950s as a business adviser to a number of US corporations. He was also a prolific writer on management.

3.4   Drucker argued that the manager of a business has a basic function - **economic performance**. In this respect, the business manager is different from the manager of any other type of organisation. Management can only justify its existence and its authority by the economic results it produces, even though as a consequence of its actions, significant non-economic results occur as well.

3.5   He then described the jobs of management within this basic function of economic performance as follows.

(a)   **Managing a business.** The purposes of the business are:

- To create a customer
- Innovation

(b)   **Managing managers.** The requirements here are:

- Management by objectives
- Proper structure of managers' jobs
- Creating the right spirit in the organisation
- Making a provision for the managers of tomorrow
- Arriving at sound principles of organisation structure

(c)   **Managing worker and work.**

3.6   A manager's performance in all areas of management, including management of the business, can be enhanced by a study of the principles of management, the acquisition of 'organised knowledge' (eg management techniques) and the systematic self-assessment.

3.7   Later Drucker grouped the work of the manager into five categories.

(a)   **Setting objectives for the organisation.** Managers decide what the objectives of the organisation should be and quantify the targets of achievement for each objective. They must then communicate these targets to other people in the organisation.

(b)   **Organising the work.** The work to be done in the organisation must be divided into manageable activities and manageable jobs. The jobs must be integrated into a formal organisation structure, and people must be selected to do the jobs.

(c)   **Motivating** employees and communicating information to them to enable them to do their work.

(d)   **The job of measurement.** Management must:

- Establish **objectives** or yardsticks of performance for every person in the organisation
- Analyse **actual performance**, appraise it against the objectives or yardsticks which have been set, and analyse the comparison
- Communicate the findings and explain their significance both to subordinate employees and also to superiors

(e)   **Developing people.** The manager 'brings out what is in them or he stifles them. He strengthens their integrity or he corrupts them'.

3.8   Every manager performs all five functions listed above, no matter how good or bad a manager he is. However a bad manager performs these functions badly, whereas a good manager performs them well. Drucker emphasised the importance of *communication* in the functions of management, which should be evident in items (a), (c) and (d) above.

BPP
PUBLISHING

Ouchi: Theory Z

3.9 McGregor labelled two typical American approaches to management 'Theory X' and 'Theory Y' (see Chapter 13 of this Study Text). When the Japanese economy was performing well, a generation ago, it became fashionable to study Japanese management methods and promote them as a solution to the West's then seemingly intractable industrial problems. *Ouchi* called these methods 'Theory Z'.

3.10 The characteristics of a Theory Z organisation offer some interesting contrasts with the Western way of doing things.

   (a) Long term, often lifetime employment with one company, with a high value placed on mutual loyalty.

   (b) Relatively slow promotion.

   (c) Fairly specialised career paths for managers and the development of company-specific skills.

   (d) Implicit, informal control systems supported by explicit measures of performance.

   (e) Decision by consensus but ultimate individual responsibility.

   (f) Attention to the welfare of subordinates.

   (g) Informal relationships.

3.11 Theory Z was welcomed as a more human and therefore more effective way of managing people. It has had no lasting effect on Western management practice, unlike Japanese engineering and the JIT phenomenon.

Peters and Waterman: excellence

3.12 *Peters and Waterman* designated certain companies as **excellent** because over a 20 year period they had given an above average return on investment and they had a reputation for innovation.

3.13 Peters and Waterman identified eight **attributes of excellence**.
   - **A bias for action** rather than analysis
   - **Closeness to customers**
   - **Autonomy and entrepreneurship**
   - **Productivity through people**
   - **Hands-on, value driven**. There is a commitment to shared corporate value
   - **Stick to the knitting**: avoid conglomerate diversification
   - **Simplicity.** Excellent companies are not over-complicated
   - **Simultaneous loose-tight properties**: few rules and procedures but strong values

3.14 Peters and Waterman found that the '**dominance and coherence of culture' was an essential feature of the 'excellent'** companies they observed. A 'handful of guiding values' was more powerful than manuals, rule books, norms and controls formally imposed (and resisted).

3.15 **Excellence theories have been criticised**. Key problems are:
   - Many 'excellent' companies, such as IBM, have stumbled.
   - It concentrates on operational issues rather than long term strategy.
   - Strong cultures can impede necessary change.
   - It proposes that there is 'one best way' to succeed.

3.16   Excellence does not appear to involve any long-term strategic thinking, other than as a by-product of 'sticking to the knitting' and keeping 'close to customers' and sharing 'core values'. IBM was close to its customers because customers had no alternative: IBM had control of a proprietary and expensive technology.

4   MODERN WRITERS: MINTZBERG AND THE MANAGER'S TASK

4.1   Managerial **functions** are those activities necessary for the **organisation** to be managed. As we saw in the exercise above, however, a manager will do a number of **tasks** in each day. Henry Mintzberg (1989) did a study of a relatively small sample of US corporations to see how senior managers actually spend their time. He suggests that in their daily working lives, managers fulfil three **types** of managerial role.

Role category	Role	Comment
Interpersonal role	**Figurehead** (or ceremonial)	A large part of a Chief Executive's time is spent representing the company at dinners, conferences and so on.
	Leader	Hiring, firing and training staff, motivating employees, and reconciling individual needs with the requirements of the organisation
	Liaison	Making contacts outside the vertical chain of command. Some managers spend up to half their meeting time with their peers rather than with their subordinates and as such are the ambassadors or spies of the departments they control
Informational role Managers have: • Access to all their staff • Many external contacts	**Monitor**	The manager *monitors* the environment, and receives information from subordinates, superiors and peers in other departments. Much of this information is of an informal nature, derived from the manager's network of contacts. It might be gossip or speculation.
	Spokesperson	The manager provides information to interested parties either within or outside the organisation
	Disseminator	The manager *disseminates* this information to subordinates
Decisional role The manager's formal authority and access to information mean that no one else is in a position to take decisions relating to the work of the department as a whole.	**Entrepreneur**	A manager initiates possibly small scale projects, a number of which may be on the go at any one time, to improve the department or to help it react to a changed environment.

BPP PUBLISHING

Role category	Role	Comment
	Disturbance handler	A manager has to respond to pressures over which the department has no control, taking decisions in unusual or unexpected situations.
	Resource allocator	A manager takes decisions relating to the allocation of scarce resources. The manager determines the department's direction and authorises decisions taken by subordinates.
	Negotiator	Both inside and outside the organisation, negotiation takes up a great deal of management time.

4.2 Debunking myths about management work

Mintzberg's researches challenged the received wisdom of the time.

(a) Managers are **not reflective, systematic planners.**

(b) **Managerial work is disjointed** and discontinuous.

(c) Managers **do** have **routine** duties to perform, especially of a ceremonial nature (receiving important guests) or related to authority (signing cheques as a signatory) contrary to the myth that all routine work is done by juniors.

(d) Managers **prefer verbal** and informal information to the formal output of management information systems. Verbal information is 'hotter' and probably easier to grasp.

(e) **Management cannot be a science** or a profession. According to Mintzberg we do not know what procedures managers use, so they cannot be analysed scientifically or codified into an examinable body of theory.

4.3 Mintzberg states that general management is, in practice, a matter of **judgement and intuition**, gained from **experience** in **particular situations** rather than from abstract principles. 'Fragmentation and verbal communication' characterise the manager's work.

Question 2

'Mintzberg's findings completely invalidate the notion that there are distinct management functions'. Discuss.

Answer

Despite the fact that the managerial work might be as Mintzberg describes it, organisations are planned, directed and controlled, largely by managers. Mintzberg seems to be saying that much management knowledge is inherently personal (or tacit, as in paragraph 1.14). The ways in which individual managers or organisations perform those functions vary. (As has been said, there may be a separate group of strategic planners.) Individual managers implement strategy (eg in the **entrepreneurial** aspect of the **decision role**) and co-ordinate activities (indirectly perhaps by **negotiation** with other departments).The informational role is also necessary for proper co-ordination.

Rosemary Stewart: managerial behaviour

4.4 *Rosemary Stewart* developed a model for the analysis of managerial work that considers three elements.

- **Demands** are the duties and responsibilities that *must* be discharged.
- **Constraints** are factors that place limitations upon freedom of action.
- **Choices** represent areas of freedom or discretion.

4.5 Using these elements as a basis for studying managerial work leads Stewart to conclude, rather as Mintzberg does, that management is not a rational, ordered process. It consists much more of responding to random stimuli, exerting influence, trading, compromising and manoeuvring.

Kanter: managers and innovation

4.6 Many large companies seek to retain some of the innovation and flexibility supposedly characteristic of small firms. They are converging on a balance between bureaucracy (the old order) and entrepreneurial innovation (the new order) based on **synergies, alliances** and '**newstreams**'.

(a) A **synergy** is a combination of businesses, internal services and organisation structures which means that the whole is worth more in value than the sum of the parts. People at all levels focus on doing what they do best.

(b) Organisations are also seeking to extend their reach without increasing their size by forming closer working relationships or **strategic alliances** with other organisations. This involves partnerships and joint ventures as well as contracting out services to outside suppliers.

(c) A flow of new business possibilities within the organisation is termed a '**newstream**' by Moss Kanter. Instead of relying on innovation just happening, **official channels are created to speed the flow of new ideas such as special funds, creativity centres and incentives**. This implies a management approach which is sensitive, flexible, persistent and autonomous.

4.7 In *When Giants Learn to Dance, Moss Kanter* described some of the impossible or incompatible demands made on managers when seeking improved performance and excellence through innovation.

DEMANDS MADE ON MANAGERS

Be entrepreneurial and risk taking	*but*	Don't lose money
Invest in the future	*but*	Keep profitable now
Do everything you're doing now but even better	*but*	Spend more time communicating, on teams and new projects
Lead and direct	*but*	Participate, listen, co-operate
Know everything about your business	*but*	Delegate more
Work all hours	*but*	Keep fit
Be single-minded in your commitment to ideas	*but*	Be flexible and responsive

DEMANDS MADE ON ORGANISATIONS

Be 'lean and mean'	*but*	Be a good employer
Be creative and innovative	*but*	'Stick to the knitting'
Decentralise to small, simple autonomous units	*but*	Centralise to be efficient and integrative
Have a sense of urgency	*but*	Deliberately plan for the future

5 MANAGEMENT AND SUPERVISION: ACHIEVING TASKS

5.1 There are different levels of management in most organisations. A **finance department** in an organisation might be headed by the **finance director** (A) supported by a chief **financial accountant** (B) and chief **management accountant** (C). Lower down in the hierarchy assistant accountants might report to (B) and (C).

5.2 The supervisor is the lowest level of management.

5.3 **Features of supervision**

(a) A supervisor is usually a front-line manager, dealing with the levels of the organisation where the bread-and-butter work is done. The supervisor's **subordinates are non-managerial employees**.

(b) A supervisor does not spend all his or her time on the managerial aspects of his job. Much of the time will be spent doing **technical/operational work** himself.

(c) A supervisor is a **gatekeeper** or filter for communication in the organisation.

(d) The supervisor monitors and controls work by means of **day-to-day, frequent and detailed information:** higher levels of management plan and control using longer-term, less frequent and less detailed information, which must be 'edited' or selected and reported by the supervisor.

(e) The managerial aspects and responsibilities of a supervisor's job are often ill-defined, and given no precise targets for achievement.

5.4 Above the supervisor there may be several levels of management. Authority, responsibility and the timescale for decision-making all increase as the scalar chain is ascended. However, all managerial work may be considered to have some elements of similarity. Management as a subject has attracted considerable attention from with academics and practitioners. We shall consider some of their ideas in the sections that follow.

What do supervisors do?

5.5 As a supervisor's job is a junior management job, the tasks of supervision can then be listed under similar headings to the **tasks of management**.

5.6 **Planning**
- Planning **work** so as to **meet work targets** or schedules set by more senior management
- Planning the **work for each employee;** making estimates of overtime required
- Planning the total **resources** required by the section to meet the total work-load
- Planning work **methods and procedures**
- Attending departmental planning **meetings**
- Preparing **budgets** for the section
- Planning **staff training** and staff development
- Planning the **induction** of new staff
- Planning **improvements** in the work

5.7 **Organising and overseeing the work of others**
- **Ordering** materials and equipment from internal stores or external suppliers
- **Authorising spending** by others on materials, sundry supplies or equipment
- **Interviewing** and selecting staff
- Authorising overtime

- **Allocating work** to staff
- **Allocating equipment** to staff
- Reorganising work (for example when urgent jobs come in)
- Establishing **performance standards** for staff
- Organising transport
- Deciding **job priorities**
- General 'housekeeping' duties
- Maintaining **liaison** with more senior management

Question 3

Bert Close has decided to delegate the task of identifying the reasons for machine 'down' time (when machines are not working) over the past three months to Brenda Cartwright. This will involve her in talking to operators, foremen and supervisors and also liaising with other departments to establish the effects of this down time. What will Bert need to do to delegate this task effectively? List at least four items he will need to cover with Brenda.

Answer

- Identify task objectives
- Explain limits within which Brenda will work
- Deadlines
- Formats of reporting results
- Progress monitoring

5.8 **Controlling: making sure the work is done properly**
- **Keeping records** of total time worked on the section
- Deciding when sub-standard work must be re-done
- Attending progress control meetings
- Dealing with trade union representatives
- Dealing with personal problems of staff
- Disciplining staff (for late arrival at work and so on)
- Counselling staff
- Ensuring that work procedures are followed
- Ensuring that the quality of work is sustained to the required levels
- Ensuring that safety standards are maintained
- Checking the progress of new staff/staff training, on-the-job training
- Co-ordinating the work of the section with the work of other sections
- Ensuring that work targets are achieved, and explaining the cause to senior management of any failure to achieve these targets

5.9 **Motivating employees, and dealing with others: appraisal**
- Dealing with staff problems
- Dealing with people in other sections
- Reporting to a senior manager
- Dealing with customers
- Motivating staff to improve work performance
- Applying disciplinary measures to subordinates who act unreasonably or work badly
- Helping staff to understand the organisation's goals and targets
- Training staff, and identifying the need for more training

5.10 **Communicating**
- Telling employees about plans, targets and work schedules

39

- Telling managers about the work that has been done
- Filling in reports (for example absentee reports for the personnel department)
- Writing memos, notes and reports
- Passing information between employees and managers, and between sections
- Collecting information and distributing it to the other persons interested in it.
- Keeping up-to-date with developments

5.11 **'Doing'**

- Doing operations work
- Standing in for a senior manager when he or she is on holiday or otherwise absent
- Giving advice to others to help solve problems

Question 4

Look at the job of the supervisor (or similar position) in your office (your own job, if you are in such a position).

(a) Identify the (i) managerial and (ii) technical aspects of the job, and list as many as you can. Think of the duties they entail.

(b) Get hold of a copy of the **job description** of a supervisory job (or have a look at one in the organisation manual). Does it bear any relation to the list you compiled yourself? Is it a realistic description of the actual work of the supervisor? Is the 'supervisory' part of the job well-defined (as compared with the technical part)? Are there targets or standards, and training requirements?

(c) Consider your own experience of promotion to a supervisory post (or ask your supervisor). What preparation, training, coaching, and/or advice was given by the manager for this first step into managerial work - was it 'sink or swim'?

The resources at the manager's supervisor's disposal to achieve results

5.12 A supervisor is asked to get a piece of work done, or organise other people to get the work done. A supervisor has resources, as follows.

(a) **Human resources.** A supervisor can deploy his or her staff to do different tasks at different times.

(b) **Material resources,** for example. Some discretion over the use of machinery.

(c) **Financial resources,** within budget guideline.

Work planning

5.13 **Work planning** is the establishment of work methods and practices to ensure that predetermined objectives are efficiently met at all levels.

(a) **Task sequencing or prioritisation** (ie considering tasks in order of importance for the objective concerned).

(b) **Scheduling or timetabling tasks,** and allocating them to different individuals within appropriate time scales.

(c) **Establishing checks and controls** to ensure that:

(i)   Priority deadlines are being met and work is not 'falling behind'
(ii)   Routine tasks are achieving their objectives

(d) **Contingency plans:** arrangements for what should be done if a major upset were to occur, eg if the company's main computer were to break down.

(e) **Co-ordinating the efforts of individuals.**

(f) **Reviewing and controlling performance of individuals and group.**

5.14 Some jobs (eg assembly line worker), are entirely routine, and can be performed one step at a time, but for most people, some kind of planning and judgement will be required.

Assessing where resources are most usefully allocated

5.15 A manager or supervisor is responsible for allocating resources between:

(a) **Different ways** to achieve the same objective (eg to increase total profits, sell more, or cut costs etc).

(b) **Competing areas,** where total resources are limited.

5.16 **ABC analysis (Pareto analysis)** suggests that only a small proportion of items will be significant. For example a business might have 99 customers who each spend £10 per month and 1 customer who spends £100,000 per month. Pareto's Law assumes that, for sales, approximately 80% of sales volume is accounted for by 20% of the customers. This means that the manager will:

(a) Concentrate scarce resources on the crucial 20%.

(b) Devise policies and procedures for the remaining 80%, or delegate.

5.17 A piece of work will be **high priority** in the following cases.

- **If it has to be completed by a certain time** (ie a deadline)
- **If other tasks depend on it**
- **If other people depend on it**

5.18 **Routine priorities** or regular peak times (eg tax returns etc) can be **planned ahead of time,** and other tasks planned around them.

5.19 **Non-routine priorities** occur when **unexpected demands** are made. Thus planning of work should cover routine scheduled peaks and contingency plans for unscheduled peaks and emergencies.

Projects

> **KEY TERM**
>
> A **project** is 'an undertaking that has a beginning and an end and is carried out to meet established goals within cost, schedule and quality objectives' (Haynes, *Project Management*).

5.20 The difference between project planning and other parts of planning is that a **project is not a repetitive activity. Characteristics of projects are:**

- Specific start and end points
- Well-defined objectives
- The project endeavour is to a degree unique and not repetitious
- The project usually contains costs and time schedules
- A project cuts across many organisational and functional boundaries

BPP PUBLISHING

5.21 **Examples of projects**

Project	Comment
Building and construction	Any building project, such as the construction of 'Cyberjaya', a new high-tech city in Malaysia.
Management	Development of an information system.
Supervision	Installing new machinery

The role of the project manager or supervisor

5.22 The job of **project management** is to foresee as many dangers as possible, and to plan, organise, co-ordinate and control activities.

Duty	Comment
Outline project planning	• Developing project targets such as overall costs or timescale (eg project should take 20 weeks). • Dividing the project into activities (eg analysis, programming, testing), and placing these activities into the right sequence, often a complicated task if overlapping. • Developing the procedures and structures, manage the project (eg plan weekly team meetings, performance reviews etc).
Detailed planning	Identifying the tasks, resource requirements, network analysis for scheduling.
Teambuilding	The project manager has to meld the various people into an effective team.
Communication	The project manager must let superiors know what is going on, and ensure that members of the project team are properly briefed.
Co-ordinating project activities	Between the project team and users, and other external parties (eg suppliers of hardware and software).
Monitoring and control	The project manager should estimate the causes for each departure from the standard, and take corrective measures.
Problem-resolution	Unforeseen problems may arise, and it falls upon the project manager to sort them out, or to delegate the responsibility for so doing to a subordinate.
Quality control	There is often a short-sighted trade-off between getting the project out on time and the project's quality.

Chapter roundup

- **Management** is responsible for using the organisation's resources to meet its goals. It is accountable to the owners, in a business, to government in the public sector.

- **Supervision** is the lowest level of management.

- The classical writers were largely concerned with **efficiency.**

    ○ **Taylor** was an engineer and sought the most efficient methods.
    ○ **Fayol** was an administrator and proposed universal rules.
    ○ **Mayo** and his colleagues investigated the complexity of individual and group behaviour.

- Recently writers have examined what managers **actually** do, and theorised about what they **should** do.

    ○ **Drucker** emphasised the economic objective of managers in businesses.
    ○ **Mintzberg** described three categories of management role.
    ○ **Stewart** examined the **demands, constraints** and **choices** influencing managers.
    ○ **Ouchi** described the Japanese way of management
    ○ **Peters and Waterman** analysed the similarities between excellent organisations.
    ○ **Kanter** was concerned with innovation and its demands on managers.

Quick quiz

1 State Fayol's functions of management

2 State Taylor's principles of scientific management

3 What advance did the Hawthorne studies make in the management of people?

4 What overriding responsibility does the management of a business have, according to Drucker?

5 What managerial roles did Mintzberg describe and what categories did he group them into?

6 What types of influence on managerial work did Stewart examine?

7 What did Ouchi call the Japanese approach to management?

8 What criticisms have been made of Peters and Waterman's ideas about excellence?

Answers to quick quiz

1 Planning, organising, commanding, co-ordinating, controlling

2 The development of a true science of work; the scientific selection and progressive development of workers; the bringing together of the science and the workers; constant and intimate co-operation between management and workers.

3 **Individual attitudes** and **group relationships** help determine the level of output.

4 Economic performance.

5

Category	Roles
Interpersonal:	Figurehead; Leader; Liaison
Informational:	Monitor; Spokesperson; Disseminator
Decisional	Entrepreneur; Disturbance handler; Resource allocator; Negotiator

6 Demands, constraints, choices

7 Theory Z

8 Many excellent companies have stumbled. Long term strategy is ignored. Strong culture can impede change. It supports a single solutions to success

Now try the question below from the Exam Question Bank

Question to try	Level	Marks	Time
3	Exam	15	27

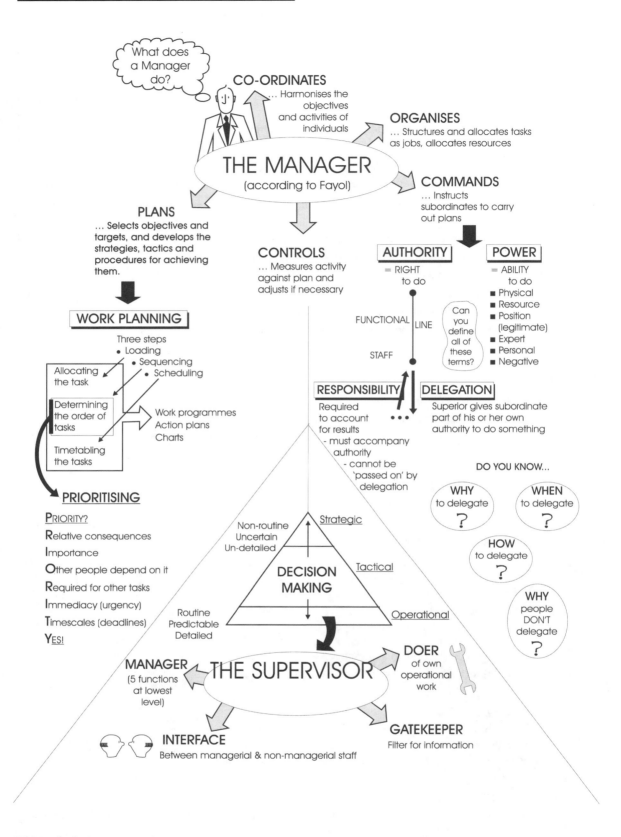

This mindmap covers the management task, and integrates several chapters' work.

Chapter 3

GROUP BEHAVIOUR: ORGANISATION CULTURE

Topic list	Syllabus reference
1 Organisation culture	1(d)
2 The informal organisation	1(d)

Introduction

Like chapter 1, this chapter contains background material that underpins the rest of the Study Text. The concept of culture is particularly important when thinking about how organisations work. **Culture is an aspect of group behaviour as it denotes how people interact.**

Study guide

Section 4(d) – Individual and group behaviour

- Explain the concept of organisation culture

- Discuss the differences between individual and group behaviour

Exam guide

Like the material in Chapter 1, the contents of this chapter could form part of the background to questions on most parts of the syllabus.

1 ORGANISATION CULTURE

> **KEY TERM**
>
> **Organisation culture:** the complex body of shared beliefs attitudes and values in an organisation.

1.1 Elements of organisation culture

Item	Example
Beliefs and values, which are often unquestioned	'The customer always prefers good quality to a cheaper price'
Customs: acceptable ways of behaviour, sometimes enforced by rules	Few organisations have a dress code as explicit as BT's. In the City of London, standard business dress is still taken for granted and even 'dress down Fridays' have their rules.

BPP
PUBLISHING

Item	Example
Artefacts: tools, buildings office layout	**Microsoft** encourages communication between employees by setting aside spaces for the purpose.
Rituals: formal, repeated behaviour	In some firms, sales people compete with each other, and there is a reward, given at a ceremony, for the salesperson who does best in any period.
Symbols: signs which stand in for other signs	**Corporate logos** are an example of symbols, but they are directed **outwards**. **Within** the organisation, symbols can represent power; dress, make and model of car, office size and equipment and access to facilities can all be important symbols.

1.2 **Manifestations of culture**
- How formal the organisation **structure** is
- **Communication:** are senior managers approachable?
- Office **layout**
- The type of **people** employed
- **Symbols, legends,** corporate **myths**
- **Management** style
- **Freedom** for subordinates to show initiative
- Attitudes to **quality**
- Attitudes to **risk**
- Attitudes to the **customer**
- Attitudes to **technology**

Question 1

What do you think would differentiate the culture of:

- A regiment in the army
- An advertising agency?

Answer

Here are some hints. The army is very disciplined. Decisions are made by officers; behaviour between ranks is sometimes very formal. The organisation values loyalty, courage and discipline and team work.

An advertising agency, with a different mission, is more fluid. Individual creativity, within the commercial needs of the firm, is expected.

1.3   **Characteristics of culture**

Characteristic	Comment
Exclusive	Organisation culture reinforces a sense of identity, but can suppress important information inconsistent with the culture
Group	A culture is shared: it sets criteria by which people are judged
Coherent	The assumptions of a culture should reinforce each other
Consistent over time	A culture gives its participants a sense of continuity
Consequences	The group's or the individual's actions follows on from the culture
Supportive	Some activities are justified if they are consistent with the culture
Pattern	The way a member of staff treats a customer might reflect the way a member of staff is treated by his or her superior
Offers solutions to dilemmas	A culture helps people act on persistent problems (eg cost vs quality)
Cultures can learn	Cultures can change over time

Culture and structure

1.4   Writing in 1972, *Roger Harrison* suggested that organisations could be classified into four types. His work was later popularised by *Charles Handy* in his book 'Gods of Management' (Harrison). The four types are differentiated by their structures, processes and management methods. The differences are so significant as to create **distinctive cultures**, to each of which Handy gives the name of a Greek God.

1.5   **Zeus** is the god representing the **power culture** or **club culture**. Zeus is a dynamic entrepreneur who rules with snap decisions. Power and influence stem from a central source, perhaps the owner-directors or the founder of the business. The degree of formalisation is limited, and there are few rules and procedures. Such a firm is likely to be organised on a **functional** basis.

(a)   The organisation is capable of adapting quickly to meet change.

(b)   Personal influence decreases as the size of an organisation gets bigger. **The power culture is therefore best suited to smaller entrepreneurial organisations, where the leaders have direct communication with all employees**.

(c)   Personnel have to get on well with each other for this culture to work. These organisations are clubs of 'like-minded people introduced by the like-minded people, working on empathetic initiative with personal contact rather than formal liaison.'

1.6   Apollo is the god of the **role culture** or bureaucracy. There is a presumption of logic and rationality.

BPP
PUBLISHING

(a) These organisations have a formal structure, and operate by well-established rules and procedures. Individuals are required to perform their job to the full, but not to overstep the boundaries of their authority. Individuals who work for such organisations tend to learn an expertise without experiencing risk; many do their job adequately, but are not over-ambitious.

(b) **The bureaucratic style can be very efficient** in a stable environment, when the organisation is large and when the work is predictable.

1.7 **Athena** is the goddess of the **task culture. Management is seen as completing a succession of projects or solving problems**.

- The task culture is reflected in project teams and task forces. In such organisations, **there is no dominant or clear leader. The principal concern in a task culture is to get the job done.** Therefore the individuals who are important are the **experts** with the ability to accomplish a particular aspect of the task.

- Performance is judged by results.

- Task cultures are expensive, as experts demand a market price.

- Task cultures also depend on variety, and to tap creativity requires a tolerance of perhaps costly mistakes.

1.8 **Dionysus** is the god of the **existential** or **person culture**. In the three other cultures, the individual is subordinate to the organisation or task. **An existential culture is found in an organisation whose purpose is to serve the interests of the individuals within it.** These organisations are rare, although an example might be a partnership of a few individuals who do all the work of the organisation themselves (with perhaps a little secretarial or clerical assistance).

- Barristers (in the UK) work through chambers. The clerk co-ordinates their work and hands out briefs, but does not control them.

- Management in these organisations are often lower in status than the professionals and are labelled secretaries, administrators, bursars, registrars and chief clerk.

- The organisation depends on the **talent of the individuals;** management is derived from the consent of the managed, rather than the delegated authority of the owners.

1.9 When thinking about these four types of culture, remember that they do not necessarily equate to specific organisation types, though some styles of organisation culture may accompany particular organisation structures. Also, it is quite possible for different cultures to prevail in different parts of the same organisation, especially large ones with many departments and sites.

Cultures, management traditions and organisational effectiveness

1.10 The descriptions above interrelate four different strands.

- The **individual**
- The type of **work** the organisation does
- The **culture** of the organisation
- The **environment**

1.11 Organisational effectiveness perhaps depends on an **appropriate fit** of all of them.

Case example

Handy cites a pharmaceutical company which at one time had all its manufacturing subcontracted, until the turnover and cost considerations justified a factory of its own. The company hired nine talented individuals to design and run the factory. Result:

(a) The **design team** ran on a task culture, with a democratic/consultative leadership style, using project teams for certain problems. This was successful while the factory was being built.

(b) After its opening, the factory, staffed by 400, was run on similar lines. There were numerous problems. Every problem was treated as a project, and the workforce resented being asked to help sort out 'management' problems. In the end, the factory was run in a slightly more autocratic way. Handy states that this is a classic case of an **Athenian** culture to create a factory being superseded by an **Apollonian** culture to run it. Different cultures suit different businesses.

Question 2

Review the following statements. Ascribe each of them to one of Harrison's four corporate cultures.

People are controlled and influenced by:

(a) the personal exercise of rewards, punishments or charisma;

(b) impersonal exercise of economic and political power to enforce procedures and standards of performance;

(c) communication and discussion of task requirements leading to appropriate action motivated by personal commitment to goal achievement;

(d) intrinsic interest and enjoyment in the activities to be done, and/or concern and caring for the needs of the other people involved.

Answer

(a) Zeus
(b) Apollo
(c) Athena
(d) Dionysus

1.12 Organisations, says Handy, have a tendency to develop Apollonian cultures because of **comparability** and **consistency**.

(a) **Consistency** in behaviour enables better planning and greater cost-effectiveness.

(c) **Comparability** is necessary so that effort can be directed at the most needy areas. Operational efficiency in different locations can be compared.

1.13 **Large size and consistency** are desirable from the control standpoint. However, 'Size ... brings formality, impersonality and rules and procedures in its train... Similarly, consistency implies budgets, norms, standardised methods, fixed reporting periods, common documents and the whole barrage of bureaucracy.' Handy believes that there are three 'strands of resistance' to Apollo.

(a) As an organisation gets larger, it becomes internally more complex and unmanageable.

(b) Apollonian cultures put the **role above the individual**. Individuals resent it. Here are some of the perverse consequences of Apollonian culture, outlined in *Rosabeth Moss Kanter's* Rules for Stifling Innovation.

1	Regard any new idea from below with suspicion.
2	Insist that people who need your approval first go through several other levels of management.
3	Get departments/individuals to challenge each other's proposals.
4	Express criticism freely, withhold praise, instil job insecurity.
5	Treat identification of problems as signs of failure.
6	Control everything carefully. Count everything in sight - frequently.
7	Make decisions in secret, and spring them on people.
8	Do not hand out information to managers freely.
9	Get lower-level managers to implement your threatening decisions.
10	Above all, never forget that you, the higher-ups, already know everything important about the business.

(c) **Changes in society**. 'There is in other words a growing clash in Western Society between organisation logic and the feelings of the individual'. Handy goes on to say that this is encouraged by an education system that values self-expression and team work as opposed to rote learning.

Tradition and management

1.14 Tradition is a part of culture in a society, and may also be a distinctive part of the management culture of an organisation

Management culture

1.15 Different countries have different ways of doing business.

Case example

'French managers see their work as an intellectual challenge, requiring the remorseless application of individual brainpower. They do not share the Anglo-Saxon view of management as an interpersonally demanding exercise, where plans have to be constantly "sold" upward and downward using personal skills.' This is especially relevant in the cross-border merger and acquisitions congruent on the Single European Market. For example, is a meeting called to **make a decision** or to **exchange views**?

(Harvard Business Review)

Case example

Another example of tradition in management cultures, also quoted in the *Harvard Business Review* (March-April 1993), is provided by the possible influence of Confucianism (the official ideology of the Chinese Empire until 1905) on some Asian companies. The article identifies certain core values in certain companies run by overseas Chinese. It bears some similarities to 'Zeus'.

(a) Thrift ensures survival.

(b) A high (even irrational) level of savings is desirable.

(c) Hard work.

(d) An incompetent relative is better than a competent stranger. Examples of this tradition are as follows.

(i) Poor managers all retained because they are 'family'.

(ii)   Family members sit in on decisions that 'non-family' members do not, even though, in Western practice, the non-family members would have more right to be there than some of the family members.

(iii)   Outsiders are not trusted.

(f)   Obedience to patriarchal authority is essential to maintain order and direction.

(g)   Investment is based on clan affiliations.

(h)   Tangible property is preferable to intangible property.

(i)   Be prepared to move.

The organisation's traditions

1.16   **Influences on culture**

(a)   The organisation's **founder**. A strong set of values and assumptions is set up by the organisation's founder, and even after he or she has retired, these values have their own momentum. Or, to put it another way, an organisation might find it hard to shake off its original culture.

(b)   The organisation's **history**.

(i)   Culture reflects the **era when the organisation was founded**.

(ii)   The effect of history can be determined by **stories, rituals and symbolic behaviour**. They legitimise behaviour and promote priorities.

(c)   **Leadership and management style**. An organisation with a strong culture recruits managers who naturally conform to it, who perpetuate the culture.

(d)   **Structure and systems**

The importance of culture: excellence

1.17   In 1982 *Tom Peters and Robert Waterman* published *In Search of Excellence*. By an anecdotal technique they set about describing and analysing what it was that made successful companies successful.

1.18   Excellent companies, according to Peters and Waterman, are good at two things:

- Producing commercially viable **new products**
- Responding to **changes in their environment**

1.19   Peters and Waterman noted that **excellent companies share certain characteristics**.

1	A bias for action and experimentation, for 'getting on with it'.
2	Closeness to the customer - quality, service and reliability. Many get their best ideas from customers.
3	Autonomy and entrepreneurship.
4	Productivity through people; at Texas Instruments, every worker is 'seen as a source of ideas, not just a pair of hands'.
5	Hands-on management, driven by value: managers walking factory floors to find out what is going on.
6	'An inclination to stick to the knitting' - stick with what they know and can run.
7	Simple structures, small numbers of top-level staff. Matrix structures are unpopular; most are very simple, often with many relatively small autonomous divisions.
8	Simultaneous loose-tight properties - they are at once centralised and decentralised. Autonomy is allowed on the shop-floor and in project teams but all parts of the organisation must adhere to core values.

1.20   These attributes were associated with the **leaders**, often the founders of the company. The role of managers is to manage the **values** of the company. A later work by Tom Peters with Nancy Austin, *A Passion For Excellence*, focuses on the importance of leadership and values. In particular, it advocates **management by wandering about** (MBWA), by which it means that managers should keep in touch with what customers want, how products are produced and how employees are carrying out their work.

2   THE INFORMAL ORGANISATION

The informal organisation

2.1   An **informal organisation** exists side by side with the formal one. When people work together, they establish social relationships and customary ways of doing things:

(a) Social **groups**, or cliques are formed, sometimes acting against one another.

(b) **Informal ways of getting things done** develop, which are different in character from the rules which are **imposed** by the formal organisation.

2.2   The informal organisation can improve communications and facilitate the co-ordination of various individuals or departments. Informal methods may be more flexible and adaptable to required changes than the formal ways of doing things.

2.3   Certain **individuals can have an important informal influence** in an organisation. For instance, in small organisations, there is often a trusted, long service employee, doing a job like payroll or production control, whose formal role is quite routine but who is used by the owners as a combination of sounding board, gossip conduit and repository of common sense. The person's main informal role is to act as a safety valve for non-unionised shop floor opinion.

2.4   The **informal structure supplements the formal structure** which improves the way in which top management sets about its job. The informal structure of a company may take over from the formal organisation when the formal structure is slow to adapt to change.

2.5 An **informal organisation** is **loosely structured, flexible and spontaneous**. Membership is gained consciously or unconsciously and it is often hard to determine the time when a person becomes a member.

2.6 **Section summary**

- Informal organisations exist in conjunction with formal ones.
- They can improve the working environment by supplementing the formal procedures for doing something.
- They introduce a degree of flexibility and spontaneity into a workplace.

Chapter roundup

- Culture in an organisation is found in the formalisation of its structure, how decisions are taken, the degree to which authority and responsibility are delegated, and the degree to which initiative is allowed.

- Harrison notes four **cultures**, to which he gives the names of Greek deities. The **power culture (Zeus)** is run by one individual, who makes snap decisions, with people who share his or her outlook and values. The **role culture** describes a rule-driven specialised bureaucracy. A **task culture** is one in which people group and regroup into teams to accomplish specific projects. An **existential culture** is one in which management serves employees who are professionals or experts. Some companies or tasks require more than one of these cultures.

- The importance of corporate culture for organisation success has been highlighted by **excellence** theories. However, while culture can help success it can be disadvantageous, as it **resists change**.

- In most organisations, there is an informal structure, derived out of a network of personal relations. The formal structure of authority might be subverted by the informal structure.

Quick quiz

1 What are the elements of culture?

2 What characterises a 'power' culture?

3 What do Handy's descriptions integrate?

4 What are excellent companies good at?

5 What is the informal organisation?

Answers to quick quiz

1 Beliefs and values, customs, artefacts, rituals, symbols.

2 Based on personalities; adaptable and informal; small businesses.

3 The individual, the work, the organisation, the environment.

4 Innovation; responding to change.

5 A network of personal relationships in which individuals have more or less influence than would be suggested by their function in the organisation hierarchy.

Now try question 2 from the Exam Question Bank at the end of the Text

Question to try	Level	Marks	Time
2	Exam		

Chapter 4

INDIVIDUALS, GROUPS AND TEAMS

Topic list	Syllabus reference
1 Individuals	1(a)
2 Groups and teams	1(d)
3 Membership and composition of the team	1(a)
4 Development of the team	1(d)
5 Building the team	1(d)
6 Successful teams	1(d)

Introduction

Teams are the basic building blocks of organisations and promoting team work is an important part of the management of people. In this chapter we look at the ways in which people associate with one another both in informal groups and in the more structured environment of the team. We consider in particular, how to create and maintain **effective** teams at work.

Study guide

Section 2(b) – The role of management

- Identify the difference between individual and group contribution to work performance:

Section 4(d) – Individual and group behaviour

- Discuss the differences between individual and group behaviour

- Outline the contribution of individuals and teams to organisational success

- Identify individual and team approaches to work

- Understand perception and role theory

Section 5(e) – Team management

- Explain the role of the manager in building the team and developing individuals

- Define the purpose of a team

- Outline the composition of successful teams: Belbin, Peters and Waterman

- Explain the development of a team: (Tuckman)

- List team building tools

Exam guide

Relationships within a team and the management of teams are likely to figure prominently in the examination. The pilot paper included a question on groups and teams in Section B.

1 INDIVIDUALS

Personality

1.1 In order to identify, describe and explain the differences between people, psychologists use the concept of **personality**.

> **KEY TERM**
>
> **Personality** is the total pattern of characteristic ways of thinking, feeling and behaving that constitute the individual's distinctive method of relating to the environment.

1.2 **Self and self-image**

Personality develops from dynamic process whereby the individual interacts with the environment and other people, through experience.

(a) **Self-image.** If people regularly praise your hard work, for example, you may have an image of yourself as a successful worker. People tend to behave, and expect to be treated, in accordance with their self-image.

(b) **Personality development.** People tend, as they mature, to become more actively independent, to take on more equal or superior relationships (moving from child-adult, to adult-adult and adult-child relationships) and to develop self control and self awareness.

1.3 **Personality and work behaviour**

An individual should be compatible with work in three ways.

Compatibility	Comments
With the task	Different personality types suit different types of work. A person who appears unsociable and inhibited will find sales work, involving a lot of social interactions, intensely stressful - and will probably not be very good at it.
With the systems and management culture of the organisation	Some people hate to be controlled, for example, but others want to be controlled and dependent in a work situation, because they find responsibility threatening.
With other personalities in the team	Personality clashes are a prime source of conflict at work. An achievement-oriented personality, for example, tends to be a perfectionist, is impatient and unable to relax, and will be unsociable if people seem to be getting in the way of performance: such a person will clearly be frustrated and annoyed by laid-back sociable types working (or not working) around him.

1.4 Where incompatibilities occur, the manager or supervisor has three options.

(a) **Restore compatibility**: this may be achieved by reassigning an individual to tasks more suited to his personality type, for example, or changing management style to suit the personalities of the team.

(b) **Achieve a compromise**: individuals should be encouraged to:

(i) **Understand the nature** of their differences. Others have the right to be themselves (within the demands of the team); personal differences should not be taken personally, as if they were adopted deliberately to annoy.

(ii) **Modify their behaviour** if necessary.

(c) **Remove the incompatible personality.** In the last resort, obstinately difficult or disruptive people may simply have to be weeded out of the team.

Question 1

Look at the following list and number the qualities in priority order. 1 is very important, 2 is quite important, 3 is unimportant.

(a) Good appearance
(b) Ability to do the job
(c) Ability to answer questions clearly
(d) A pleasant speaking voice
(e) Being objective

(f) A pleasant personality
(g) The ability to reason
(h) Being interested in further training
(i) Being used to working in a team
(j) Being a good listener

Answer

You probably felt as we did that none of the qualities listed were unimportant. You probably had similar priorities to ours, as follows.

Perception

1.5 Different people see things differently and human beings behave in (and in response to) the world, not as it really is, but as they see it.

KEY TERM

Perception is the psychological process by which stimuli or in-coming sensory data are selected and organised into patterns which are meaningful to the individual.

1.6 Perception may be determined by any or all of the following.

(a) **The context.** People see what they want to see: whatever is necessary or relevant in the situation in which they find themselves. You might notice articles on management in the newspapers while studying this module which normally you would not notice.

(b) **The nature of the stimuli.** Our attention tends to be drawn to large, bright, loud, unfamiliar, moving and repeated (not repetitive) stimuli. Advertisers know it.

(c) **Internal factors.** Our attention is drawn to stimuli that match our personality, needs, interests, expectations and so on If you are hungry, for example, you will pick the smell of food out of a mix of aromas.

(d) **Fear or trauma.** People are able to avoid seeing things that they don't want to see: things that are threatening to their security of self-image, or things that are too painful for them.

1.7 A complementary process of **perceptual organisation** deals with the **interpretation** of the data which has been gathered and filtered.

Perception and work behaviour

1.8 People do not respond to the world as it really is, but as they **perceive it to be**. If people act in ways that seem illogical or contrary to you, it is probably not because of stupidity or defiance, but because they simply do not see things in the same way you do.

(a) Consider whether **you** might be misinterpreting the situation.

(b) Consider whether **others** might be misinterpreting the situation or interpreting it differently from you.

(c) When tackling a task or a problem get the people involved to **define the situation** as they see it.

(d) Be aware of the most common clashes of perception at work.

  (i) **Managers and staff.** The experience of work can be very different for managerial and non-managerial personnel. Efforts to bridge the gap may be viewed with suspicion.

  (ii) **Work cultures.** Different functions in organisations may have very different time-scales and cultures of work, and will therefore perceive the work, and each other, in different ways.

  (iii) **Race and sex.** A joke, comment or gesture that one person may see as amusing may be offensive - and construed as harassment under the law - to another.

Question 2

Identify the perceptual problem(s) in the following cases.

(a) An autocratic manager tries to adopt a more participative style of management, in order to improve the morale of his staff. He tells them they will be given more responsibility, and will be 'judged and rewarded accordingly'. For some reason, morale seems to worsen, and several people ask to transfer to other departments.

(b) A woman has just be promoted to the management team. At the first management meeting, the chairman introduces her to her new colleagues - all male - and says: 'At least we'll get some decent tea in these meetings from now on, eh?' Almost everyone laughs. For some reason, the woman does not contribute much in the meeting, and the chairman later tells one of his colleagues: 'I hope we haven't made a mistake. She doesn't seem to be a team player at all.'

(c) A new employee wanders into the office canteen, and is offered a cup of coffee by a youngster in jeans and an T-shirt, who has been chatting to the canteen supervisor. The youngster joins the man at his table (to his surprise) and asks how he likes working there so far. After a while, glancing uneasily at the man behind the serving counter, the new employee asks: 'Is it OK for you to be sitting here talking to me? I mean, won't the boss mind?' The youngster replies: 'I am the boss. Actually, I'm the boss of the whole company. Biscuit?'

Answer

The perceptual problems in the situations given are as follows.

(a) The manager perceives himself as 'enlightened', and his style as an opportunity and gift to his staff. he clearly thinks that assessment and reward on the basis of more responsibility is a positive thing, probably offering greater rewards to staff. He does not perceive his use of the work 'judged' as potentially threatening: he uses it as another word for 'assessed'. His staff obviously see things differently. 'More responsibility' means their competence - maybe their jobs - are on the line. Feeling this way, and with the expectations they have of their boss (based on past experience of his autocratic style), they are bound to perceive the work 'judged' as threatening.

(b) The chairman thinks he is being funny. Maybe he is only joking about the woman making the tea - but he may really perceive her role that way. He lacks the perception that his new colleague may find his remark offensive. From the woman's point of view, she is bound to be sensitive and insecure in her first meeting and with all male colleague: small wonder that, joke or not, she perceives the chairman's comment as a slap in the face. The chairman later fails to perceive the effect his joke has had on her, assuming that her silence is a sign of poor co-operation or inability to communicate.

(c) This is a case of closure leading to misinterpretation. The new employee sees the informal dress, the position behind the counter, and the offer of coffee: his brain fills in the gaps, and offers the perception that the youngster must be the tea-boy. Perceptual selectivity also plays a part filtering out awkward information that does not fit his expectations (like the fact that the 'tea-boy' comes to chat with him).

Attitudes

1.9 Attitudes are our general standpoint on things: the positions we have adopted in regard to particular issues, things and people, as we perceive them.

> **KEY TERM**
>
> An **attitude** is 'a mental state ... exerting a directive or dynamic influence upon the individual's response to all objects and situations with which it is related.'

1.10 **Attitudes** are thought to contain three basic components.

- Knowledge, beliefs or disbeliefs, perceptions
- Feelings and desires (positive or negative)
- Volition, will or the intention to perform an action

Attitudes and work

1.11 Behaviour in a work context will be influenced by:

(a) **Attitudes to work:** the individual's standpoint on working, work conditions, colleagues, the task, the organisation and management.

(b) **Attitudes at work:** all sorts of attitudes which individuals may have about other people, politics, education, religion among other things, and which they bring with them into the work place - to act on, agree, disagree or discuss.

1.12 Positive, negative or neutral attitudes to other workers, or groups of workers, to the various systems and operations of the organisation, to learning - or particular training initiatives - to communication or to the task itself will obviously influence performance at work. In particular, they may result in varying degrees of:

- Co-operation or conflict between individuals and groups, or between departments
- Co-operation with or resistance to management
- Success in communication - interpersonal and organisation wide
- Commitment and contribution to the work

Question 3

Suggest four elements which would make up a positive attitude to work. (An example might be the belief that you get a fair day's pay for a fair day's work.)

Answer

Elements of a positive attitude to work may include a willingness to:

(a) Commit oneself to the objectives of the organisation, or adopt personal objectives that are compatible with those of the organisation.

(b) Accept the right of the organisation to set standards of acceptable behaviour for its members.

(c) Contribute to the development and improvement of work practices and performance.

(d) Take advantages of opportunities for personal development at work.

1.13 **Non-work factors that might influence attitudes to work, or affecting work**

(a) **Class and class consciousness:** attitudes about the superiority or inferiority of others, according to birth, wealth and education; attitudes to money and work (necessity or career?).

(b) **Age**. Attitudes to sexual equality, family and morality can vary widely from one generation to the next.

(c) **Race, culture or religion**. These will affect the way people regard each other and their willingness to co-operate in work situations. Culture and religion are also strong influences on attitudes to work.

(d) **Lifestyle and interests**. Attitudes to these areas affect interpersonal relations and self-image, as well as the relative importance of work and leisure to the individual.

(e) **Sex**. Attitudes to the equality of the sexes and their various roles at work and in society may be influential in:

   (i) **Interpersonal relations at work**: sexist attitudes and language

   (ii) **The self concept of the individual:** women at work may be made to feel inferior, incompetent or simply unwelcome, while men working for female managers might feel threatened

   (iii) **Attitudes to work.** Stereotypical role profiles ('a women's place is in the home', 'the man has to support the family') may be held by both sexes and may create feelings of guilt, resentment or resignation about wanting or having to work.

1.14 **Intelligence** is a wide and complex concept. Sensible analysis of its complexity is not helped by the current fashion for labelling personal qualities is types A intelligence, when more precise terminology is available.

(a) **Analytic intelligence**: measured by IQ test

(b) **Spatial intelligence**: the ability to see patterns and connections, most obvious in the creative artist or scientist

(c) **Musical intelligence**: musical ability

(d) **Physical intelligence**: strength, speed agility, dexterity

(e) **Practical intelligence**: practical aptitude, handiness

(f) **Intra-personal intelligence**: self-awareness, self expression

(g) **Inter-personal intelligence**: empathy, sympathy, understanding

Role theory

1.15 Many people behave in any situation according to the roles they are expected to perform, and the role tends to influence the type of interpersonal relationships that people have.

(a) A **role set** is a group of people who respond to a person in a particular way. As a supervisor or manager, your subordinates and superiors are likely to respond to you as a supervisor or manager rather than according to the other roles that you play.

(b) **Role signs** indicate what role people are in at any particular time. A good example is office dress. Some firms are very strict about this.

(c) **Role ambiguity**. There is confusion about the roles a person plays.

(d) People select role **models** on which to base themselves throughout life. An individual's attraction as role model may come from their:

- Charisma, or personality
- Expertise or talent
- Success
- Dominance

Question 4

Choose one role in which your regularly interact with other people. (The role of 'student', say?)

(a) Identify your role set and role signs.

(b) Identify any areas of ambiguity, compatibility or conflict the role presents. What could be done about each (if anything)? Could the other members of your role set help?

Answer

Your answer might be along the following lines.

(a) If you chose 'student' your role set would consist of fellow students, lecturers, library and administrative staff. Your role signs may include dressing and acting informally with your colleagues, but being rather more formal with others.

(b) Lecturers who dress and act informally with their students may cause problems. Mature students with partners and children may find role incompatible when study interferes with personal life.

Question 5

Managers could exert a powerful influence over team members if they could establish themselves as role models. What kind of example could they set that might be helpful for the team members and for the organisation?

Answer

You may have your own views on examples managers could set. Basically, successful managers provide an aspirational model: showing junior staff that it is possible for them to achieve organisational success and the lifestyle that may go with it. A manager may also model the roles of popular leaders, a person who combines work and home/leisure life, a person who does not panic in a crises, a person who is developing their skills and so on. Models are, after all, in the eye of the beholder!

---

2 GROUPS AND TEAMS

2.1 As an employee your relationship with the organisation is as an individual: after all, the employment contract is with you as an individual, and you are recruited as an individual. In your working life, though, you will generally find yourself working as part of a group or **team**. If you are a supervisor or a manager, you may direct a **team**.

Groups

> **KEY TERM**
>
> A **group** is any collection of people who perceive themselves to be a group.

2.2   Groups have certain attributes that a random crowd does not possess.

(a) **A sense of identity**. There are acknowledged boundaries to the group which define who is in and who is out, who is us and who is them.

(b) **Loyalty to the group,** and acceptance within the group. This generally expresses itself as conformity or the acceptance of the norms of behaviour and attitudes that bind the group together and exclude others from it.

(c) **Purpose and leadership.** Most groups have an express purpose, whatever field they are in: most will, spontaneously or formally, choose individuals or sub-groups to lead them towards the fulfilment of those goals.

2.3   Any organisation is composed of many groups, with attributes of their own. People in organisations will be drawn together into groups by a variety of forces.

- A **preference for small groups,** where closer relationships can develop
- The **need to belong** and to make a contribution that will be noticed and appreciated
- **Familiarity:** a shared office or canteen
- **Common** rank, specialisms, objectives and interests
- The attractiveness of a particular group **activity** (joining an interesting club, say)
- **Resources** offered to groups (for example sports facilities)
- **Power** greater than the individuals could muster alone (trade union, pressure group)
- **Formal** directives

2.4   **Informal** groups will invariably be present in any organisation. Informal groups include workplace cliques, and networks of people who regularly get together to exchange information, groups of 'mates' who socialise outside work and so on. They have a constantly fluctuating membership and structure.

2.5   **Formal** groups will be consciously organised by the organisation, for a task which they are held responsible - they are task oriented, and become **teams**. Although many people enjoy working in teams, their popularity in the work place arises because of their effectiveness in fulfilling the organisation's work.

Question 6

What primary groups are you a member of in your study or work environment(s)? How big are these groups? How does the size of your class, study group, work-team - or whatever- affect your ability to come up with questions or ideas and give you the help and support to do something you couldn't do alone?

Answer

The primary groups are probably your tutor group or class. If at work, it would be the section in which you work. If the groups are large, you may feel reluctant to put forward ideas or ask questions, but even within a large group you should feel there is support and that help is at hand if you need it.

BPP PUBLISHING

Teams

> **KEY TERM**
>
> A **team** is a small number of people with complementary skills who are committed to a *common purpose*, performance *goals* and approach for which they hold themselves basically accountable.

2.6 Purpose of teams

Type of role	Comments
Work organisation	Combine skills of different individuals.
	Avoids complex communication between different business functions.
Control	Fear of letting down the team can be a powerful motivator - teams can be used to control the performance and behaviour of individuals.
	Teams can be used to resolve conflict
Knowledge generation	Teams can generate ideas.
Decision-making	Decisions can be evaluated from more than one viewpoint.
	Teams can be set up to investigate new developments.

Teamworking

2.7 The basic work units of organisations have traditionally been specialised functional departments. In more recent times, organisations are adopting small, flexible teams. Teamworking allows work to be **shared** among a number of individuals, so it gets done faster than by individuals working alone. Individuals working alone may achieve less.

- They lose sight of their whole tasks
- They have to co-ordinate their efforts through lengthy channels of communication

2.8 A team may be called together temporarily, to achieve specific task objectives (**project team**), or may be more or less permanent, with responsibilities for a particular product, product group or stage of the production process (a **product or process team**).

There are two basic approaches to the organisation of team work: multi-skilled teams and multi-disciplinary teams.

Multi-disciplinary teams

2.9 **Multi-disciplinary teams** bring together individuals with **different skills and specialisms**, so that their skills, experience and knowledge can be **pooled** or exchanged.

2.10 Multi-disciplinary teams do three things.

(a) Increase workers' **awareness of their overall objectives** and targets

(b) **Aid co-ordination** between different areas of the business

(c) **Help to generate solutions to problems,** and suggestions for improvements, since a multi-disciplinary team has access to more pieces of the jigsaw

Multi skilled teams

2.11 A multi-skilled team brings together a number of individuals who can **perform *any* of the** group's tasks. These tasks can then be shared out in a more flexible way between group members, according to who is available and best placed to do a given job at the time it is required.

2.12 The recognition that greater autonomy can - and perhaps should - be given to work teams is reflected clearly in the comparatively recent concept of **empowerment,** which is discussed in the next chapter.

2.13 Teams and teamworking are very much in fashion, but there are potential drawbacks.

(a) Teamworking is **not suitable for all jobs** - some managers do not like to admit this.

(b) Teamwork should be introduced because it leads to better performance, not because people feel better or more secure.

(c) The teams can delay good decision-making. The team might produce the compromise decision, not the right decision.

(d) Social relationships might be maintained at the expense of other aspects of performance.

(e) **Group norms** may **restrict individual personality** and flair.

(f) **Group think.** The cosy consensus prevents consideration of alternatives or constructive criticism.

(g) Personality clashes and political behaviour can get in the way of decision making.

Individual and group contribution

Question 7

Identify some differences between your contribution as an individual to your organisation and your contribution as a team member.

Answer

Individuals contribute:	Groups contribute:
• A set of skills	• A mix of skills
• Objectives set by manager	• Some teams can set their own objectives under the corporate framework
• A point of view	• A number of different points of view, enabling a swift overview of different ways of looking at a problem
• Creative ideas related to the individual's expertise	• Creative ideas arising from new combinations of expertise
• 'I can't be in two places at once'	• Flexibility as team members can be deployed in different ways
• Limited opportunity for self-criticism	• Opportunity for exercising control

Question 8

Before reading on, list five 'types' of people that you would want to have on a project team, involved (say) in organising an end-of-term party.

Answer

For your ideal team, you might have listed: a person with originality and ideas; a 'get up and go' type, with energy and enthusiasm; a quite logical thinker who can be sensible about the ideas put forward; a plodder who will be happy to do the routine leg-work; and a team player who can organise the others and help them reach agreement on ideas.

3 MEMBERSHIP AND COMPOSITION OF THE TEAM

Who should belong?

3.1 Team members should be good at getting things done and establishing good working relationships. Here is what determines membership.

(a) The technical specialist **skills needed**. A team might exist to combine expertise from different departments.

(b) **Power** in the wider organisation. Team members may have influence.

(c) Access to **resources**.

(d) The **personalities** and goals of the individual **members** of the team will help to determine the group's and goals.

(e) The **blend** of the individual skills and abilities of its members.

3.2 **Belbin** (1981) drew up a list of the most effective character-mix in a team. This involves eight necessary roles which should ideally be **balanced** and evenly 'spread' in the team.

Member	Role
Co-ordinator	Presides and co-ordinates; balanced, disciplined, good at working through others.
Shaper	Highly strung, dominant, extrovert, passionate about the task itself, a spur to action.
Plant	Introverted, but intellectually dominant and imaginative; source of ideas and proposals but with disadvantages of introversion.
Monitor-evaluator	Analytically (rather than creatively) intelligent; dissects ideas, spots flaws; possibly aloof, tactless - but necessary.
Resource-investigator	Popular, sociable, extrovert, relaxed; source of new contacts, but not an originator; needs to be made use of.
Implementer	Practical organiser, turning ideas into tasks; scheduling, planning and so on; trustworthy and efficient, but not excited; not a leader, but an administrator.
Team worker	Most concerned with team maintenance – supportive, understanding, diplomatic; popular but uncompetitive - contribution noticed only in absence.
Finisher	Chivvies the team to meet deadlines, attend to details; urgency and follow-through important, though not always popular.

The **specialist** joins the team to offer expert advice when needed.

How do people contribute?

3.3 Analysing the functioning of a team

(a) Assess who (if anybody) is performing each of Belbin's **team roles**. Who is the team's plant? co-ordinator? monitor-evaluator? and so on.

(b) Analyse the **frequency and type** of individual members' contributions to group discussions and interactions.

(i) Identify which members of the team habitually make the most contributions, and which the least. (You could do this by taking a count of contributions from each member, during a sample 10-15 minutes of group discussion.)

(ii) If the same people tend to dominate discussion **whatever** is discussed, the team has a problem.

3.4 Neil Rackham and Terry Morgan have developed a helpful categorisation of the types of contribution people can make to team discussion and decision-making.

Category	Behaviour	Example
Proposing	Putting forward suggestions, new concepts or courses of action	'Why don't we look at a flexi-time system?'
Building	Extending or developing someone else's proposal.	'Yes. We could have a daily or weekly hours allowance, apart from a core period in the middle of the day.'
Supporting	Supporting another person or his/her proposal.	'Yes, I agree, flexi-time would be worth looking at.'
Seeking information	Asking for more facts, opinions or clarification.	'What exactly do you mean by "flexi-time"?'
Giving information	Offering facts, opinions or clarification.	'There's a helpful outline of flexi-time in this article.'
Disagreeing	Offering criticism or alternative factors or opinions which contradict a person's proposals or opinions.	'I don't think we can take the risk of not having any staff here at certain periods of the day.'
Attacking	Attempting to undermine another person or their position: more emotive than disagreeing.	'In fact, I don't think you've thought this through at all.'
Defending	Arguing for one's own point of view.	'Actually, I've given this a lot of thought, and I think it makes sense.'
Blocking/ difficulty stating	Putting obstacles in the way of a proposal, without offering any alternatives.	'What if the other teams get jealous? It would only cause conflict.'
Open behaviour	Risking ridicule and loss of status by being honest about feelings and opinions.	'I thing some of us are afraid that flexi-time will show up how little work they really do in a day.'

Cont'd/......

BPP PUBLISHING

Category	Behaviour	Example
Shutting-out behaviour	Interrupting or overriding others; taking over.	'Nonsense. Let's move onto something else - we've had enough of this discussion.
Bringing-in behaviour	Involving another member; encouraging contribution.	'Actually, I'd like to hear what Fred has to say. Go on, Fred.'
Testing understanding	Checking whether points have been understood.	'So flexi-time could work over a day or a week; have I got that right?'
Summarising	Drawing together or summing up previous discussion.	'We've now heard two sides to the flexi-time issue: on the one hand, flexibility; on the other side possible risk. Now ... '

3.5 Each type of behaviour may be appropriate in the right situation at the right time. A team may be low on some types of contribution - and it may be up to the team leader to encourage, or deliberately adopt, desirable behaviours (such as bringing-in, supporting or seeking information) in order to provide balance.

4 DEVELOPMENT OF THE TEAM

4.1 You probably have had experience of being put into a group of people you do not know. Many teams are set up this way and it takes some time for the team to become effective.

4.2 Four stages in this development were identified by Tuckman (1965).

Step 1. **Forming**
The team is just coming together. Each member wishes to impress his or her **personality** on the group. The individuals will be trying to find out about each other, and about the aims and norms of the team. There will at this stage probably be a **wariness about introducing new ideas**. The **objectives** being pursued may as yet be **unclear** and a leader may not yet have emerged. This period is essential, but may be time wasting: the team as a unit will not be used to being autonomous, and will probably not be an efficient agent in the planning of its activities or the activities of others.

Step 2. **Storming**
This frequently involves more or less open **conflict** between team members. There may be **changes** agreed in the original objectives, procedures and norms established for the group. If the team is developing successfully this may be a fruitful phase as more realistic targets are set and **trust** between the group members increases.

Step 3. **Norming**
A period of **settling down**: there will be agreements about work sharing, individual requirements and expectations of output. Norms and procedures may evolve which enable methodical working to be introduced and maintained.

Step 4. **Performing**
The team sets to work to execute its task. The difficulties of growth and development no longer hinder the group's objectives.

Question 9

Read the following statements and decide to which category they belong (forming, storming, norming, performing, dorming).

(a)   Two of the group arguing as to whose idea is best.
(b)   Progress becomes static.
(c)   Desired outputs being achieved.
(d)   Shy member of group not participating.
(e)   Activities being allocated.

Answer

Categorising the behaviour of group members in the situations described results in the following: (a) storming, (b) dorming, (c) performing, (d) forming, (e) norming.

5   BUILDING THE TEAM

5.1   In Section 3, we suggested that teams have a natural evolutionary life cycle, and that four stages can be identified. Not all teams develop into mature teams, and might be stuck, stagnating, in any one of the stages.

5.2   So, it often falls to the supervisor or manager to build the team. There are three main issues involved in team building.

Issues	Comments
Team identity	Get people to see themselves as part of this group
Team solidarity	Encourage loyalty so that members put in extra effort for the sake of the team
Shared objectives	Encourage the team to commit itself to shared work objectives and to co-operate willingly and effectively in achieving them.

5.3   **Teambuilding tools** should seek to achieve these objectives. However, with the best will in the world, problems can develop. **Woodcock** refers to **blockages** and **building blocks** in the team building process. Adapted, these are as follows.

Issue	Blockage	Building block
Leadership	Inappropriate	The leader can adopt a suitable leadership style. See Chapter 10
Membership	Insufficient mix of skills and personalities	Ensure team members are suitably qualified; if necessary, get them to adopt another role than what they would normally
Climate	Unconstructive	Strive to achieve an atmosphere of co-operation
Objectives	Not clear	The team has been brought together for some organisational purpose, so this can be clarified and developed into sub-objectives which are agreed

Issue	Blockage	Building block
Achievement	Poor achievement	Performance is improved in a climate of trust and learning
Work methods	Ineffective	Develop sensible procedures for carrying out the team's business
Communications	Not open; people are afraid to challenge or confront key issues	Develop a climate in which people can speak their minds, constructively
Individuals	Development needs not attended to	Individuals are given opportunities to grow or develop within the team; easier in multi-skilled teams
Creativity	Low	Techniques such as brainstorming can enhance creativity, but a lot depends on how new ideas are treated
Interpersonal relations	Poor and unconstructive	Some people will never get on or have much in common, but they can still work together effectively. Exercises might be needed to break the ice
Review and control	Non-existent	The performance of the team can be reviewed at regular intervals

5.4 We can now discuss some of the techniques for building team identity, team solidarity and the commitment to shared-objectives. But first try the question below.

Question 10

Why might the following be effective as team-building exercises?

(a) Sending a project team (involved in the design of electronic systems for racing cars) on a recreational day out karting.

(b) Sending two sales teams on a day out playing 'War Games, each being an opposing combat team trying to capture the other's flag, armed with paint guns.

(d) Sending a project team on a conference at a venue away from work, with a brief to review the past year and come up with a vision for the next year.

These are actually commonly-used techniques. If you are interested, you might locate an activity centre or company near you which offers outdoor pursuits, war games or corporate entertainment and ask them about team-building exercises and the effect they have on people.

Answer

(a) Recreation helps the team to build informal relationships: in this case, the chosen activity also reminds them of their tasks, and may make them feel special, as part of the motor racing industry, by giving them a taste of what the end user of their product does.

(b) A team challenge purses the group to consider its strengths and weaknesses, to find it's natural leader. This exercise creates and 'us' and 'them' challenge: perceiving the rival team as the enemy heightens the solidarity of the group.

(c) This exercise encourages the group the raise problems and conflicts freely, away from the normal environment of work and also encourages brainstorming and the expression of team members' dreams for what the team can achieve in the future.

5.5 A manager might seek to reinforce the sense of identity of the group. Arguably this is in part the creation of boundaries, identifying who is in the team and who is not.

(a) **Name**. Staff at McDonald's restaurants are known as the Crew. In other cases, the name would be more official describing what the team actually does (eg Systems Implementation Task Force)

(b) **Badge or uniform**. This often applies to service industries, but it is unlikely that it would be applied within an organisation

(c) Expressing the team's **self-image:** teams often develop their own jargon, especially for new projects

(d) Building a team **mythology** - in other words, stories from the past ('classic mistakes' as well as successes.)

(e) **A separate space**: it might help if team members work together in the same or adjacent offices, but this is not always possible.

Question 11

Consider the group of people you are studying with. Do you feel you are a team? Appoint a leader - someone you think is a 'co-ordinator' type, who will keep the discussion on track and under control - and try another brainstorming session. This time you are going to organise the end of term party.

5.6 **Team solidarity** implies cohesion and loyalty inside the team. A team leader might be interested in:

(a) Expressing solidarity

(b) Encouraging interpersonal relationships - although the purpose of these is to ensure that work does get done.

(c) Dealing with conflict by getting it out into the open; disagreements should be expressed and then resolved

(d) Controlling competition. The team leader needs to treat each member of the team fairly and to be seen to do so; favouritism undermines solidarity.

(e) Encouraging some competition with other groups if appropriate. For example, sales teams might be offered a prize for the highest monthly orders; London Underground runs best-kept station competitions.

Question 12

Can you see any dangers in creating a very close-knit group? Think of the effect of strong team cohesion:

(a) what the group spends its energies and attention on;
(b) how the group regards outsiders, and any information or feedback they supply;
(c) how the group makes decisions.

What could be done about these dangerous effects?

Answer

Problems may arise in an ultra close-knit group because:

(a) The group's energies may be focused on its own maintenance and relationships, instead of on the task.

(b) The group may be suspicious or dismissive of outsiders, and may reject any contradictory information or criticism they supply; the group will be blinkered and stick to its own views, no matter what; cohesive groups thus often get the impression that they are infallible: they can't be wrong - and therefore can't learn from this mistake.

(c) The group may squash any dissent or opinions that might rock the boat. Close-knit groups tend to preserve a consensus - falsely if required - and to take risky decisions, because they have suppressed alternative facts and viewpoints.

This phenomenon is called **'groupthink'**. In order to limit its effect, the team must be encouraged:

(a) Actively to seek outside ideas and feedback;
(b) To welcome self-criticism within the group; and
(c) Consciously to evaluate conflicting evidence and opinions.

5.7 Getting commitment to the team's objectives

- Clearly set out the objectives of the team
- Allowing the team to participate in setting objectives
- Regular feedback on progress and results with constructive criticism
- Get the team involved in providing feedback
- Positive reinforcement (praise etc) can encourage the team
- Where appropriate, champion the success of the team within the organisation

6 SUCCESSFUL TEAMS

6.1 Some teams work more effectively than others, for a variety of reasons, and we can identify ways **of evaluating** whether a team is effective and successful.

	Quantifiable factors	
Factor	**Effective team**	**Ineffective team**
Labour turnover	Low	High
Accident rate	Low	High
Absenteeism	Low	High
Output and productivity	High	Low
Quality of output	High	Low
Individual targets	Achieved	Not achieved
Stoppages and interruptions to the work flow	Low	High (eg because of misunderstandings, disagreements)
Commitment to targets and organisational goals	High	Low
Understanding of team's work and why it exists	High	Low
Understanding of individual roles	High	Low

	Qualitative factors	
Factor	Effective team	Ineffective team
Communication between team members	Free and open	Mistrust
Ideas	Shared for the team's benefit	'Owned' (and hidden) by individuals for their own benefit
Feedback	Constructive criticism	Point scoring, undermining
Problem-solving	Addresses causes	Only looks at symptoms
Interest in work decisions	Active	Passive acceptance
Opinions	Consensus	Imposed solutions
Job satisfaction	High	Low
Motivation in leader's absence	High	'When the cat's away...'

Rewarding effective teams

6.2 Organisations may try to encourage effective team performance by designing reward systems that recognise **team**, rather than **individual** success. Indeed, individual performance rewards may act against team performance.

(a) They **emphasise** individual rather than team performance.

(b) They encourage team leaders to think of team members only as individuals rather than relating to them as a team.

6.3 For **team rewards** to be effective, the team must have certain characteristics.

(a) Distinct roles, targets and performance measures
(b) Significant autonomy and thus influence over performance
(c) Maturity and stability co-operation
(d) Interdependence of team members

6.4 **Reward schemes**

(a) **Profit sharing** schemes are based on a pool of cash related to profit.

(b) **Gainsharing** schemes use a formula related to a suitable performance indicator, such as added value. Improvements in the performance indicator must be within the employees control.

(c) **Employee share option** schemes give the right to acquire shares in the employing company at an attractive price.

6.5 We cover these in more detail in a later chapter.

Chapter roundup

- Personality is the total pattern of an individual's thoughts, feelings and behaviours. It is shaped by a variety of factors, both inherited and environmental.

- **Perception** is the process by which the brain selects and organises information in order to make sense of it. People behave according to what they perceive - not according to what really is.

- People develop attitudes about things, based on what they think, what they feel and what they want to do about it. Attitudes are formed by perception, experience and personality which in turn are shaped by wider social influences.

- A **group** is a collection of individuals who perceive themselves as a group. It thus has a sense of **identity**.

- A **team** is more than a group. It has an **objective**, and may be set up by the organisation under the supervision or coaching of a team leader, although (as we saw in the Nationwide example at the end of the chapter) **self-managed teams** are growing in popularity.

- Teamworking has four main roles: **organising** work; **controlling** activities; **generating** knowledge; **decision-making**.

- **Multidisciplinary** teams contain people from different departments, pooling the skills of specialists.

- **Multi-skilled** teams contain people who themselves have more than one skill.

- Problems with teams include **conflict** on the one hand, and **group think** on the other.

- Ideally teams should have a **mix** of personalities and roles. **Belbin** suggests: co-ordinator, shaper, plant, monitor-evaluator, resource-investigator, implementer, team-worker, finisher and, occasionally, specialist.

- Team members make different types of **contribution** (eg proposing, defending, blocking)

- A team develops in **stages**: forming, storming, norming, performing and dorming. (Alternatively, try undeveloped team, experimenting team, consolidating team, mature team.) These processes can be enhanced by active **team building** measures to support team identity, solidarity and commitment to objectives.

- A team can be evaluated on the basis of quantifiable and qualitative factors, covering its **operations** and its **output**.

Quick quiz

1 What is a trait cluster, and why might it be useful in everyday social interaction?

2 List three factors for a manager to consider in managing 'personality' at work.

3 Give three examples of areas where people's perceptions commonly conflict.

4 What are the three components of an 'attitude'?

5 Give three examples of non-work factors that might influence attitudes to work.

6 What is a team?

7 What are Belbin's eight roles for a well-rounded team?

8 Outline what happens in the 'storming' stage of the team development.

9 Describe a mature team.

10 List teambuilding issues.

11 Suggest five ways in which a manager can get a team 'behind' task objectives.

12 List six of Rackham and Morgan's categories of contribution to group discussion.

13 Suggest five quantifiable characteristics of effective teams and five qualitative characteristics of ineffective teams.

Answers to quick quiz

1   A number of related or compatible traits which form a personality type.

2   The compatibility of an individual's personality with the task, with the systems and culture of the organisation and with other members of the team.

3   Managers and staff, work culture, race and gender.

4   Knowledge, feelings and desires, volition.

5   Class, age, race, culture or religion, interests and sex,

6   A small number of people with complementary skills who are committed to a common purpose, performance goals and approach for which they hold themselves basically accountable.

7   Co-ordinator, shaper, plant, monitor-evaluator, resource-investigator, implementer, teams worker, finisher.

8   Storming brings out members' own ideas and attitudes. There may be conflict as well as creativity.

9   Members work well together; objectives and procedures are clear.

10 Leaders, Members. Climate. Objectives. Achievement. Work methods. Communications. Individuals, Creativity. Interpersonal communications. Review and control.

11 Set clear objectives, get the team to set targets/standard, provide information and resources, give feedback, praise and reward, and champion the team in the organisation.

12 Proposing, building, supporting, seeking information, giving information, disagreeing.

13 Refer to Paragraph 5.1

Now try the question below from the Exam Question Bank

Number	Level	Marks	Time
4	Exam	15	27 mins

BPP PUBLISHING

Chapter 5

AUTHORITY, POWER AND DELEGATION

Topic list	Syllabus reference
1 Power and authority	1(f)
2 Responsibility and accountability	1(f)
3 Delegation	1(f)
4 Empowerment	1(f)

Introduction

Power and authority are found in all organisations: they are what enables managers to get things done. They also form an important part of relationships between the people in organisation and are an essential part of the definition of their roles.

Study guide

Section 7(b) – Authority, responsibility and delegation

- Define the items authority, responsibility and delegation

- Explain the term legitimised power: Weber

- Describe the process of determining authority and responsibility

- Examine the case of responsibility without authority

Exam guide

This is an important topic and formed the basis of a Section B question in the pilot paper.

1   POWER AND AUTHORITY

1.1 Organisations feature a large number of different activities to be co-ordinated, and large numbers of people whose **co-operation and support** is necessary for the manager to get anything done. As you have probably noticed if you have worked for any length of time, organisations rarely run as clockwork, and all depend on the directed energy of those within them.

KEY TERM

Power is the **ability** to get things done.

1.2   A manager without power, of whatever kind, cannot do his/her job properly, and this applies to supervisors too. Power is not something a person has in isolation: it is exercised over other individuals or groups.

1.3   **Types of power**

Type of power	Description
Physical, coercive power	This is the power of physical force or punishment. Physical power is absent from most organisations, but organisations can sometimes use hidden forms of coercion to get what they want
Resource power	Access to or control over valued resources is a source of power. For example, managers have a resource of information or other contacts. The amount of resource power a person has depends on the scarcity of the resource, how much the resource is valued by others, and how far the resource is under the manager's control
Position power	This is power associated with a particular job or position in the hierarchy. For example, your boss has the power to authorise certain expenses, or organise work. This is equivalent to **authority, in which case** power is legitimate.
Expert power	A person may have power if his/her experience, qualifications or expertise are recognised. Typically, accountants have a type of expert power because of their knowledge of the tax system.
Personal power	A person may be powerful simply by force of personality, which can influence other people, inspire them etc.
Negative power	This is the power to disrupt operations, such as strike, refusal to communicate information

KEY TERM

Authority is the *right* of a person to ask someone else to do something and expect it to be done. Authority is thus another word for position power.

1.4   Managerial authority consists of:

(a) **Making decisions within the scope of authority** given to the position. For example, a supervisor's authority is limited to his/her team and with certain limits. For items of expenditure more than a certain amount, the supervisor may have to go to someone else up the hierarchy.

(b) **Assigning tasks** to subordinates, and expecting satisfactory performance of these tasks.

Question 1

What types of power are being exercised in the following case?

Marcus is an accountant supervising a team of eight technicians. He has to submit bank reconciliation statements every week to the chief accountant. However, the company runs four different bank accounts and Marcus gets a team member, Dave, to do it for him. Marcus asks Isabella to deal with the purchase ledger - the company obtains supplies from all over the world, and Isabella, having worked once for an international bank, is familiar with letters of credit and other documentation involved with overseas trade. Isabella has recently told Marcus that Maphia Ltd, a supplier, should not be paid because of problems with the import documentation, even though Marcus has promised Maphia to pay them. Marcus is getting increasingly annoyed with Sandra who seems to be leaving Marcus's typing until last, although she says she has piles of other work to do. 'Like reading the newspaper,' thinks Marcus, who is considering pulling rank by giving her an oral warning.

Answer

Marcus exercises position power because he has the right, given to him by the chief accountant, to get his staff, such as Dave, to do bank reconciliations. Dave does not do bank recs because of Marcus's personality or expertise, but because of the simple fact that Marcus is his boss. Marcus also exercises position power by getting Isabella to do the purchase ledger. However, Isabella exercises expert power because she knows more about import/export documentation than Marcus. She does not have the authority to stop the payment to Maphia, and Marcus can ignore what she says, but that would be a bad decision. Sandra is exercising negative power as far as Marcus is concerned, although she is claiming, perhaps, to exercise resource power - her time is a scarce resource. No-one appears to be exercising physical power as such, although Marcus's use of the disciplinary procedures would be a type of coercive power.

1.5 When analysing the types of authority which a manager or a department may have, the terms **line, staff** and **functional authority** are often used.

KEY TERMS

- **Line authority** is the authority a manager has over a subordinate.

- **Staff authority** is the authority one manager or department may have in giving specialist advice to another manager or department, over which there is no line authority. Staff authority does not entail the right to make or influence decisions in the advisee department.

- **Functional authority** is a hybrid of line and staff authority, whereby the technostructure manager or department has the authority, in certain circumstances, to direct, design or control activities or procedures of another department. An example is where a finance manager has authority to require timely reports from line managers.

Question 2

What sort of authority is exercised:

(a) by the financial controller over the chief accountant?
(b) by the production manager over the production workforce?
(c) by the financial controller over the production manager?

Answer

(a) and (b) are both examples of line authority.
(c) is staff or perhaps functional authority.

1.6 There are inevitable tensions involved in asserting staff authority.

Problem	Possible solution
The technostructure can **undermine** the **line managers'** authority, by empire building.	**Clear** demarcations of line, staff and functional authority should be created.
Lack of seniority: middle line managers may be more senior in the hierarchy than technostructure advisers.	Use **functional authority** (via procedures). Experts should be seen as a resource, not a threat.
Expert managers may **lack realism,** going for technically prefect, but commercially impractical solutions.	Technostructure planners should **be fully aware** of **operations issues.**
Technostructure experts **lack responsibility** for the success of their ideas.	Technostructure experts should be involved in **implementing** their suggestions and should take responsibility for their success.

Legitimised power

1.7 Legitimacy was covered in Chapter 1 when we covered types of organisation and bureaucracy legitimate power is thus power that someone has the **right** to exercise. That right may be granted in a number of ways. In most cases of organisational life, legitimate power is based on your position in the organisation hierarchy.

2 RESPONSIBILITY AND ACCOUNTABILITY

> **KEY TERMS**
>
> **Responsibility** is the **obligation** a person has to fulfil a task, which (s)he has been given.
>
> **Accountability** is a person's liability to be called to account for the fulfilment of tasks they have been given.

2.1 The definitions given above have been created because **responsibility** is used in two ways.

   (a) A person is said to be responsible **for** a piece of work when he or she is required to ensure that the work is done.

   (b) The same person is said to be responsible **to** a superior when he or she is given work by that superior.

   One is thus responsible **to** a superior **for** a piece of work.

2.2 The word **accountable** has come to be used instead of **responsible** in the meaning given in 2.1 (b) above. A person is thus **accountable to** a superior and **responsible for** work.

2.3 **Delegation**. We will discuss the process of delegation further in the next section. The principle of delegation is that a manager may make subordinates **responsible for** work, but remains **accountable to** his or her own superior for ensuring that the work is done. Appropriate decision-making **authority** must be delegated alongside the delegated responsibility.

Responsibility without authority

2.4 In practice, matters are rarely clear-cut, and in many organisations responsibility and authority are:

	Comments
Not clear	When the organisation is doing something new or in a different way, its existing rules and procedures may be out of date or unable to cope with the new development. Various people may try to 'empire build'. The managers may not have designed the organisation very well.
Shifting	In large organisations there may be real conflict between different departments; or the organisation may, as it adapts to its environment, need to change.

2.5 Authority without accountability is a recipe for arbitrary and irresponsible behaviour. The subordinate who has responsibility without authority is placed in an impossible position.

Question 3

You have just joined a small accounts department. The financial controller keeps a very close eye on expenditure and, being prudent, believes that nothing should be spent that is not strictly necessary. She has recently gone on a three week holiday to Venezuela. You have been told that you need to prepare management accounts, and for this you have to obtain information from the payroll department in two weeks time. This is standard procedure. However, there are two problems. One of the other people in your department has gone sick, and a temporary replacement will be needed very shortly. The personnel department say: 'We need a staff requisition from the Financial Controller before we can get in a temp. Sorry, you'll just have to cancel your weekend'. The payroll department is happy to give you the information you need - except directors' salaries, essential for the accounts to be truly accurate.

What is the underlying cause of the problem and what, in future, should you ask the Financial Controller to do to put it right?

Answer

The immediate problem is that the Financial Controller should have considered these issues before she went to Venezuela. The underlying cause, as far as you are concerned, is that you have responsibility to do a task but without the authority - to obtain all the information you need and to hire a temp - to do the job. In future the Financial Controller should, when delegating the task, delegate the authority to do it.

3 DELEGATION

KEY TERM

Delegation of authority occurs when a superior gives to a subordinate part of his or her own authority to make decisions.

3.1 Note that delegation can only occur if the superior initially possesses the authority to delegate; a subordinate cannot be given organisational authority to make decisions unless it would otherwise be the superior's right to make those decisions personally.

3.2 Managers and supervisors must delegate some authority for three reasons.

(a) There are **physical and mental limitations** to the work load of any individual or group in authority.

(b) Managers and supervisors are free to **concentrate on the aspects of the work** (such as planning), which only they are competent (and paid) to do.

(c) The **increasing size and complexity** of some organisations calls for specialisation, both managerial and technical.

3.3 However, by delegating authority to assistants, the supervisor takes on two extra tasks:
- **Monitoring their performance**
- **Co-ordinating** the efforts of different assistants.

3.4 **The process of delegation**

Step 1. **Specify the expected performance** levels of the assistant, keeping in mind the assistant's level of expertise.

Step 2. **Formally assign tasks** to the assistant, who should formally agree to do them.

Step 3. **Allocate resources and authority** to the assistant to enable him or her to carry out the delegated tasks at the expected level of performance.

Step 4. **Maintain contact** with the assistant to review the progress made and to make constructive criticism. **Feedback** is essential for control, and also as part of the learning process.

3.5 Remember that ultimate **accountability** for the task remains with the supervisor: if it is not well done it is at least partly the fault of poor delegation, and it is still the supervisor's responsibility to get it re-done.

Problems of delegation

3.6 Many managers and supervisors are **reluctant to delegate** and attempt to do many routine matters themselves in addition to their more important duties.

(a) **Low confidence and trust** in the abilities of their staff: the suspicion that 'if you want it done well, you have to do it yourself'.

(b) The burden of **accountability for the mistakes of subordinates**, aggravated by (a) above.

(c) A **desire to 'stay in touch'** with the department or team - both in terms of workload and staff - particularly if the manager does not feel 'at home' in a management role.

(d) **Feeling threatened.** An unwillingness to admit that assistants have developed to the extent that they could perform some of the supervisor's duties. The supervisor may feel threatened by this sense of 'redundancy'.

(e) **Poor control and communication systems** in the organisation, so that the manager feels he has to do everything himself, if he is to retain real control and responsibility for a task, and if he wants to know what is going on.

(f) An **organisational culture** that has failed to reward or recognise effective delegation, so that the manager may not realise that delegation is positively regarded (rather than as shirking responsibility).

(g) **Lack of understanding** of what delegation involves - not giving assistants total control, or making the manager himself redundant.

3.7 As an accountant, you might like the idea of a **trust-control dilemma** in a superior-subordinate relationship (Handy, 1993). The sum of trust and control is a constant amount:

$$T + C = Y$$

where $T =$ the trust the superior has in the subordinate, and the trust which the subordinate feels the superior has in him;

$C =$ the degree of control exercised by the superior over the subordinate;

$Y =$ a constant, unchanging value;

If there is any increase in C (if the superior retains more 'control' or authority), the subordinate will immediately recognise that he is being trusted less. If the superior wishes to show more trust in the subordinate, he can only do so by reducing C: by delegating more authority.

3.8 **Overcoming the reluctance of managers to delegate**

(a) **Train the subordinates** so that they are capable of handling delegated authority in a responsible way. If assistants are of the right 'quality', supervisors will be prepared to trust them more.

(b) Have a system of **open communications**, in which the supervisor and assistants freely interchange ideas and information. If the assistant is given all the information needed to do the job, and if the supervisor is aware of what the assistant is doing:

(i) The assistant will make better-informed decisions.

(ii) The supervisor will not panic because he does not know what is going on.

(c) **Ensure that a system of control is established**. If responsibility and accountability are monitored at all levels of the management hierarchy, the dangers of relinquishing authority and control to assistants are significantly lessened.

3.9 **When to delegate**

(a) Is the **acceptance** of staff affected required for morale, relationships or ease of implementation of the decision?

(b) Is the **quality** of the decision most important? Many technical financial decisions may be of this type, and should be retained by the supervisor if he or she alone has the knowledge and experience to make them.

(c) Is the **expertise or experience** of assistants relevant or **necessary** to the task, and will it enhance the quality of the decision?

(d) Can **trust** be placed in the competence and reliability of the assistants?

(e) Does the **decision** require tact and confidentiality, or, on the other hand, maximum exposure and assimilation by employees?

3.10 In instances where **reference upwards** to the manager's own superior may be necessary, the manager should consider:

(a) Whether the decision is **relevant** to the superior: will it have any impact on the boss's area of responsibility, such as strategy, staffing, or the departmental budget?

(b) Whether the superior has **authority** or **information** relevant to the decision that the manager does not possess: for example, authority over issues which affect other departments or interdepartmental relations, or information only available at senior levels.

(c) The **political climate** of the organisation: will the superior expect to be consulted, and resent any attempt to make the decision without his authority?

Question 4

You are the manager of an accounts section of your organisation and have stopped to talk to one of the clerks in the office to see what progress he is making. He complains bitterly that he is not learning anything. He gets only routine work to do and it is the same routine. He has not even been given the chance to swap jobs with someone else. You have picked up the same message from others in the office. You discuss the situation with Jean Howe the recently appointed supervisor. She appears to be very busy and harassed. When confronted with your observations she says that she is fed up with the job. She is worked off her feet, comes early, goes late, takes work home and gets criticised behind her back by incompetent clerks.

What has gone wrong?

Answer

The problem appears to be that the new supervisor is taking too much of the department's work on to herself. While she is overworked, her subordinates are apparently not being stretched and as a result motivation and morale amongst them are poor. The supervisor herself is unhappy with the position and there is a danger that declining job satisfaction will lead to inefficiencies and eventually staff resignations.

There could be a number of causes contributing to the problem.

(a)   Jean Howe may have been badly selected, ie she may not have the ability required for a supervisory job.

(b)   Alternatively she may just be unaware of what is involved in a supervisor's role. She may not have realised that much of the task consists of managing subordinates; she is not required to shoulder all the detailed technical work herself.

(c)   There may be personality problems involved. Jean Howe regards her clerks as incompetent and this attitude may arise simply form an inability to get on with them socially. (Another possibility is that her staff actually are incompetent.)

(d)   The supervisor does much of the department's work herself. This may be because she does not understand the kind of tasks which can be delegated and the way in which delegation of authority can improve the motivation and job satisfaction of subordinates.

As manager you have already gone some way towards identifying the actual causes of the problem You have spoken to some of the subordinates concerned and also to the supervisor. You could supplement this by a review of personnel records relating to Jean Howe to discover how her career has progressed so far and what training she had received (if any) in the duties of a supervisor. You may then be in a position to determine which of the possible causes of the problems are operating in this case.

4   EMPOWERMENT

4.1   Empowerment and delegation are related.

> ### KEY TERM
>
> **Empowerment** is the current term for making workers (and particularly work teams) responsible for achieving, and even setting, work targets, with the freedom to make decisions about how they are to be achieved.

4.2   **Empowerment** goes in hand in hand with:

(a) **Delayering** or a cut in the number of levels (and managers) in the chain of command, since responsibility previously held by middle managers is, in effect, being given to operational workers.

(b) **Flexibility**, since giving responsibility to the people closest to the products and customer encourages responsiveness - and cutting out layers of communication, decision-making and reporting speeds up the process.

(c) **New technology**, since there are more 'knowledge workers'. Such people need less supervision, being better able to identify and control the means to clearly understood ends. Better information systems also remove the mystique and power of managers as possessors of knowledge and information in the organisation.

4.3 Reasons for empowerment

'The people lower down the organisation possess the knowledge of what is going wrong with a process but lack the authority to make changes. Those further up the structure have the authority to make changes, but lack the profound knowledge required to identify the right solutions. The only solution is to change the culture of the organisation so that everyone can become involved in the process of improvement and work together to make the changes.' (Max Hand)

The change in organisation structure and culture as a result of empowerment can be shown in the diagram below.

Traditional hierarchical structure: fulfilling management requirements

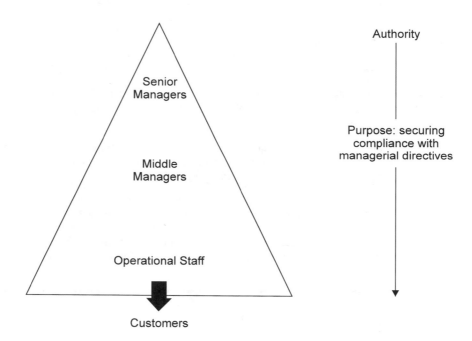

Empowerment structure: supporting workers in serving the customer

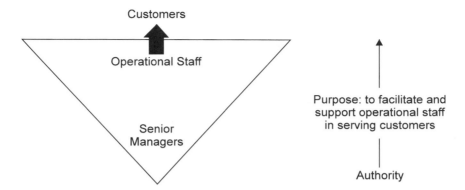

4.4 The argument, in a nutshell, is that by empowering workers (or 'decentralising' control of business units, or devolving/delegating responsibility, or removing levels in hierarchies that restrict freedom), not only will the job be done more effectively but the people who do the job will get more out of it.

Case example

The validity of this view and its relevance to modern trends appears to be borne out by the approach to empowerment adopted by *Harvester Restaurants*, as described in *Personnel Management*. The management structure comprises a branch manager and a 'coach', while everyone else is a team member. Everyone within a team has one or more 'accountabilities' (these include recruitment, drawing up rotas, keeping track of sales targets and so on) which are shared out by the team members at their weekly team meetings. All the team members at different times act as 'co-ordinator' to the person responsible for taking the snap decisions that are frequently necessary in a busy restaurant. Apparently all of the staff involved agree that empowerment has made their jobs more interesting and has hugely increased their motivation and sense of involvement.

Chapter roundup

- **Power** is the ability to get things done.

- There are many types of power in organisations: position or **legitimate power**, expert power, personal power, resource power and negative power are examples.

- **Authority** is related to position power. It is the right to take certain decisions within certain boundaries.

- A person with **responsibility** is given a task to get done. Such a person must have the necessary authority to command resources and staff to get the job. Responsibility without authority is stressful for the individual.

- Responsibility can be **delegated**, but the person delegating responsibility still remains accountable to his or her boss that the job has been done to the right standard. Accountability is not delegated.

- **Delegation** is necessary to get work distributed throughout the organisation. Successful delegation requires the resolution of the Trust-Control dilemma. Some managers and supervisors are reluctant to delegate.

- Successful delegation requires that people have the right skills and the authority to do the job, and are given feedback.

- **Empowerment** takes the process of delegation further. Its advantages are not simply that it releases managers to do more important things, but that front line staff are closest to customers are best able to take decisions concerning them.

Quick quiz

1 What is position power?

2 Give an example of negative power

3 How can uncertainty give power to managers in one department as opposed to another?

4 Why might functional authority be a good thing for the organisation?

5 Why can't accountability be delegated?

6 Why are there problems in determining authority and responsibility?

7 List the stages in the process of delegation.

8 List some problems in delegation.

Answers to quick quiz

1 Legitimate power is power arising from formal position in the organisation hierarchy; authority, in other words.

2 Going on strike; refusal to communicate; withhold information; delaying etc.

3 If the department reduces the level of uncertainty other departments face.

4 Because it is exercised impersonally, impartially and automatically.

5 Because the delegator has been given the task by his/her own boss.

6 Because the boundaries are often unclear and shifting.

7 Specify performance levels; formally assign task; allocate resources and authority; give feedback.

8 Low trust, low competence, fear, worry about accountability.

Now try the question below from the Exam Question Bank

Number	Level	Marks	Time
5	Exam	15	27 mins

Chapter 6

PERFORMANCE, OBJECTIVES AND TARGETS

Topic list	Syllabus reference
1 Introducing control systems	1(e)
2 Organisational objectives and targets	1(e)
3 Personal objectives and targets	1(g)
4 Performance management: an introduction	1(g)

Introduction

Where the work of an organisation is fragmented and disorganised, it is likely that the organisation's objectives are unclear, confused or even in conflict. Setting objectives, goals or targets is fundamental to organising work.

Study guide

Section 6(f) – Objective setting

- Explain the importance of objective setting

- Compare and contrast profit and other objectives: Drucker, Cyert and March, Marginalist Theories, Simon

- Explain the behavioural theories of objective setting

- Explain the importance of understanding ethics and social responsibility

- Compare and contrast the difference between corporate objectives and personal objectives

- Illustrate the difference between quantitative and qualitative target setting

- Outline the management role in identifying performance standards and accountability

- Identify methods to measure achievement of objectives

Section 8(h) – Standard setting and performance management

- Define the term performance management

- Identify a process for establishing work standards and performance management

- Outline a method to establish performance indicators

Exam guide

A question devoted to objectives is unlikely, but this topic could form the background to questions on a variety of management topics.

BPP PUBLISHING

1   INTRODUCING CONTROL SYSTEMS

1.1   Let's recap to the definition of organisation in Chapter 1: **it is a social arrangement for the controlled performance of collective goals**. In this chapter we look at 'controlled performance' and various sorts of goal, in the context of the organisation and the individual within it.

> ## Exam focus point
>
> A look at the wider context of the management function of control will help you to get a grasp of this topic, and to understand why it is important for organisations and individuals, and for your exam.

1.2   Because organisations have **goals** they want to satisfy, they need to direct their activities by:

- Deciding what they want to achieve
- Deciding how and when to do it and who is to do it
- Checking that they do achieve what they want, by monitoring what has been achieved and comparing it with the plan
- Taking action to correct any deviation

1.3   The overall framework for this is a system of **planning and control**. This is best demonstrated by means of a diagram.

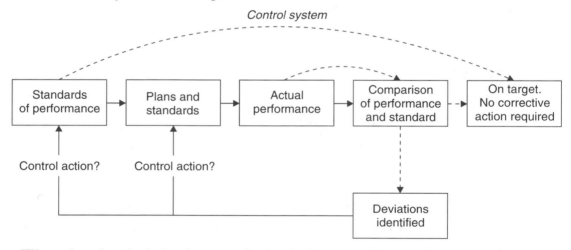

Where there is a deviation from standard, a decision has to be made as to whether to adjust the plans or the standard, or whether it is the performance itself that needs correction.

2   ORGANISATIONAL OBJECTIVES AND TARGETS

Mission

2.1   Overall, the main direction of an organisation is set by its mission.

> ## KEY TERM
>
> **Mission** 'the organisation's basic function in society'.

2.2   Mission has four elements.

Elements	Comments
Purpose	Why does the organisation exist and for whom (eg shareholders)
Strategy	Mission provides the operational logic for the organisation. It answers TWO questions. • What do we do? • How do we do it?
Policies and standards of behaviour	Mission should influence what people actually do and how they behave: the mission of a hospital is to save lives, and this affects how doctors and nurses interact with patients
Values	What the organisation believes to be important, that is, its principles. These should not clash with the individual values of its people.

2.3   Even though the mission can be very general, you can see it does have real implications for how individuals go about what they do.

Goals, aims and objectives

2.4   Many different writers use different terminology to describe the same thing. In this area you have to be especially careful.

> **KEY TERMS**
>
> **Goals**: 'The intentions behind decision or actions' (Henry Mintzberg) or 'a desired end result' (Shorter Oxford English Dictionary)

2.5   There are two types of goal.

- Non-operational, **qualitative** goals (**aims**)
- Operational, **quantitative** goals (**objectives**)

2.6   **Aims** are qualitative goals. In other words they are not quantified. For example, a university's may be: 'to seek truth'. (You would not see: 'increase truth by 5%')

2.7   **Objectives** are operational goals. In other words they can be expressed in quantitative form.

Characteristics	Example
Objectives are SMART • Specific • Measurable • Attainable • Realistic • Time-bounded	• Operational goal: cut costs. • Objective: reduce budgeted expenditure on paper-clips by 5% by December 31 2000

2.8   In practice, people often use the words goals, aims and objectives interchangeably. But remember that some goals fulfil SMART criteria and others do not, even though they are still meaningful.

Question 1

Most organisations establish closed or quantifiable objectives.

(a)   Give reasons why aims (non-operational goals) might still be important.
(b)   Give an example of when SMART targets might be essential.

Answer

(a)   Aims can be just as helpful: customer satisfaction is not something which is achieved just once. Some goals are hard to quantify, for example 'to retain technological leadership'. Quantified objectives are hard to change when circumstances change, as changing them looks like an admission of defeat. Not everything can be measured easily.

(b)   An example of when a SMART, quantified target is essential was the need to repair many computer programs by the Year 2000, so that they did not crash. There was a definite deadline, and all relevant software had to be replaced or changed.

The purpose of and objective setting

2.9   'Objectives are needed in every area where performance and results directly and vitally affect the survival and prosperity of the business' (Drucker). Objectives in these key areas should enable management to:

(a)   **Implement** the mission, by outlining what needs to be achieved

(b)   **Publicise** the direction of the organisation to managers and staff, so that they know where their efforts should be directed

(c)   **Appraise** the validity of decisions about **strategies** (by assessing whether these are sufficient to achieve the stated objectives)

(d)   **Assess and control actual performance**, as objectives can be used as targets for achievement

2.10   There is a **hierarchy of objectives/goals,** with one primary corporate objective (restricted by certain constraints on corporate activity) and a series of subordinate objectives/goals which should combine to ensure the achievement of the overall objective.

Primary objectives

2.11   People might disagree on the choice of the overall corporate objective, although for a **business** it must be a **financial objective,** such as **profitability,** return on capital employed or earnings per share.

(a)   Profit, in its broadest sense, measures the creation of value, the relationship of **inputs** to **outputs**. It thus integrates cost behaviour and revenue performance for the whole organisation.

(b)   **Profit** also is a key indicator for shareholders.

(c)   **Profit** is one of several measures that can be compared across organisations.

Secondary objectives

2.12 Secondary or **subordinate** goals and objectives can be listed under the following broad headings. They support the primary goal.

(a) **Market position**
Total market share of each market, growth of sales, customers or potential customers, the need to avoid relying on a single customer for a large proportion of total sales, what markets should the company be in.

(b) **Product development**
Bring in new products, develop a product range, investment in research and development, provide products of a certain quality at a certain price level.

(c) **Technology**
Improve productivity, reduce the cost per unit of output, exploit appropriate technology.

(d) **Employees and management**
Train employees in certain skills, reduce labour turnover.

Question 2

Review the list of goals and objectives above. How do you think of each of them relates to the financial objectives in 2.11? What conflicts are there?

Answer

(a) Market position. Markets are customers. Customers are source of revenue. Markets are where organisations compete with each other. Gaining market share *now* helps future profitability - but this market share may be expensive in the short term.

(b) Product development is another way of competing, to make profits to satisfy the corporate objectives. This, too, is expensive.

(c) and (d) are to do with organising the production process. This means making operations efficient and effective.

Plans and standards

2.13 Plans state what should be done to achieve the objectives. Standards and targets specify a desired level of performance. Here are some examples.

(a) **Physical standards** eg units of raw material per unit produced.

(b) **Cost standards**. These convert physical standards into a money measurement by the application of standard prices. For example, the standard labour cost of making product X might be 4 hours at £5 per hour = £20.

(c) **Capital standards**. These establish some form of standard for capital invested (eg the ratio of current assets to current liabilities) or a desired share price.

(d) **Revenue standards**. These measure expected performance in terms of revenue earned (such as turnover per square metre of shelf space in a supermarket).

(e) **Deadlines for programme completion**. Performance might be measured in terms of actual completion dates for parts of a project compared against a budgeted programme duration.

(f) The **achievement of stated goals** (eg meeting profit objective).

(g) **Intangible standards**. Intangible standards might relate to employee motivation, quality of service, customer goodwill, corporate image, product image etc. It is possible to measure some of these by attitude surveys, market research etc.

2.14 Standards and targets are used in the **control system** to monitor whether performance is in fact proceeding according to plan.

2.15 EXAMPLE: BUDGETARY CONTROL

We now relate the control system to a practical example, such as **monthly budgetary control variance reports.**

(a) Standard costs and a master budget are prepared for the year. Management organises the resources of the business (inputs) so as to achieve the budget targets.

(b) At the end of each month, actual results (output, sales, costs, revenues etc) are reported back to management. The reports are the measured output of the control system, and the process of sending them to the managers responsible provides the feedback loop.

(c) Managers compare actual results against the plan and where necessary, take corrective action to adjust the workings of the system, probably by amending the inputs to the system.

Organisational and pesonal objectives

2.16 The American management writers *Cyert and March* suggest that traditional ideas on organisational objectives are too simplistic and do not recognise managerial and economic reality. Many business organisations have market power and therefore **discretion** as to their objectives.

(a) The firm is a **connection of groups, so** therefore **multiple goals**, especially as this network changes over time.

(b) There is **unresolved conflict** because of the existence of this network.

(c) Objectives are rarely thought through and are often stated in **non-operational terms**. In practice, objectives tend to be stable because of:

- Limited bargaining time
- Control systems
- Departmentalisation
- Precedents becoming institutionalised as 'the way things are always done'.

(d) One reason why firms fail to achieve optimal results is the development of **'organisational slack'**.

- Payment is based only on what is necessary
- Maximum efficiency is not known
- Because of limited market information, it is not possible to maximise profit

(e) In general, Cyert and March identify the following goals for any organisation.

- Production
- Inventory
- Market and market share
- Profit

(f) They conclude that **'Organisations cannot have objectives, only people have objectives'**.

Ethics and social responsibility

> **KEY TERM**
>
> **Ethics** are the moral principles by which people act or do business.

> **KEY TERM**
>
> This is a hard term to pin down, but here's one definition.
>
> **Social responsibility**: actions which the organisation is not obliged to take, taken for the well-being of stakeholders and the public.

2.17 Managers need to take into account the effect of organisational outputs into the market and the wider **social community,** for several reasons.

   (a) The modern **marketing concept** says that in order to survive and succeed, organisations must satisfy the needs, wants and **values** of customers and potential customers. Communication and education have made people much more aware of issues such as the environment, the exploitation of workers, product safety and consumer rights. Therefore an organisation may have to be **seen** to be responsible in these areas in order to retain public support for its products.

   (b) There are skill shortages in the labour pool and employers must compete to attract and retain high quality employees. If the organisation gets a reputation as a **socially responsible** employer it will find it easier to do this, than if it has a 'poor employer' brand.

   (c) Organisations **rely** on the society, and local community of which they are a part, for access to facilities, business relationships, media coverage, labour, supplies, customers and so on. Organisations which acknowledge their responsibilities as part of the community may find that many areas of their operation are facilitated.

   (d) The law, regulations and Codes of Practice **impose** certain social responsibilities on organisations, in areas such as employment protection, equal opportunities, environmental care, health and safety, product labelling and consumer rights. There are financial and operational **penalties** for organisations which fail to comply.

2.18 The **social responsibilities of a business,** depending on the nature of its operations, may include:

   (a) The impact of its operations on the **natural environment**

   (b) Its treatment of **staff** and potential staff, for example, the hiring and promotion of people from minority groups, policies on sexual harassment, refusal to exploit cheap labour in developing countries

   (c) Non-reliance on contracts with **military** or adverse **political connotations.**

   (d) **Charitable support** and activity in the local community or in areas related to the organisation's field of activity

   (e) **Above-minimum** standards of product health, safety and labelling

Question 3

See if you can come up with examples of socially responsible activities, in line with (a) to (e) above.

Answer

Examples (our suggestions only) include:

(a)   The Body Shop (among others) not using animal testing for ingredients, Shell (as a **negative** example) being held responsible for environmental devastation in Nigeria's river deltas, recyclable packaging

(b)   British Airways extension of married employees' benefits to homosexual partners, anti-ageist policies, the Body shop (again) building economic infrastructures in rural communities

(c)   Sanctions or boycotts of countries such as (in the past) South Africa or Iraq

(d)   Major supermarkets and retailers such as WH Smith often sponsor community facilities, charities and sporting events

(e)   Some organisations have very stringent quality standards

Question 4

Why do you think social responsibility might be difficult to pin down?

Answer

(a)   Few organisations would admit to being socially irresponsible.
(b)   There is genuine disagreement as to what it means.

2.19   **Examples of 'social responsibility' by businesses**

- Financial donations to charity
- Secondment of management staff to assist charities
- Sponsorship of the Arts or Sport
- Giving benefits to employees above the legal minimum
- Helping a supplier through a bad patch
- Business in the Community
- Exceeding compensation to customers offered under Fair Trading legislation
- Voluntary adoption of ecological best practice above the minimum legal requirements

2.20   This list seems very admirable but it is worth raising a few contrary remarks.

Against social responsibility

2.21   **'The social responsibility of business is profit maximisation'**

According to *Milton Friedman* and *Elaine Sternberg*, the only responsibility of a **business** organisation, as opposed to a public sector one, is to maximise wealth for its owners over the long term.

(a)   Shareholders may disagree with managers' choice of beneficiary.

(b)   Business profits are shareholders' wealth and amounts spent on other objectives **not** related to shareholders' wealth maximisation is theft, almost.

(c)   The public interest is served because the state levies taxes: the state is a better arbiter of the public interest than a business.

(d) In practice, many company shares are owned by pension funds, investing on behalf of small savers.

(e) Without the discipline of shareholders, managers will simply favour their own pet interests. 'Managers who are accountable to everyone are accountable to none.'

For social responsibility

2.22 'Consequently, the only justification for social responsibility is **enlightened self interest**' according to Milton Friedman.

(a) **Employee benefits** over the legal norm may be part of a remuneration package negotiated in the normal way, and may be **necessary** to attract, retain and motivate the right staff.

(b) Make a **virtue out of necessity** - voluntary activities can pre-empt government legislation.

(c) **Customer benefits** - for most businesses, getting repeat customers is cheaper than attracting new ones, so delighting customers with exceptional service makes good business sense.

(d) Sponsorship - marketers recognise the **public relations** value of sponsoring the arts and building a 'brand' image. It raises the profile of the firm in the minds of a particular audience.

2.23 **Social responsibility recognises externalities.**

Externalities are costs imposed by businesses on other people.

2.24 EXAMPLE: POLLUTION

Industrial pollution is bad for health: if someone is made ill by industrial pollution, then arguably the polluter should pay the sick person, as damages or in compensation, in the same way as if the business's builders had accidentally bulldozed somebody's house. In practice, of course, while it is relatively easy to identify **statistical** relationships between pollution levels and certain illnesses, mapping out the chain of cause and effect from an individual's wheezing cough to the dust particles emitted by Factory X, as opposed to Factory Y, is quite a different matter.

Government are beginning to introduce 'polluter pays' taxes. But tax revenue may be spent on curing the disease, rather than stopping it at its source. Use of pollution control equipment may be the **fair** way of dealing with this problem.

2.25 **Managers and shareholders are citizens, too.**

(a) Charitable donations have to be declared in the financial statements of the firm. In practice, such donations are not large in relation to turnover: shareholders rarely demand that charitable donations cease.

(b) Some shareholders regard ethical trading and a firm's stance on ethics and responsibility as very important.

2.26 **A business is a social system not just an economic machine.**

Mintzberg raises three important real-world arguments.

(a) Shareholders rarely control their investments: it is too easy for them to sell, so company managements have too much power.

(b) A business's relationship with society is not only economic, simply because a business is an open system with many other non-economic impacts.

(c) Social responsibility helps to create a social climate in which the business can prosper in the long term.

2.27 **Business ethics** are the values underlying what an organisation understands by socially responsible behaviour. An organisation may have *values* to do with non-discrimination, fairness and integrity. It is very important that managers understand:

(a) The importance of **ethical behaviour** – as outlined above

(b) The differences in what is considered ethical behaviour in **different cultures**

2.28 Theorist *Elaine Sternberg* suggests that two **ethical values** are particularly pertinent for business, because without them business could not operate at all. There are:

(a) **Ordinary decency.** This includes respect for property rights, honesty, fairness and legality.

(b) **Distributive justice.** This means that organisational rewards should be proportional to the contributions people make to organisational ends. The supply and demand for labour will influence how much a person is actually paid, but if that person is worth employing and the job worth doing, then the contribution will justify the expense.

2.29 Business ethics in a **global market place**, are however, far from clear cut. If you are working outside the UK, you will need to develop – in line with whatever policies your organisation may have in place – a kind of 'situational' ethic to cover various issues.

- **Gifts** may be construed as bribes in Western business circles, but are indispensable in others

- Attitudes to **women** in business

- The 'exploitation' of **cheap labour** in very poor countries

- The expression and nature of **agreements**

2.30 A business may operate on principles which strive to be:

- Ethical and legal (eg The Body Shop)
- Unethical but legal (eg arms sales to brutal regimes)
- Ethical but illegal (eg publishing stolen documents on government mismanagement)
- Unethical and illegal (eg the drugs trade, employing child labour)

2.31 Assuming a firm wishes to act ethically, it can embed **social responsibility** in its decision processes in the following ways.

- Include it in the **corporate culture,** or codes of practice

- Ensure that **incentive systems** are designed to support ethical behaviour (eg safety)

- Identify social responsibility in the **mission statement**, as a public declaration of what the organisation stands for

3 PERSONAL OBJECTIVES AND TARGETS

Behavioural theories of objective setting

3.1 People are purposive: that is, they act in pursuit of particular goals or purposes. The goals or objectives of an individual influence three things.

(a) **Perception**, since we filter out messages not relevant to our goals and objectives and select those which are relevant

(b) **Learning**, since learning is a process of selecting and analysing experience in order to take it into account in acting in future, so that our goals and objectives may be more effectively met

(c) **Behaviour**, since people behave in such a way as to satisfy their goals. This is the basis of motivation, since organisations can **motivate** people to behave in desirable ways (effective work performance) by offering them the means to fulfil their goals.

3.2 In order for learning and motivation to be effective, it is essential that **people know exactly what their objectives are**. This enables them.

(a) **Plan and direct their effort** towards the objectives

(b) **Monitor their performance** against objectives and adjust (or **learn**) if required

(c) Experience the **reward of achievement** once the objectives have been reached

(d) Feel that their tasks have **meaning and purpose**, which is an important element in job satisfaction

(e) Experience the **motivation of a challenge**: the need to expend energy and effort in a particular direction in order to achieve something

(f) Avoid the **de-motivation** of impossible or inadequately rewarded tasks: if objectives are vague, unrealistic or unattainable, there may be little incentive to pursue them: hence the importance of SMART objectives.

3.3 We will be discussing specific behavioural theories in relation to motivation and learning in later chapters.

The hierarchy of objectives

3.4 **Individual objectives must be directed towards, or 'dovetailed with' organisational goals.**

(a) **Direction.** Each job is directed towards the same organisational goals. Each managerial job must be focused on the success of the business as a whole, not just one part of it.

(b) **Target.** Each manager's targeted performance must be derived from targets of achievement for the organisation as a whole.

(c) **Performance measurement.** A manager's results must be measured in terms of his or her contribution to the business as a whole.

(d) **Each manager must know** what his or her targets of performance are.

3.5 The hierarchy of objectives which emerges is this.

BPP PUBLISHING

STRATEGIC PLANS (LONGER-TERM)
|
TACTICAL PLANS
(Shorter-term, for product
market development,
resource development,
operations and organisation)
|
UNIT, OR
DEPARTMENTAL PLANS
|
INDIVIDUAL MANAGERS' OBJECTIVES

Types of objectives for individuals and teams

3.6   **Work objectives**

(a)   At team level, they relate to the purpose of the team and the contribution it is expected to make to the goals of the department and the organisation.

(b)   At individual level, they are related specifically to the job. They clarify what the individual is expected to do and they enable the performance of the individual to be measured.

3.7   **Standing aims and objectives**

(a)   **Qualitative aims** cover issues such as promptness and courtesy when dealing with customer requests; they are always relevant.

(b)   A **quantified target** for a sales team would be to ensure that all phone calls are picked up within three rings.

3.8   **Output or improvement targets**

These have most of the features of SMART objectives. A sales person may be given a target of increasing the number of sales made in a particular district in a certain time. Many firms have targets which involve reducing the number of defects in goods produced, or seek to find ways of working more efficiently.

3.9   **Developmental goals**

These deal with how an individual can improve his/her own performance and skills. These goals are often set at the appraisal interview and are part of the performance management system. In the control model outlined in Section 1, setting developmental goals would be an example of action taken to improve the individual's and the organisation's performance.

Integrating the organisation's and the individual's objectives

3.10   The diagram of the hierarchy of objectives in paragraph 3.5 shows a cascade of objectives from the organisation to the individual. This is not always easy to achieve. However, a method of doing so was suggested by proponents of **management by objectives**.

Setting unit objectives for departments: Steps 1 to 4

3.11   **Unit objectives** are required for all departments.

Step 1. They must be set first of all in terms of primary targets, for example relating to achievement of production schedules and delivery dates, the quality of output or efficiency in the use of resources (labour, productivity, material usage)services, or

Step 2. For each of these primary targets, secondary targets (or sub-targets) will be set.

Step 3. **Identify which individual managers** within the unit are in a position to influence the achievement of each of them.

Step 4. Top management will then make a **unit improvement plan** for each unit of the business, setting out specifically the objectives for improvement, the performance standards and the time scale. Each unit improvement plan must be approved by the senior manager with overall responsibility for the unit.

Setting key results: Steps 5 to 7

3.12 *Step 5.* The unit improvement plan is then broken down into a series of **key results** and **performance standards**. For example, the key results of an information systems manager might be as given below.

ITEM	KEY RESULT
Service to users	To ensure that users get regular software upgrades, with appropriate helplines and training.
Use of resources and efficiency levels	The time when users cannot use the network must not exceed 5%.
Costs	The cost per operating hour must not exceed £60.
Quality	Queries from users must be responded to within ten minutes.

Step 6. A personal **job improvement plan** should be agreed with each manager, which will make a quantifiable and measurable contribution to achievement of the plans for the department, branch or company as a whole, within specified time periods.

Step 7. A systematic **performance review** is also necessary.

- A performance review must be a formal and disciplined review of the results achieved by each manager, carried out regularly on pre-determined dates. Performance standards in key results areas provide the means of comparison for actual results achieved.

- Failure to achieve satisfactory results should initiate control action first by the manager, with prompting from his or her superior.

Performance measures for individuals: some guidelines and examples

3.13 The Key Results table above indicated some examples of how a unit's objectives could be tied in with what an individual (a manager in that case) is expected to achieve. But clearly, performance has to be measured properly for any changes to be effected.

3.14 Some principles for devising performance measures are these.

BPP PUBLISHING

Principle	Comment
Job-related	They should be related to the actual job, and the key tasks outlined in the job description (see chapter 7)
Controllable	People should not be assessed according to factors which they cannot control
Objective and observable	This is contentious. Certain aspects of performance can be measured, such as volume sales, but matters such as courtesy or friendliness which are important to some businesses are harder to measure
Data must be available	There is no use identifying performance measures if the data cannot actually be collected

Question 5

A senior sales executive has a job which involves: 'building the firm's sales' and maintaining 'a high degree of satisfaction with the company's products and services'. The firm buys sports equipment, running machines and so on, which it sells to gyms and individuals. The firm also charges fees to service the equipment. Service contracts are the sales executive's responsibility, and he has to manage that side of the business.

Here some possible performance indicators to assess the sales executive's performance in the role. What do you think of them? Are they any good?

(a) Number of new customers gained per period
(b) Value of revenue from existing customers per period
(c) Renewal of service contracts
(d) Record of customer complaints about poor quality products
(e) Regular customer satisfaction survey
(f) Market share related to competitors

Answer

These measures do not all address some of the key issues of the job.

(a) *Number of new customers.* This is helpful as far as it goes but omits two crucial issues: how much the customers actually spend and what the potential is. Demand for this service might be expanding rapidly, and the firm might be increasing sales revenue but losing market share.

(b) *Revenue from existing customers* is useful - repeat business is generally cheaper than gaining new customers, and it implies customer satisfaction.

(c) *Renewal of service contracts* is very relevant to the executive's role.

(d) *Customer complaints about poor quality products.* As the company does not make its own products, this is not really under the control of the sales manager. Instead the purchasing manager should be more concerned. Complaints about the service contract are the sales executive's concern.

(e) *Customer satisfaction survey.* This is a tool for the sales manager to use as well as a performance measure, but not everything is under the sales executive's control.

3.15 In an ideal world, when setting objectives and planning the operations of the organisation, the manager will:

* Start from the facts of the situation
* Trace through all possible courses of action, and their consequences
* Choose the course of action with the greatest net benefits.

3.16 This ideal model cannot readily be realised. In practice, managers are limited by time, by the information they have and by their own skills, habits and reflexes.

3.17 **Simon** evolved a 'best practicable model' which would fit the problems of real life. This approach Simon characterised as **bounded rationality**.

(a) In this model the **manager does not optimise** (ie get the best possible solution).

(b) Instead the manager **satifices**. In other words, the manager carries on searching until he or she finds an option which appears tolerably satisfactory, and adopts it, even though it may be less than perfect.

4 PERFORMANCE MANAGEMENT: AN INTRODUCTION

KEY TERM

Performance management is: 'a means of getting better results...by understanding and managing performance within an agreed framework of planned goals, standards and competence requirements. It is a process to establish a shared understanding about what is to be achieved, and an approach to managing and developing people..[so that it]...will be achieved' (Armstrong, Handbook of Personnel Management Practice).

Exam focus point

The definition is long, but it is worth learning, because the ability to define performance management is explicitly mentioned in the ACCA's Teaching Guide.

4.1 Armstrong expands on this definition, and describes some other features of performance management.

Aspect	Comment
Agreed framework of goals, standards and competence requirements	As in MBO, the manager and the employee agree about a standard of performance, goals and the skills needed.
Performance management is a process	Managing people's performance is an everyday issue to generate real results. It is not just a system of form filling.
Shared understanding	People need to understand the nature of high levels of performance so they can work towards them.
Approach to managing and developing people	(1) How managers work with their teams (2) How team members work with managers and each other. (3) Developing individuals to improve their performance.

Aspect	Comment
Achievement	The aim is to enable people to realise their potential and maximise their contribution to the organisation's well being.
Line management	A performance management system is primarily the concern, not of experts in the personnel/HRM department, but of the managers responsible for driving the business.
All staff	Everybody is involved in the success of the organisation, so managers must be included in the system.
Specific	As each organisation has unique issues to face, performance management systems cannot really be bought off the peg.
Future-based	Performance management is forward-looking, based on the organisation's future needs and what the individual must do to satisfy them

4.2 **The process of performance management**

Step 1. From the **business plan**, identify the requirements and competences required to carry it out.

Step 2. Draw up a **performance agreement**, defining the expectations of the individual or team, covering standards of performance, performance indicators and the skills and competences people need.

Step 3. Draw up a **performance and development plan** with the individual. These record the actions needed to improve performance, normally covering development in the current job. They are discussed with job holders and will cover, typically:

- The areas of performance the individual feels in need of development
- What the individual and manager agree is needed to enhance performance
- Development and training initiatives

Step 4. **Manage performance continually throughout the year,** not just at appraisal interviews done to satisfy the personnel department. Managers can review actual performance, with more informal interim reviews at various times of the year.

  (a) High performance is reinforced by praise, recognition, increasing responsibility. Low performance results in coaching or counselling

  (b) Work plans are updated as necessary.

  (c) Deal with performance problems, by identifying what they are, establish the reasons for the shortfall, take control action (with adequate resources) and provide feedback

Step 5. Performance review. At a defined period each year, success against the plan is reviewed, but the whole point is to assess what is going to happen in future.

Question 6

What are the advantages to employees of introducing such a system.?

Answer

The key to performance management is that it is forward looking and constructive. Objective-setting gives employees the security in knowing exactly what is expected of them, and this is agreed at the outset with the manager, thus identifying unrealistic expectations. The employee at the outset can indicate the resources needed.

4.3 Organisations are introducing such systems for much the same reason as they pursued management by objectives, in other words, to:

- Tie in individual performance with the performance of the organisation
- Indicate where training and development may be necessary

4.4 Many of the issues covered in this brief outline are explored in later chapters. The purpose of introducing it here is to show how the wider goals and expectations of the organisation depend on how individuals work together.

Chapter roundup

- Organisations have **goals**, which they aspire to achieve.

- Achieving these goals requires a system of **planning and control**: deciding what should be done (goals and objectives), how it is to be done (plans and standard-setting), reviewing what is actually done, comparing actual outcome with plans, and taking corrective action.

- The **mission** is the organisation's overall purpose and reason for existence. While it seems abstract and general it has implications for the commercial strategy, the values of the organisation, and policies and actual standards of behaviour of the people within it.

- **Goals** give flesh to the mission. They can be quantified (objectives) or not quantified (**aims**). Most organisations use a combination of both. Quantified or specific **objectives** have SMART characteristics.

- There is **hierarchy of objectives**. A primary objective of a business might be profit; secondary objectives relate to ways to achieve it.

- The organisation will only achieve its goals through the work of the individuals within it. Therefore, techniques have been suggested to break down the goals into **targets for departments and individuals**. Management by objectives was one such technique, although it perhaps has been superseded by the more modern approach of performance management.

- **Standards of performance** set for individuals should be **job related, controllable, observable**.

- **Performance management** suggests that people must agree performance standards, that the responsibility for performance management is principally that of line management, and that it is a conscious commitment to developing and managing people in organisations. It is a continuous process.

Quick quiz

1 How can organisations direct their activities?

2 What are the elements of a control system?

3 What are four elements of mission?

4 What do you understand by SMART?

5 Why might an organisation wish to be 'socially responsible?

6 List four types of objectives for an individual.

7 How must objectives be interlocked?

8 Define performance management

9   List the steps in performance management

10 How can managers and staff become more committed to objectives, according to supporters of MBO and performance management?

Answers to quick quiz

1   By deciding what should be done, how it should be done, reviewing outcomes, and monitoring performance

2   Plans and standards; sensor to detect actual performance; comparator to compare performance with plans and standards; effector to take control action where necessary. Feedback is information about performance.

3   Purpose; business strategy; policies and standards of behaviour; values

4   Specific, measurable, attainable, realistic, time-bounded

5   To retain and attract customers and employees and community support. To comply with legal and policy provisions.

6   Work-based; standing; output or improvement; developmental

7   Vertically; horizontally (across departments); over time

8   Performance management is 'a means of getting better results...by understanding and managing performance within an agreed framework of planned goals, standards and competence requirements. It is a process to establish a shared understanding about what is to be achieved, and an approach to managing and developing people..[so that it]...will be achieved' (Armstrong, Handbook of Personnel Management Practice).

9   Steps in performance management

Step 1   From the business plan, identify the requirements and competences required to carry it out.

Step 2   Develop a performance agreement.

Step 3   Draw up a performance and development plan with the individual.

Step 4   Manage performance continually throughout the year,

Step 5   Performance review.

10 By participating in setting them.

Now try the question below from the Exam Question Bank

Number	Level	Marks	Time
6	Exam	15	27 mins

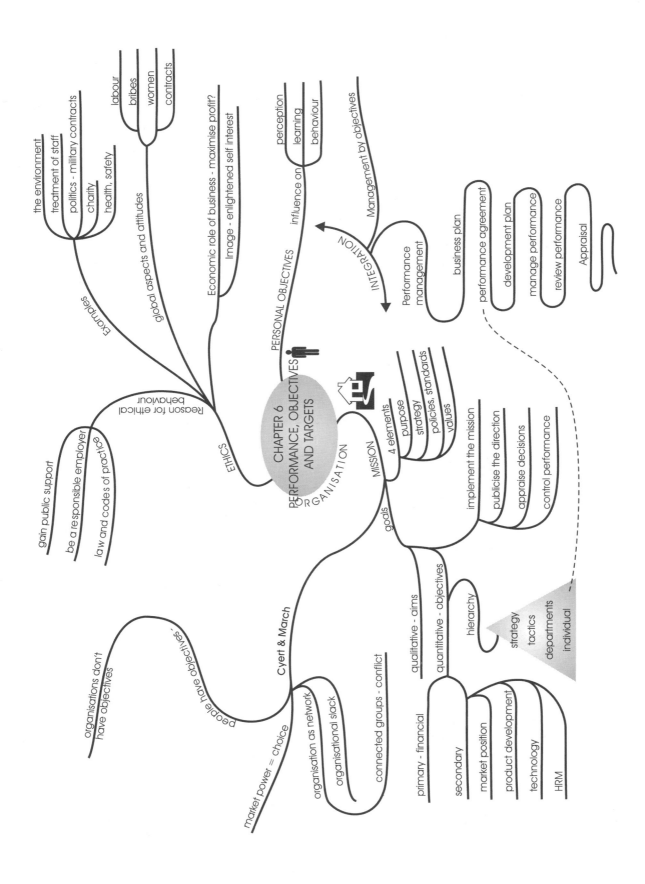

BPP PUBLISHING

Part B
Recruitment and selection

Chapter 7

RECUITMENT

Topic list		Syllabus reference
1	The importance of recruitment and selection	2(a)
2	Who is involved in recruitment and selection?	2(a)
3	The recruitment process	2(a)
4	Job analysis	2(d)
5	Job description	2(c)
6	Person specification	2(c)
7	Advertising the position	2(b)

Introduction

Recruitment and selection are two core activities in the field of human resource management (HRM). The shift from personnel management to an HRM approach has led to these activities being firmly embedded in the wider **human resource plan.**

In this chapter we examine the process of recruitment, which is about obtaining candidates, as opposed to selection, which is about choosing from the candidate pool. Selection is the subject of the next chapter.

Study guide

Sections

9a   The recruitment and section process
10b Effective recruitment.
11c The job description and personnel specification
12d Job analysis

The full detail of all these Study Guide sessions can be found in the introductory pages to this Study Text.

Exam guide

A question requirement on recruitment is likely to be combined with a requirement relating to **selection**, so you should treat this chapter and the next as a unity.

1 THE IMPORTANCE OF RECRUITMENT AND SELECTION

1.1   The process of recruitment should be part of the organisation's human resource plan. People are a major organisational resource and must be managed as such.

BPP PUBLISHING

Case example

London bus drivers

The pressures faced by recruiters is exemplified by recruiting for the bus industry, here as described in the *Financial Times* (20 August 1997).

'London bus drivers tend not to say in a job for more than a few months. The capital's bus companies are facing the highest levels of staff turnover since the 1950s. A combination of the reviving economy and the expanding London bus network means that some bus companies are having to replace up to 40 per cent of drivers a year.

Pay is one issue, shift work is another. A number of bus drivers, for instance, are skilled workers for whom the job was a welcome safety net during the recession of the early 1990s. But the pay, at £230 to £300 for a 40 hour week, is not enough to keep them now.

But the bus companies, competing in a deregulated market, are under pressure to match their services to commuter needs, rather than the body clocks of their drivers.

The squeeze on numbers of these semi-skilled workers - it takes six weeks to train a bus driver - is now so acute that some bus companies are looking outside London for staff. Go Ahead Group, which owns London General Transport with 1,400 drivers, has launched a scheme to recruit drivers from the provinces.

Some argue that what is really needed is a fundamental change of culture at London Transport. This is the authority that puts out to tender the coveted 400 London bus routes. The companies with the lowest cost base scoop the best routes as they require less public subsidy.

CentreWest, owed by FirstBus, believes that recruiting drivers from outside their local area spells trouble. Instead, it has broadened its recruitment policy to include significantly older and younger drivers, as well as more women.

Metroline hopes to keep its drivers by offering the prospect of "virtually a job for life and very high staff share ownership as well as good pension schemes".

Bus bosses agree that the work has got tougher, with congestion now blocking London's roads from 7am to midnight.'

1.2 The main belief of human resources management (HRM) approach is that **employees** are a scarce resource to be used properly.

(a) Recruitment (and training) issues are central to the **business strategy**.

(b) Organisations need to deploy **skills** in order to succeed. Although the labour market might seem a 'buyer's market', in practice there are:

- Skills shortages in key sectors (eg computing services) which drive up prices
- Mismatches between available supply and the skills demanded

(c) In most companies, recruitment is an on-going process, and so the composition of the labour force changes fairly slowly. Only rarely (as when Nissan built its first UK plant) will a firm recruit an entire labour force from scratch.

1.3 The **overall aim of the recruitment and selection process** in an organisation is to obtain the quantity and quality of employees required to fulfil the objectives of the organisation.

1.4 This process can be broken down into three main stages.

(a) Defining requirements, including the preparation of **job descriptions, job specifications and person specifications (sometimes called personnel specifications).**

(b) **Attracting potential employees,** including the evaluation and use of various methods of reaching sources of applicants.

(c) **Selecting** the appropriate people for the job or the appropriate job for the people.

KEY TERMS

Recruitment is the part of the process concerned with finding the applicants: it is a positive action by management, going into the labour market (internal and external), communicating opportunities and information, generating interest.

Selection is the part of the employee resourcing process which involves choosing between applicants for jobs: it is largely a 'negative' process, eliminating unsuitable applicants.

1.5 In times of low unemployment, employers have to compete to attract desirable categories of labour (and may also have to downgrade their selection requirements if the competition is too stiff). In times of high unemployment, and therefore plentiful supply, 'the problem is not so much of attracting candidates, but in deciding how best to select them' (Cole, *Personnel Management Theory and Practice*). In times of low demand for labour, however, socially responsible employers may have the additional policy of using existing staff (internal recruitment) rather than recruiting from outside, in order to downsize staff levels through natural wastage and redeployment.

1.6 Even in conditions of high overall employment, particular skill shortages still exist and may indeed be more acute because of recessionary pressures on education and training. Engineers and software designers, among other specialist and highly trained groups, are the target of fierce competition among employers, forcing a revaluation of recruitment and retention policies.

2 WHO IS INVOLVED IN RECRUITMENT AND SELECTION?

Question 1

Think back to when you started work or when you obtained your current position. How many people did you have to see? Were you interviewed by your immediate boss or someone else?

Answer

Large organisations tend to have standard procedures. In order to ensure a standard process, you might have seen a specialist from the personnel department only. Smaller organisations cannot afford such specialists so you might have been interviewed by your immediate boss - but perhaps someone else might also have interviewed you (your boss's boss) to check you out.

2.1 Precisely who is involved in recruitment and selection varies from organisation to organisation.

Senior managers

2.2 **Senior managers' role in recruitment and selection**

(a) Senior managers/directors are obviously involved in recruiting people - from within or outside the organisation - for **senior positions.**

(b) However, for most positions they will **not be directly involved**: but they are responsible for **human resources planning** (see below), in other words identifying the overall needs of the organisation.

The personnel/human resources department

2.3 Some firms employ **specialists** to manage their recruitment and other activities relevant to human resources. They may be congregated in a personnel department or **human resources department.** Typical job titles you might come across are **personnel manager** or **human resources manager**.

2.4 The **role of the human resources (HR) department in recruitment and selection**

- Assessing needs for human resources
- Maintaining records of people employed
- Keeping in touch with trends in the labour market
- Advertising for new employees
- Ensuring the organisation complies with equal opportunities and other legislation
- Designing application forms
- Liasing with recruitment consultants
- Preliminary interviews and selection testing

The full extent of the involvement of the HR department will vary according to the circumstances of the organisation.

Line managers

2.5 In many cases the recruit's prospective boss will be involved in the recruitment.

(a) In a small business he/she might have sole responsibility for recruitment.

(b) In larger organisations, line managers may be responsible for:

- Asking for more human resources
- Advising on requirements
- Having a final say on candidates presented in the personnel department, perhaps at a final interview

Recruitment consultants

2.6 For some firms, help from **recruitment consultants** or agencies is useful. The tasks involved in this include:

- Analysing, or being informed of, the requirements - the demands of the post, the organisation's preferences for qualifications, personality and so on
- Helping to draw up, or offering advice on, job descriptions, person specifications and other recruitment and selection aids
- Designing job advertisements
- Screening applications, so that those most obviously unsuitable are weeded out immediately
- Helping with short-listing for interview
- Advising on the constitution and procedures of the interview

- Offering a list of suitable candidates with notes and recommendations

Much will depend on whether the consultant is employed to perform the necessary tasks, or merely to **advise** and recommend.

2.7 The decision of **whether or not to use consultants** will depend on a number of factors.

(a) **Cost**.

(b) **The level of expertise** and specialist techniques or knowledge which **the consultant can bring** to the process.

(c) **The level of expertise** and specialist knowledge available **within the organisation**.

(d) Whether there is a **need for impartiality** which can only be filled by an outsider trained in objective assessment. If fresh blood is desired in the organisation, it may be a mistake to have staff selecting clones of the common organisational type.

(e) Whether the import of an outside agent will be **regarded as helpful** by in-house staff.

(f) Whether the **structure and politics of the organisation** are conducive to allowing in-house staff to make decisions of this kind. Consultants are not tied by status or rank and can discuss problems freely at all levels. They are also not likely to fear the consequences of their recommendations for their jobs or career prospects.

(g) **Time**. Consultants will need to learn about the job, the organisation and the organisation's requirements. The client will not only have to pay fees for this period of acclimatisation: it may require a post to be filled more quickly than the process allows.

(h) **Supply of labour**. If there is a large and reasonably accessible pool of labour from which to fill a post, consultants will be less valuable. If the vacancy is a standard one, and there are ready channels for reaching labour (such as professional journals), the use of specialists may not be cost effective.

3 THE RECRUITMENT PROCESS

3.1 The recruitment process is part of a wider whole which is outlined below.

(a) Detailed **human resource planning** defines what resources the organisation needs to meet its objectives.

(b) The **sources of labour** should be forecast. **Internal** and **external** sources, and media for reaching both, will be considered.

(c) **Job analysis** produces two outputs.

(i) A **job description**: a statement of the component tasks, duties, objectives and standards

(ii) A **person specification**: a reworking of the job specification in terms of the kind of person needed to perform the job.

(d) Recruitment as such begins with the identification of vacancies, from the requirements of the manpower plan or by a **job requisition** from a department, branch or office that has a vacancy.

(e) Preparation and publication of advertising **information** will have three aims.

(i)   Attract the attention and interest of potentially suitable candidates.

(ii)   Give a favourable (but accurate) impression of the job and the organisation.

(iii) Equip those interested to make an attractive and relevant application (how and to whom to apply, desired skills, qualifications and so on).

(f) Recruitment merges into selection at the stage of **processing applications** and assessing candidates.

(g) **Notifying applicants** of the results of the selection process is the final stage of the combined recruitment and selection process.

The diagram below shows in more detail how the various recruitment activities fit together.

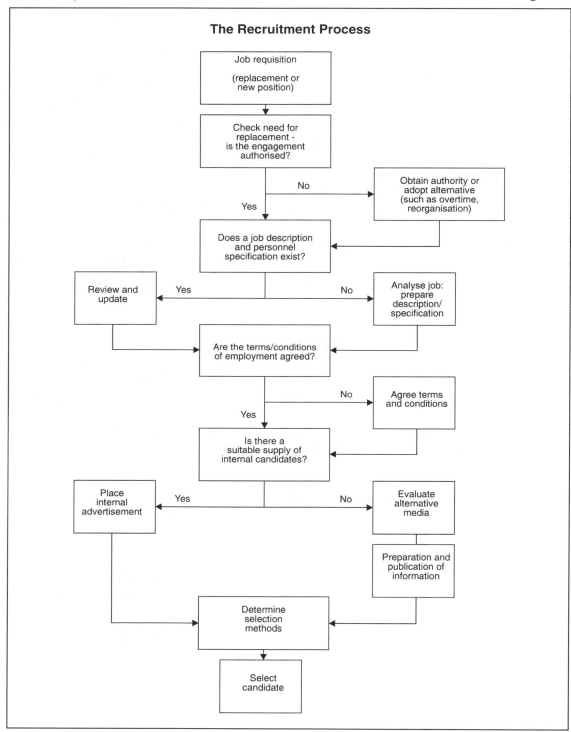

Recruitment policy

3.2 Detailed procedures for recruitment should only be devised and implemented within the context of a coherent **policy**, or code of conduct. A typical recruitment policy might deal with:

- **Internal advertisement** of vacancies
- Efficient and courteous **processing** of applications
- Fair and accurate provision of information to potential recruits
- Selection of candidates on the basis of suitability, without discrimination

3.3 The Institute of Personnel and Development has issued a Recruitment Code.

The IPD Recruitment Code

1 Job advertisements should state clearly the form of reply desired, in particular whether this should be a formal application form or by curriculum vitae. Preferences should also be stated if handwritten replies are required.

2 An acknowledgement of reply should be made promptly to each applicant by the employing organisation or its agent. If it is likely to take some time before acknowledgements are made, this should be made clear in the advertisement.

3 Applicants should be informed of the progress of the selection procedures, what there will be (eg group selection, aptitude tests, etc), the steps and time involved and the policy regarding expenses.

4 Detailed personal information (eg religion, medical history, place of birth, family background, etc) should not be called for unless it is relevant to the selection process.

5 Before applying for references, potential employers must secure permission of the applicant.

6 Applications must be treated as confidential.

7 The code also recommends certain courtesies and obligations on the part of the applicants.

3.4 Detailed **procedures** should be devised in order to make recruitment activity systematic and consistent throughout the organisation (especially where it is decentralised in the hands of line managers). Apart from the manpower resourcing requirements which need to be effectively and efficiently met, there is a **marketing** aspect to recruitment, as one 'interface' between the organisation and the outside world: applicants who feel they have been unfairly treated, or recruits who leave because they feel they have been misled, do not enhance the organisation's reputation in the labour market or the world at large.

Question 1

Find out, if you do not already know, what are the recruitment and selection procedures in your organisation, and who is responsible for each stage. The procedures manual should set this out, or you may need to ask someone in the personnel department.

Get hold of and examine some of the documentation your organisation uses. We show specimens in this chapter, but practice and terminology varies, so your own 'house style' will be invaluable. Compare your organisation's documentation with our example.

---

4 JOB ANALYSIS

4.1 The management of the organisation needs to analyse the sort of work needed to be done.

> ## KEY TERM
>
> **Job analysis** is:
>
> 'the process of collecting, analysing and setting out information about the content of jobs in order to provide the basis for a job description and data for recruitment, training, job evaluation and performance management. Job analysis concentrates on what job holders are expected to do.' (Armstrong)

4.2 The definition shows why job analysis is important - the firm has to know what people are doing in order to recruit effectively.

4.3 **Information that might be obtained from a job analysis**

Information	Comments
Purpose of the job	This might seem obvious. However, it has to be set in the context of the organisation as a whole.
Content of the job	The detailed duties and responsibilities of the job.
Accountabilities	The results for which the job holder must account to his or her spouse.
Performance criteria	These are the criteria which measure how good the holder is at the job.
Responsibility	This denotes the importance of the job. For example, a person running a department and taking decisions involving large amounts of money is more responsible that someone who only does what he or she is told.
Organisational factors	Who does the jobholder report to directly (line manager) or on grounds of functional authority?
Developmental factors	Relating to the job, such as likely promotion paths, if any, career prospects and so forth. Some jobs are 'dead-end' if they lead nowhere.
Environmental factors	Working conditions, security and safety issues, equipment and so on.

Carrying out a job analysis

4.4 A job analysis has to be done systematically - that is why it is called an **analysis -** as the purpose is to obtain facts about the job. Therefore the job analysis involves the use of a number of different techniques to gather the data. The stages should be:

Step 1. **Obtain documentary information** such as procedures manuals and written instructions

Step 2. Ask **managers** about more **general aspects** such as the job's purpose, the main activities, the responsibilities involved and the relationships with others.

Step 3. **Ask the job holders** similar questions about their jobs - perceptions might differ.

Step 4. **Observe** the job holders to see what they actually do.

Techniques of job analysis

4.5 **Interviews** establish basic facts about the job, from the job holder's point of view. There are two sorts of information.

(a) **Basic facts** about the job, such as the job title, the jobholder's manager or team leader, people reporting to the jobholder, the main tasks or duties, official targets or performance standards.

(b) More **subjective issues**, which are harder to test which are still important.

- The amount of supervision a person receives
- How much freedom a person has to take decisions
- How hard the job is
- The skills/qualifications needed to carry out the job
- How the job fits in elsewhere with the company
- How work is allocated
- Decision-making authority

This information should always be checked for accuracy.

4.6 **Advantages and disadvantages of job analysis interviewing**

Advantages	Disadvantages
Flexibility	Time consuming
Interactive	Hard to analyse
Easy to organise and carry out	Interviewee might feel on the defensive and might not be entirely frank
New or follow-on questions can be asked in the light of information received	
Reveals other organisational problems	

4.7 **Questionnaires** are sometimes used in job analysis. Their success depends on the willingness of people to complete them accurately.

- They gather purely factual information
- They can cover large numbers of staff
- They provide a structure to the process of information gathering

4.8 **Checklists and inventories.** A checklist would contain a list of activities and the job holder would have to note down how important these are in the job.

Activity description	Time spent on activity	Importance of activity
Processes sales invoices	Less than 10%	Unimportant
	10% to 20%	Not very important
	20-30%	Important
	...and so on	Very important

4.9 **Observation**. People are watched doing the job. This is easy enough for jobs which can be easily observed or which are physical, but is harder for knowledge based work. But observation is quite common in assessing performance - trainee school teachers are observed in the classroom.

4.10 **Self description**. Jobholders are asked to prepare their own job descriptions and to analyse their own jobs. This is quite difficult to do, because people often find it hard to stand back from what they are doing.

4.11 **Diaries and logs** - people keep records of what they do over a period of time, and these can be used by the analyst to develop job descriptions. You may come across something like this in your working life, if, say, you have to keep a timesheet covering work for a particular client, or if it is part of your training record.

4.12 **Which method should be used?** It depends. Any job analysis exercise might involve a variety of methods: Questionnaires or checklists save time. Interviews give a better idea of the detail. Self-description to shows how people *perceive* their jobs, which may be very different from how managers perceive their jobs. Diaries and logs are useful for management jobs, in which a lot is going on.

4.13 It is not always easy to carry out a job analysis, especially for managers and supervisors. In part of this text, we identified the growth of the use of **teams** and **flexible working** in which people are expected to exercise initiative. The case example below shows how job analysis techniques can be adapted

Case example

People Management, 6 March 1997, described **Workset**, a job analysis system developed by Belbin. Workset uses colour coding to classify work and working time into seven types.

1	Blue: tasks the job holder carries out in a prescribed manner to an approved standard
2	Yellow: individual responsibility to meet an objective (results, not means)
3	Green: tasks that vary according to the reactions and needs of others
4	Orange: shared rather than individual responsibility for meeting an objective
5	Grey: work incidental to the job, not relevant to the four core categories
6	White: new or creative undertaking outside normal duties
7	Pink: demands the presence of the job holder but leads to no useful results

The manager gives an outline of the proportion of time which the manager expects the jobholder to spend on each 'colour' of work. The job holder then briefs the manager on what has actually been done. This highlights differences: between managers' and job-holders' perceptions of jobs; between the perceptions of different jobholders in the same nominal position, who had widely different ideas as to what they were supposed to do.

Important issues arise when there is a gap in perception. Underperformance in different kinds of work can be identified, and people can be steered to the sort of work which suits them best.

Question 3

Analyse your own working time according to the Workset classification above. Do the results surprise you?

4.14 The product of the analysis is usually a *description* - a detailed statement of the activities (mental and physical) involved in the job, and other relevant factors in the social and physical environment.

4.15 Job analysis, and the job description resulting from it, may be used by managers in:

(a) Recruitment and selection - for a detailed description of the vacant job

(b) Appraisal - to assess how well an employee has fulfilled the requirements of the job

(c) Devising training programmes - to assess the knowledge and skills necessary in a job

(d) Establishing rates of pay - this will be discussed later in connection with job evaluation

(e) Eliminating risks - identifying hazards in the job

(f) Re-organising of the organisational structure - by reappraising the purpose and necessity of jobs and their relationship to each other

Competences

4.16 A more recent approach to job design is the development and outlining of **competences**.

> **KEY TERM**
>
> A person's **competence** is 'a capacity that leads to behaviour that meets the job demands within the parameters of the organisational environment and that, in turn, brings about desired results', (Boyzatis). Some take this further and suggest that a competence embodies the ability to transfer skills and knowledge to new situations within the occupational area.

4.17 **Different sorts of competences**

(a) **Behavioural/personal** competences: underlying personal characteristics people bring to work (eg interpersonal skills); personal characteristics and behaviour for successful performance, for example, 'ability to relate well to others'. Most jobs require people to be good communicators.

(b) **Work-based/occupational competences** refer to 'expectations of workplace performance and the outputs and standards people in specific roles are expected to obtain'. This approach is used in NVQ systems (see below). They cover what people have to do to achieve the results of the job. For example, a competence of a Certified Accountant includes 'produce financial and other statements and report to management'

(c) **Generic competences** can apply to all people in an occupation.

4.18 Many lists of competences confuse:

- Areas of **work** at which people are competent
- Underlying **aspects of behaviour**

4.19   **Examples of competences for managers**

Competence area	Competence
Intellectual	• Strategic perspective • Analytical judgement • Planning and organising
Interpersonal	• Managing staff • Persuasiveness • Assertiveness and decisiveness • Interpersonal sensitivity • Oral communication
Adaptability	
Results	• Initiative • Motivation to achievement • Business sense

These competences can be elaborated by identifying **positive** and **negative** indicators.

5   JOB DESCRIPTION

5.1   The job analysis is used to develop the job description.

KEY TERM

Job description. A job description sets out the purpose of a job, where it fits in the organisation structure, the context within which the job holder functions and the principal accountability of job holders and the main tasks they have to carry out.

5.2   **Purpose of job description**

Purpose	Comment
Organisational	The job description defines the job's place in the organisational structure
Recruitment	The job description provides information for identifying the sort of person needed (person specification)
Legal	The job description provides the basis for a contract of employment
Performance	Performance objectives can be set around the job description

5.3   **Contents of a job description**

(a)   **Job title** (eg Assistant Financial Controller). This indicates the function/department in which the job is performed, and the level of job within that function.

(b)   **Reporting to** (eg the Assistant Financial controller reports to the Financial Controller), in other words the person's immediate boss. (No other relationships are suggested here.)

(c)   **Subordinates** directly reporting to the job holders.

(d) **Overall purpose** of the job, distinguishing it from other jobs.

(e) **Principal accountabilities or main tasks**

    (i) Group the main activities into a number of broad areas.

    (ii) Define each activity as a statement of accountability: what the job holder is expected to achieve (eg **tests** new system to ensure they meet agreed systems specifications).

(f) The current fashion for multi-skilled teams means that **flexibility** is sometimes expected.

Examples of job descriptions are given below.

JOB DESCRIPTION

1   *Job title:* Baking Furnace Labourer.

2   *Department:* 'B' Baking.

3   *Date:* 20 November 19X0.

4   *Prepared by:* H Crust, baking furnace manager.

5   *Responsible to:* baking furnace chargehand.

6   *Age range:* 20-40.

7   *Supervises work of:* N/A.

8   *Has regular co-operative contract with:* Slinger/Crane driver.

9   *Main duties/responsibilities:* Stacking formed electrodes in furnace, packing for stability. Subsequently unloads baked electrodes and prepares furnace for next load.

10   *Working conditions:* stacking is heavy work and requires some manipulation of 100lb (45kg) electrodes. Unloading is hot (35° - 40°C) and very dusty.

11   *Employment conditions:*

    Wages £3.60 ph + group bonus (average earnings £219.46 pw).

    Hours: Continuous rotating three-shift working days, 6 days on, 2 days off. NB must remain on shift until relieved.

    Trade Union: National Union of Bread Bakers, optional.

BPP
PUBLISHING

MIDWEST BANK PLC

1   *Job title:*   Clerk (Grade 2).

2   *Branch:*   All branches and administrative offices.

3   *Job summary:*   To provide clerical support to activities within the bank.

4   *Job content:*   Typical duties will include:

    (a)   Cashier's duties;
    (b)   Processing of branch clearing;
    (c)   processing of standing orders;
    (d)   support to branch management.

5   *Reporting structure*

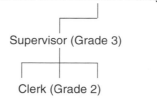

Administrative officer/assistant manager

Supervisor (Grade 3)

Clerk (Grade 2)

6   *Experience/education:* experience not required, minimum 3 GCSEs or equivalent.

7   *Training to be provided:* initial on-the-job training plus regular formal courses and training.

8   *Hours:* 38 hours per week.

9   *Objectives and appraisal:* Annual appraisal in line with objectives above.

10 *Salary:* refer to separate standard salary structure.

Job description prepared by: Head office personnel department.

Question 4

Studying has placed you in a role in which you have to perform a fairly consistent set of duties, in fairly consistent conditions, within a structure that requires you to interact with other people, both superiors and peers (and possibly subordinates). Draw up a job description for yourself.

Alternatives to job descriptions

5.4   **Detailed** job descriptions are perhaps only suited for jobs where the work is largely repetitive and therefore performed by low-grade employees: once the element of **judgement** comes into a job description it becomes a straitjacket. Many difficulties arise where people adhere strictly to the contents of the job description, rather than responding flexibly to task or organisational requirements.

5.5   Perhaps job descriptions should be written in terms of the **outputs and performance levels** expected. Some firms are moving towards **accountability profiles** in which outputs and performance are identified explicitly.

5.6   Armstrong suggests a crucial difference between:

- A job - a group of tasks.

- A role - a part played by people in meeting their objectives by working competently and flexibly within the context of the organisation's objectives, structures and processes

5.7   A **role definition** is wider than a job description. It is less concerned with the details of the job content, but how they interpret the job, and how they perceive them.

Case example

Guinness

According to *People Management*, 11 September 1997, in May 1996 Guinness Brewing Great Britain introduced a new pay system based on competences.

Restrictive job definitions, lengthy job descriptions and a 24-grade structure were replaced by broad role profiles and three pay bands. Roles are now specified in terms of 'need to do' (primary accountabilities), 'need to know' (experience and knowledge requirements) and 'need to be' (levels of competence).

Competences are defined as 'the skill, knowledge and behaviours that need to be applied for effective performance'. There are seven of them, including commitment to results and interpersonal effectiveness. Roles are profiled against each relevant competence and individuals' actual competences are compared with the requirements through the performance management process.

Question 5

Without looking at the real thing, to start with, draw up a job description for your own job and for the job of a personnel officer in your organisation. Now look at the official job descriptions. Are they true, detailed and up-to-date, compared with the actual jobs as you saw them? If not, what does this tell you about (a) job descriptions and (b) perceptions of the personnel function?

6 PERSON SPECIFICATION

> **KEY TERM**
>
> 'A **person specification** sets out the education, qualifications, training, experience personal attributes and competences a job holder requires to perform her or his job satisfactorily.' (Armstrong)

6.1 The job description outlines the **job**: the person specification describes the **person** needed to do the job. For example, a position of secretary or personal assistant normally requires the holder to have word processing skills.

Traditional approaches to the person specification

6.2 The **Seven Point Plan** put forward by Professor Rodger in 1951 draws the selector's attention to seven points about the candidate.

- **Physical attributes** (such as neat appearance, ability to speak clearly)
- **Attainment** (including educational qualifications)
- **General intelligence**
- **Special aptitudes** (such as neat work, speed and accuracy)
- **Interests** (practical and social)
- **Disposition** (or manner: friendly, helpful and so on)
- Background **circumstances**

6.3 **Problems with the Seven Point Plan**.

(a) Physical attributes or disposition might include a person's demeanour. **Eye contact** is considered a sign of honesty and frankness in some cultures, but a sign of disrespect in others.

(b) **General intelligence** is not something that can be measured easily. A criticism of IQ tests is that test scores tell you that you are good at doing IQ tests - and not much else.

(c) **Attainment**: educational qualifications - no attention is paid to the circumstances in which these were obtained.

The plan does not identify a person's **potential**, or suggest how it can be aligned precisely to the organisation's requirements.

Five-Point Pattern

6.4 Munro-Fraser's Five Point Pattern is one alternative.

- **Impact on others**: physical attributes, speech, manner

- **Acquired knowledge** and qualifications

- **Innate abilities**: ability to learn, mental agility

- **Motivation**: What sort of goals does the individual set, how much effort goes into achieving them, how successful.

- **Adjustment**: emotional stability, tolerance of slips.

New approaches: competences

6.5 The two methods described above have been in use for many years. More recruiters are using **competences** (see paragraph 4.15) in designing the person specification.

Preparing the specification

6.6 Each feature in the person specification should be classified as essential, desirable or contra indicated.

Information	Comments
Essential	For instance, honesty in a cashier is essential whilst a special aptitude for conceptual thought is not.
Desirable	For instance, a reasonably pleasant manner should ensure satisfactory standards in a person dealing with the public.
Contra-indicated	Some features are actively disadvantageous, such as an inability to work in a team when acting as project leader.

PERSON SPECIFICATION: Customer Accounts Manager

	ESSENTIAL	DESIRABLE	CONTRA-INDICATED
Physical attributes	Clear speech Well-groomed Good health	Age 25-40	Age under 25 Chronic ill-health and absence
Attainments	2 'A' levels GCSE Maths and English Thorough knowledge of retail environment	Degree (any discipline) Marketing training 2 years' experience in supervisory post	No experience of supervision or retail environment
Intelligence	High verbal intelligence		
Aptitudes	Facility with numbers Attention to detail and accuracy Social skills for customer relations	Analytical abilities (problem solving) Understanding of systems and IT	No mathematical ability Low tolerance of technology
Interests	Social: team activity		Time-consuming hobbies 'Solo' interests only
Disposition	Team player Persuasive Tolerance of pressure and change	Initiative	Anti-social Low tolerance of responsibility
Circumstances	Able to work late, take work home	Located in area of office	

Question 6

Turn your job description for A student into a corresponding Personnel Specification, using the 'essential; desirable; contra-indicated' framework, and either the Seven Point Plan or Five Point Pattern. If you did not do Activity 7.5, do it now! (You might like to consider into which section of your personnel specification 'laziness' would fall....)

Limitations of person specifications

6.7 A wide number of variables may be included in a person specification. If it is not used flexibly, however, and the specification fails to evolve as business and employment conditions change, it may swiftly lose its relevance. For example:

(a) Attainments are often focused on **educational** achievements, since there has traditionally been a strong correlation between management potential and higher education. However, as recent (January 1999) editions of *People Management* suggest, graduate recruitment is now in crisis, as more people enter higher education, with more diverse educational backgrounds, and more diverse educational standards.

(b) **Physical attributes** and **background circumstances** may suggest criteria which can now be interpreted as discriminatory.

(c) The category of **general intelligence** has traditionally been based on IQ, a narrow definition of intelligence as mental dexterity.

6.8 In addition, person specifications were explicitly developed in order to match the aptitudes of job applicants to the requirements of an occupation. If employees are recruited and deployed on a **project** or **consultancy basis,** a different package of attributes will be required for each project in each organisation.

6.9 The competence approach goes some way to overcoming these problems.

7 ADVERTISING THE POSITION

7.1 The object of recruitment advertising is to attract suitable candidates and deter unsuitable candidates.

7.2 **Characteristics of the job advertisement**

(a) **Concise,** but comprehensive enough to be an accurate description of the job, its rewards and requirements.

(b) **Attractive** to the maximum number of the right people.

(c) **Positive and honest** about the organisation. Disappointed expectations will be a prime source of dissatisfaction when an applicant actually comes into contact with the organisation.

(d) **Relevant and appropriate to the job and the applicant**. Skills, qualifications and special aptitudes required should be prominently set out, along with special features of the job that might attract - on indeed deter - applicants, such as shiftwork or extensive travel.

7.3 **Content of the advertisement**

(a) The **organisation**: its main business and location, at least.

(b) The **job**: title, main duties and responsibilities and special features.

(c) **Conditions**: special factors affecting the job.

(d) **Qualifications and experience** (required, and preferred); other attributes, aptitudes and/or knowledge required.

(e) **Rewards**: salary, benefits, opportunities for training, career development, and so on.

(f) **Application process**: how to apply, to whom, and by what date.

7.4 It should encourage a degree of **self-selection,** so that the target population begins to narrow itself down. The information contained in the advertisement should deter unsuitable applicants as well as encourage potentially suitable ones.

7.5 **Factors influencing the choice of advertising medium**

(a) **The type of organisation**. A factory is likely to advertise a vacancy for an unskilled worker in a different way to a company advertising for a member of the Institute of Personnel and Development for an HRM position.

(b) **The type of job.** Managerial jobs may merit national advertisement, whereas semi--skilled jobs may only warrant local coverage, depending on the supply of suitable candidates in the local area. Specific skills may be most appropriately reached through trade, technical or professional journals, such as those for accountants or computer programmers.

(c) **The cost of advertising.** It is more expensive to advertise in a national newspaper than on local radio, and more expensive to advertise on local radio than in a local newspaper etc.

(d) The **readership and circulation** (type and number of readers/listeners) of the medium, and its suitability for the number and type of people the organisation wants to reach.

(e) The **frequency** with which the organisation wants to advertise the job vacancy, and the duration of the recruitment process.

Question 7

Dealing with individuals demands a certain... ...um...

You've heard the old line...
'You don't have to be mad to work here, but it helps'. It's like that at AOK, but in the nicest possible way. We believe that our Personnel Department should operate for the benefit of our staff, and not that staff should conform to statistical profiles. It doesn't make for an easy life, but dealing with people as individuals, rather than numbers, certainly makes it a rewarding one.

We're committed to an enlightened personnel philosophy. We firmly believe that our staff are our most important asset, and we go a long way both to attract the highest quality of people, and to retain them.

AOK is a company with a difference. We're a highly progressive, international organisation, one of the world's leading manufacturers in the medical electronics field.

...Character

As an expanding company, we now need another experienced Personnel Generalist to join us at our UK headquarters in Reigate, Surrey.

Essentially we're looking for an individual, a chameleon character who will assume an influential role in recruitment, employee relations, salary administration, compensation and benefits, or whatever the situation demands. The flexibility to interchange with various functions is vital. Within your designated area, you'll experience a large degree of independence. You'll be strong in personality, probably already experienced in personnel management in a small company. Whatever your background you'll certainly be someone who likes to help people help themselves and who is happy to get involved with people at all levels within the organisation.

Obviously, in a fast growing company with a positive emphasis on effective personnel work, your prospects for promotion are excellent. Salaries are highly attractive and benefits are, of course, comprehensive.

So if you're the kind of personnel individual who enjoys personal contact, problem solving, and will thrive on the high pace of a progressive, international organisation, such as AOK, get in touch with us by writing or telephoning, quoting ref: 451/BPD, to AOK House, Reigate, Surrey.

What do you think of this advertisement? How can you improve it?

Answer

(a) Goods points about the advertisement and points for improvement

    (i) It is attractively designed in terms of page layout.

(ii)   The tone of the headline and much of the body copy is informal, colloquial and even friendly. It starts with a joke, implying that the company has a sense of humour.

(iii)   The written style is fluent and attractive.

(iv)   It appears to offer quite a lot of information about the culture of the company - how it feels about personnel issues, where it's going etc - as well as about the job vacancy.

Improvement that could be made

Job advertisements carry certain 'responsibilities': they are a form of pre-selection, and as such should be not be just attractive and persuasive, but accurate and complete enough to give a realistic and relevant picture of the post and the organisation.

(i)   There is too much copy. Readers may not have the patience to read through so much (rather wordy) prose, particularly since the same phrases are repeated ('progressive international organisation', for example), or look rather familiar in any case ('in the nicest possible ways', 'our staff are our most important asset', 'a company with a difference' etc) and there is very little 'hard' information contained in the ad.

(ii)   There are many words and expressions which sound good, and seem to **imply** good things, but are in fact empty of substance, and commit the organisation to nothing. They are usually the 'stock' expressions like 'committed to an enlightened personnel philosophy': what does that actually **mean**?

(iii)   There are confusing contradictions, eg between the requirements for flexibility, 'interchange with various functions', do 'whatever the situation demands' etc and the more cautious 'within your designated area ...'.

(iv)   The copywriters are in places too 'clever' for their own good. The first three lines, for example, could backfire quite badly if a reader failed to catch the next line, or simply didn't appreciate the self-deprecating tone.

(v)   The advertisement does not give enough 'hard' information to make effective response likely - and then fails to do its job of facilitating response at all! Despite the invitation to telephone, no number is given. No named corespondent is cited, merely a reference number - despite the claimed emphasis on people as people, not numbers.

(b)   What is learnt about AOK

The advertisement **claims** to say quite a lot about AOK, its culture, its people-centredness, its expansion and progressive outlook, flexibility, sense of humour etc. Such claims should always be taken with a pinch of salt. We may, however, infer some things about the company.

(i)   It has a strong cultural 'flavour', and believes in 'selling' that culture quite hard. It likes, for example, telling people what it is 'committed to', what it 'firmly believes' etc.

(ii)   It tends to stress its good points and opportunities: it certainly sees itself (even allowing for advertising hyperbole) as go-ahead, successful and expanding, flexible, people-oriented.

(iii)   It is possibly not as deeply people oriented as it tries to project. The areas of involvement for the Personnel Department enumerated, for example, seem rather limited and administrative: there is no suggestion of a wider strategic role for personnel, such as would indicate that 'people issues' really do affect management outlook.

7.6   Media for recruitment advertising

(a)   **In-house magazine, notice-boards,** e-mail or intra-net. An organisation might invite applications from employees who would like a transfer or a promotion to the particular vacancy advertised.

(b)   **Professional and specialist newspapers or magazines,** such as *Accountancy Age, Marketing Week* or *Computing.*

(c)   **National newspapers** are used for senior management jobs or vacancies for skilled workers, where potential applicants will not necessarily be found through local advertising.

(d) **Local newspapers** would be suitable for jobs where applicants are sought from the local area.

(e) **Local radio, television and cinema.** These are becoming increasingly popular, especially for large-scale campaigns for large numbers of vacancies.

(f) **Job centres.** Vacancies for unskilled work (rather than skilled work or management jobs) are advertised through local job centres, although in theory any type of job can be advertised here.

(g) **School and university careers offices.** Ideally, the manager responsible for recruitment in an area should try to maintain a close liaison with careers officers. Some large organisations organise special meetings or **careers fairs** in universities and colleges, as a kind of showcase for the organisation and the careers it offers.

(h) The **Internet**. Many businesses advertise vacancies on their websites.

Chapter roundup

- Effective recruitment practices ensure that a firm has enough **people with the right skills**.

- Most recruitment practices aim to **fit the person to the job** by identifying the needs of the job and finding a person who satisfies them.

- The recruitment process involves **personnel specialists** and **line managers**, sometimes with the help of recruitment **consultants**.

- First the overall **needs of the organisation** have been identified in the recruitment process.

- The account for each individual position a **job analysis** is prepared, which identifies through various investigative techniques, the content of the job.

- A **job description** is developed from the job analysis. The job description outlines the **tasks** of the job and its place within the organisation.

- A **person specification** identifies the characteristics of a person who will be recruited to do the job identified in the job description.

- The person specification can be used to develop the **job advertisement**. The Seven Point Plan and Five Point Pattern are examples.

- In recent years, recruiters have been using the **competences** as a means to select candidates. A **competence** is a person's capacity to behave in a particular way for example to fulfil the requirements of a job, or to motivate people. Work-based competences directly relate to the job (eg the ability to prepare a trial balance); behavioural competences relate to underlying issues of personality.

BPP PUBLISHING

Quick quiz

1 What is the underlying principle of human resources management?

2 What, in brief, are the stages of the recruitment and selection process?

3 What is the role of line managers in the recruitment process?

4 List the factors determining whether a firm should use recruitment consultants.

5 Briefly summarise:

(a) job analysis
(b) job description
(c) person specification

6 What is a currently fashionable approach to drawing up jobs analysis, job descriptions etc?

7 List the components of the Five Point Pattern.

8 What are the characteristics of a good job advertisement?

Answers to quick quiz

1 People are a scarce resource and need to be managed effectively.

2 Identifying/defining requirements; attracting potential employees; selecting candidates.

3 It depends - making a requisition, identifying departmental needs, interviewing, reviewing the job analysis, job description etc.

4 Cost: expertise; impartiality; organisation structure and politics; time; supply of labour.

5 (a) **Job analysis**. The process of examining a 'job' to identify the component parts and the circumstances in which it is performed.

(b) **Job description**. A broad statement of the purpose, scope, duties and responsibilities of a particular 'job'.

(c) **Personnel specification**. The kind of person suitable for the job.

6 The use of competences - work based and behavioural.

7 Impact on others; acquired knowledge and qualifications; innate abilities; motivation; adjustment.

8 Concise; reaches the right people; gives a good impression; relevant to the job, identifying skills required etc.

Now try the question below from the Exam Question Bank

Question to try	Level	Marks	Time
7	Exam	15	27 mins

Chapter 8

SELECTION

Topic list	Syllabus reference
1 The selection process in outline	2(a)
2 Application forms	2(a)
3 Selection methods in outline	2(e)
4 Interviews	2(f)
5 Tests	2(e)
6 Other selection methods	2(e)
7 Which selection method is best?	2(e)
8 References	2(e)
9 Evaluating and improving recruitment and selection practices	2(a)

Introduction

Once potential recruits have been attracted to apply, there must be a careful winnowing process to separate out those that are most suitable. Most organisations use interviews for this, but other techniques are probably more appropriate.

Study guide

Section 13 – Selection methods

Section 14 – Selection interview

The full details of these sessions can be found in the introductory pages to this Study Text.

Exam guide

Selection was covered in outline in the pilot paper. Bear in mind that there are a number of procedures and techniques.

BPP PUBLISHING

1 THE SELECTION PROCESS IN OUTLINE

1.1 In brief we can outline the main steps.

Step 1. Deal with responses to job advertisements. This might involve sending **application forms** to candidates. preferring to review CVs.

Step 2. Assess each application against **key criteria** in the job advertisement and specification. Critical factors may include age, qualifications, experience or whatever.

Step 3. **Sort applications** into 'possible', 'unsuitable' and 'marginal.

'Possibles' will then be more closely scrutinised, and a shortlist for interview drawn up. Ideally, this should be done by both the personnel specialist and the prospective manager of the successful candidate.

Step 4. **Invite candidates for interviews.**

Step 5. Reinforce interviews with **selection testing,** if suitable.

Step 6. Review un-interviewed 'possibles', and 'marginals', and put potential future candidates on hold, or in reserve.

Step 7. Send standard letters to unsuccessful applicants, and inform them simply that they have not been successful. Reserves will be sent a holding letter: 'We will keep your details on file, and should any suitable vacancy arise in future...'.

Step 8. Make a provisional offer to the recruit.

1.2 Sometimes Steps 4 and 5 will be reversed, so that **testing** comes before **interviewing.** There are good reasons for this, as we shall see.

2 APPLICATION FORMS

2.1 Job advertisements usually ask candidates to fill in a **job application form,** or to send information about themselves and their previous job experience (their **curriculum vitae (CV)**), usually with a covering letter briefly explaining why they think they are qualified to do the job.

2.2 **Purposes of application forms**

- Weeding out unsuitable candidates
- Identifying possible candidates

2.3 Application forms fulfil these jobs in two ways.

Asking specific questions	• The application form will be designed around the personnel specification. So, if a certain number of GCSE's are needed, the applicant will be asked to list educational qualifications.
	• Certain questions **cannot** be asked by law, BECAUSE of equal opportunities legislation.
Finding out more	Candidates should be given the ability to **write about themselves,** their ambitions, why they want the job. Some application forms ask people to write about key successes and failures. This gives information about the candidate's underlying personality as well as matters such as neatness, literacy and the ability to communicate in writing.

AOK PLC

APPLICATION FORM

Post applied for ....

PERSONAL DETAILS

Surname Mr/ Mrs/ Miss/Ms

First name

Address

Post code

Telephone   (Daytime)   (Evenings)

Date of birth

Nationality

Marital status

Dependants

Education (latest first)

Date		Institution	Exams passed/qualifications
From	To		

TRAINING AND OTHER SKILLS

Please give details of any specialised training courses you have attended.

Please note down other skills such as languages (and degree of fluency), driving licence (with endorsements if any), keyboard skills (familiarity with software package).

BPP PUBLISHING

Part B: Recruitment and selection

EMPLOYMENT

| Dates | | Employer | Title |
From	To	name and address	and duties

Current salary and benefits ...

INTERESTS

Please describe your leisure/hobby/sporting interests

YOUR COMMENTS

Why do you think you are suitable for the job advertised?

ADDITIONAL INFORMATION

Do you have any permanent health problems? If so, please give details.

When would you be able to start work?

REFERENCES

Please give two references. One should be a former employer.

Name	Name
Address	Address
Position	Position

Signed	Date

Question 1

Suggest four possible design faults in job application forms - you may be able to draw on your own personal experience.

Answer

(a) Boxes too small to contain the information asked for.

(b) Forms which are (or look) so lengthy or complicated that a prospective applicant either completes them perfunctorily or gives up (and applies to another employer instead).

(c) Illegal (eg discriminatory) or offensive questions.

(d) Lack of clarity as to what (and how much) information is required.

Application forms and CVs

2.4 Many firms are either **too small** or cannot be bothered to design a standard application form for all posts. The requirements of a business employing, say, 30 people, are very different from a large employer such as the Civil Service or British Airways. This is why many job advertisements ask for a CV and a covering letter.

2.5 How a CV is presented tells a great deal about the candidate - not only the information on the CV but the candidate's neatness and ability to structure information.

2.6 **Application forms** have the merit of being **standardised,** so that all candidates are asked the same information. Gaps can thus be identified clearly, and essential information can be asked for. CVs on the other hand are easy to mould and manipulate.

Sifting application forms and CVs: biodata

2.7 For some jobs, hundreds or even thousands of people might apply, and so to reduce all this to manageable proportion, recruiters can use structured ways of sifting the data. Some firms even use computers to identify items on CVs or application forms in order to rank the candidates in order to generate a shortlist.

2.8 **Biodata** is the term given to techniques which aim to score and structure biographical information about a candidate in order to predict work performance.

(a) A **biodata questionnaire**, which might even be appended to the application form, asks specific questions.

- Demographic details (age, sex, family circumstances)
- Education and professional qualifications
- Previous employment history and work experience
- Positions of responsibility outside work
- Leisure interests
- Career and job motivation

(b) **Each item is given a weight**. For example, education and professional qualifications might account for up to 20 marks; leisure interests might account for up to ten marks. Within each weight the candidate is given a score.

(c) The **scores are added up**, to give the candidate a total. A candidate who scores below a certain level will not be accepted.

2.9 Biodata is only really suitable when large numbers of applicants have to be screened. Furthermore, the biodata weights are based on the scores of existing employees, so a large workforce is needed for any meaningful correlation to be made between biodata and work performance.

3 SELECTION METHODS IN OUTLINE

3.1 We will briefly list the main selection methods here. The more important are discussed in the following sections.

Methods	Examples
Interviewing	• Individual (one-to-one)
	• Interview panels
	• Selection boards
	• Assessment centres
Biodata	
Selection tests	• Intelligence
	• Aptitudes
	• Personality
	• Proficiency
Work sampling	
Group selection methods	

4 INTERVIEWS

4.1 Most firms use the selection interview as their main source for decision-making.

4.2 **Purpose of the interview**

(a) Finding the best person for the job, by giving making the organisation a chance to assess applicants (and particularly their interpersonal communication skills) directly

(b) Making sure that applicants understand what the job, what the career prospects are and have suitable information about the company

(c) Giving the best possible impression of the organisation - after all, the candidate may have other offers elsewhere

(d) Making all applicants feel that they have been given **fair treatment** in the interview, whether they get the job or not

4.3 **Conducting selection interviews: matters to be kept in mind**

(a) The **impression** of the organisation given by the interview arrangements

(b) The **psychological effects** of the location of the interview and seating arrangements

(c) The **manner and tone** of the interviewers

(d) Getting the candidates to talk freely (by asking open questions) and honestly (by asking probing questions), in accordance with the organisation's need for **information**

(e) The **opportunity for the candidate to learn** about the job and organisation

(f) The control of **bias** or hasty judgement by the interviewer

Preparation of the interview

4.4 Candidates should be given clear instructions about the date, time and location - perhaps with a map, and the name of the person they should contact on arriving.

4.5 **The interview room.** The interview is where the organisation sells itself and the candidate aims to give a good impression. The layout of the room should be carefully designed. Being interrogated by two people from the other side of a desk may be completely unsuitable. However. some interviews are **deliberately** tough, to see how a candidate performs under pressure.

4.6 **The agenda.** The agenda and questions will be based on three things.

(a) The job description and what abilities are required of the jobholder.

(b) The personnel specification. The interviewer must be able to judge whether the applicant matches up to the personal qualities required from the jobholder.

(c) The application form or the applicant's CV: the qualities the applicant claims to possess.

Conduct of the interview

4.7 Questions should be paced and put carefully. The interviewer should not be trying to confuse the candidate, plunging immediately into demanding questions or picking on isolated points; neither, however, should the interviewee be allowed to digress or gloss over important points. The interviewer must retain control over the information-gathering process.

Type of question	Comment
Open questions	('Who...? What...? Where...? When...? Why....?') These force candidates to put together their own responses in complete sentences. This encourages them to talk, keeps the interview flowing, and is most revealing ('Why do you want to be an accountant?')
Probing questions	Similar to open questions, these aim to discover the deeper significance of the candidate's answers, especially if they are initially dubious, uninformative, too short, or too vague. ('But what was it about accountancy that **particularly** appealed to you?')
Closed questions	Invite only 'yes' or 'no' answers: ('Did you...?', 'Have you...?'). (a) They elicit an answer **only** to the question asked. This may be useful where there are small points to be established ('Did you pass your exam?') (b) Candidates cannot express their personality, or interact with the interviewer on a deeper level. (c) They make it easier for candidates to conceal things ('You never **asked** me...'). (d) They make the interviewer work very hard.

BPP PUBLISHING

Type of question	Comment
Multiple questions	Two or more questions are asked at once. ('Tell me about your last job? How did your knowledge of accountancy help you there, and do you think you are up-to-date or will you need to spend time studying?'). This encourages the candidate to talk at some length, without straying too far from the point. It might also test the candidate's ability to listen, and to handle large amount of information.
Problem solving questions	Present the candidate with a situation and ask him/her to explain how he/she would deal with it. ('How would you motivate your staff to do a task that they did not want to do?'). Such questions are used to establish whether the candidate will be able to deal with the sort of problems that are likely to arise in the job.
Leading questions	Encourage the candidate to give a certain reply. ('We are looking for somebody who likes detailed figure work. How much do you enjoy dealing with numbers?' or 'Don't you agree that...?' 'Surely...?). The danger with this type of question is that the candidate will give the answer that he thinks the interviewer wants to hear.

Question 2

Identify the type of question used in the following examples, and discuss the opportunities and constraints they offer the interviewee who must answer them.

(a) 'So, you're interested in a Business Studies degree, are you, Jo?'

(b) 'Surely you're interested in Business Studies, Jo?'

(c) 'How about a really useful qualification like a Business Studies degree, Jo? Would you consider that?'

(d) 'Why are you interested in a Business Studies degree, Jo?

(e) 'Why particularly Business Studies, Jo?'

Answer

(a) Closed. (The only answer is 'yes' or 'no', unless Jo is prepared to expand on it, at his or her own initiative.)

(b) Leading. (Even if Jo was interested, (s)he should get the message that 'yes' would not be what the interviewer wanted, or expected, to hear.)

(c) Leading closed multiple! ('Really useful' leads Jo to think that the 'correct' answer will be 'yes': There is not much opportunity for any other answer, without expanding on it unasked.)

(d) Open. (Jo has to explain, in his or her own words.)

(e) Probing. (If Jo's answer has been unconvincing, short or vague, this question forces a more specific answer.)

4.8 **Evaluating the response**

(a) The interviewer must **listen carefully** to the responses and evaluate them so as to judge what the **candidate** is:

  • Wanting to say

- Trying **not** to say
- Saying, but does not mean, or is lying about
- Having difficulty saying

(b) In addition, the interviewer will have to be aware when he/she is hearing:

- Something he/she needs to know
- Something he/she **doesn't** need to know
- Only what he/she **expects** to hear
- Inadequately - when his or her own attitudes, perhaps prejudices, are getting in the way of an objective response to the candidate

4.9 **Candidates should be given the opportunity to ask questions.** The choice of questions might well have some influence on how the interviewers assess a candidate's interest in and understanding of the job. Moreover, there is information that the candidate will need to know about the organisation, the job, and indeed the interview process.

Types of interview

4.10 **Individual** or **one-to-one interviews** are the **most common** selection method.

(a) **Advantages**

(i) **Direct** face-to-face communication

(ii) **Rapport** between the candidate and the interviewer: each has to give attention solely to the other, and there is potentially a relaxed atmosphere, if the interviewer is willing to establish an informal style.

(b) The **disadvantage** of a one-to-one interview is the scope it allows for a biased or superficial decision.

(i) The **candidate** may be able to **disguise** lack of knowledge in a specialist area of which the interviewer knows little.

(ii) The **interviewer's** perception may be selective or **distorted**, and this lack of objectivity may go unnoticed and unchecked.

(iii) The greater opportunity for personal rapport with the candidate may cause a **weakening of the interviewer's objective judgement**.

4.11 **Panel interviews** are designed to overcome such disadvantages. A panel may consist of two or three people who together interview a single candidate: most commonly, an HR specialist and the departmental manager who will have responsibility for the successful candidate. This saves the firm time and enables better assessment.

4.12 Large formal panels, or **selection boards**, may also be convened where there are a number of individuals or groups with an interest in the selection.

(a) **Advantage.** A number of people see candidates, and share information about them at a single meeting: similarly, they can compare their assessments on the spot, without a subsequent effort at liaison and communication.

(b) **Drawbacks**

(i) Questions tend to be more varied, and more random, since there is **no single guiding force** behind the interview strategy. The candidate may have trouble switching from one topic to another so quickly, especially if questions are not led up to, and not clearly put - as may happen if they are unplanned. Candidate are also seldom allowed to expand their answers and so may not be able to do justice to themselves.

(ii)   If there is a **dominating member** of the board, the interview may have greater continuity - but that individual may also influence the judgements of other members.

(iii)   Some candidates may not perform well in a formal, artificial situation such as the board interview, and may find such a situation extremely stressful.

(iv)   Research shows that **board members rarely agree** with each other in their judgements about candidates.

The limitations of interviews

4.13   Interviews are criticised because **they fail to provide accurate predictions** of how a person will perform in the job, partly because of the nature of interviews, partly because of the errors of judgement by interviewers.

Problem	Comment
Scope	• An interview is **too brief** to 'get to know' candidates in the kind of depth required to make an accurate prediction of work performance.
	• An interview is an **artificial situation**: candidates may be on their best behaviour or, conversely, so nervous that they do not do themselves justice. Neither situation reflects what the person is really like.
The halo effect	A tendency for people to make an initial **general judgement** about a person based on a **single obvious attribute,** such as being neatly dressed or well-spoken. This single attribute will colour later perceptions, and might make an interviewer mark the person up or down on every other factor in their assessments
Contagious bias	The interviewer changes the behaviour of the applicant by suggestion. The applicant might be led by the wording of questions or non-verbal cues from the interviewer, and change what (s)he is doing or saying in response.
Stereotyping	Stereotyping groups people together who are assumed to share certain characteristics (women, say, or vegetarians), then attributes certain traits to the group as a whole. It then assumes that each individual member of the supposed group will possess that trait.
Incorrect assessment	Qualitative factors such as motivation, honesty or integrity are very difficult assess in an interview.
Logical error	For example, an interviewer might decide that a young candidate who has held two or three jobs in the past for only a short time will be unlikely to last long in any job.

Problem	Comment
Inexperienced interviewers	• Inability to evaluate information about a candidate properly
	• Failure to compare a candidate against the requirements for a job or a personnel specification
	• Bad planning of the interview
	• Failure to take control of the direction and length of the interview
	• A tendency either to act as an inquisitor and make candidates feel uneasy or to let candidates run away with the interview
	• A reluctance to probe into fact and challenge statements where necessary

4.14 While some interviewers may be experts for the human resources function, it is usually thought desirable to include **line managers** in the interview team. They cannot be full-time interviewers, obviously: they have their other work to do. No matter how much training they are given in the interview techniques, they will lack continuous experience, and probably not give interviewing as much thought or interest as they should.

Question 3

What assumptions might an interviewer make about **you**, based on your:

(a) Accent, or regional/national variations in your spoken English
(b) School
(c) Clothes and hair-style
(d) Stated hobbies, interest, 'philosophies'
(e) Taste in books and TV programmes

For objectivity, you might like to conduct this Activity in class. What assumptions do you make about the person sitting next to you?

Exam focus point

Interviews are relevant to many areas of personnel management. The issues described above are relevant to appraisal interviews, disciplinary interviews and so on.

5 TESTS

5.1 In some job selection procedures, an interview is supplemented by some form of **selection test**. Tests must be:

(a) **Sensitive** enough to discriminate between different candidates

(b) **Standardised** on a representative sample of the population, so that a person's results can be interpreted meaningfully

(c) **Reliable**: in that the test should measure the same thing whenever and to whomever it is applied

(d) **Valid**: measuring what they are supposed to measure

5.2 The science of measuring mental capacities and processes is called 'psychometrics'; hence the term **psychometric testing**. Types of test commonly used in practice are:

- Intelligence tests
- Aptitude tests
- Personality tests;
- Proficiency tests.

5.3 **Intelligence tests.** Tests of **general intellectual ability** typically test memory, ability to think quickly and logically, and problem solving skills.

(a) Most people have experience of IQ tests and the like, and few would dispute their validity as good measure of **general** intellectual capacity.

(b) However, there is **no agreed definition of intelligence**.

5.4 **Aptitude tests.** Aptitude tests are designed to **measure** and predict an individual's potential for performing a job or learning new skills.

- **Reasoning**: verbal, numerical and abstract
- **Spatio-visual ability**: practical intelligence, non-verbal ability and creative ability
- **Perceptual speed and accuracy**: clerical ability
- **'Manual' ability**: mechanical, manual, musical and athletic

5.5 **Personality tests.** Personality tests may measure a variety of characteristics, such as an applicant's skill in dealing with other people, his ambition and motivation or his emotional stability.

Case example

Probably the best known example is the 16PF, originally developed by Cattell in 1950.

The 16PF comprises 16 scales, each of which measure a factor that influences the way a person behaves.

The factors are functionally different underlying personality characteristics, and each is associated with not just one single piece of behaviour but rather is the source of a relatively broad range of behaviours. For this reason the factors themselves are referred to as source traits and the behaviours associated with them are called surface traits.

The advantage of measuring source traits, as the 16PF does, is that you end up with a much richer understanding of the person because you are not just describing what can be seen but also the characteristics underlying what can be seen.

The 16PF analyses how a person is likely to behave generally including, for example, contribution likely to be made to particular work contexts, aspects of the work environment to which the person is likely to more or less suited, and how best to manage the person.

Personnel Management February 1994

5.6 The validity of such tests has been much debated, but is seems that some have been shown by research to be valid predictors of job performance, so long as they are used **properly.**

5.7 **Proficiency tests.** Proficiency tests are perhaps the most closely related to an assessor's objectives, because they **measure ability to do the work involved.** An applicant for an audio typist's job, for example, might be given a dictation tape and asked to type it.

5.8 **Trends in the use of tests**

(a) Continuing **enthusiasm for personality tests**.

(b) The continuing influence of **cognitive ability intelligence** tests.

(c) A focus on certain popular themes - sales ability or aptitude, customer orientation, motivation, teamworking and organisational culture are mentioned.

(d) The growing diversity of test producers and sources (meaning more choice, but also more poor quality measures).

(e) Expanded packages of tests, including tapes, computer disks, workbooks and so on.

(f) A growing focus on **fairness**: the most recent edition of the 16PF test, for example, has been scrutinised by expert psychologists to exclude certain types of content that might lead to bias. *(Fletcher)*

5.9 Limitations of testing

(a) There is not always a direct relationship between ability in the test and ability in the job: the job situation is very different from artificial test conditions.

(b) The **interpretation of test results is a skilled task,** for which training and experience is essential. It is also highly subjective (particularly in the case of personality tests), which belies the apparent scientific nature of the approach.

(c) Additional difficulties are experienced with particular kinds of test. For example:

    (i) An aptitude test measuring arithmetical ability would need to be constantly revised or its content might become known to later applicants.

    (ii) Personality tests can often give misleading results because applicants seem able to guess which answers will be looked at most favourably.

    (iii) It is difficult to design intelligence tests which give a fair chance to people from different cultures and social groups and which test the **kind** of intelligence that the organisation wants from its employees: the ability to **score highly in IQ** tests does not necessarily correlate with desirable traits such as mature **judgement** or **creativity**, merely mental ability.

    (d) Most tests are subject to coaching and practice effects.

(d) **It is difficult to exclude bias from tests**. Many tests (including personality tests) are tackled less successfully by women than by men, or by some candidates born overseas than by indigenous applicants because of the particular aspect chosen for testing.

6 OTHER SELECTION METHODS

Group selection methods

6.1 **Group selection methods** might be used by an organisation as the final stage of a selection process as a more 'natural' and in-depth appraisal of candidates. Group assessments tend to be used for posts requiring leadership, communication or teamworking skills: advertising agencies often use the method for selecting account executives, for example.

6.2 They consist of a series of tests, interviews and group situations over a period of two days, involving a **small number of candidates for a job**. After an introductory session to make the candidates feel at home, they will be given one or two tests, one or two individual interviews, and several group situations in which the candidates are invited to discuss problems together and arrive at solutions as a management team.

6.3 **Techniques in such programmes**

(a) **Group role-play exercises,** in which they can explore (and hopefully display) interpersonal skills and/or work through simulated managerial tasks.

BPP PUBLISHING

(b) **Case studies**, where candidates' analytical and problem-solving abilities are tested in working through described situations/problems, as well as their interpersonal skills, in taking part in (or leading) group discussion of the case study.

6.4 These group sessions might be thought useful because:

(a) They give the organisation's **selectors a longer opportunity to study the candidates**.

(b) **They reveal more than application forms, interviews and tests alone** about the ability of candidates to persuade others, negotiate with others, and explain ideas to others and also to investigate problems efficiently. These are typically **management skills**.

(c) They reveal more about how the **candidate's personalities and attributes will affect the work team** and his own performance.

Work sampling

6.5 Work sampling involves getting the candidate to spend **some time doing the job**, in actual or simulated conditions. A firm wanting to recruit someone to do typesetting work can simply sit that person down in front of a wordprocessor or PC for a few hours to see how they do the job.

7   WHICH SELECTION METHOD IS BEST?

7.1 Smith and Abrahamsen in 1994 referred to a scale that predicts how well a candidate will perform at work if offered that job. This is known as a **predictive validity** scale. The scale ranges from 1 (meaning a method that is right every time) to 0 (meaning a method that is no better than chance). On this basis, they produced the following results.

Method	*% use*	*Predictive validity*
Interviews	92	0.17
References	74	0.13
Work sampling	18	0.57
Assessment centres	14	0.40
Personality tests	13	0.40
Cognitive tests	11	0.54
Biodata	4	0.40
Graphology	3	0.00

7.2 The results are most revealing as they show a pattern of employers relying most heavily on the **least** valid selection methods for their recruitment purposes. Interviews, in particular (and for the reasons given earlier) seem not much better than tossing a coin.

8   REFERENCES

8.1 References provide further confidential information about the prospective employee. This may be of varying value, as the reliability of all but the most factual information must be in question. A reference should contain two types of information.

(a) Straightforward **factual information.** This confirms the nature of the applicant's previous job(s), period of employment, pay, and circumstances of leaving.

(b) **Opinions** about the applicant's personality and other attributes. These should obviously be treated with some caution. Allowances should be made for prejudice (favourable or unfavourable), charity (withholding detrimental remarks), and possibly fear of being actionable for libel (although references are privileged, as long as they are factually correct and devoid of malice).

At least two **employer** references are desirable, providing necessary factual information, and comparison of personal views. **Personal** references tell the prospective employer little more than that the applicant has a friend or two.

8.2 **Written references** save time, especially if a standardised letter or form has been pre-prepared. A simple letter inviting the previous employer to reply with the basic information and judgements required may suffice. A standard form to be completed by the referee may be more acceptable, and might pose a set of simple questions about:

- Job title
- Main duties and responsibilities
- Period of employment
- Pay/salary
- Attendance record

If a judgement of character and suitability is desired, it might be most tellingly formulated as the question: 'Would you re-employ this individual? (If not, why not?)'

8.3 **Telephone references** may be time-saving if standard reference letters or forms are not available. They may also elicit a more honest opinion than a carefully prepared written statement. For this reason, a telephone call may also be made to check or confirm a poor or grudging reference which the recruiter suspects may be prejudiced.

Question 4

(a) At the end of a recent selection process one candidate was outstanding, in the view of everyone involved. However, you have just received a very bad reference from her current employer. What do you do?

(b) For fun, rephrase the following comments in the way that you might expect to see them appear in a letter of reference. Mr Smith is:

    (i) Habitually late
    (ii) Remains immature
    (iii) Socially unskilled with clients

Answer

(a) It is quite possible that her current employer is desperate to retain her. Disregard the reference, or question the referee by telephone, and seek another reference from a previous employer if possible.

(b) The phrases given are 'translations' by Adrian Furnham (*Financial Times,* December 1991) of the following.

    (i) 'Mr Smith was occasionally a little lax in time keeping'
    (ii) 'Clearly growing out of earlier irresponsibility'

---

9 EVALUATING AND IMPROVING RECRUITMENT AND SELECTION PRACTICES

9.1 Good recruitment practices might seem like common sense; but common sense, for example that interviews are the best mechanism, can be wrong sometimes.

9.2 To get a clear idea as to how good a firm's recruitment and selection practices are, firms can ask themselves these questions.

- Can we identify human resources requirements from business plans?
- How fast do we respond to demands from line managers for human resources?
- Do we give/receive good advice on labour market trends?
- Do we select the right advertising media to reach the market?
- How effective is our recruitment advertising?
- How long does it take from the initial request for staff to filling the position?
- How do our recruits actually perform - do we end up employing the right people
- Do we retain our new recruits?

9.3 Recruitment and selection practices can be reviewed in these ways.

Review	Comment
Performance indicators	Each stage of the process can be assessed by performance indicators, for example the time it takes to reply to the application. Data can be collected to check any deviation from standard. Delays in replying to applications might encourage candidates to look elsewhere.
Cost-effectiveness	For example, number of responses per advert or, more usefully, number of *relevant* responses. An advert which attracted large numbers of unsuitable candidates might have been badly worded.
Monitoring the workforce	High staff turnover (ie the number and frequency of people leaving) may reflect poor recruitment, if people joined with the wrong expectations
Attitude surveys	The firm can ask its recruits what they thought of the process
Actual performance	A person's actual performance can be compared with what was expected when he/she was recruited

9.4 **Improving the effectiveness of recruitment and selection**

If, as we mentioned in Chapter 1, organisations are seeking to empower their staff and give them more responsibility, then the cost of bad recruitment policies increases.

9.5 Consequently, improving recruitment processes involves:

- Specifying **much more carefully** what is expected of the employee

- Employing a variety of methods, as outlined in section 7, as opposed to relying on interviews alone

Chapter roundup

- The process of selection begins when the recruiter receives details of candidates interested in the job, in response, for example, to a job advert, or possibly enquiries made to the recruitment consultant.

- Many firms require candidates to fill out an **application form**. This is standardised and the firm can ask for specific information about **work experience** and **qualifications**, as well as other **personal data**. Some firms do not bother with an application form, being happy to accept CVs with a covering letter.

- Application forms and CVs are then sifted, to weed out unsuitable candidates and to identify others whose applications can be taken further. **Biodata** techniques give weight to the data submitted giving applicants a score.

- Most firms use **interviews**, on a one-to-one basis, using a variety of **open** and **closed questions**. The interviewer should avoid bias in assessing the candidate.

- **Selection tests** can be used before or after interviews. Intelligence tests measures the candidate's general intellectual ability, and personality tests identify the type of person. Other tests are more specific to the job (eg proficiency tests)

- Interviews are unreliable as predictors of actual job performance for many posts, but they are traditional and convenient. A combination of interviews with other methods may be used.

Quick quiz

1   What should application forms achieve?

2   Why are bio-data techniques useful?

3   What factors should be taken into account in an organisation's interview strategy?

4   Why are open questions useful?

5   Why do interviews fail to predict performance accurately?

6   List the desirable features of selection tests.

7   Give examples of group selection methods.

8   'Personality and cognitive tests are more reliable predictors of job performance than interviews.' True or False?

9   What should be obtained in a reference?

10 How can firms improve their recruitment and selection practices?

Answers to quick quiz

1   They should give enough information to identify suitable candidates and weed out no-hopers, by asking specific questions and by getting the candidate to volunteer information.

2   Bio-data techniques enable data in application forms/CVs to be weighted and scored, making it easier to sift candidates' applications.

3   In brief, giving the right impression on the organisation and obtaining a rounded, relevant assessment of the candidate.

4   They allow the candidate to volunteer more, and open avenues for further questions.

5   Brevity and artificiality of interview situation combined with the bias and inexperience of interviewers.

6   Sensitive; standardised; reliable; valid

7   Role play exercises; case studies

8   True

9   Facts, corroborating other data supplied by the candidate; opinions about the candidate

10   Clearly identifying what they want from the candidate; not relying on interviews alone.

Now try the question below from the Exam Question Bank

Question to try	Level	Marks	Time
8	Exam	15	27 mins

Chapter 9

DIVERSITY AND EQUAL OPPORTUNITIES

Topic list	Syllabus reference
1 Discrimination at work	2(a)
2 The legislative framework	2(a)
3 The practical implications	2(e)
4 Diversity	2(e)

Introduction

Sexual and racial discrimination have become such high-profile issues that you should be aware of obvious abuses: 'White Anglo-Saxon Protestant Males only need apply' is not an acceptable recruitment policy!

However, recent years have seen the range of **discrimination issues** widening to include disability, age and sexual orientation. Moreover, the concept of indirect discrimination has forced employers to examine the implications of other practices. (If you encourage word-of-mouth recruitment, for example, in a predominantly white male workforce, you are indirectly discriminating against women and ethnic minorities by not allowing them the same opportunity to hear about the jobs.)

Employers still need to comply with the law and Codes of Practice by which they could be taken to an Industrial Tribunal in the event of a dispute. But they are also starting (slowly) to realise that discriminatory policies and practices risk alienating not only existing and potential employees, but the customers on whom their business depends.

Diversity is thus a wider issue than just equal opportunities.

Note. In this chapter there is frequent reference to the situation in the UK, particularly with reference to the legal position. Non-UK students may choose to use this material or may prefer to make use of their knowledge of similar matters in their own countries.

Study guide

Section 15 – Equal opportunities

Section 15(g) - Equal opportunities and the management of diversity

- Understanding equal opportunities
- Measuring equal value
- The legal position
- The appropriateness of managing diversity in the workplace
- Understanding individual circumstances

Exam guide

Discrimination and equal opportunities are topics of great importance for managers in real life. We include them in this part of the study text because that is where the syllabus puts them. However, you should be aware that they are relevant to all aspects of people management and therefore, potentially to **any question** in the examination.

BPP PUBLISHING

1 DISCRIMINATION AT WORK

Women in employment

1.1   The acceptance of women in paid employment on an equal footing to men has been a slow process which is even now having to be enforced by law.

1.2   The distribution of women in the UK workforce today is still heavily concentrated in categories such as textiles, footwear, clothing and leather, hotel and catering, retail distribution, professional and scientific services, and miscellaneous services. A significant percentage of the women employed in these categories work part-time.

1.3   Only in recent decades has there been a widespread challenge to sex segregation in employment - the idea that there are men's jobs and women's jobs, with only a few genuinely unisex categories of work. There are many reasons for this discrimination.

   (a) **Social pressures** on the woman to bear and rear children, and on the man to make a lifetime commitment to paid work as the breadwinner led employers to assume - and sometimes still assume - that women's paid work would be short-term or interrupted, and that training and development was therefore hardly worthwhile.

   (b) The nature of **earlier industrial work**, which was physically heavy: legal restrictions were placed on women's employment in areas such as mines and night work in factories.

   (c) **Lack of organisation** of women at work and influence in trade unions (except in industries like textiles), until recently.

   (d) The reinforcing of **segregation** at home and at school: for example, lack of encouragement to girls to study mathematical and scientific subjects.

   (e) **Career ladders which fail to fast-track women**. Apprenticeships, for example, are rarely held by girls.

        Some employers have tended to assume that women are unlikely to want such a career. Commitments to geographical mobility are similarly assumed to be undesirable to women.

   (f) **Child-bearing and family responsibilities**. Part-time work has enabled many women to continue in paid employment, but tends to apply to jobs which carry little prospect for promotion.

   Many of these assumptions are being re-examined, and we will look a bit later at some of the measures being taken to remove the barriers to women in employment.

Ethnic minorities in employment

1.4   The 1999 edition of *Social Trends* (Office of National Statistics) shows that while 6% of the UK's white population was unemployed in 1997, the black and Pakistani/Bangladeshi ethnic groups were much worse off, with 19% and 21% unemployment respectively. In the 16-24 age group black unemployment was three times as high as white.

   (a) The **ethnic minority** population is **much younger than the population** as a whole: young people find it particularly hard to get jobs when vacancies are scarce.

   (b) **Concentration** of minorities in **certain industrial sectors**, types of firm and occupations, which are contracting (hitherto mainly in the manufacturing sector), insecure or low-status.

(c)   Direct **racial discrimination** in favour of white labour, when this is in ample supply.

It is likely that the first two factors will diminish with time, highlighting further the need to address the issue of **racial discrimination**. That racial discrimination is still alive is suggested by the fact that unemployment is higher among ethnic minorities, including those still who have attained levels of qualification.

1.5   In January 1995, the Commission for Racial Equality (CRE) launched an initiative in the drive for equal opportunities, with its benchmarking standard for employers, *Racial Equality Means Business*. This aims to move the issue beyond compliance with legislation, and even beyond commitment to the moral principle of equality, to a recognition of its business benefits. Companies which have implemented practical policies and action plans on racial equality claim to have found measurable benefits in terms of staff morale and performance, and customer loyalty.

1.6   **Reasons for adopting such equal opportunities**

(a)   Good HR practice, in attracting and retaining the best people

(b)   Compliance with the CRE's Code of Practice, which is used by industrial tribunals

(c)   Widening the recruitment pool

(d)   Other potential benefits to the business through its image as a good employer, and through the loyalty of customers in areas of ethnic diversity

At the launch, however, the CRE Chairman also criticised companies that did nothing except use 'equal opportunities designer labels' to make recruitment advertisements look good.

Other areas of discrimination

1.7   Discrimination may operate in all kinds of areas: not just on grounds of sex, but of sexual orientation or marital status; on grounds of religion or politics as well as race and colour; and on grounds of age.

Question 1

Have you ever felt discriminated against at school, work or your university/ college? On what grounds: your sex, colour, age, background? What was the effect of the discrimination on your plans and attitudes?

1.8   Two further forms of discrimination are specifically legislated against.

(a)   Failure to provide equal opportunities to suitably qualified disabled persons

(b)   Non-engagement or dismissal on the grounds of a conviction for a criminal offence, once the offender is rehabilitated and his conviction 'spent'

(The relevant legislation in these cases is discussed below in Section 2 of this chapter.)

Age and employment

1.9   Despite demographic and educational changes and associated skill shortages among the younger population, a certain amount of discrimination is still directed at more mature workers.

1.10 In 1996, the Chartered Institute of Personnel and Development (CIPD) issued a statement, *Age and Employment*, to encourage policies and practices which lead to the employment of qualified individuals regardless of age. The CIPD statement says that the use of age-related criteria should be challenged in every aspect of employment decision-making, including recruitment, selection for training, counselling, development, and promotion, and selection for redundancy. However, it is still not against the law in the UK to specify age requirements in recruitment.

2 THE LEGISLATIVE FRAMEWORK

Equal Pay Act 1970

2.1 The Equal Pay Act (passed in 1970, but effective from 1975) was the first major attempt to tackle sexual discrimination. It was intended 'to prevent discrimination as regards terms and conditions of employment between men and women'.

(a) Where there is an element of sex discrimination in a collective agreement, this must be removed to offer a unisex pay rate.

(b) Where a job evaluation scheme is operated to determine pay rates, a woman can claim equal pay for a job which has been rated as equivalent under the scheme.

(c) Where job evaluation is not used, a women can claim equal pay for work that is 'the same or broadly similar' as the work of a man in the same establishment, ('broadly similar' having to be interpreted in the courts, in many cases. The defending employer must show differences of 'practical importance' in the two jobs).

2.2 The Equal Pay (Amendment) Regulations 1984 established the right to equal pay for 'work of equal value', so that a woman would no longer have to compare her work with that of a man in the same or broadly similar work, but could establish that her work has equal value to that of a man in the same establishment.

2.3 Legal example: equal pay for work of equal value

> *Case: Hayward v Cammell Laird Shipbuilders Ltd.* The applicant, a trained canteen cook, claimed that her work was equal in value to that of male tradesmen employed as painter, thermal installation engineer and joiner. The industrial tribunal found in her favour. (The employers subsequently appealed to the Employment Appeals Tribunal, which ruled that the same pay and overtime rates did not in fact have to be paid to the cook since, when her terms and conditions of work overall were taken into account, she was not unfavourably treated.)

Equal opportunity

2.4 In Britain, two main Acts have been passed to deal with inequality of opportunity.

(a) The Sex Discrimination Act 1975 (SDA), outlawing certain types of discrimination on the grounds of sex or marital status.

(b) The Race Relations Act 1976 (RRA), outlawing certain types of discrimination on grounds of colour, race, nationality, or ethnic or national origin.

There are two types of discrimination, under the Acts.

KEY TERMS

Direct discrimination occurs when one interested group is treated less favourably than another (except for exempted cases). It is unlikely that a prospective employer will practise direct discrimination unawares.

Indirect discrimination occurs when a policy or practice is fair in form, but discriminatory in operation: for example, if requirements or conditions are imposed, with which a substantial proportion of the interested group cannot comply.

2.5 The employer must, if challenged, justify the conditions on non-racial or nonsexual grounds. It is often the case that employers are not aware that they are discriminating in this way and this concept was a major breakthrough when introduced by the Acts.

Question 2

Suggest four examples of practices that would constitute indirect discrimination on the grounds of sex.

Answer

(a) Advertising a vacancy in a primarily male environment, where women would be less likely to see it.

(b) Offering less favourable terms to part-time workers (given that most of them are women).

(c) Specifying age limits which would tend to exclude women who had taken time out of work for child-rearing.

(d) Asking in selection interviews about plans to have a family (since this might be to the detriment of a woman, but not a man.

2.6 In both Acts, the obligation of non-discrimination applies to all aspects of employment, including advertisements, recruitment and selection programmes, access to training, promotion, disciplinary procedures, redundancy and dismissal.

2.7 In both Acts, too, there are certain exceptions, in which discrimination of a sort may be permitted.

(a) In relation to women, the most important of these are '**genuine occupational qualifications**', which include:

   • Reasons of physiology (not physical strength)

   • Reasons of **decency** or **privacy**, closely defined

   • Special **welfare** consideration

   • The provision of **personal** services promoting welfare or education

   • **Legal restrictions**, eg work outside the UK, where 'laws or customs are such that the duties could not, or could not effectively, be performed by a woman'

(b) In the case of ethnic minorities, the exceptions are:

   • **Dramatic performances**, where the **dramatis personae** requires a person of a particular racial group

   • **Artists' or photographic models** for advertising purposes, for reasons of authenticity

   • Where **personal services** are rendered for the welfare of the particular group

2.8   The legislation does *not* (except with regard to training) permit **positive discrimination** - actions which give preference to a protected person, regardless of genuine suitability and qualification for the job. In particular, there is no quota scheme such as operates for registered disabled persons (as discussed a bit later): there is no fixed number or percentage of jobs that must be filled by women or members of ethnic minorities, regardless of other criteria.

> ### Exam focus point
>
> Bear in mind that the above situation reflects the UK. Other countries, for reasons of social policy, may require some organisations to operate quotas for members of particular ethnic groups.

2.9   The organisation may, however, set itself *targets* for the number of such persons that they will *aim* to employ - if the required number of eligible and suitably qualified people can be recruited - as part of an equality action plan.

2.10   **Training** may (RRA ss 37-38, SDA ss 47-48) be given to particular groups exclusively, if the group has in the preceding year been substantially under-represented. It is also permissible to encourage such groups to apply for jobs where such exclusive training is offered; and to apply for jobs in which they are under-represented.

2.11   A training body (other than the employer) running such a positively discriminating scheme must be either permitted by the Act, or specially designated by application to the Secretary of State for Employment.

2.12   The Equal Opportunities Commission and Commission for Racial Equality have powers, subject to certain safeguards, to investigate alleged breach of the Acts, to serve a 'non-discrimination notice', and to follow-up the investigation until satisfied that undertakings given (with regard to compliance and information of persons concerned) are carried out.

Marital status

2.13   The Sex Discrimination Act also makes it unlawful to discriminate against married people, for example if an employer believes that a single man will be able to devote more time to the job. (Oddly, perhaps, there is no equivalent protection for single people.)

Disability

2.14   The Disability Discrimination Act 1995 contains the following key points.

(a)   A disabled person is defined as a person who has a physical or mental impairment that has a substantial and long-term (more than 12 months) adverse effect on his ability to carry out normal day to day activities. Severe disfigurement is included, as are progressive conditions such as HIV even though the current effect may not be substantial.

(b)   The effect includes mobility, manual dexterity, physical co-ordination, and lack of ability to lift or speak, hear, see, remember, concentrate, learn or understand or to perceive the risk of physical danger.

(c)   The Act makes it **unlawful to discriminate against a disabled person/employee** in three respects.

- In deciding who to interview or who to employ, or in the terms of an employment offer

- In the terms of employment and the opportunities for promotion, transfer, training or other benefits, or by refusing the same

- By dismissal or any other disadvantage

(d) The employer has a duty to make reasonable adjustments to working arrangements or to the physical features of premises where these constitute a disadvantage to disabled people.

(e) The provisions regarding employment do not apply to an employer who has fewer than 20 employees.

Question 3

Examine any large shop (like a supermarket) you know well. What facilities have been provided for disabled people (staff and customers)? What problems remain? Are there any disabled people on the staff? If so, what are their jobs?

Rehabilitation of Offenders Act 1974

2.15 A conviction for criminal offences is 'spent' after a period of time (which varies according to the severity of the offence). After this period, an offender is 'rehabilitated' and is not obliged to disclose the nature of his offence or details of his conviction. Failure to disclose is therefore not justifiable grounds for non-engagement (or dismissal). There are exceptions, however, including life imprisonment, prison sentences over 30 months, and convictions for doctors, lawyers, teachers, accountants and police officers.

2.16 The Police Act 1997 will make it easier for recruiters to screen out applicants who have a criminal record. It will establish the Criminal Records Agency, administering a new system of conviction certificates that employers can ask job applicants to provide.

Religion

2.17 Under the Fair Employment Act of 1989, employers in **Northern Ireland** are required to monitor the religious composition of their workforce and draw up affirmative action programmes, with targets, to ensure equal opportunity given the sectarian divisions.

Part time staff

2.18 At the time of writing there are a number of developments regarding part-time workers who may be accorded similar pro-rated rights to full time workers, under the EU's **Part-time working Regulation** (eg on holiday pay).

3 THE PRACTICAL IMPLICATIONS

3.1 The **practical implications** of the legislation for employers are set out in **Codes of Practice**, issued by the Commission for Racial Equality and the Equal Opportunities Commission. These do not have the force of law, but may be taken into account by Industrial Tribunals, where discrimination cases are brought before them. Many organisations now establish their own policy statements or codes of practice on equal opportunities: apart from anything else, a statement of the organisation's position may provide some protection in the event of complaints.

Formulating an effective equal opportunities policy

3.2 Some organisations make minimal efforts to avoid discrimination, paying lip-service to the idea only to the extent of claiming 'We are an Equal Opportunities Employer' on advertising literature. He goes on to explore the factors necessary to turn such a claim into reality.

(a) **Support** from the top of the organisation for the formulation of a practical policy

(b) A **working party** drawn from - for example - management, unions, minority groups, the HR function and staff representatives. This group's brief will be to produce a draft Policy and Code of Practice, which will be approved at senior level

(c) **Action plans and resources** (including staff) to implement and monitor the policy, publicise it to staff, arrange training and so on

(d) **Monitoring**. The numbers of women and ethnic minority staff can easily be monitored

- On entering (and applying to enter) the organisation
- On leaving the organisation
- On applying for transfers, promotions or training schemes

(It is less easy to determine the ethnic origins of the workforce through such methods as questionnaires: there is bound to be suspicion about the question's motives, and it may be offensive to some workers.)

(e) **Positive action**: the process of taking active steps to encourage people from disadvantaged groups to apply for jobs and training, and to compete for vacancies. (Note that this is not positive discrimination.) Examples might be: using ethnic languages in job advertisements, or implementing training for women in management skills

Recruitment and selection

3.3 This is an area of particular sensitivity. There is always a risk that a disappointed job applicant, for example, will attribute his lack of success to discrimination, especially if the recruiting organisation's workforce is conspicuously lacking in representatives of the same ethnic minority, sex or group. The implications are obviously wide.

(a) **Advertising**

   (i) Any wording that suggests preference for a particular group should be avoided (except for genuine occupational qualifications).

   (ii) Employers must not indicate or imply any 'intention to discriminate'.

   (iii) Recruitment literature should state that the organisation is an Equal Opportunities employer.

   (iv) The placing of advertisements only where the readership is predominantly of one race or sex is construed as indirect discrimination. This includes word-of-mouth recruiting from the existing workforce, if it is not broadly representative.

(b) **Recruitment agencies.** Instructions to an agency should not suggest any preference

(c) **Application forms.** These should include no questions which are not work-related (such as domestic details) and which only one group is asked to complete

(d) **Interviews**

    (i) Any non-work-related question must be asked of all subjects, if at all, and even then, some types of question may be construed as discriminatory. (You cannot, for example, ask only women about plans to have a family or care of dependants, or ask - in the most offensive case - about the Pill or PMT.)

    (ii) It may be advisable to have a witness at interviews, or at least to take detailed notes, in the event that a claim of discrimination is made.

(e) **Selection tests**. These must be wholly relevant, and should not favour any particular group. Even personality tests have been shown to favour white male applicants.

(f) **Records**. Reasons for rejection, and interview notes, should be carefully recorded, so that in the event of investigation the details will be available.

Other initiatives

3.4 In addition to responding to legislative provisions, some employers have begun to address the underlying problems of equal opportunities, with measures such as the following.

(a) Putting equal opportunities higher on the agenda by appointing Equal Opportunities **Managers** (and even Directors) who report directly to the Personnel Director.

(b) **Flexible hours** or part-time work, term-time or annual hours contracts (to allow for school holidays) to help women to combine careers with family responsibilities. Terms and conditions, however, must not be less favourable.

(c) **Career-break or return-to-work** schemes for women.

(d) **Fast-tracking school-leavers**, as well as graduates, and posting managerial vacancies internally, giving more opportunities for movement up the ladder for groups (typically women and minorities) currently at lower levels of the organisation.

(e) **Training for women-returners** or women in management to help women to manage their career potential. Assertiveness training may also be offered as part of such an initiative.

(f) Awareness training for managers, to encourage them to think about equal opportunity policy.

(g) The provision of **workplace nurseries** for working mothers.

(h) **Positive action** to encourage job and training applications from minority groups.

(i) Alteration of premises to accommodate wheelchair users, blind or partially sighted workers and so on.

(j) Practices to be reviewed for discrimination against employees of a particular marital status or sexual orientation. (For example, British Airways' extension of its concessionary travel scheme to partners of gay employees. Entitlement to a dead partner's pension is another big issue for partners in homosexual and even heterosexual partnerships: most schemes only recognise husbands or wives as beneficiaries.)

Case example

In his inauguration speech, [as London's first directly elected Mayor] Ken Livingstone called on businesses working in the capital to develop and implement genuine equal opportunities policies at all levels of their organisations.

'Glass ceilings for women and discrimination against Asian and black businesses weaken the potential prosperity of every Londoner,' he said. 'Every citizen of the capital must find that the only limit to their achievement is their own talent, energy and determination.

In a BBC interview 24 hours earlier, the mayor suggested that he was ready to 'name and shame' companies that failed to meet equal opportunity standards. This raised the threat of such firms being barred from contracts with the new London Authority.

The Institute of Directors branded Livingstone's television comments 'absurd and unworkable.' The institute's head of policy, Ruth Lea, said that as a woman she found the idea of quotas for women managers 'patronising'.

Dinah Worman, CIPD adviser on equal opportunities, warned that Livingstone's plans were negative and possibly counterproductive.

'He is doing it with organisations he thinks have to take a close look at what they are doing, and I can see why he might want to pressurise them over that change,' she said. 'Yet, on the other hand, how do you know that an organisation that has not got very good representation of women, disabled people or ethnic minorities at senior levels is not actually looking jolly hard at improving? This sort of thing is not always a way of getting people to think about issues. It also puts the frighteners on. Doing that to well-intentioned organisations is not necessarily going to help them move forward.'

4   DIVERSITY

4.1   **Diversity** in employment, as a concept, goes further than equal opportunities. Some companies try to ensure - within what is legally acceptable - that the composition of the workforce reflects the population as a whole. The rationale is that a **diverse** organisation will understand its customers better.

Case example

Procter & Gamble employ a diversity manager in the UK to increase the proportion of ethnic minorities and women in the workforce. P & G's record in the UK is good (6% of UK workforce are from ethnic minorities, compared to 5.4% of the population) but P & G wishes to increase this representation at management levels. As well as an ethical focus, the rationale is to increase P&G's effectiveness.

Chapter roundup

- Discrimination of certain types is illegal in the UK on grounds of:

    ○ Sex and marital status (Sex Discrimination Act 1975)
    ○ Colour, race, nationality and ethnic or national origin (Race Relations Act 1976)
    ○ Disability (Disability Discrimination Act 1995)
    ○ spent convictions (Rehabilitation of Offenders Act 1975).

- In addition, age discrimination has recently been highlighted as an undesirable feature of employment practice, and sexual harassment has been ruled to be sexual discrimination under UK law.

- Employers should note the implications of the Acts for both:

    ○ Direct discrimination - less favourable treatment of a protected group

    ○ Indirect discrimination - when requirements or conditions cannot be justified on non-racial grounds and work to the detriment of a protected group.

- Specific legislation (Equal Pay Act 1970) covers the offer of equal pay to a woman as to a man for work that is:

    ○ Similarly evaluated in a job evaluation scheme
    ○ 'The same or broadly similar' to the man's
    ○ 'Of equal value' (Equal Pay (Amendment) Regulations).

Quick quiz

1   Matt Black and Di Gloss run a small DIY shop. They're recruiting an assistant. Matt puts up an ad on the notice board of his Men's Club. It says: 'Person required to assist in DIY shop. Fulltime. Aged under 28. Contact...' Two candidates turn up for interview the following day: a man and a woman (who's heard about the job by word of mouth, through Di). Matt interviews them both, asking work-related questions. He also asks the woman whether she has children and how much time she expects to spend dealing with family matters.

Under the Sex Discrimination Act 1975, Matt has laid himself open to allegations of:

A   one count of discrimination
B   two counts of discrimination
C   three counts of discrimination
D   no discrimination at all

2   List four causes of high minority unemployment in the UK.

3   List five possible measures that might support an equal opportunities policy in an organisation.

4   What is sexual harassment?

5   What are the implications of Part-Time Workers regulations?

Answers to quick quiz

1   C   Advertising in a place where the readership is predominately male. Asking the women about (1) children and (2) time spent on family matters.

2   Low average age of minority populations; lack of UK recognised skills and qualifications; racial discrimination; concentrations of minority populations in places and industries with falling or static economic activity.

3   Support from top management; a policy and code of practice on equal opportunities; resources to implement the policy; monitoring of implementation; positive action to encourage minority applications.

4   Any unwanted conduct with physical or verbal connotations.

5   Part-time workers are entitled to the same benefits as a full-time 'comparator'.

Now try the question below from the Exam Question Bank

Question to try	Level	Marks	Time
9	Exam	10	18 mins

Part C
Training and development

Chapter 10

EMPLOYEE DEVELOPMENT AND TRAINING

Topic list	Syllabus reference
1 Development and the role of training	3(c)
2 Identifying training and development needs	3(c)
3 Methods of development and training	3(c)
4 The learning process	3(a)
5 People involved in training and development	3(b)
6 Evaluating training	3(c)

Introduction

All organisations provide training, though the extent of the provision varies. There is a close link between training and recruitment, since induction training is one of the commonest forms of training provision. There is also a close link with appraisal, since much training is targeted on individual needs with the aim of improving performance.

Study guide

Section 16(a) The learning process

Section 17(b) Retention, training and development

Section 18(c) Effective training and development

Full detail of the Study Guide for these sections can be found at the front of the text.

Section 8(h) – Standard setting and performance management

- Describe management contribution to personal development planning

Section 21(f) – Individual skills and development

- Identify the methods used to develop skills

- Outline how to plan a skills development programme

- Explain the role of mentoring in the process of skills development

Exam guide

Training and development could form the basis of a complete question. It is also likely to be linked with appraisal and performance management.

BPP PUBLISHING

1   DEVELOPMENT AND THE ROLE OF TRAINING

Factors affecting job performance

1.1   There are many factors affecting a person's performance at work, as shown in the diagram below. Training and development are the ways by which organisations seek to improve the performance of their staff and, it is hoped, of the organisation.

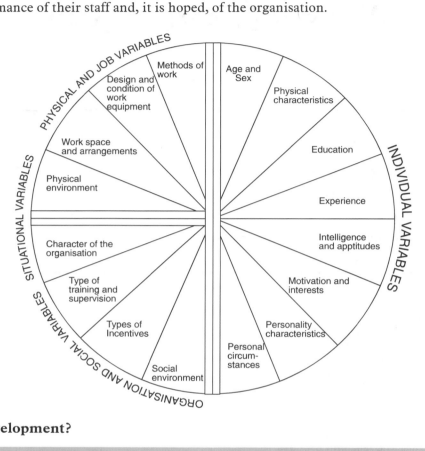

What is development?

> **KEY TERMS**
>
> **Development** is 'the growth or realisation of a person's ability and potential through the provision of learning and educational experiences'.
>
> **Training** is 'the planned and systematic modification of behaviour through learning events, programmes and instruction which enable individuals to achieve the level of knowledge, skills and competence to carry out their work effectively'.
>
> (Armstrong)

1.2   **Overall purpose of employee and management development**

- **Ensure** the firm meets current and future performance objectives by...
- **Continuous improvement** of the performance of individuals and teams, and...
- **Maximising people's** potential for growth (and promotion).

1.3   **Development activities**
- Training, both on and off the job
- Career planning
- Job rotation
- Appraisal (see next chapter)
- Other learning opportunities

Question 1

Note down key experiences which have developed your capacity and confidence at work, and the skills you are able to bring to your employer (or indeed a new employer!)

Answer

Few employers throw you in at the deep end – it is far too risky for them! Instead, you might have been given induction training to get acclimatised to the organisation, and you might have been introduced slowly to the job. Ideally, your employer would have planned a programme of tasks of steadily greater complexity and responsibility to allow you to grow into your role(s).

1.4   Organisations often have a **training and development strategy,** based on the overall strategy for the business. We can list the following steps.

Step 1.   Identify the skills and competences are needed by the **business plan**

Step 2.   Draw up the **development strategy** to show how training and development activities will assist in meeting the targets of the corporate plan.

Step 3.   **Implement** the training and development strategy.

The advantage of such an approach is that the training is:

- Relevant
- Problem-based (ie corrects a real lack of skills)
- Action-oriented
- Performance-related

Training and the organisation

1.5   **Benefits for the organisation of training and development programmes**

Benefit	Comment
Minimise the learning costs of obtaining the skills the organisation needs	Training supports the business strategy.
Lower costs and **increased productivity,** thereby improving performance	Some people suggest that higher levels of training explain the higher productivity of German as opposed to many British manufacturers
Fewer accidents, and better health and safety	EU health and safety directives require a certain level of training. Employees can take employers to court if accidents occur or if unhealthy work practices persist.
Less need for detailed supervision	If people are trained they can get on with the job, and managers can concentrate on other things. Training is an aspect of **empowerment.**
Flexibility	Training ensures that people have the **variety** of skills needed – multi-skilling is only possible if people are properly trained.
Recruitment and succession planning	Training and development attracts new recruits and ensures that the organisation has a supply of suitable managerial and technical staff to take over when people retire.

Benefit	Comment
Change management	Training helps organisations manage change by letting people know why the change is happening and giving them the skills to cope with it.
Corporate culture	(1) Training programmes can be used to build the corporate culture or to direct it in certain ways, by indicating that certain **values** are espoused.
	(2) Training programmes can **build relationships** between staff and managers in different areas of the business
Motivation	Training programmes can increase commitment to the organisation's goals

1.6 Training cannot do everything. Look at the wheel below paragraph 1.1 again. Training only really covers:

Aspect of performance	Areas covered
Individual	Education; Experience; possibly Personal Circumstances (if successful completion of training is accompanied by a higher salary
Physical and job	Methods of work
Organisational and social	Type of training and supervision

1.7 In other words, **training cannot improve performance problems** arising out of:
- Bad management
- Poor job design
- Poor equipment, factory layout and work organisation
- Other characteristics of the employee (eg intelligence)
- Motivation – training gives a person the ability but not necessarily the willingness to improve
- Poor recruitment

Question 2

Despite all the benefits to the organisation, many are still reluctant to train. What reasons can you give for this?

Answer

Cost: training can be costly. Ideally, it should be seen as an investment in the future or as something the firm has to do to maintain its position. In practice, many firms are reluctant to train because of poaching by other employers – their newly trained staff have skills which can be sold for more elsewhere. This got so bad that staff at one computer services firm were required to pay the firm £4,000 if they left (to go to another employer) within two years of a major training programme.

Training and the individual

1.8 For the individual employee, the benefits of training and development are more clear-cut, and few refuse it if it is offered.

Benefit	Comment
Enhances portfolio of **skills**	Even if not specifically related to the current job, training can be useful in other contexts, and the employee becomes more attractive to employers and more promotable
Psychological benefits	The trainee might feel reassured that he/she is of continuing value to the organisation
Social benefit	People's social needs can be met by training courses – they can also develop networks of contacts
The job	Training can help people do their job better, thereby increasing job satisfaction

Training and retention

1.9   In chapter 1 we described flat organisation structures in which there are few opportunities for promotion. It is also the case that many people **feel** less secure in their jobs and are concerned about deskilling.

1.10   Training makes employees more marketable, giving the employee the opportunity to develop skills of greater value. Training programmes mean that talented staff do not have to look outside for **self development** in the short term, and therefore the organisation can retain them.

1.11   Training can thus be considered a motivational issue according to two theories, which we shall cover in Part D.

(a)   **Maslow**

- Self actualisation needs
- Security needs (makes employee more employable; may lead to pay rise

(b)   **Herzberg**

- A part of job enrichment or job enlargement

2   IDENTIFYING TRAINING AND DEVELOPMENT NEEDS

The training process in outline

2.1   In order to ensure that training meets the real needs of the organisation, large firms adopt a planned approach to training. This has the following steps.

Step 1.   Identify and define the **organisation's training needs**. It may be the case that recruitment might be a better solution to a problem than training

Step 2.   **Define the learning required** – in other words, specify the knowledge, skills or competences that have to be acquired. For technical training, this is not difficult: for example all finance department staff will have to become conversant with a new accounting system.

Step 3.   **Define training objectives** – what must be learnt and what trainees must be able to do after the training exercise

BPP PUBLISHING

Step 4. **Plan training programmes** – training and development can be planned in a number of ways, employing a number of techniques, as we shall learn about in Section 3. (Also, people have different approaches to learning, which have to be considered.) This covers:

- Who provides the training
- Where the training takes place
- Divisions of responsibilities between trainers, managers and the individual.

Step 5. **Implement the training**

Step 6. **Evaluate** the training: has it been successful in achieving the learning objectives?

Step 7. Go back to Step 2 if more training is needed.

Question 3

Draw up a training plan for introducing a new employee into your department. Repeat this exercise after you have completed this chapter to see if your chosen approach has changed.

Training needs analysis

2.2 Training needs analysis covers three issues.

Current state	Desired state
Organisation's current results	Desired results, standards
Existing knowledge and skill	Knowledge and skill needed
Individual performance	Required standards

2.3 The difference between the two columns is the **training gap**. Training programmes are designed to improve individual performance, thereby improving the performance of the organisation.

Case example: training standards

Training for quality

The British Standards for Quality Systems (BS EN ISO 9000: formerly BS 5750) which many UK organisations are working towards (often at the request of customers, who perceive it to be a 'guarantee' that high standards of quality control are being achieved) includes training requirements. As the following extract shows, the Standard identifies training needs for those organisations registering for assessment, and also shows the importance of a systematic approach to ensure adequate control.

The training, both by specific training to perform assigned tasks and general training to heighten quality awareness and to mould attitudes of all personnel in an organisation, is central to the achievement of quality.

The comprehensiveness of such training varies with the complexity of the organisation. The following steps should be taken:

1 Identifying the way tasks and operations influence quality in total

2 Identifying individuals; training needs against those required for satisfactory performance of the task

3 Planning and carrying out appropriate specific training

4 Planning and organising general quality awareness programmes

5   Recording training and achievement in an easily retrievable form so that records can be updated and taps in training can be readily identified

BSI, 1990

2.4   **Training surveys** combine information from a variety of sources to discern what the training needs of the organisation actually are. These sources are:

(a)   The **business strategy** at corporate level.

(b)   **Appraisal and performance reviews** – the purpose of a performance management system (see Chapter 6) is to improve performance, and training maybe recommended as a remedy.

(c)   **Attitude surveys** from employees, asking them what training they think they need or would like.

(d)   **Evaluation of existing training** programmes.

(e)   **Job analysis** (see Chapter 7) can be used. To identify training needs from the job analysis, the job analysis can pay attention to:

(i)   Reported difficulties people have in meeting the skills requirement of the job

(ii)   Existing performance weaknesses, of whatever kind, which could be remedied by training

(iii)   Future changes in the job.

The job analysis can be used to generate a training specification covering the knowledge needed for the job, the skills required to achieve the result, attitudinal changes required.

Setting training objectives

2.5   The **training manager** will have to make an initial investigation into the problem of the gap between job or competence **requirements** and current performance of **competence**.

2.6   If training would improve work performance, training **objectives** can then be defined. They should be clear, specific and related to observable, measurable targets, ideally detailing:

- **Behaviour** - what the trainee should be able to do
- **Standard** - to what level of performance?
- **Environment** - under what conditions (so that the performance level is realistic)?

2.7   EXAMPLE

'At the end of the course the trainee should be able to describe ... or identify ... or distinguish x from y ... or calculate ... or assemble ...' and so on. It is insufficient to define the objectives of training as 'to give trainees a grounding in ...' or 'to encourage trainees in a better appreciation of ...': this offers no target achievement which can be measured.

2.8   Training objectives link the identification of training needs with the content, methods and technology of training. Some examples of translating training needs into learning objectives are given in *Personnel Management, A New Approach* by D Torrington and L Hall.

BPP PUBLISHING

Training needs	Learning objectives
To know more about the Data Protection Act	The employee will be able to answer four out of every five queries about the Data Protection Act without having to search for details.
To establish a better rapport with customers	The employee will immediately attend to a customer unless already engaged with another customers.
	The employee will greet each customer using the customer's name where known.
	The employee will apologise to every customer who has had to wait to be attended to.
To assemble clocks more quickly	The employee will be able to assemble each clock correctly within thirty minutes.

Having identified training needs and objectives, the manager will have to decide on the best way to approach training: there are a number of types and techniques of training, which we will discuss below.

3 METHODS OF DEVELOPMENT AND TRAINING

Incorporating training needs into an individual development programme

> **KEY TERM**
>
> A **personal development plan** is a 'clear developmental action plan for an individual which incorporates a wide set of developmental opportunities including formal training.'

3.1 The purpose of a personal development plan will cover:

- Improving performance in the existing job
- Developing skills for future career moves within and outside the organisation.

> **KEY TERM**
>
> **Skills:** what the individual needs to be able to do if results are to be achieved. Skills are built up progressively by repeated training. They may be manual, intellectual or mental, perceptual or social.

3.2 **Preparing a personal development plan.**

Step 1. **Analyse the current position**. You could do a personal SWOT (strengths, weaknesses, opportunities, threats) analysis. The supervisor can have an input into this by categorising the skills use of the employee on a grid as follows, in a **skills analysis**.

	Performance	
	High	Low
Liking of skills — High	Like and do well	Like but don't do well
Liking of skills — Low	Dislike but do well	Dislike and don't do well

The aim is to try to incorporate more of the employees' interests into their actual roles.

Step 2. **Set goals to cover performance in the existing job,** future changes in the current role, moving elsewhere in the organisations, developing specialist expertise. Naturally, such goals should have the characteristic, as far as possible of SMART objectives (ie specific, measurable, attainable, realistic and time-bounded).

Step 3. **Draw up action plan** to achieve the goals, covering the developmental activities listed in paragraph 3.1

Question 4

Draw up a personal development plan for yourself over the next month, the next year, and the next five years. You should include your CAT activities.

Formal training

3.3 Formal training

(a) **Courses** may be run by the organisation's training department or may be provided by external suppliers.

(b) **Types of course**

   (i) **Day release**: the employee works in the organisation and on one day per week attends a local college or training centre for theoretical learning.

   (ii) **Distance learning, evening classes and correspondence courses,** which make demands on the individual's time outside work.

   (iii) **Revision courses** for examinations of professional bodies.

   (iv) **Block release** courses which may involve four weeks at a college or training centre followed by a period back at work.

   (v) **Sandwich courses,** usually involve six months at college then six months at work, in rotation, for two or three years.

   (vi) A **sponsored full-time course** at a university for one or two years.

(c) **Computer-based training** involves interactive training via PC. The typing program, Mavis Beacon, is a good example.

(d) **Techniques** used on the course might include lecturers, seminars, role play and simulation.

3.4 Disadvantages of formal training

(a) An individual will not benefit from formal training unless he or she **is motivated to learn.**

(b) If the **subject matter** of the training course does not **relate to an individual's job**, the learning will quickly be forgotten.

On the job training

3.5 Successful on the job training

(a) The assignments should have a **specific purpose** from which the trainee can learn and gain experience.

(b) The organisation must **tolerate any mistakes** which the trainee makes. Mistakes are an inevitable part of on the job learning.

(c) The work should **not be too complex**.

3.6 Methods of on the job training

(a) **Demonstration/instruction:** show the trainee how to do the job and let them get on with it. It should combine **telling** a person what to do and **showing** them how, using appropriate media. The trainee imitates the instructor, and asks questions.

(b) **Coaching:** the trainee is put under the guidance of an experienced employee who shows the trainee how to do the job.

    (i) **Establish learning targets**. The areas to be learnt should be identified, and specific, realistic goals (eg completion dates, performance standards) stated by agreement with the trainee.

    (ii) **Plan a systematic learning and development programme.** This will ensure regular progress, appropriate stages for consolidation and practice.

    (iii) **Identify opportunities for broadening the trainee's knowledge and experience:** eg by involvement in new projects, placement on interdepartmental committees, suggesting new contacts, or simply extending the job, adding more tasks, greater responsibility etc.

    (iv) **Take into account the strengths and limitations of the trainee** in learning, and take advantage of learning opportunities that suit the trainee's ability, preferred style and goals.

    (v) **Exchange feedback**. The coach will want to know how the trainee sees his or her progress and future. He or she will also need performance information in order to monitor the trainee's progress, adjust the learning programme if necessary, identify further needs which may emerge and plan future development for the trainee.

(c) **Job rotation:** the trainee is given several jobs in succession, to gain experience of a wide range of activities. (Even experienced managers may rotate their jobs, to gain wider experience; this philosophy of job education is commonly applied in the Civil Service, where an employee may expect to move on to another job after a few years.)

(d) **Temporary promotion:** an individual is promoted into his/her superior's position whilst the superior is absent due to illness. This gives the individual a chance to experience the demands of a more senior position.

(e) **'Assistant to' positions:** a junior manager with good potential may be appointed as assistant to the managing director or another executive director. In this way, the individual gains experience of how the organisation is managed 'at the top'.

(f) **Action learning:** a group of managers are brought together to solve a real problem with the help of an 'advisor' who exposes the management process that actually happens.

(g) **Committees:** trainees might be included in the membership of committees, in order to obtain an understanding of inter-departmental relationships.

(h) **Project work.** work on a project with other people can expose the trainee to other parts of the organisation.

Question 5

Suggest a suitable training method for each of the following situations.

(a) A worker is transferred onto a new machine and needs to learn its operation.

(b) An accounts clerk wishes to work towards becoming qualified with the relevant professional body.

(c) An organisation decides that its supervisors would benefit from ideas on participative management and democratic leadership.

(d) A new member of staff is about to join the organisation.

Answer

Training methods for the various workers indicated are as follows.

(a) Worker on a new machine: on-the-job training, coaching.

(b) Accounts clerk working for professional qualification: external course - evening class or day-release.

(c) Supervisors wishing to benefit from participative management and democratic leadership: internal or external course. However, it is important that monitoring and evaluation takes place to ensure that the results of the course are subsequently applied in practice.

(d) New staff: induction training.

Induction training

3.7 On the first day, a manager or personnel officer should welcome the new recruit. He/she should then introduce the new recruit to the person who will be their **immediate supervisor.**

3.8 The immediate supervisor should commence the **on-going process of induction.**

Step 1. Pinpoint the areas that the recruit will have to learn about in order to **start the job.** Some things (such as detailed technical knowledge) may be identified as areas for later study or training.

Step 2. Explain first of all the nature of the job, and the goals of each task, both of the recruit's job and of the department as a whole.

Step 3. Explain about hours of work, and stress the importance of time-keeping. If flexitime is operated, the supervisor should explain how it works.

Step 4. Explain the structure of the department: to whom the recruit will report, to whom he/she can go with complaints or queries and so on.

Step 5. Introduce the recruit to the people in the office. One particular colleague may be assigned to the recruit as a **mentor**, to keep an eye on them, answer routine queries, 'show them the ropes'.

Step 6. Plan and implement an appropriate **training programmes** for whatever technical or practical knowledge is required. Again, the programme should have a clear schedule and set of goals so that the recruit has a sense of purpose, and so that the programme can be efficiently organised to fit in with the activities of the department.

Step 7. Coach and/or train the recruit; and check regularly on their progress, as demonstrated by performance, as reported by the recruit's mentor, and as perceived by the recruit him or herself.

3.9 Note that induction is an **on-going process**, embracing mentoring, coaching, training, monitoring and so on. It is not just a first day affair! After three months, six months or one year the performance of a new recruit should be formally appraised and discussed with them. Indeed, when the process of induction has been finished, a recruit should continue to receive periodic appraisals, just like every other employee in the organisation.

Coaching and mentoring

3.10 **Coaching** is an important aspect of communication and particularly relevant to management development. It is an appropriate part of a senior-junior line management relationship. Senior managers coach their subordinates by providing challenging **opportunities** and **guidance** on tackling them. The junior managers range and depth of competence is thus enhanced.

KEY TERM

Mentoring is the use of specially trained individuals to provide guidance and advice which will help develop the careers of those allocate to them. A person's line manager should not be his or her mentor.

3.11 **Mentoring** differs from coaching in two ways.

(a) The mentor is not usually the protégé's immediate superior.

(b) Mentoring covers a much wider range of functions. Coaching is one aspect of mentoring.

3.12 *Kram* identifies two broad functions for the mentor.

(a) **Career functions**

- Sponsoring within the organisation and providing exposure at higher levels
- Coaching and influencing progress through appointments
- Protection
- Drawing up personal development plans
- Advice with administrative problems people face in their new jobs
- Help in tackling projects, by pointing people in the right direction

(b) **Psychosocial functions**

- Creating a sense of acceptance and belonging
- Counselling and friendship
- Providing a role model

3.13 Organisational arrangements for coaching and mentoring will vary, but in general a coach needs to be an expert in the trainee's professional field. Mentors are often drawn from other areas of the organisation but can open up lines of communication to those with power and influence across it. **For this reason, a mentor is usually in a senior position.**

Question 6

'Joining an organisation with around 8,500 staff, based on two sites over a mile apart and in the throes of major restructuring, can be confusing for any recruit. This is the situation facing the 20 to 30 new employees recruited each month by the Hospital Trust, which was formed by the merger of the two hospitals in April.

In a climate of change, new employees joining the NHS can be influenced by the negative attitudes of other staff who may oppose the current changes. So it has become increasingly important for the trust's management executive to get across their view of the future and to understand the feelings of confusion new staff may be experiencing.'

See if you can design a **one day** induction programme for these new recruits, in the light of the above. The programme is to be available to **all** new recruits, from doctors and radiographers to accountants, catering and cleaning staff and secretaries.

Answer

9.00	Welcome	
9.05	Introduction	*Ground rules and objectives for the day*
9.25	Presentation	*The history of the hospital*
10.25	Presentation	*Talk on structure of the management team, trust board and executive*
10.45	Group exercise	*With chief executive Mr Y on patient care, funding, hospital processes and measuring the care provided*
12.20	Lunch	
1.15	First tour	
2.30	Presentation	*Looking at trust with new eyes - suggestions for change*
2.20	Presentation	*Information on staff organisations*
3.10	Presentation	*Security issues, fire drills, health and safety (including handouts)*
3.30	Presentation	*Session on occupational health*
3.40	Presentation	*Local areas and staff benefits*
3.45	Seasonal tour	
4.30	Presentation	*Facilities management and patient care*
4.45	Closing session	*Evaluation and finish*

Particularly important is the focus on patient care and the group exercises. Also, people enjoy the discussions and learn a lot more about their colleagues and the trust by participating rather than being talked at.

4   THE LEARNING PROCESS

4.1   There are different schools of learning theory which explain and describe how people learn.

(a)   **Behaviourist psychology** concentrated on the relationship between **stimuli** (input through the senses) and **responses** to those stimuli. 'Learning' is the formation of **new** connections between stimulus and response, on the basis of **conditioning**. We modify our responses in future according to whether the results of our behaviour in the past have been good or bad.

(b)   The **cognitive approach** argues that the human mind takes sensory information and imposes organisation and meaning on it: we interpret and rationalise. We use feedback information on the results of past behaviour to make **rational decisions** about whether to maintain successful behaviours or modify unsuccessful behaviours in future, according to our goals and our plans for reaching them.

4.2 Whichever approach it is based on, learning theory offers certain useful propositions for the design of **effective training programmes**.

Proposition	Comment
The individual should be **motivated** to learn	The advantages of training should be made clear, according to the individual's motives - money, opportunity, valued skills or whatever.
There should be clear **objectives and standards** set, so that each task has some meaning	Each stage of learning should present a challenge, without overloading the trainee or making them lose confidence. Specific objectives and performance standards for each will help the trainee in the planning and control process that leads to learning, and providing targets against which performance will constantly be measured.
There should be timely, relevant **feedback** on performance and progress	This will usually be provided by the trainer, and should be concurrent - or certainly not long delayed. If progress reports or performance appraisals are given only at the year end, for example, there will be no opportunity for behaviour adjustment or learning in the meantime.
Positive and negative **reinforcement** should be judiciously used	Recognition and encouragement enhance an individuals confidence in their competence and progress: punishment for poor performance - especially without explanation and correction - discourages the learner and creates feelings of guilt, failure and hostility
Active **participation** is more telling than passive reception (because of its effect on the motivation to learn, concentration and recollection).	If a high degree of participation is impossible, practice and repetition can be used to reinforce receptivity. However, participation has the effect of encouraging 'ownership' of the process of learning and changing - committing the individual to it as their **own** goal, not just an imposed process.

Learning styles

4.3 The way in which people learn best will differ according to the type of person. That is, there are **learning styles** which suit different individuals. Peter **Honey** and Alan **Mumford** have drawn up a popular classification of four learning styles.

(a) **Theorists** seek to understand basic principles and to take an intellectual, 'hands-off' approach based on logical argument. They prefer training to be:

- Programmed and structured
- Designed to allow time for analysis
- Provided by teachers who share his/her preference for concepts and analysis

(b) **Reflectors**

- Observe phenomena, think about them and then choose how to act
- Need to work at their own pace
- Find learning difficult if forced into a hurried programme
- Produce carefully thought-out conclusions after research and reflection
- Tend to be fairly slow, non-participative (unless to ask questions) and cautious

(c) **Activists**

- Deal with practical, active problems and do not have patience with theory
- Require training based on hands-on experience
- Are excited by participation and pressure, such as new projects
- Flexible and optimistic, but tend to rush at something without due preparation

(d) **Pragmatists**

- Only like to study if they can see its direct link to practical problems
- Good at learning new techniques in on-the-job training
- Aim is to implement action plans and/or do the task better
- May discard good ideas which only require some development

Training programmes should ideally be designed to accommodate the preferences of all four styles. This can often be overlooked especially as the majority of training staff are activists.

Question 7

With reference to the four learning styles drawn up by Honey and Mumford, which of these styles do you think most closely resembles your own? What implications has this got for the way you learn?

Answer

Depending on your answer you will learn most effectively in particular given situations. For example, the theorist will learn best from lectures and books, whereas the activist will get most from practical activities.

The learning cycle

4.4 Another useful model is the **experiential learning cycle** devised by David **Kolb**. Experiential learning involves **doing**, however, and puts the learners in an active problem-solving role: a form of **self-learning** which encourages the learners to formulate and commit themselves to their own learning objectives.

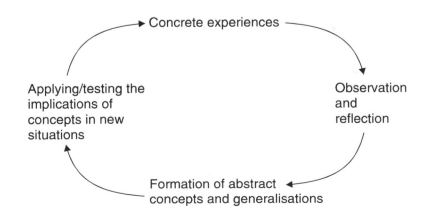

BPP
PUBLISHING

4.5 EXAMPLE

An employee interviews a customer for the first time (concrete experience). He observes his own performance and the dynamics of the situation (observation) and afterwards, having failed to convince the customer to buy his product, the employee analyses what he did right and wrong (reflection). He comes to the conclusion that he failed to listen to what the customer really wanted and feared, underneath his general reluctance: he realises that the key to communication is listening (abstraction/ generalisation). In his next interview he applies his strategy to the new set of circumstances (application/testing). This provides him with a new experience with which to start the cycle over again.

4.6   Simplified, this learning by doing approach involves:

Act: Analyse action: Understand principles: Apply principles:

Barriers to learning

4.7   According to Peter **Senge**, there are seven sources of **learning disability** in organisations which prevent them from attaining their potential - which trap them into 'mediocrity', for example, when they could be achieving 'excellence'.

(a) **'I am my position'**. When asked what they do for a living, most people describe the tasks they perform, not the **purposes** they fulfil; thus they tend to see their responsibilities as limited to the boundaries of their position.

(b) **'The enemy is out there'**. If things go wrong it is all too easy to imagine that somebody else 'out there' was at fault.

(c) **The illusion of taking charge.** The individual decides to be more active in fighting the enemy out there, trying to destroy rather than to build.

(d) **The fixation on events**. Conversations in organisations are dominated by concern about events (last month's sales, who's just been promoted, the new product from our competitor), and this focus inevitably distracts us from seeing the longer-term patterns of change.

(e) **The parable of the boiled frog.** Failure to adapt to gradually building threats is pervasive. (If you place a frog in a pot of boiling water, it will immediately try to scramble out; but if you place the frog in room temperature water, he will stay put. If you heat the water gradually, the frog will do nothing until he boils: this is because 'the frog's internal apparatus for sensing threats to survival is geared to sudden changes in his environment, not to slow, gradual changes'.)

(f) **The delusion of learning from experience.** We learn best from experience, but we never experience the results of our most important and significant decisions. Indeed, we never know what the outcomes would have been had we done something else.

(g) **The myth of the management team.** All too often, the management 'team' is not a team at all, but is a collection of individuals competing for power and resources.

Question 8

How far do Senge's seven learning disabilities apply to your own organisation, or to some other significant organisation with which you may be familiar?

4.8 For individuals, the barriers may be:

- 'A waste of time': people see no personal benefit from training
- Training programmes employ the wrong techniques for people's learning styles
- Unwillingness to change

Encouraging learning: what managers can do

4.9 Managers can try to **develop the learning organisation**.

- Encourages continuous learning and knowledge generation at all levels
- Has the processes to move knowledge around the organisation
- Can transform knowledge into actual behaviour

> **KEY TERM**
>
> **Learning organisation** is 'An organisation that facilitates the learning of all its members and continuously transforms itself'.

4.10 **The building of the learning organisation**

Characteristics	Comments
Systematic problem solving	Problems should be tackled in a scientific way.
Experimentation	Experimentation can generate new insights.
Learn from experience	Knowledge from past failures can help avoid them in future.
Learn from others	Customers and other firms can be a good source of ideas. Learning opportunities should be sought out.
Knowledge transfer	Knowledge should be transferred throughout the organisation.

5 PEOPLE INVOLVED IN TRAINING AND DEVELOPMENT

The trainee

5.1 Many people now believe that the ultimate responsibility for training and development lies, not with the employer, but with the **individual**. People should seek to develop their own skills, to improve their own careers rather than wait for the organisation to impose training upon them. Why? The current conventional wisdom is that:

(a) **Delayering** means there are fewer automatic promotion pathways; promotion was once a source of development but there might not be further promotions available.

(b) Technological change means that new skills are always needed, and people who can find new work will be learning new skills.

The human resources department or training department

5.2 The human resources department is ideally concerned with developing people. Some organisations have extensive development and career planning programmes. These shape the progression of individuals through the organisation, in accordance with the performance and potential of the individual and the needs of the organisation. Of course, only large organisations can afford or use this sort of approach.

5.3 The HR department also performs an **administrative** role by recording what training and development opportunities and individual might be given – in some firms, going on a training programme is an entitlement that the personnel department might have to enforce.

Supervisors, managers and training

5.4 **Line managers** and **supervisors** bear some of the responsibility for training and development within the organisation by identifying:

- The training needs of the department or section
- The current competences of the individuals within the department
- Opportunities for learning and development on the job
- When feedback is necessary.

5.5 The **supervisor** may be required to organise training programmes for staff.

The training manager

5.6 The training manager is a member of staff appointed to arrange and sometimes run training. The training manager generally reports to the **human resources** or **personnel director**, but also needs a good relationship with line managers in the departments where the training takes place.

5.7 **Responsibilities of the training manager**

Responsibility	Comment
Liaison	With HRM department and operating departments
Scheduling	Arranging training programmes at convenient times
Skills identifying	Discerning existing and future skills shortages
Programme design	Develop tailored training programmes
Feedback	The trainee, the department and the HR department

6 TRAINING EVALUATION

KEY TERM

Validation of training means observing the results of the course and measuring whether the training objectives have been achieved.

Evaluation of training means comparing the actual costs of the scheme against the assessed benefits which are being obtained. If the costs exceed the benefits, the scheme will need to be redesigned or withdrawn.

6.1 **Ways of validating and evaluating a training scheme**

(a) **Trainees' reactions to the experience.** This form of monitoring is rather inexact, and it does not allow the training department to measure the results for comparison against the training objective.

(b) **Trainee learning:** measuring what the trainees have learned on the course by means of a test at the end of it.

(c) **Changes in job behaviour following training.** This is possible where the purpose of the course was to learn a particular skill.

(d) **Organisational change as a result of training:** finding out whether the training has affected the work or behaviour of **other** employees not on the course - seeing whether there has been a general change in attitudes arising from a new course in, say, computer terminal work. This form of monitoring would probably be reserved for senior managers in the training department.

(e) **Impact of training on organisational goals:** seeing whether the training scheme has contributed to the overall objectives of the organisation. This too is a form of monitoring reserved for senior management, and would perhaps be discussed at board level in the organisation. It is likely to be the main component of a cost-benefit analysis.

Question 9

Outline why it is important to evaluate and validate a training programme and describe possible methods for achieving this.

Answer

Validation of a new course is important to ensure that objectives have been achieved. Evaluation of it is more difficult, but at least as important because it identifies the value of the training programme to the organisation.

Taking the example of a one-day customer-service training programme for all staff, you could use the following methods of validation and evaluation.

BPP PUBLISHING

Chapter roundup

- In order to achieve its goals, an organisation requires a **skilled workforce**. This is partly achieved by training.

- The main purpose of training and development is to **raise competence and therefore performance standards**. It is also concerned with **personal development**, helping and motivating employees to fulfil their potential.

- A thorough analysis of **training needs** should be carried out as part of a systematic approach to training, to ensure that training programmes meet organisational and individual requirements. Once training needs have been identified, they should be translated into **training objectives**.

- Individuals can incorporate training and development objectives into a personal development plan.

- There are different schools of thought as to how people learn. Different people have different learning styles.

- There are a variety of training methods. These include:

  ° Formal education and training
  ° On-the-job training
  ° Awareness-oriented training

- Managers can design and manager the organisation to encourage learning.

Quick quiz

1   List examples of development opportunities within organisations.

2   List how training can contribute to:

   (a)   Organisational effectiveness
   (b)   Individual effectiveness and motivation

3   According to ISO 9000, what are the main steps to be adopted in a systematic approach to training?

4   Define the term 'training need'.

5   How should training objectives be expressed?

6   What does learning theory tell us about the design of training programmes?

7   List the four learning styles put forward by Honey and Mumford.

8   List the four stages in Kolb's experiential learning cycle.

9   List the available methods of on-the-job training.

10   What are the levels of training validation/evaluation?

11   What is the supervisor's role in training?

Answers to quick quiz

1   Career planning, job rotation, deputising, on-the-job training, counselling, guidance, education and training.

2   (a)   Increased efficiency and productivity; reduced costs, supervisory problems and accidents; improved quality, motivation and morale.

    (b)   Demonstrates individual value, enhances security, enhances skills portfolio, motivates, helps develop networks and contacts.

3   Identify how operations influence quality; identify individual training needs against performance requirements; plan and conduct training; plan and organise quality awareness programmes; record training and achievement.

4   The required level of competence minus the present level of competence.

5   Actively - 'after completing this chapter you should understand how to design and evaluate training programmes'.

6   The trainee should be motivated to learn, there should be clear objectives and timely feedback. Positive and negative reinforcement should be used carefully, to encourage active participation where possible.

7   Theorist, reflector, activist and pragmatist.

8   Concrete experience, observation/reflection, abstraction/generalisation, application/testing.

9   Induction, job rotation, temporary promotion, 'assistant to' positions, project or committee work

10   Reactions, learning, job behaviour, organisational change, ultimate impact.

11   Identifying training needs of the department or section. identifying the skills of the individual employee, and deficiencies in performance. Providing or supervising on-the-job training (eg coaching). Providing feedback on an individuals performance.

Now try the question below from the Exam Question Bank

Question to try	Level	Marks	Time
10	Exam	15	27 mins

BPP PUBLISHING

Chapter 11

APPRAISAL AND COMPETENCE ASSESSMENT

Topic list	Syllabus reference
1 Appraisal and performance management	3(d)
2 The purpose of appraisal	3(d)
3 The process of appraisal	3(d)
4 The appraisal report	3(f)
5 The appraisal interview	3(e)
6 Follow-up	3(f), 3(g)
7 Barriers to effective appraisal	3(d)
8 New approaches to appraisal	3(d)
9 How effective is the appraisal scheme?	3(g)

Introduction

The general purpose of performance appraisal is to improve the efficiency of the organisation by ensuring that the individuals within it are performing to the best of their ability, and (perhaps) also developing their potential for improvement. Within this overall aim, staff appraisals are used for three purposes.

(a) **Reward review** - assessing whether an employee is deserving of a bonus or pay increase

(b) A review of **past performance**, for identifying problems and unutilised potential, planning and following-up training and development programmes

(c) The identification of **potential**, as an aid to planning career development

This used to be regarded as a process which started with an appraisal form and ended with a (frequently perfunctory) chat about it. But in the late 1980s, emphasis shifted more towards the setting of the goals and priorities on which performance would be assessed: an approach known as **performance management**.

Study guide

Section 8(h) – Standard setting and performance management

- Illustrate ways of applying performance management

Section 19(d) – Competitive assessment

Section 20(e) – Conducting the appraisal process

Section 21(f) – Individual skills and development

- Explain the link between the appraisal process and effective employee development
- Describe the role of the appraisee in the process
- Suggest ways in which self-development can be part of the process

---

Exam guide

The process of appraisal and the detailed procedures associated with it could form a question in either Section A or Section B.

---

1   APPRAISAL AND PERFORMANCE MANAGEMENT

Performance management: set objectives for the future

1.1   **Performance management** is an approach which aims 'to get better results from the organisations, teams and individuals by measuring and managing performance within agreed frameworks of objectives and competence requirements, assessing and improving performance'. **Performance management is part of the control system of the organisation.**

Appraisal: review past performance to establish the current position.

1.2   The process of appraisal is part of this system of performance management.

> **KEY TERM**
>
> Whilst performance management as a whole is forward looking, the process of **appraisal** is designed to review performance over the past period, with a view to identifying any deficiencies, and improving it in the future.

2   THE PURPOSE OF APPRAISAL

2.1   The general purpose of any appraisal system is to improve the efficiency of the organisation by ensuring that the individuals within it are performing to the best of their ability and developing their potential for improvement.

(a)   **Reward review.** Measuring the extent to which an employee is deserving of a bonus or pay increase as compared with his or her peers.

(b)   **Performance review**, for planning and following-up training and development programmes, ie identifying training needs, validating training methods and so on.

(c)   **Potential review**, as an aid to planning career development and succession, by attempting to predict the level and type of work the individual will be capable of in the future.

2.2   **Objectives of appraisals**

(a)   Establishing what **the individual has to do** in a job in order that the objectives for the section or department are realised.

(b)   Establishing the **key or main results** which the individual will be expected to achieve in the course of his or her work over a period of time.

(c)   **Comparing the individual's level of performance against a standard**, to provide a basis for remuneration above the basic pay rate.

(d)   Identifying the individual's training and **development needs** in the light of actual **performance**.

(e) Identifying **potential candidates for promotion.**

(f) Identifying **areas of improvement**.

(g) Establishing an **inventory of actual and potential performance** within the undertaking to provide a basis for manpower planning.

(h) Monitoring the undertaking's **initial selection procedures** against the subsequent performance of recruits, relative to the organisation's expectations.

(i) **Improving communication** about work tasks between different levels in the hierarchy.

2.3 The benefits of formal appraisal systems

(a) Managers and supervisors may obtain **random impressions** of subordinates' performance (perhaps from their more noticeable successes and failures), but rarely form a coherent, complete and objective picture.

(b) They may have a fair idea of their subordinates' shortcomings - but may not have devoted **time and attention** to the matter of improvement and development.

(c) Judgements are **easy to make**, but **less easy to justify** in detail, in writing, or to the subject's face.

(d) **Different assessors** may be applying a **different set of criteria**, and varying standards of objectivity and judgement. This undermines the value of appraisal for comparison, as well as its credibility in the eyes of the appraisees.

(e) Unless stimulated to do so, managers rarely give their subordinates adequate **feedback** on their performance.

Question 1

List four disadvantages to the individual of not having a formal appraisal system.

Answer

Disadvantages to the individual of not having an appraisal system include: the individual is not aware of progress or shortcomings, is unable to judge whether s/he would be considered for promotion, is unable to identify or correct weaknesses by training and there is a lack of communication with the manager.

2.4 Three basic problems

(a) The **formulation and appreciation of desired traits and standards** against which individuals can be consistently and objectively assessed.

(b) **Recording assessments**. Managers should be encouraged to utilise a standard and understood framework, but still allowed to express what they consider important, and without too much form-filling.

(c) **Getting the appraiser and appraisee together,** so that both contribute to the assessment and plans for improvement and/or development.

3 THE PROCESS OF APPRAISAL

3.1 A typical appraisal system

Step 1. **Identification of criteria** for assessment, perhaps based on job analysis, performance standards, person specifications and so on.

Step 2. The preparation by the subordinate's manager of an **appraisal report**. In some systems both the appraisee and appraiser prepare a report. These reports are then compared.

Step 3. An **appraisal interview,** for an exchange of views about the appraisal report, targets for improvement, solutions to problems and so on.

Step 4. **Review of the assessment** by the assessor's own superior, so that the appraisee does not feel subject to one person's prejudices. Formal appeals may be allowed, if necessary to establish the fairness of the procedure.

Step 5. The preparation and implementation of **action plans** to achieve improvements and changes agreed.

Step 6. **Follow-up:** monitoring the progress of the action plan.

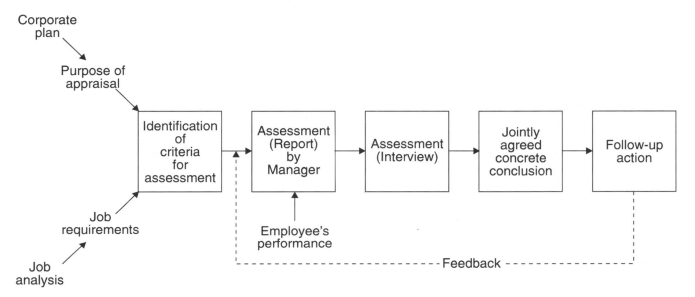

4   THE APPRAISAL REPORT

What is appraised?

4.1   Assessments must be related to a **common standard,** in order for comparisons to be made between individuals: on the other hand, they should be related to **meaningful performance criteria,** which take account of the **critical variables in each different job.**

4.2   An **appraisal report** is written before the interview. An example of a report is given on the next page.

(a)   Key issues relate to the **job description**

(b)   **Personality**: not relevant unless specifically related to performance.

(c)   **Competences**. It can include the ability to transfer skills and knowledge to new situations.

> **KEY TERM**
>
> A **competence** is an observable skill or ability to complete a particular task successfully.

4.3   Some competences for **managers and supervisors** might be adapted for appraisal as follows.

APPRAISAL REPORT						
Name:		Time in position				
Position:		Period of review:				
Company:		Age:				

	A	B	C	D	E	Comment
Overall assessment						
Job knowledge						
Effective output						
Co-operation						
Initiative						
Time-keeping						
Other relevant facts (specify)						

A= Outstanding   A = above standard   C = To required standard
D = Shot of standard in some respects   E= Not up to required standard

Potential	A	B	C	D	E	Comment

A = Overdue for promotion   B = Ready for promotion   C = Potential for promotion
D = No evidence of promotion potential at present
E = Has not worked long enough with me for judgement

Training, if any, required

Assessment discussed with employee?   Yes   No

Signed   Date

Confirmed   Date

Management competence	Comment
Intellectual	(1) Ability to see the wider picture
	(2) Analysis and judgement (eg seeks relevant information, due attention to detail)
	(3) Planning and organising (eg scheduling and delegating)
Interpersonal	(1) Managing staff (eg leadership style, developing people)
	(2) Persuasiveness (good in negotiation)
	(3) Assertiveness and decisiveness
	(4) Interpersonal sensitivity (is flexible in dealing with others)
	(5) Oral communication
Adaptability and resilience	Can operate under pressure and adversity
Results-orientation	(1) Energy and initiative (is a 'self starter', maintains a high level of activity)
	(2) Achievement motivation (sets demanding goals)
	(3) Business sense

Many competences are obviously **more detailed and technical**. It is possible to assess competences in the appraisal process by judging the individual's performance against the competences he or she is *supposed* to have.

Question 2

Identify specific competences which may be relevant to some jobs of your choice.

Answer

You might have identified such things as:

(a) Numerical ability applicable to accounts staff, say, more than to customer contact staff.
(b) Ability to drive safely, essential for transport workers - not for desk-bound ones.
(c) Report-writing (not applicable to manual labour, say).

4.4 Appraisal techniques

(a) **Overall assessment**. The manager writes in narrative form his judgements about the appraisee. There will be no guaranteed consistency of the criteria and areas of assessment, however, and managers may not be able to convey clear, effective judgements in writing.

(b) **Guided assessment**. Assessors are required to comment on a number of specified characteristics and performance elements, with guidelines as to how terms such as 'application', 'integrity' and 'adaptability' are to be interpreted in the work context. This is more precise, but still rather vague.

(c) **Grading**. Grading adds a comparative frame of reference to the general guidelines, whereby managers are asked to select one of a number of levels or degrees to which the individual in question displays the given characteristic. These are also known as **rating scales**.

Numerical values may be added to ratings to give rating scores. Alternatively a less precise **graphic scale** may be used to indicate general position on a plus/minus scale.

Factor: job knowledge

High _____√_____ Average _____ Low

(d) **Behavioural incident methods**. These concentrate on **employee behaviour**, which is measured against typical behaviour in each job, as defined by common **critical incidents** of successful and unsuccessful job behaviour reported by managers.

(e) **Results-orientated schemes**. This reviews performance against specific targets and standards of performance **agreed in advance by manager and subordinate together**.

    (i) The subordinate is more involved in appraisal because he/she is able to evaluate his/her progress in achieving, jointly-agreed targets.

    (ii) The manager is relieved of a critic's role, and becomes a counsellor.

    (iii) Clear and known targets help modify behaviour.

The effectiveness of the scheme will depend on the **targets set** (are they clearly defined? realistic?) and the **commitment** of both parties to make it work.

Question 3

What sort of appraisal systems are suggested by the following examples?

(a) The Head Teacher of Dotheboys Hall sends a brief report at the end of each term to the parents of the school's pupils. Typical phrases include 'a satisfactory term's work', and 'could do better'.

(b) A firm of auditors assess the performance of their staff in four categories: technical ability, relationships with clients, relationships with other members of the audit team, and professional attitude. On each of these criteria staff are marked from A (= excellent) to E (= poor).

(c) A firm of insurance brokers assesses the performance of its staff by the number of clients they have visited and the number of policies sold.

Answer

(a) Overall assessment of the blandest kind.
(b) This is a grading system, based on a guided assessment.
(c) Results orientated scheme.

Self-appraisals

4.5 Self-appraisals occur when individuals carry out their own self-evaluation as a major input into the appraisal process.

(a) **Advantages** of self appraisal

    (i) It **saves the manager time** as the employee identifies the areas of competence which are relevant to the job and his/her relative strengths.

    (ii) It offers **increased responsibility** to the individual which may improve motivation.

    (iii) This reconciles the goals of the individual and the organisation.

    (iv) It may overcome the problem of needing skilled appraisers, thus cutting training costs and reducing the managerial role in appraisal.

(v) In giving the responsibility to an individual, the scheme may offer more **flexibility** in terms of timing, with individuals undertaking ongoing self-evaluation.

(b) **Disadvantage**

People are often not the best judges of their own performance.

4.6 Many schemes combine the two - manager and subordinate fill out a report and compare notes.

5 THE APPRAISAL INTERVIEW

5.1 The process of the interview is given below.

Step 1. Prepare
- Plan and place, time and environment
- Review employee's history
- Consult other managers - let employee prepare
- Prepare report. Review employee's self-appraisal

Step 2. Interview
- Listen to employee. Discuss, don't argue
- Encourage employee to talk, identify problems and solutions
- Be fair

Step 3.
- Gain employee commitment
- Agree plan of action
- Summarise to check understanding

Step 4.
- Complete appraisal report, if not already prepared

Step 5.
- Take action as agreed
- Monitor progress
- Keep employee informed

Interview and counselling

5.2 The extent to which any interview is based on the written report varies in practice.

(a) The report may be distributed to the appraisee in advance of the interview, so that he has a chance to make an independent assessment for discussion with his manager. The appraisee may complete the self-appraisal form.

(b) Maier *(The Appraisal Interview)* identifies three types of approach to appraisal interviews. Most appraisees prefer the third (option 5.5, below) of the alternatives suggested.

5.3 **The tell and sell method**. The manager tells the subordinate how he/she has been assessed, and then tries to 'sell' (gain acceptance of) the evaluation and the improvement plan. This requires unusual human relations skills in order to convey constructive criticism in an acceptable manner, and to motivate the appraisee to alter his/her behaviour.

5.4 **The tell and listen method**. The manager tells the subordinate how he/she has been assessed, and then invites the appraisee to respond. The manager therefore no longer dominates the interview throughout, and there is greater opportunity for **counselling** as opposed to pure **direction**.

BPP PUBLISHING

(a) The employee is **encouraged to participate** in the assessment and the working out of improvement targets and methods: it is an accepted tenet of behavioural theory that participation in problem definition and goal setting increases the individual's commitment to behaviour and attitude modification.

(b) This method does not assume that a change in the employee will be the sole key to improvement: the manager may receive helpful feedback about how job design, methods, environment or supervision might be improved.

5.5 **The problem-solving approach**. The manager abandons the role of critic altogether, and becomes a helper. The discussion is centred not on the assessment, but on the employee's **work problems**. The employee is encouraged to think solutions through, and to commit himself to the recognised need for personal improvement. This approach encourages intrinsic motivation through the element of self-direction, and the perception of the job itself as a problem-solving activity. It may also stimulate creative thinking on the part of employee and manager alike, to the benefit of the organisation's adaptability and methods.

Question 4

What approach was taken at your last appraisal interview? Could it have been better?

6 FOLLOW-UP

6.1 After the appraisal interview, the manager may complete the report, with an overall assessment, assessment of potential and/or the jointly-reached conclusion of the interview, with **recommendations for follow-up action**. The manager should then discuss the report with the counter-signing manager (usually his or her own superior), resolving any problems that have arisen in making the appraisal or report, and agreeing on action to be taken. The report form may then go to the management development adviser, training officer or other relevant people as appropriate for follow-up.

6.2 **Follow-up procedures**

(a) **Informing appraisees of the results** of the appraisal, if this has not been central to the review interview.

(b) **Carrying out agreed actions** on training, promotion and so on.

(c) **Monitoring the appraisee's progress** and checking that he/she has carried out agreed actions or improvements.

(d) Taking necessary steps to **help the appraisee to attain improvement objectives**, by guidance, providing feedback, upgrading equipment, altering work methods or whatever.

Question 5

What would happen without follow-up?

Answer

The appraisal would merely be seen as a pleasant chat with little effect on future performance, as circumstances change. Moreover the individual might feel cheated.

6.3 The appraisal can also be used as an input to the employee's **personal development plan**.

7   BARRIERS TO EFFECTIVE APPRAISAL

Problems in practice

7.1   In theory, such appraisal schemes may seem very fair to the individual and very worthwhile for the organisation, but in practice the **appraisal system often goes wrong**. L Lockett (in *Effective Performance Management*) suggests that these appraisal barriers can be identified as follows.

Appraisal barriers	Comment
Appraisal as confrontation	Many people dread appraisals, or use them 'as a sort of show down, a good sorting out or a clearing of the air.'
	• There is a lack of agreement on performance levels.
	• The feedback is subjective - in other words the manager is biased, allows personality differences to get in the way of actual performance etc.
	• The feedback is badly delivered.
	• Appraisals are 'based on yesterday's performance not on the whole year'.
	• Disagreement on long-term prospects.
Appraisal as judgement	The appraisal 'is seen as a one-sided process in which the manager acts as judge, jury and counsel for the prosecution'. The subordinate is defensive. However, the process of performance management 'needs to be jointly operated in order to retain the commitment and develop the self-awareness of the individual.'
Appraisal as chat	The superior is defensive. The appraisal is a friendly chat 'without ... purpose or outcome ... Many managers, embarrassed by the need to give feedback and set stretching targets, reduce the appraisal to a few mumbled "well dones!" and leave the interview with a briefcase of unresolved issues.'
Appraisal as bureaucracy	Appraisal is a form-filling exercise, to satisfy the personnel department. Its underlying purpose, improving individual and organisational performance, is forgotten.
Appraisal as unfinished business	Appraisal should be part of a continuing process of performance management.
Appraisal as annual event	Many targets set at annual appraisal meetings become irrelevant or out-of-date.

Appraisal and pay

7.2   Another problem is the extent to which the appraisal system is related to the **pay and reward system**. Many employees consider that the appraisal system should be definitely linked with the reward system, on the ground that extra effort should be rewarded. Although this appears, superficially, a 'common sense' and fair view, there are major drawbacks to it.

(a) **Funds available** for pay rises rarely depend on one individual's performance alone - the whole company has to do well.

(b) **Continuous improvement** is always necessary - many firms have 'to run to stand still'. Continuous improvement should perhaps be expected of employees as part of their work, not rewarded as extra.

(c) In low-inflation environments, **cash pay rises are fairly small**.

(d) **Comparisons between individuals** are hard to make, as many smaller firms cannot afford the rigour of a job evaluation scheme.

(e) Performance management is about a lot more than pay for *past* performance - it is often **forward looking** with regard to future performance.

Appraisal, management expertise and empowerment

7.3 In 7.1 above, we suggested that appraisals could be subverted by managers who were biased, badly briefed or who only looked at yesterday's performance.

7.4 In organisations where **empowerment** is practised and employees are given more responsibility:

(a) Many **managers may not have the time** to keep a sufficiently close eye on individual workers to make a fair judgement.

(b) In some jobs, **managers do not have the technical expertise** to judge an employee's output.

(c) Employees depend on **other people** in the workplace/organisation to be effective - in other words, an individual's results may not be entirely under his/her control. A person's performance is often indirectly or directly influenced by the **management style** of the person doing the appraisal.

Question 6

This activity shows some of the problems of operating appraisal schemes in practice.

It is time for Pauline Radway's annual performance appraisal and Steve Taylor, her manager, has sought your advice on two problem areas which he has identified as 'motivation' and 'the organisation's systems'.

The appraisal system has a six point rating scale:

1	Excellent	4	Acceptable
2	Outstanding	5	Room for improvement
3	Competent	6	Unacceptable

The annual pay increase is determined, in part, by the overall rating of the employee.

Pauline was recruited into Steve's section 18 months ago. She took about five months to learn the job and achieve competence. Accordingly, at last year's appraisal she and Steve agreed that an overall rating of '4' was appropriate.

Over the next six months Pauline worked hard and well and in effect developed her job so she was able to accept more responsibility and expand her range of activities into areas which were both interesting and demanding.

During the last six months the section has been 'rationalised' and the workforce has been reduced (although the workload has increased). Steve is under pressure to contain costs - particularly in the area of salary increases.

Steve now has to rely on Pauline performing her enriched job which, taking the past six months as a whole and given the increased pressure, she performs 'satisfactorily' rather than 'outstandingly'; there are aspects of her performance in this enriched job which she could improve.

When Steve met Pauline to agree the time for the appraisal interview she said - only half jokingly - 'I warn you, I'm looking forward to a respectable pay rise this year.

Task

(a) Outline the problems for Steve that arise from the above scenario:

    (i)   in relation to Pauline's feelings;

    (ii)   in relation to the organisation's systems.

(b) Suggest how Steve should proceed.

Answer

(a) Steve's problems

    (i)   Pauline's feelings

        Pauline, not unreasonably, makes a connection between performance and reward. She feels she has worked hard and that this should be recognised in financial terms. Steve, on the other hand, is under pressure to keep costs under control. In fact, one of the reasons for Pauline's increased responsibility is the rationalisation of the department.

        Pauline, however, does make a crude assumption that effort equals performance. She is highly motivated at the moment, but her performance is not outstanding. Her performance is only satisfactory in her changed job, and therefore it would not be appropriate to tell her otherwise. However, using expectancy theory, we can assert that a pay increase for her is an important motivating factor to get her to work hard.

        Steve is thus faced with a dilemma. If she is not rewarded, it is likely that she will make less effort to perform well, and this would be suggested by expectancy theory. Steve will suffer, as the rationalised department depends on her continual hard work. In short, this is a hygiene factor.

        Another factor is fairness. Pauline cannot expect special treatment, when compared to other workers, who may have made an equal effort. Over-rewarding average performance, despite the effort, might demotivate other staff who will accuse Steve of favouritism.

    (ii)   The organisation's systems

        It is clear that Steve is having to negotiate the requirements and failings of four different systems here.

        (1)   The budgetary control system, restricting pay rises.

        (2)   The appraisal system, which conflates effort and performance.

        (3)   The remuneration system, by which pay rises are awarded.

        Finally, Pauline's job is very different from what it was when she first started.

        The source of the problem is the failure to recognise that Pauline is now doing a different job. Her job should have been re-evaluated. If this were the case, Steve could assess her reward on the basis of the performance in this re-evaluated job. She would have higher pay, commensurate with her enhanced responsibilities, but not an unfairly favourable grading.

        However, Steve realises that the appraisal system is the one over which he has most direct control. He is in a position to reward her effort, but this would be anomalous as her performance in the new job is not exceptional. Her rating would not be appropriate to her performance. Yet her enhanced responsibilities need to be recognised somehow, although Steve, under pressure from the budgetary control system, may not be able to reward it financially.

        There is little Steve can do about the budgetary factors, apart from stating to Pauline that everybody is in the same boat. There might be non-financial rewards that he can offer her. Pauline might like to have her own separate office space, for example, if it were available, or Steve might be able to offer her increased annual leave or a unique job title.

        Pauline might also resent waiting for the outcome of a job re-evaluation exercise, as, from her point of view, that is the organisation's problem, not hers.

(b) *What Steve should do*

Steve has a choice either to overrate Pauline, according to the appraisal system, in recognition of her efforts rather than her performance in the changed job, or, alternatively, to try and negotiate a job re-evaluation first, with the risk that Pauline will become demotivated.

Steve needs to consider the effects of an unfairly favourable appraisal grading on the other staff. There are good reasons to believe that, while it might let him off the hook immediately, it would have bad long term repercussions, as it would send the wrong signals to Pauline about her current performance. Next year, for example, if her performance had not improved, he would have to downgrade her.

He will have to try and persuade Pauline of the complexities of the situation.

Pauline is obviously strongly motivated by money. Steve has to give some guarantee that her efforts will be recognised. While a low pay rise may be a negative hygiene factor, Steve should try and invoke motivator factors to counterbalance this effect.

Steve can promise Pauline that the job will be re-evaluated. This might be a long term objective. He can promise Pauline that he will be supportive in the re-evaluation exercise, and involve her in any input to it.

Steve can also suggest new targets for Pauline to achieve in her changed job, to give her something to aim for. This might still motivate her, providing Steve can explain to her the slightly difficult situation he is in.

He might give her formal recognition of her status, and allow her more autonomy in planning her work, if she is sufficiently competent.

Obviously he cannot guarantee the result of the job evaluation system, but he can make some effort to solve the problem.

8 NEW APPROACHES TO APPRAISAL

Improving the system

8.1 The appraisal scheme should itself be assessed (and regularly re-assessed) according to the following general criteria for evaluating appraisal schemes.

Criteria	Comment
Relevance	• Does the system have a useful purpose, relevant to the needs of the organisation and the individual?
	• Is the purpose clearly expressed and widely understood by all concerned, both appraisers and appraisees?
	• Are the appraisal criteria relevant to the purposes of the system?
Fairness	• Is there reasonable standardisation of criteria and objectivity throughout the organisation?
	• Is it reasonably objective?
Serious intent	• Are the managers concerned committed to the system - or is it just something the personnel department thrusts upon them?
	• Who does the interviewing, and are they properly trained in interviewing and assessment techniques?
	• Is reasonable time and attention given to the interviews - or is it a question of 'getting them over with'?
	• Is there a genuine demonstrable link between performance and reward or opportunity for development?

Criteria	Comment
Co-operation	• Is the appraisal a participative, problem-solving activity - or a tool of management control? • Is the appraisee given time and encouragement to prepare for the appraisal, so that he can make a constructive contribution? • Does a jointly-agreed, concrete conclusion emerge from the process? • Are appraisals held regularly?
Efficiency	• Does the system seem overly time-consuming compared to the value of its outcome? • Is it difficult and costly to administer?

Upward appraisal

8.2   A notable modern trend, adopted in the UK by companies such as BP and British Airways, is **upward appraisal**, whereby employees are not rated by their superiors but by their subordinates. The followers appraise the leader.

8.3   **Advantages of upward appraisal**

(a)   Subordinates tend to know their superior better than superiors know their subordinates.

(b)   As all subordinates rate their managers statistically, these ratings tend to be more reliable - the more subordinates the better. Instead of the biases of individual managers' ratings, the various ratings of the employees can be converted into a representative view.

(c)   Subordinates' ratings have more impact because it is more unusual to receive ratings from subordinates. It is also surprising to bosses because, despite protestations to the contrary, information often flows down organisations more smoothly and comfortably than it flows up. When it flows up it is qualitatively and quantitatively different. It is this difference that makes it valuable.

8.4   **Problems** with the method include fear of reprisals, vindictiveness, and extra form processing. Some bosses in strong positions might refuse to act, even if a consensus of staff suggested that they should change their ways.

Customer appraisal

8.5   In some companies part of the employee's appraisal process must take the form of **feedback from 'customers' (whether internal or external).** This may be taken further into an influence on remuneration (at Rank-Xerox, 30% of a manager's annual bonus is conditional upon satisfactory levels of 'customer' feedback). This is a valuable development in that customers are the best judges of customer service, which the appraisee's boss may not see.

360 degree appraisal

8.6   Taking downwards, upwards and customer appraisals together, some firms have instituted **360 degree appraisal** (or multi-source appraisal) by collecting feedback on an individual's performance from the following sources.

(a)   The person's immediate boss

BPP
PUBLISHING

(b) People or groups of people who report to the appraisee

(c) Peers (co-workers): They can offer useful feedback.

(d) Customers (internal and external)

(e) The manager personally by self-appraisal

8.7 Sometimes the appraisal results in a counselling session, especially when the result of the appraisals are conflicting. For example, an appraisee's boss may have a quite different view of the appraisee's skills than subordinates do.

Case example

W H Smith (reported by Mike Thatcher, *People Management*, 21 March 1996), decided to supplement their existing upwards appraisal system (introduced 1990), covering 1,200 managers, with 360 degree appraisal. The personnel function was chosen.

'Between eight and fifteen people filled in forms covering each manager's competences and personal objectives. The appraisers were asked to rate them on a scale of one to five and give anecdotal examples to support the marks. The forms were sent to an independent third party for collating.

Ainley is pleased with the results, which have sharpened the developmental aspects of W H Smiths standard appraisal meetings. But there have been problems: a minimum of eight people commenting on 15 managers means at least 120 forms - a significant increase in administration; many appraisers found it difficult to comment on the individual manager's objectives; and there was a reluctance to back up ratings with anecdotal comments.

The second trial involving senior IT managers has just finished and the results are currently being evaluated. This time, the processing has been done in house to save costs, whilst a computerised system is being developed to cut down on the bureaucracy.

Ainley is now considering extending 360 degree appraisal to the rest of the organisation.'

9 HOW EFFECTIVE IS THE APPRAISAL SCHEME?

9.1 A survey by Saville and Holdsworth (cited by Mike Thatcher in *People Management*, 21 March 1996) indicated the mixed success of appraisal schemes in meeting objectives.

%	Very good/good	Adequate	Poor/very poor
Review past performance	84	12	3
Set individual objectives	76	19	5
Improve current performance	64	32	4
Determine one-off bonus	63	26	10
Identify training and development needs	64	32	4
Motivate staff	52	25	23
Set group goals	46	46	8
Assist career or succession	38	28	34
Determine salary rise	36	27	36
Assess potential	33	37	30

9.2 Evaluating the appraisal scheme can involve the following.

(a) Asking appraisers and appraisees what they felt.

(b) Checking to see if there have been enhancements in performance by the individual and the organisation.

(c) Reviewing other factors such as staff turnover. The appraisal scheme ought to pick up promotable people - if many talented people leave on the grounds that there are no job opportunities the overall scheme of development may be at fault.

9.3   However, firms should not expect too much of the appraisal scheme. Appraisal systems, because they target the individual's performance, concentrate on the **lowest level of performance feedback**. They ignore the organisational and systems context of that performance. (For example, if an army is badly led, no matter how brave the troops, it will be defeated.) Appraisal schemes would seem to regard most **organisation problems** as a function of the **personal characteristics** of its members, rather than the **problem** of its overall design.

Chapter roundup

- **Appraisal** is part of the system of **performance management**.

- The main difference in emphasis is that appraisals are **backward** looking, whereas performance management as a whole looks to the **future**.

- Appraisal can be used to **reward** but also to identify **potential**.

- Three **basic problems** are defining what is to be appraised, recording assessments, and getting the appraiser and appraisee together.

- A variety of appraisal **techniques** can be used.

- Normally a **report** is written - but both manager and appraisee can contribute to the process, hence the value of self-appraisal.

- **Problems** with appraisal are its implementation in practice and the fact that it ignores, by and large, the context of performance.

- **New techniques** of appraisal aim to monitor the appraisee's effectiveness from a number of perspectives.

Quick quiz

1   What are the purposes of appraisal?

2   What bases or criteria of assessment might an appraisal system use?

3   Outline a results-oriented approach to appraisal, and its advantages.

4   What is a 360-degree feedback, and who might be involved?

5   What is upward appraisal?

6   What follow-up should there be after an appraisal?

7   How can appraisals be made more positive and empowering to employees?

8   What kinds of criticism might be levelled at appraisal schemes by a manager who thought they were a waste of time?

9   What is the difference between performance appraisal and performance management?

10   What techniques might be used to measure an employee's potential to become a successful senior manager?

BPP PUBLISHING

Answers to quick quiz

1   Identifying performance levels, improvements needed and promotion prospects; deciding on rewards; assessing team work and encouraging communication between manager and employee.

2   Job analysis, job description, plans, targets and standards.

3   Performance against specific mutually agreed targets and standards.

4   Refer to paragraph 8.6

5   Subordinates appraise superiors.

6   Appraisees should be informed of the results, agreed activity should be taken, progress should be monitored and whatever resources or changes are needed should be provided or implemented.

7   Ensure the scheme is relevant, fair, taken seriously, and co-operative.

8   The manager may say that he has better things to do with his time, that appraisals have no relevance to the job and there is no reliable follow-up action, and that they involve too much paperwork.

9   Appraisal *on its own* is a backward-looking performance review. But it is a vital input into performance management, which is forward-looking.

10 Key indicators of performance should be determined and the employee should be assessed against them. The employee could be placed in positions simulating the responsibilities of senior management.

Now try the question below from the Exam Question Bank

Question to try	Level	Marks	Time
11	Exam	15	27 mins
16	Exam	40 (scenario)	72 mins

Chapter 12

THE MANAGEMENT OF HEALTH AND SAFETY

Topic list	Syllabus reference
1 Health and safety	3(h)
2 Accidents and other hazards	3(h)

Introduction

In the ACCA syllabus, health and safety is included under training and development. However, it would be a mistake to see it exclusively as a training matter. All managers, and indeed all staff, have a direct responsibility for health and safety. This is particularly the case in developed countries, where there is usually extensive legislation on the matter.

Study guide

Section 22(h) – The management of health and safety

- Preventative and protective measures

- Safety awareness and training

- Working conditions and hazards

- The legal context and the obligation of management

Exam guide

The management of health and safety is perhaps most likely to be examined as a factual question in Section B. A knowledge of the various legal requirements could be quite important.

1 HEALTH AND SAFETY

Surely health and safety precautions are obvious?

1.1 In 1972, the Royal Commission on Safety and Health at Work reported that unnecessarily large numbers of days were being lost each year through industrial accidents, injuries and diseases, because of the 'attitudes, capabilities and performance of people and the efficiency of the organisational systems within which they work'.

1.2 Since 1972, **major legislation** has been brought into effect in the UK, most notably the Health and Safety at Work Act 1974, plus Regulations and Codes of Practice under the Act, which implement the provisions of six EU directives on health and safety issues: the Management of Health and Safety at Work Regulations 1992.

1.3   Since 1972, there have been several stimuli causing society as a whole to become more aware of health and safety.

    (a)   Legislation requiring health warnings and descriptions of contents of goods

    (b)   The raising of issues such as unsafe toys, food labelling, flammable materials in furniture, and asbestos poisoning

    (c)   Experience of notorious disasters in factories, railway stations and so on

    (d)   Improvements in the general quality of life and environments.

1.4   However, it would be wrong to paint too optimistic a picture of employers' performance on health and safety.

    (a)   **Legislation sets bare minimum standards** for (and levels of commitment to) health and safety. ('The law is a floor'). It does not represent satisfactory - let alone best - practice for socially responsible organisations.

    (b)   Health and safety are still regarded with a negative attitude by many managers. Provisions are costly, and have no immediately quantifiable benefit.

    (c)   Positive discipline (setting mechanisms and systems which theoretically prevent hazardous behaviour) only goes so far, and irresponsible or ignorant behaviour can still cause accidents.

    (d)   New health and safety concerns are constantly emerging, as old ones are eradicated.

        (i)   New technology and ergonomics may make physical labour less stressful, but it creates new hazards and health risks, such as a sedentary, isolated lifestyle, and problems associated with working long hours at VDUs or shift working.

        (ii)   New issues in health are constantly arising, such as passive smoking in the workplace or alcohol abuse, with the increasing stress of work in highly competitive sectors.

Question 1

How many notorious workplace disasters can you think of? What were the main costs to the organisations concerned?

Answer

You may have thought of the Bhopal chemical plant explosion, Chernobyl reactor explosion, Kings Cross station fire, Piper Alpha oil rig disaster, various bombings by terrorist groups, and so on. The main costs are reconstruction, compensation for death and injury, lost production, and loss of reputation.

The Health and Safety at Work Act (HWSA) 1974

1.5   In the UK, the Health and Safety at Work Act 1974 provides for the introduction of a system of approved codes of practice, prepared in consultation with industry, so that an employee, whatever his employment, should find that his work is covered by an appropriate code of practice. The codes have a legal status but are not statutory in the sense that they must be followed. They are more like the Highway Code, in the sense that in a road accident, failure to obey the Highway Code would be evidence of failure in the driver's duty of care, and so open the driver to prosecution and awards for damages.

1.6   Employers' duties under the 1974 HSWA.

(a) All systems (work practices) must be safe.

(b) The work environment must be safe and healthy (well-lit, warm, ventilated and hygienic).

(c) All plant and equipment must be kept up to the necessary standard (with guards on machines and so on).

In addition, information, instruction, training and supervision should be directed towards safe working practices, and the safety policy should be clearly communicated to all staff.

1.7 Employee duties

- To take reasonable care of himself and others
- To allow the employer to carry out his duties (including enforcing safety rules)
- Not to interfere intentionally or recklessly with any machinery or equipment

Safety Representative Regulations 1978

1.8 The Safety Representative Regulations provide for safety representatives to be appointed by a recognised trade union, and for Safety Committees to be set up at the request of employee representatives, to monitor safety measures and to assist (or 'police') the employer in providing a healthy and safe place of work.

1.9 The employer must:

(a) Produce a **written statement of safety measures** and the means used to implement them and bring this statement to the notice of employees (only an employer who has less than five employees is exempt from this requirement)

(b) **Consult with safety representatives** appointed by recognised trade unions with a view to the effective maintenance of adequate safety measures

(c) Appoint a **safety committee** if requested to do so by the safety representatives, to keep safety measures under review

An employer may not make any charge to his employees for the cost of safety measures or equipment which it is his legal duty to take or provide.

Question 2

What aspects of your studying environment (if any) do you think are:

- A hindrance to your work?
- A source of dissatisfaction?
- A hazard to your health and/or safety?

EU directives

1.10 In 1989 and 1990 the European Council of Ministers agreed to a framework directive on health and safety, together with five other directives.

- Health and safety requirements for the workplace

- Safety and health requirements for the use of work equipment at work

- The use of personal protective equipment

- The manual handling of loads where there is a risk, particularly of back injury to workers

- Health and safety requirements for work with display screen equipment

1.11 The EU directives were implemented on 31 December 1992. In fact, most of the matters addressed by the directives were already covered to some extent by existing UK legislation and regulations, in particular the Health and Safety at Work Act 1974, but the requirements of the display screen equipment directive were new. (These are discussed in more detail below.)

1.12 Under the EU directives **employers have the following additional general duties**.

(a) They must carry out risk assessment, generally in writing, of all work hazards. Assessment should be continuous.

(b) They must introduce controls to reduce risks.

(c) They must assess the risks to anyone else affected by their work activities.

(d) They must share hazard and risk information with other employers, including those on adjoining premises, other site occupiers and all subcontractors coming on to the premises.

(e) They should revise safety policies in the light of the above, or initiate safety policies if none were in place previously.

(f) They must identify employees who are especially at risk.

(g) They must provide fresh and appropriate training in safety matters.

(h) They must provide information to employees (including temps) about health and safety.

(i) They must employ competent health and safety advisers.

1.13 Employees also have an additional duty under the new regulations to inform their employer of any situation which may be a danger, although this does not reduce the employer's responsibilities in any way because his risk assessment programme should have spotted the hazard in any case.

The Workplace directive

1.14 The Workplace directive deals with matters that have been statutory requirements for many years in the UK under legislation such as the Offices, Shops and Railway Premises Act 1963, although in some cases the requirements have been more clearly defined. The following provisions are made.

(a) **Equipment**. All equipment should be properly maintained.

(b) **Ventilation**. Air should be fresh or purified.

(c) **Temperature**. The temperature must be 'reasonable' inside buildings during working hours. This means not less than 16° where people are sitting down, or 13° if they move about to do their work.

(d) **Lighting** should be suitable and sufficient, and natural, if practicable. Windows should be clean and unobstructed.

(e) **Cleaning and decoration**. Floors, walls, ceilings, furniture, furnishings and fittings must be kept clean.

(f) **Room dimensions and space.** Each person should have at least 11 cubic metres of space, ignoring any parts of rooms more than 3.1 metres above the floor or with a headroom of less than 2.0 metres.

(g) **Floors** must be properly constructed and maintained (without holes, not slippery, properly drained and so on).

(h) **Falls or falling objects.** These should be prevented by erecting effective physical safeguards (fences, safety nets, ground rails and so on).

(i) **Glazing.** Windows should be made of safe materials and if they are openable it should be possible to do this safely.

(j) **Traffic routes.** These should have regard to the safety of pedestrians and vehicles alike.

(k) **Doors and gates.** These should be suitably constructed and fitted with any necessary safety devices (especially sliding doors and powered doors and doors opening in either direction).

(l) **Escalators and travelators** should function safely and have readily accessible emergency stop devices.

(m) **Sanitary conveniences and washing facilities** must be suitable and sufficient. This means that they should be properly ventilated and lit, properly cleaned and separate for men and women. 'Sufficient' means that undue delay is avoided!

(n) **Drinking water.** An adequate supply should be available with suitable drinking vessels.

(o) **Clothing.** There should be suitable accommodation for outdoor clothing, which should be able to dry out if wet. Facilities for changing clothing should be available where appropriate.

(p) **Rest facilities and eating facilities.** These must be provided unless the employees' workstations are suitable for rest or eating, as is normally the case for offices.

Question 3

Reassess your answer to Question 2 in the light of these specific provisions!

Manual handling and protective equipment

1.15 The manual handling regulations are summarised below.

(a) The Manual Handling Operation Regulations will in the first instance require every employer, so far as is reasonably practicable, to avoid the need for his employees to undertake any manual handling activities which will involve the risk of their becoming injured.

(b) However, if the cost of avoiding such risk is unreasonable the employer will be required to carry out an assessment of all manual handling operations which are to be retained.

(c) Where the (compulsory) assessment reveals risk to employees, steps must be taken to reduce those risks to the lowest level reasonably practicable.

(d) Employees will have two duties under these regulations:

    (i) Make full and proper use of equipment and systems provided by the employer

    (ii) and to inform their employer of any injury or conditions which may affect their ability to safely undertake manual handling operations.

1.16 The regulations on protective equipment require employers to provide such equipment where necessary, maintain it properly, and provide training in its use. Employees have a duty to report defects.

Health and safety and workstations

1.17 If you have ever worked for a long period at a VDU you may personally have experienced some discomfort. Backache, eye strain and stiffness or muscular problems of the neck, shoulders, arms or hands are frequent complaints. The common, if somewhat inaccurate, term for this is Repetitive Strain Injury or RSI.

1.18 Although the Health and Safety Commission (HSC) issued helpful guidelines on working with VDUs some time ago, these did not have legal force, and employers had remained free to ignore the problem if they wished. However, the EU directive on workstations was implemented at the end of 1992.

1.19 **Main provisions of the directive**

(a) **VDUs** must not flicker, must be free from glare, and must swivel and tilt.

(b) **Keyboards** must tilt and must be free from glare; the workspace in front of them must be sufficient for the operators to rest their forearms.

(c) **Desks** must be free from glare; there must be enough space to allow flexible arrangement of all equipment and documents. Measurements are not specified.

(d) **Chairs**: the seat must be adjustable in height, and the back in height and angle; footrests must be made available if required.

(e) **Lighting**: there must be appropriate contrast between the screen and its background; windows must have some form of blinds.

(f) **Heat and humidity** levels must be adequate on the one hand and not uncomfortable on the other.

(g) **Radiation** must be reduced to negligible levels.

(h) **Breaks**: screen work must be 'periodically interrupted by breaks or changes in activity'.

(i) **Eyesight**: the employer must offer free eyesight testing at regular intervals and provide any special glasses that may be needed for screen work.

(j) **Consultation**: employees must be consulted about health and safety measures.

(k) **Training** in the proper use of equipment must be provided.

Health and safety in pregnancy

1.20 The EU directive on pregnancy and maternity (discussed in connection with maternity leave in Chapter 9) also tackled the issue of health and safety. Pregnant women, those who have recently given birth and those who are breastfeeding are recognised as special groups requiring protection. The provisions have been incorporated into UK law in the Management of Health and Safety at Work (Amendment) Regulations, 1994.

(a) **Every employer must undertake a risk assessment if the workforce includes women of child-bearing age (c.20-45),** and if the work is of a kind that could involve risk to women in any of the three categories mentioned above. All risks to health and safety must be taken into account, whether from processes, working conditions or physical, biological or chemical agents. (Risks already specifically mentioned in legislation, regulations and codes include working with lead, lifting objects, excessive use of VDUs, exposure to radiation, changes in air pressure and so on.) Heat, stress, exhaustion and mental stress are also potential hazards.

(b) **The work of pregnant women must be adjusted to remove the risk**. This may involve transferring night workers to day work, removing the need to lift heavy objects, or reducing travel in the job.

(c) If the work hours or conditions cannot be made safer, **alternative safer work** must be offered. This must be suitable for the woman and not substantially less favourable in terms and conditions.

(d) If no safer alternative work exists, the woman must be suspended on **full terms and conditions,** for the period of risk.

(e) The woman has the right to **refuse night work** on medical grounds.

1.21 These duties apply once the employer has been notified in writing that a woman is pregnant or falls into one of the other categories. The employee must, on request, product a certificate from a registered medical practitioner or midwife. Failure to identify and eliminate risks is a criminal offence under the Act, and is also a failure of the general duty to provide a safe system of work, opening the employer to various statutory claims for damages.

2   ACCIDENTS AND OTHER HAZARDS

2.1 Apart from obviously dangerous equipment in offices, there are many hazards to be found in the modern working environment. Many accidents could be avoided by the simple application of common sense and consideration by employer and employee; and by safety consciousness encouraged or enforced by a widely acceptable and well-publicised safety policy.

2.2 **Common causes of injury**

- Slippery or poorly maintained floors
- Frayed carpets
- Trailing electric leads
- Obstacles in gangways
- Standing on chairs (particularly swivel chairs) to reach high shelving
- Staircases used as storage facilities
- Lifting heavy items without bending properly
- Removing the safety guard on a machine to free a blockage

The cost of accidents

2.3 The costs of accidents to the employer are significant.

- **Time lost** by the injured **employee**

- **Time lost by other employees** who choose to, or must of necessity, stop work at the time of or following the accident

- **Time lost by supervision,** management and technical staff following the accident

- A proportion of the **cost of first aid materials, or even medical staff**

- The cost of **disruption to operations** at work

- The cost of any damage to the equipment or any cost associated with the subsequent modification of the equipment

- The costs associated with increased **insurance premiums**

- **Reduced output** from the injured employee on return to work

- The cost of possible **reduced morale,** increased absenteeism, increased labour turnover among employees

- The cost of recruiting and training a replacement for the injured worker.

2.4 Although the injured employee's damages may be reduced if his injury was partly a consequence of his own contributory **negligence,** due allowance is made for ordinary human failings.

(a) An employee is **not deemed to consent to the risk of injury because he is aware of the risk.** It is the employer's duty to provide a safe working system.

(b) Employees can become inattentive or careless in doing **work which is monotonous** or imposes stress. This factor too must be allowed for in the employer's safety precautions.

(c) It is not always a sufficient defence that the employer provided safety equipment and rules: the employer has some duty to encourage if not to insist on its proper use.

(d) Many dangers can be **caused by carelessness** or other fault of an otherwise competent employee, possibly by mere thoughtlessness. It is the employer's duty to be watchful and to keep such tendencies in check.

(e) **Employees do not work continuously.** The employer's duty is to take reasonable care for their safety in all acts which are normally and reasonably incidental to the day's work.

Question 4

If a person went to wash a tea-cup after use, at his or her office, and slipped on a slippery surface in the kitchen and was injured, who would be at fault?

Answer

This was a real case. It was held that the employee's injury had occurred in the course of her work, and that the employer had failed in his duty to take reasonable care to provide safe premises.

Preventive action

2.5 The prevention of accidents requires efforts on the part of employees and management, including those responsible for the design of the operating system and its staffing. Some of the steps, which might be taken to reduce the frequency and severity of accidents are:

(a) Developing a **safety consciousness** among staff and workers and encouraging departmental pride in a good safety record

(b) Developing effective **consultative participation** between management, workers and unions so that safety and health rules can be accepted and followed

(c) Giving **adequate instruction in safety rules** and measures as part of the training of new and transferred workers, or where working methods or speeds of operation are changed

(d) **Materials handling**, a major cause of accidents, to be **minimised** and designed as far as possible for safe working and operation

(e) Ensuring a **satisfactory standard** from the safety angle for both basic plant and auxiliary fittings such a guards and other devices

(f) **Good maintenance** - apart from making sound job repairs, temporary expedients to keep production going should not prejudice safety.

2.6 In general, the appropriate code of practice for the industry/work environment should be implemented in full.

Factories Act 1961

2.7 The 1961 Act applies only to a factory, defined as a place where manufacturing or processing work is done for the purposes of gain, and where the main purpose of the premises involves manual labour. This includes buildings ancillary to a place of manufacture and also a slaughterhouse, a laundry, a shipyard, a film set and premises where packing takes place (among other specified categories).

2.8 The occupier of a factory has an absolute duty to fence securely all prime movers (machines which provide power), all transmission machinery and every dangerous part of any machinery. Machinery is dangerous if it can be reasonably foreseen that injury to any person can occur in the ordinary course of use.

(a) It is no defence to show that there is no practicable means of fencing the machine. If it cannot be used when adequately fenced, then it should not be used at all.

(b) The fencing should be substantial and kept in position at all times when the machine is in motion, although not when it is being examined or lubricated.

(c) It is only the dangerous parts which need to be fenced. If that is done there is no duty to fence the rest of the machine.

(d) A fence is sufficiently secure even though it does not prevent reckless employees from circumventing it.

Investigation and report of accidents

2.9 Safety inspections should be carried out to locate and define faults in the system that allow accidents to occur. They may be carried out as a comprehensive audit, working through a checklist, or by using random spot checks, regular checks of particular risk points or statutory inspections of particular areas, such as lifts, hoists, boilers or pipelines.

2.10 It is essential that checklists used in the inspection process should identify corrective action to be taken, and allocate responsibility for that action. There should be reporting systems and control procedures to ensure that inspections are taking place and that findings are being acted on.

2.11 Accident-reporting systems will be particularly important, but it must be emphasised to staff that the report is not an exercise in itself but a management tool, designed to:

* Identify problems
* Indicate corrective action.

2.12   Statistical trends should be monitored to reveal areas where recurring accidents suggest the need for special investigation, but only more serious incidents will have to be followed-up in depth. Follow-up should be clearly aimed at preventing recurrence - not placing blame.

2.13   The general regulations relating to fire, contained in the Offices, Shops and Railway Premises Act 1963, were reinforced in the Fire Precautions Act 1971 and the Fire and Safety at Sports Places Act 1987.

(a)   There must be adequate means of escape kept free from obstructions.

(b)   All doors out of the building must be capable of opening from the inside.

(c)   All employees should know the fire alarm system.

(d)   There must be an effective and regularly tested fire alarm system.

(e)   There must be fire-fighting equipment easily available and in working order.

2.14   **Fire represents a further area for preventive action**. The main causes of fire in industry and commerce tend to be associated with electrical appliances and installations, and smoking is a major source of fires in business premises. The Fire Protection Association (of the UK) suggests the following guidelines for fire prevention and control.

(a)   Management should accept that fire prevention policies and practices must be established and reviewed regularly.

(b)   Management should be aware of the possible effects and consequences of fires, in terms of loss of buildings, plant and output, damage to records, effects on customers and workers, etc.

(c)   Fire risks should be identified, particularly as regards sources of ignition, presence of combustible materials, and the means by which fires can spread.

(d)   The responsibility for fire prevention should be established.

(e)   A fire officer should be appointed.

(f)   A fire evacuation drill should be established and practised.

Stress

KEY TERM

Stress is a term which is often loosely used to describe feelings of tension of exhaustion - usually associated with too much, or overly-demanding, work. In fact, stress is the product of demands made on an individual's physical and mental energies: monotony and feelings of failure or insecurity are sources of stress, as much as the conventionally considered factors of pressure, overwork and so on.

2.15   It is worth remembering, too, that demands on an individual's energies may be stimulating as well as harmful: many people, especially those suited to managerial jobs, work well under pressure, and even require some form of stress to bring out their best performance.

2.16   Harmful stress, or strain, can be identified by its effects on the individual and his performance.

(a)   **Nervous tension**. This may manifest itself in various ways: irritability and increased sensitivity, preoccupation with details, a polarised perspective on the issues at hand, or sleeplessness. Various physical symptoms - such as skin and digestive disorders - are also believed to be stress-related.

(b) **Withdrawal**. This is essentially a defence mechanism which may manifest itself as unusual quietness and reluctance to communicate, or as physical withdrawal in the form of absenteeism, poor time-keeping, or even leaving the organisation.

(c) **Low morale**: low confidence, dissatisfaction, expression of frustration or hopelessness.

(d) Signs that the individual is repressing the problem, trying to deny it. Forced cheerfulness, boisterous playfulness or excessive drinking may indicate this.

2.17 Some of these symptoms - say, absenteeism - may or may not be **correctly identified with stress**. There are many **other possible causes of such problems**, both at work (lack of motivation) and outside (personal problems). The same is true of physical symptoms such as headaches and stomach pains: these are not invariably correlated with personal stress.

2.18 All these things can adversely affect performance, however, which is why stress management has become a major workplace issue. Considerable research effort has been directed to:

- Investigating the causes of stress
- Increasing awareness of stress in organisations
- Designing techniques and programmes for stress control

2.19 **Causes or aggravators of stress**

Cause	Comment
Personality	Competitive, sensitive and insecure people feel stress more acutely.
Ambiguity or conflict in the roles required of an individual	If a person is unsure what is expected of him at work, or finds conflict between two incompatible roles (employee and mother of small children, say), role stress may be a problem.
Insecurity, risk and change	A manager with a high sense of responsibility who has to initiate a risky change, and most people facing career change, end or uncertainty, will feel this kind of stress.
Management style	A recent American report pointed out particular management traits that were held responsible by workshop interviewees for causing stress and health problems (high blood pressure, insomnia, coronary heart disease and alcoholism). • Unpredictability - constant threat of an outburst • Destruction of workers' self esteem - making them feel helpless and insecure • Setting up win/lose situations - turning work relationships into a battle for control • **Providing too much** - or too little - stimulation

Question 5

What sources of stress are there in your own lifestyle? Are you aware of the symptoms of stress in yourself? What do you do (if anything) to control your stress?

Answer

You may have spotted the following hazards (if not others as well...)

(a) Heavy object on high (secure?) shelf
(b) Standing on swivel chair
(c) Lifting heavy object incorrectly
(d) Open drawers blocking passage
(e) Trailing wires
(f) Electric bar fire
(g) Unattended lit cigarette - passive smoking AND fire hazard
(h) Overfull waste bin
(i) Overloaded electric socket
(j) Overloaded tray of hot liquids
(k) Dangerous spike

2.20 Greater awareness of the nature and control of stress is a feature of the modern work environment. Stress management techniques are increasingly taught and encouraged by organisations, and include the following.

- Counselling
- Time off or regular rest breaks
- Relaxation techniques (breathing exercises, meditation)
- Physical exercise and self-expression as a safety valve for tension
- Delegation and planning (to avoid work-load related stress)
- Assertiveness (to control stress related to insecurity in personal relations)

2.21 In addition, **job training** can increase the individual's sense of competence and security and ecological control can be brought to bear on the problem of stress, creating conditions in which stress is less likely to be a problem: well-designed jobs and environments, and an organisation culture built on meaningful work, mutual support, communication and teamwork.

> A survey conducted by the Industrial Society in 1996 revealed that, while 53 per cent of respondents agreed that stress had increased, 76 per cent admitted that it had never been measured in their organisation. Similarly, 76 per cent thought that absenteeism was the most damaging effect of stress, while only 7 per cent reported that they measured the amount of absence cased by stress. It seems that many of us - HR managers and employees alike - simply assume that stress levels are high and have detrimental effects on people's wellbeing and performance.
>
> But what are organisations actually doing about stress - and is it working? We need first to clarify what counts as stress management intervention (SMI), because we cannot simply label any health-related practice as such. A broadly accepted definition of SMI is any activity that aims to do one or more of the following: reduce exposure to psychologically harmful working conditions; and treat people who have been harmed in some way by work.
>
> This may seem a narrow definition, but providing gymnasium facilities, salads in the canteen or advice about quitting smoking do not seem to be to constitute stress management. While these may well make employees feel better, they are not aimed at tackling either the causes or effects of work stress.
>
> People Management, 30 September 1999

Sick Building Syndrome (SBS)

2.22 SBS is an illness (comparatively recently identified) associated with the workplace. Symptoms include lethargy, stuffy nose, dry throat, headache and itching eyes: once away from the workplace, staff are free from these problems. Factors in the workplace suspected to contribute to SBS include air-conditioning, and open-plan office space where there is perceived to be little control over the indoor environment. A report by the Health and Safety Executive (HSE) (reported in *Personnel Management*, September 1992) found that 30-50% of new or refurbished buildings may affect people in this way, but that the causes (and therefore the cure) are uncertain.

Passive smoking

2.23 Following a 1992 Australian court case in which an employer was held to have been negligent in not protecting a non-smoking employee from the ill-effects of exposure to colleagues' smoking, smoking policies have rapidly been introduced by many organisations.

2.24 One report suggests that 'The risks of passive smoking are greater than these posed by any other indoor man-made pollutant released into the general environment'. A recent Health Education Authority campaign has called for environmental tobacco smoke to be added to the list of substances which can be controlled in the workplace under the Control of Substances Hazardous to Health (COSHH) Regulations.

2.25 Amid the publication of conclusive scientific evidence as to the harmful effects, of smoking and the publicity surrounding it (including advice on segregation of smokers and nonsmokers from the HSE), there is considerable pressure on employers to act. It is no longer possible for an employer to plead ignorance of the risks as a defence against civil action by an employee whose health has been damaged by passive smoking at work. However, the only current legal requirement is that non-smokers shall not suffer discomfort from smoking in rest areas.

2.26 The options for a smoking policy were identified as a total smoking ban, or the provision of separate smoking rooms.

Case example

Chase Manhattan introduced a smoking policy in its Bournemouth headquarters. The policy was devised by a working party (including a consultant) with the agreed aims: 'To introduce a smoking policy which would:

(a)   Recognise the employer's obligations to its employees regarding health and safety

(b)   Improve the working environment at Chase Manhattan with regard to general cleanliness etc

(c)   Best attempt to respect the wishes of smokers.'

After communication and consultation, it was decided to make the office a non-smoking site with designated smoking areas (which were designed to be well-ventilated and pleasant, but away from areas of public circulation). A policy statement was inserted in the staff handbook, and given to all potential recruits: breach of smoking regulations was to be considered a matter for disciplinary action. Details of assistance were given for those smokers who wished to give up, but there was no pressure on people to change their behaviour - other than its location.

Chase Manhattan have found that the necessity for smoking breaks has not caused a significant drop in performance. The working environment is considered cleaner and more pleasant. Health hazard awareness has risen. Initial worries - about alienating smokers, handling the need for smoking breaks, fire hazards and so on - were overcome by systematic consultation and briefing.

2.27 In December 1998, the Government published a white paper called 'Smoking Kills'. As part of the consultation process, the Health and Safety Commission is sounding opinion on whether to introduce an Approved Code of Practice on passive smoking.

Alcohol policy

2.28 Alcoholism and alcohol awareness is a major and growing issue. (As far back as 1981, the Government suggested the need for an agreed policy on alcohol, in its booklet The Problem Drinker at Work). Recent research suggests that 70% of organisations in the UK had formal or informal policies on alcohol.

2.29 Reasons given for introducing an alcohol policy.

- The introduction of a wider programme of health promotion and awareness
- Health and safety concerns
- Concerns about inefficiency caused by alcohol misuse

2.30 Most alcohol policies embrace the following areas.

(a) **Positive aims** and objectives - including statistics on alcohol-related harm.

(b) **Restrictions on alcohol** possession or consumption.

    (i) A total ban on alcohol consumption on company premises

    (ii) A total ban on alcohol consumption on and off (eg in company cars) the premises during working hours

    (iii) Restriction of alcohol consumption to certain areas of the premises (say, visitors' dining rooms or a licensed canteen) and/or hours

    (iv) Selective restrictions on certain employees - usually for health and safety reasons

    (v) Specific provisions for workplace social events

Question 7

What categories of employees would you think it advisable to ban from drinking at or before work?

Answer

The two most common categories are those involving driving and operating heavy or dangerous machinery

Chapter roundup

- Legislation is not designed to represent best practice but offers a floor below which standards of conduct cannot drop, for the protection of employees.

- Health and safety legislation requires that the systems, environment, equipment and conduct of organisations be such as to minimise the risk to the health and safety of employees and visitors alike.

- Employees share responsibility for health and safety with employers, although the latter take responsibility for the environment, systems, equipment and training.

Systematic approach to health and safety

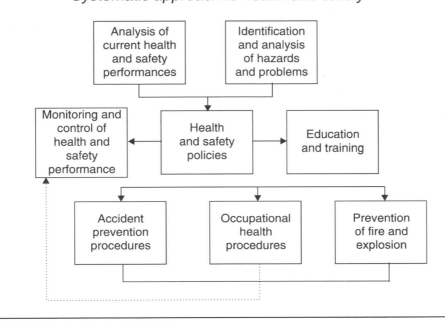

Quick quiz

1   What are employees' legal duties in respect of health and safety?

2   What areas of health and safety are covered by EU directives?

3   What three categories of female employees have special protection under new Health and Safety at Work regulations?

4   List some of the symptoms of stress.

5   List the elements of an alcohol policy at work.

BPP PUBLISHING

Answers to quick quiz

1   To take reasonable care of themselves and of others. To allow the employer to discharge his duties. Not to interfere with any machinery or equipment.

2   Framework
    Workplace
    Work equipment
    Personal protective equipment
    Manual handling
    Display screen equipment

3   Women who are pregnant, who have recently given birth or who are breastfeeding.

4   Tension, withdrawal, low morale, repression

5   Restrictions on possession or consumption; relationship between policy and disciplinary procedures; role of managers in implementing policy; counselling services.

Now try the question below from the Exam Question Bank

Question to try	Level	Marks	Time
12	Tutorial	5	9 mins

Part D

Motivation and leadership

Chapter 13

MOTIVATION AT WORK

Topic list	Syllabus reference
1 Needs and goals	4(a)
2 Theories of motivation	4(a)
3 Rewards and incentives	4(a)
4 Pay as a motivator	4(a)

Introduction

Human behaviour can be a complex phenomenon. It is important for managers that they have some knowledge and appreciation of the factors that produce specific behaviour. This is particularly important in the context of promoting high quality work performance. There has been considerable academic research into and practical observation of the processes of motivation.

Study guide

Section 2(b) – The role of management

- List the systems of performance reward for individual and group contribution

Section 2(b) – Team management

- Examine ways of rewarding a team

Section 23(a) – Motivation, concepts, models and practices

- Covered in its entirety; see the front of the text for full details

Exam guide

Motivation is likely to appear regularly in the exam since it is an essential aspect of managerial responsibility. Since there is a large body of academic work, you must be prepared to outline theories and quote authorities. Motivation is likely to be examined in the context of a scenario.

1   NEEDS AND GOALS

Needs

1.1   Individual behaviour is partly influenced by human biology, which requires certain basics for life. When the body is deprived of these essentials, biological forces called **needs** or **drives** are activated (eg hunger), and dictate the behaviour required to end the deprivation: each, drink, flee and so on. However, we retain freedom of choice about **how** we satisfy our drives: they do not dictate specific or highly predictable behaviour. (Say you are hungry: how many specific ways of satisfying your hunger can you think of?)

Goals

1.2 Each individual has a different set of goals. The relative importance of those goals to the individual may vary with time, circumstances and other factors including the following.

Influence	Comment
Childhood environment and education	Aspiration levels, family and career models and so on are formed at early stages of development
Experience	This teaches us what to expect from life: we will either strive to repeat positive experiences, or to avoid or make up for negative ones.
Age and position	There is usually a gradual process of goal shift with age. Relationships and exploration may preoccupy young employees. Career and family goals tend to conflict in the 20-40 age group: career launch and take-off may have to yield to the priorities associated with forming permanent relationships and having children.
Culture	Some studies suggest that Japanese goals show a greater concern than in Europe for relationships at work and a lesser preoccupation with power and autonomy.
Self-concept	All the above factors are bound up with the individual's own self-image. The individual's assessments of his own abilities and place in society will affect the relative strength and nature of his needs and goals.

1.3 You should now be able to identify some of the needs and goals that people might have, where they might come from and why the might change. So why are they relevant to a manager?

1.4 **The significance of personal goals**

(a) People behave in such a way as to **satisfy their needs and fulfil their goals**.

(b) An **organisation is in a position to offer some of the satisfactions** people might seek: relationships and belonging, challenge and achievement, progress on the way to self-actualisation, security and structure and so on.

(c) The **organisation can therefore influence people** to behave in ways it desires (to secure work performance) by **offering them the means to satisfy their needs** and fulfil their goals **in return for** that behaviour. This process of influence is called **motivation.**

(d) If people's needs are being met, and goals being fulfilled, at work, they are more likely to have a positive attitude to their work and to the organisation.

2 THEORIES OF MOTIVATION

KEY TERMS

Motivation is 'a decision-making process through which the individual chooses the desired outcomes and sets in motion the behaviour appropriate to acquiring them'. (Huczynski and Buchanan).

Motives: 'learned influences on human behaviour that lead us to pursue particular goals because they are socially valued'. (Huczynski and Buchanan).

2.1 **Douglas MacGregor** suggested that managers in the USA tended to behave as though they subscribed to one of two opposing philosophies about people's attitudes to work: **Theory X** and **Theory Y**.

(a) **Theory X.** This is the theory that most people **dislike work and responsibility and will avoid both if possible.** Because of this, most people must be coerced, controlled, directed and/or threatened with punishment to get them to make an adequate effort. Managers who believe in this theory brandish the stick.

(b) **Theory Y. Physical and mental effort in work is as natural as play or rest.** The ordinary person does not inherently dislike work: according to the conditions it may be a source of satisfaction or punishment. At present the potentialities of the average person are not being fully used. A manager with this sort of attitude to his staff is likely to be a democratic, consultative type.

2.2 Both are rather crude simplifications, resting on assumptions as to how people are motivated.

2.3 **Chris Argyris** felt that the way that bureaucratic organisations were structured positively encouraged **psychological immaturity**, and suggested that management could encourage people to grow.

Immaturity	Maturity
Possivity	Activity
Dependence	Independence
Able to behave in few ways	Capable of belonging in many ways
Shallow interests	Deep interests
Short term perspective	Long-term perspective
Subordinate position	Superordinates position
Lack of self-awareness	Self awareness and control

(a) Argyris believed that people have strong needs to fulfil their potential (self-actualisation, see Maslow below) but that organisations hold them back.

(b) The greater the disparity between organisational needs and company needs, the greater the degree of demotivation.

(c) Organisations should therefore encourage people to grow.

2.4 We can develop this in two ways.

(a) Argyris perhaps takes a Theory Y view of people, but suggests that most organisations pursue a Theory X agenda.

(b) Argyris appears to suggest that **work** should bring psychological maturity, whereas this might be developed elsewhere in life.

Question 4

What factors in yourself or your organisation motivate you to:

(a) Turn up to work at all?
(b) Do an average day's work?
(c) 'Bust a gut' on a task or for a boss?

Motives

2.5 In practice the words **motives** and **motivation** are commonly used in different contexts to mean the following.

(a) **Goals or outcomes** that have become desirable for a particular individual. We say that money, power or friendship are motives for doing something.

(b) The **mental process of choosing desired outcomes,** deciding how to go about them (and whether the likelihood of success warrants the amount of effort that will be necessary) and **setting in motion** the required behaviours.

(c) The **social process** by which **other people motivate us** to behave in the ways they wish. Motivation in this sense usually applies to the attempts of organisations to get workers to put in more effort.

2.6 Many theories try to explain motivation and why and how people can be motivated. One classification is between content and process theories.

(a) **Content theories** ask the question: '**what** are the things that motivate people?'

They assume that human beings have a *set* of needs or desired outcomes. Maslow's hierarchy theory and Herzberg's two-factor theory, both discussed shortly, are two of the most important approaches of this type.

(b) **Process theories** ask the question: '**how** can people be motivated?'

They explore the process through which outcomes **become** desirable and are pursued by individuals. This approach assumes that people are able to select their goals and choose the paths towards them, by a conscious or unconscious process of calculation. Expectancy theory and Handy's 'motivation calculus', discussed soon, are theories of this type.

Content theories

Maslow's hierarchy of needs

2.7 Maslow described five needs, as in the diagram below, and put forward certain propositions about the motivating power of each need.

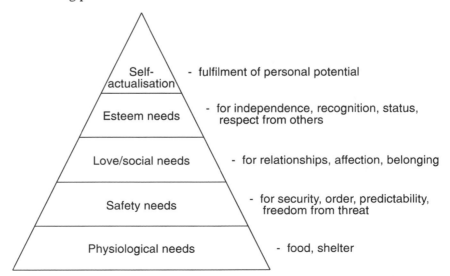

(a) Any individual's needs can be arranged in a '**hierarchy** of relative pre-potency'.

(b) Each level of need is **dominant until satisfied**; only then does the next level of need become a motivating factor.

(c) A need which has been satisfied no longer motivates an individual's behaviour. The need for self-actualisation can rarely be satisfied.

(d) In addition, Maslow described:

(i) Freedom of enquiry and expression needs (for social conditions permitting free speech, and encouraging justice, fairness and honesty)

(ii) Knowledge and understanding needs (to gain knowledge of the environment, to explore, learn).

Question 5

Decide which of Maslow's categories the following fit into.

(a) Receiving praise from your manager
(b) A family party
(c) An artist forgetting to eat
(d) A man washed up on a desert island
(e) A pay increase
(f) Joining a local drama group
(g) Being awarded the OBE
(h) Buying a house

Answer

Maslow's categories for the listed circumstances are as follows.

(a) Esteem needs
(b) Social needs
(c) Self-actualisation needs
(d) He will have physiological needs
(e) Safety needs initially; esteem needs above in a certain income level
(f) social needs or self-actualisation needs
(g) Esteem needs
(h) Safety needs or esteem needs

2.8 **Problems with Maslow's hierarchy**

(a) An individual's behaviour may be in response to **several needs**. Work, after all, can either satisfy or thwart the satisfaction of a number of needs.

(b) The **same need may cause different behaviour** in different individuals.

(c) It ignores the concept of **deferred gratification** by which people are prepared to ignore current suffering for the promise of future benefits.

(d) **Empirical verification is hard to come by.** In particular tests revealed it had a bias towards US and UK cultures.

McClelland

2.9 McClelland identified three rather different types of motivating need.

(a) **The need for power.** People with a high need for power usually seek positions in which they can influence and control others.

(b) **The need for affiliation.** People who need a sense of belonging and membership of a social group tend to be concerned with maintaining good personal relationships.

(c) **The need for achievement**. People who need to achieve have a strong desire for success and a strong fear of failure.

Herzberg's two-factor theory

2.10 **Herzberg's** two-factor theory identified **hygiene factors** and **motivator factors**.

(a) **Hygiene factors** are based on a **need to avoid unpleasantness.**

If inadequate, they cause **dissatisfaction** with work. They work analogously to sanitation, which minimises threats to health rather than actively promoting 'good health'. Unpleasantness demotivates: pleasantness is a steady state. Hygiene factors (the conditions of work) include:

- Company policy and administration
- Salary
- The quality of supervision
- Interpersonal relations
- Working conditions
- Job security

(b) **Motivator factors** are based on a **need for personal growth.**

They actively create job satisfaction and are effective in motivating an individual to superior performance and effort. These factors are:

- Status (this may be a hygiene factor too)
- Advancement
- Gaining recognition
- Responsibility
- Challenging work
- Achievement
- Growth in the job

A lack of motivators at work will encourage employees to concentrate on bad hygiene factors such as to demand more pay.

2.11 Herzberg suggested that where there is evidence of poor motivation, such as low productivity, poor quality and strikes, management should not pay too much attention to hygiene factors such as pay and conditions. Despite the fact that these are the traditional target for the aspirations of organised labour, their potential for bringing improvements to attitudes to work is limited. Instead, management should rearrange systems of work so that motivator factors could have effect. Herzberg suggested three ways in which this could be done.

- Job enlargement
- Job rotation
- Job enrichment

2.12 Herzberg's original study was concerned with 203 Pittsburgh engineers and accountants. His theory has therefore been criticised as relevant only to the relatively well educated middle-class.

Process theories

Expectancy theory

2.13 Expectancy theory (Victor Vroom) states that people will decide how much they are going to put into their work, according to two factors (Vroom, 1964)

(a) **Valence:** the value that they place on this outcome (whether the positive value of a reward, or the negative value of a punishment)

(b) **Expectancy:** the strength of their expectation that behaving in a certain way will in fact bring out the desired outcome.

Expectancy × Valence = Force of motivation

2.14 EXAMPLE: EXPECTANCY THEORY IN ACTION

This example illustrates the complexity of expectancy theory when applied to, say, the case of an insurance company sales representative who is male and in his 50s. For a given level of effort (E), he may perceive the possible outcomes as follows.

(a) A 75% chance of selling 17 policies in a week
(b) a 15% chance of selling 13 policies in a week
(c) A 10% chance of selling 30 policies in a week

There is 100% probability that this given level of effort (E) will produce the following effects.

(a) Exhaustion
(b) Sarcastic comments from his colleagues
(c) Aggravation to his sciatica

If he succeeds in selling 17 policies a week, the perceived outcomes will be as follows.

(a) Praise from his manager
(b) Accusations from colleagues about setting impossibly high standards
(c) Sufficient earnings (from commission) to buy a present for his wife

If he only sells 13 policies in the week, the perceived outcomes will be as follows.

(a) Criticism from his manager

(b) Tacit approval from colleagues

(c) A poor level of commission on earnings and income, leading to disapproval from his wife.

Selling 20 policies in a week will generate these perceived outcomes:

(a) Loud praise from his manager
(b) Extreme hostility from his colleagues
(c) Family expectations that income on this level will be sustained

The sales representative must assign a probability to each of these outcomes, eg a 75% probability that selling 17 policies will produce accusations from colleagues, and a 60% probability that selling 17 policies will produce praise from his manager.

Finally, the sales representative must attach a **valence** to each of the expected outcomes. Earning enough money to buy a present for his wife may have **high valence** for him; attracting the disapproval of colleagues may have **low valence.**

It can be seen from this (much simplified) example that trying to predict which choice will be made, in any given situation, becomes impossibly arduous.

Equity theory

2.15 'Equity theory focuses on people's feelings of how fairly they have been treated in comparison with the treatment received by others. It is based on exchange theory --- People expect certain outcomes in exchange for certain contributions ... when the ratio of a person's total outcomes to total inputs equals the *perceived* ratio of other people's total outcomes to total inputs, there is equity.'

Handy's motivation calculus

2.16 Charles Handy suggests that for any individual decision, there is a conscious or unconscious **motivation calculus** which is an assessment of three factors.

(a) The **individual's own set of needs**.

(b) The **desired results** - what the individual is expected to do in his job.

(c) **'E' factors** (effort, energy, excitement in achieving desired results, enthusiasm, emotion, and expenditure).

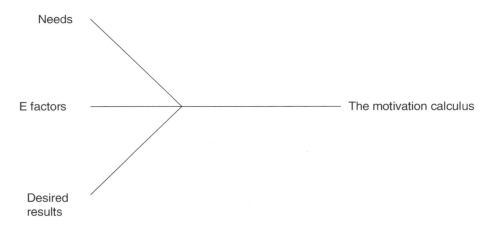

2.17 The **motivation decision** will depend on:

- The **strength of the individual's needs**
- The **expectancy** that expending 'E' will lead to a desired result
- How far the result will be **instrumental** in satisfying the individual's needs

2.18 **Consequences for management**

(a) **Intended results should be made clear,** so that the individual can complete the calculation by knowing **what is expected,** the **reward,** and **how much 'E'** it will take.

(b) Individuals are more committed to **specific goals** which they **have helped to set themselves**.

(c) **Feedback.** Without knowledge of **actual results,** there is no check that the 'E' expenditure was justified (and will be justified in future).

(d) If an individual is **rewarded** according to performance tied to standards (management by objectives), however, he or she may well set lower standards: the instrumentality part of the calculus (likelihood of success and reward) is greater if the standard is lower, so less expense of 'E' is indicated.

Motivation and performance

2.19 Motivation, from the manager's view, is the controlling of the work and the work environment, and the offering of rewards in such a way as to encourage extra performance from employees.

(a) Motivation is about getting *extra* levels of commitment and performance from employees, over and above mere compliance with rules and procedures. If individuals can be motivated, by one means or another, they might work more efficiently (and productivity will rise) or they will produce a better quality of work.

(b) The case for **job satisfaction** as a factor in improved performance is not proven.

(c) The key is to work 'smarter'.

2.20 Motivation can be a negative process (appealing to an individual's need to **avoid** unpleasantness, pain, fear etc) as well as a positive one (appealing to the individual's need to attain certain goals).

(a) **Negative motivation** is the threat of punishment.

(b) **Positive motivation** is dangling the carrot, and may be achieved in two ways.

    (i) The offer of extrinsic rewards, such as pay incentives, promotion, better working conditions etc

    (ii) Internal or psychological satisfaction for the individual (in the form of a sense of achievement, responsibility, being appreciated and so on.

Morale and team motivation

KEY TERM

Morale is a term drawn primarily from a military context, to denote the state of mind or spirit of a group, particularly regarding discipline and confidence. It can be related to satisfaction, since **low morale** implies a state of dissatisfaction.

Morale relates to how a group feels.

2.21 The signs by which morale is often gauged are by no means clear cut.

(a) **Low productivity** is not invariably a sign of low morale. In fact there may be **little correlation between morale and output**.

(b) **High labour turnover** is not a reliable indicator of low morale: the age structure of the workforce and other factors in natural wastage will need to be taken into account. Low turnover, likewise, is no evidence of high morale: people may be staying because of lack of other opportunities in the local job market, for example.

(c) There is some evidence that satisfaction correlates with mental health - so that symptoms of **stress or psychological failure** may be a signal to management that all is not well, although again, a range of non-work factors may be contributing.

(d) **Attitude surveys** may indicate workers' perception of their job satisfaction, by way of interview or questionnaire.

BPP PUBLISHING

3   REWARDS AND INCENTIVES

> ### KEY TERMS
>
> A **reward** is a token (monetary or otherwise) given to an individual or team in recognition of some contribution or success.
>
> An **incentive** is the offer or promise of a reward for contribution or success, designed to motivate the individual or team to behave in such a way as to earn it. (In other words, the 'carrot' dangled in front of the donkey!)

3.1   Not all the incentives that an organisation can offer its employees are directly related to **monetary** rewards. The satisfaction of **any** of the employee's wants or needs maybe seen as a reward for past of incentive for future performance.

3.2   **Different individuals have different goals,** and get different things out of their working life: in other words they have different **orientations** to work. There are any number of reasons why a person works, or is motivated to work well.

(a)   The **human relations** school of management theorists regarded **work relationships** as the main source of satisfaction and reward offered to the worker.

(b)   Later writers suggested a range of **higher** motivations, notably:

- **Job satisfaction**, interest and challenge in the job itself - rewarding work
- **Participation** in decision-making - responsibility and involvement

(c)   **Pay** has always occupied a rather ambiguous position, but since people need money to live, it will certainly be part of the reward package.

Intrinsic and extrinsic factors

3.3   **Rewards offered to the individual** at work

(a)   **Extrinsic rewards**

These are external to the individual, and given by others, such as wage or salary, bonuses and prizes, working conditions, a car, training opportunities.

(b)   **Intrinsic rewards**

There arises within individual: feelings of companionship, comfort, sense of achievement, enjoyment of status and recognition, interest in the job, responsibility, pride in the organisation's success and so on.

3.4   The system of rewards used in an organisation or in the department will depend on two things.

- The **assumptions the managers make** about their subordinates' working life
- The **employees' goals**

3.5   **Child** has outlined **management criteria for a reward system**. Such a system should do six things.

(a)   Encourage people to **fill job vacancies** and not leave.

(b)   Increase the **predictability of employees' behaviour**, so that employees can be depended on to carry out their duties consistently and to a reasonable standard.

(c) Increase **willingness to accept change** and flexibility. (Changes in work practices are often 'bought' from trade unions with higher pay.)

(d) Foster and **encourage innovative behaviour**.

(e) **Reflect the nature of jobs** in the organisation and the skills or experience required. The reward system should therefore be consistent with seniority of position in the organisation structure, and should be thought fair by all employees.

(f) **Motivate**, that is, increase commitment and effort.

The job as a motivator

3.6 The job itself can be used as a motivator, or it can be a cause of dissatisfaction.

3.7 One of the consequences of mass production was what might be called a micro-division of labour, or **job simplification**.

(a) **Little training**. A job is divided up into the smallest number of sequential tasks possible. Each task is so simple and straightforward that it can be learned with very little training.

(b) **Replacement**. If labour turnover is high, this does not matter because unskilled replacements can be found and trained to do the work in a very short time.

(c) **Flexibility**. Since the skill required is low, workers can be shifted from one task to another very easily. The production flow will therefore be unaffected by absenteeism.

(d) **Control**. If tasks are closely defined and standard times set for their completion, production is easier to predict and control.

(e) **Quality**. Standardisation of work into simple tasks means that quality is easier to predict. There is less scope for doing a task badly, in theory.

3.8 **Disadvantages**

(a) The work is **monotonous** and makes employees tired, bored and dissatisfied. The consequences will be high labour turnover, absenteeism, spoilage, unrest.

(b) **People work better** when their work is **variable**, unlike machines.

(c) An individual doing a simple task feels like a small cog in a large machine, and has no **sense of contributing to the organisation's end product** or service.

(d) Excessive specialisation **isolates** the individual in his or her work and inhibits not only social contacts with 'work mates', but knowledge generation.

(e) In practice, excessive job simplification leads to **lower quality, through inattention**.

3.9 Herzberg suggest three ways of improving job design, to make jobs more interesting to the employee, and hopefully to improve performance: job enrichment, job enlargement and job rotation.

Job enrichment

> **KEY TERM**
>
> **Job enrichment** is planned, deliberate action to build greater responsibility, breadth and challenge of work into a job. Job enrichment is similar to **empowerment** although the emphasis of job enrichment is on the individual rather than on the team.

3.10 A job may be enriched by:

(a) Giving the job holder **decision-making capabilities of a higher order**. What is, mundane detail at a high level can represent significant job interest at a lower level.

(b) Giving the **employee greater freedom** to decide how the job should be done.

(c) Encouraging employees **to participate** in the planning decisions of their superiors.

(d) Giving the employee regular **feedback**.

3.11 Job enrichment alone will not **automatically** make employees more productive. 'Even those who want their jobs enriched will expect to be rewarded with more than job satisfaction. Job enrichment is not a cheaper way to greater productivity. Its pay-off will come in the less visible costs of morale, climate and working relationships'. (Handy).

Job enlargement

> **KEY TERM**
>
> **Job enlargement** is the attempt to widen jobs by increasing the number of operations in which a job holder is involved.

3.12 By reducing the number of repetitions of the same work, the dullness of the job should also be reduced. Job enlargement is therefore a **horizontal extension** of an individual's work, whereas job enrichment is a vertical extension.

(a) Just by giving an employee tasks which span a larger part of the total production work should **reduce boredom**.

(b) Enlarged jobs can provide a **challenge and incentive**. For example, a trusted employee might be given added responsibilities, for example:

- **Checking the quality of output**
- **On the job training** of new recruits

(c) Enlarged jobs might also be regarded as having higher status within the department, and as stepping stones towards promotion.

Job rotation

3.13 **Job rotation** might take two forms.

(a) An employee might be **transferred to another job** after a period of, say, two to four years in an existing job, in order to give him or her a new interest and challenge, and to bring a fresh person to the job being vacated.

(b) **Job rotation might be regarded as a form of training**. Trainees might be expected to learn a bit about a number of different jobs, by spending six months or one year in each job before being moved on. The employee is regarded as a trainee rather than as an experienced person holding down a demanding job.

Job optimisation

3.14 A **well designed job** should therefore provide the individual with five things.

- **Scope** for setting his own work standards and targets
- **Control** over the pace and methods of working
- **Variety** by allowing for inter-locking tasks to be done by the same person
- **Voice**: A chance to add his comments about the design of the product, or his job
- **Feedback** of information to the individual about his performance

Participation as a motivator

3.15 People want more interesting work and to have a say in decision-making. These expectations are a basic part of the movement towards greater **participation** at work.

3.16 The methods of achieving increased involvement have largely crystallised into two main streams.

(a) **Immediate participation** is used to refer to the involvement of employees in the **day-to-day** decisions of their work group.

(b) **Distant participation** refers to the process of including company employees at the top levels of the organisation which deal with long-term policy issues including investment and employment. Typical examples of this type of participation would be found in any major German company with the **two-tier** board structure. although firms in the EU are to have **works councils**.

3.17 Participation can involve employees and make them feel committed to their task, given the following conditions (5 Cs).

- **Certainty**. Participation should be genuine.
- **Consistency**. Efforts to establish participation should be made consistently over a long period.
- **Clarity**. The purpose of participation is made quite clear.
- **Capacity**. The individual has the ability and information to participate effectively.
- **Commitment**. The manager believes in participation.

3.18 Motivation through **employee satisfaction** is not a useful concept because employee satisfaction is such a **vague idea**. Drucker suggested that employee satisfaction comes about through encouraging - if need be, by pushing - employees to accept responsibility. There are four ingredients to this.

(a) **Careful placement of people in jobs** so that an individual is suited to the role.

(b) **High standards of performance in the job,** so that the employee should know what to aim for.

(c) **Providing the worker with feedback control information.** The employee should receive routine information about how well or badly he or she is doing without having to be told by his boss.

(d) **Opportunities for participation** in decisions that will give the employee managerial vision.

(Drucker, 1968)

4 PAY AS A MOTIVATOR

4.1 Extrinsic rewards include:

- Basic pay and overtime
- Bonuses
- Performance-related pay
- Share-ownership schemes
- Benefit car or allowance
- Holiday entitlement

- Sick pay and maternity pay over the legal minimum
- Contributions to a pension scheme
- Private health care
- Sickness and disability insurance
- Crèches
- Season ticket loans

You may be able to think of some more.

4.2 **Pay is important** because:

- It is an important cost
- People feel strongly about it
- It is a legal issue (minimum wage, equal opportunities legislation)

How is pay determined?

4.3 As pay is such a **complex** issue, there are a number of ways by which organisations determine pay.

(a) **Job evaluation** is a systematic process for establishing the relative worth of jobs within an organisation. It has four purposes.

(i) Provide a rational basis for the design and maintenance of an equitable and defensible pay structure

(ii) Help manage differences existing between jobs within the organisation

(iii) Enable consistent decisions to be made on grading and rates of pay

(iv) Establish the extent to which there is comparable worth between jobs so that equal pay can be provided for work of equal value.'

The salary structure is based on **job content**, and **not on the personal merit** of the job-holder. (The individual job-holder can be paid extra personal bonuses in reward for performance.)

(b) **Fairness.** Pay must be **perceived** and felt to match the level of work, and the capacity of the individual to do it.

(c) **Negotiated pay scales**. Pay scales, differentials and minimum rates may have been negotiated at plant, local or national level, according factors such as legislation, government policy, the economy, trade unions, the labour market.

(d) **Market rates.** Market rates of pay will have most influence on pay structures where there is a standard pattern of supply and demand in the open labour market. If an organisation's rates fall below the benchmark rates in the local or national labour market from which it recruits, it will have trouble attracting and holding employees.

(e) **Individual performance in the job**.

What do people want from pay?

4.4   **Pay has a central - but ambiguous - role in motivation theory.** It is not mentioned explicitly in any need list, but it **offers the satisfaction of many of the various needs**

(a)   Physiological - pay for food, shelter

(b)   Security

(c)   Esteem needs - pay might be a mark of status, but also a level of pay may be a sign of fairness

(d)   Self-actualisation - pay gives people resources to pursue self-actualisation outside the working environment

4.5   Individuals may also have needs unrelated to money, however, which money cannot satisfy, or which the pay system of the organisation actively denies. So to what extent is pay an inducement to better performance: a motivator or incentive?

4.6   Although the size of their income will affect their standard of living, most people tend not to be concerned to **maximise** their earnings. They may like to earn more but are probably more concerned to:

(a)   Earn **enough**

(b)   Know that their pay is **fair** in comparison with the pay of others both inside and outside the organisation

4.7   Pay is more of a 'hygiene' factor than a motivator factor. It gets taken for granted, and so is more usually a source of dissatisfaction than satisfaction. However, pay is the **most important of the hygiene factors**, according to Herzberg. It is valuable not only in its power to be converted into a wide range of other satisfactions but also as a consistent measure of worth or value, allowing employees to compare themselves and be compared with other individuals or occupational groups inside and outside the organisation. But this clearly **conflicts with performance-related pay**.

4.8   Research illustrated an instrumental orientation to work (the attitude that work is not an end in itself but a means to other ends).

Case example

The highly-paid Luton car assembly workers experienced their work as routine and dead-end. The researchers concluded that they had made a rational decision to enter employment offering high monetary reward rather than intrinsic interest: they were getting out of their jobs what they most wanted from them.

The Luton researchers did not claim that all workers have an instrumental orientation to work, however, but suggested that a person will seek a suitable balance of:

- The rewards which are important to him
- The deprivations he feels able to put up with

Even those with an instrumental orientation to work have limits to their purely financial aspirations, and will cease to be motivated by money if the deprivations - in terms of long working hours poor conditions, social isolation or whatever- become too great. In other words, if the 'price' of pay is too high.

High taxation rates may also weigh the deprivation side of the calculation; workers may perceive that a great deal of extra effort will in fact earn them little extra reward.   (Goldthorpe)

4.9 Unlike other 'hygiene' or 'motivator' factors at work, pay is the only factor which is impossible to 'leave behind' at the office.

    (a) Furthermore, if pay is a dominant motivator, then you would expect **difficulties in recruiting** for certain lower paid jobs. Academic research is not particularly well paid, but the job has other satisfactions, such as interest, status or esteem.

    (b) Pay is thus only one of several **intrinsic or extrinsic rewards** offered by work. If pay is used to motivate, it can only do so in a **wider context of the job** and the other rewards. **Thanks, praise and recognition** are also relevant.

Question 6

Hertzberg says that money is a **hygiene** factor in the motivation process. if this is true, it means that lack of money can demotivate, but the presence of money will not in itself be a motivator.

How far do you agree with this proposition? Can individual be motivated by a pay rise? What are the arguments against trying to motivate people purely by means of monetary incentives?

Performance related pay (PRP)

> **KEY TERM**
>
> **Performance related pay (PRP)** is related to output (in terms of the number of items produced or time taken to produce a unit or work), or results achieved (performance to defined standards in key tasks, according to plan).

4.10 The most common individual PRP scheme for wage earners is straight **piecework**: payment of a fixed amount per unit produced, or operation completed.

4.11 For managerial and other salaried jobs, however, a form of **management by objectives** will probably be applied. PRP is often awarded at the discretion of the line manager, subject to the budget overall. Guidelines may suggest, for example, that those rated exceptional get a rise of 10% whereas those who have performed less well only get, say, 3%.

    (a) Key results can be identified and specified, for which merit awards will be paid.

    (b) There will be a clear model for evaluating performance and knowing when, or if, targets have been reached and payments earned.

    (c) The exact conditions and amounts of awards can be made clear to the employee, to avoid uncertainty and later resentment.

4.12 For service and other departments, a PRP scheme may involve **bonuses** for achievement of key results, or **points schemes**, where points are awarded for performance of various criteria (efficiency, cost savings, quality of service and so on). Certain points totals (or the highest points total in the unit, if a competitive system is used) then win cash or other awards.

4.13 Here are the supposed benefits and problems of performance related pay.

    (a) **Benefits of PRP cited**

        • Improves **commitment** and capability
        • **Complements other HR initiatives**
        • Improves focus on the business's performance objectives

- Better **two-way communications**
- Greater **supervisory responsibility**
- It **recognises achievement** when other means are not available

(b) **Potential problems cited**

- Subjectivity
- Supervisors' commitment and ability
- Translating appraisals into pay
- Divisive/against team working
- Union acceptance/employee attitudes

Case example

People Management (September 1996) reported several local authorities who had withdrawn from their PRP schemes. PRP was adopted by around 70 councils between 1988 and 1991: the figure is now in decline. The London Borough of Brent dropped PRP because of the difficulty in measuring performance and a general unease about its position in local government. Cambridgeshire Country Council axed its PRP scheme as part of an overhaul of salary policy, while the London Borough Lewisham abandoned PRP in favour of other programmes such as Investors in People, and ISO 9000, claiming that it demotivated more people than it inspired.

Question 7

Why might PRP fail to motivate?

Answer

(a) The rewards from PRP are often too small to motivate effectively. Anyhow, some employees may not expect to receive the rewards and hence will not put in the extra effort.

(b) It is often unfair, especially in jobs where success is determined by uncontrollable factors.

(c) As people are rewarded individually, they are less willing to work as a team. Consequently 'teamwork' might be included as a factor to be rewarded - but this is hard to measure.

(d) People concentrate on performance indicators rather than on longer-term issues such as innovation or quality. In other words, people put all their energy into hitting the target rather than doing their job better.

(e) PRP schemes have to be well designed to ensure performance is measured properly, people consider them to be fair and there is consent to the scheme.

(f) Performance is often hard to measure.

(g) If too many factors have to be taken into account, the whole process becomes subjective and unfair.

Rewarding the team

Group bonus schemes

4.14 **Group incentive schemes** typically offer a bonus for a which achieves or exceeds specified targets. Offering bonuses to a **whole team** may be appropriate for tasks where individual contributions cannot be isolated, workers have little control over their individual output because tasks depend on each other, or where team-building is particularly required. It may enhance team-spirit and co-operation as well as provide performance incentives, but it may also create pressures within the group if some individuals are seen to be not pulling their weight.

Profit-sharing schemes

4.15 Profit-sharing schemes offer employees (or selected groups of them) bonuses, directly on profits or value added. Profit sharing is based on the belief that all employees can contribute to profitability, and that that contribution should be recognised. The effects may include profit-consciousness and motivation in employees, commitment to the future prosperity of the organisation and so on.

4.16 The actual incentive value and effect on productivity may be wasted, however, if the scheme is badly designed.

(a) The sum should be **significant**.

(b) There should be a **clear and timely link** between effort or performance and reward. Profit shares should be distributed as frequently as possible with the need for reliable information on profit forecasts, targets etc and the need to amass significant amounts for distribution.

(c) The scheme should only be introduced if profit forecasts indicate a **reasonable chance of achieving** the above: profit sharing is welcome when profits are high, but the potential for disappointment is great.

(d) The greatest effect on productivity arising from the scheme may in fact arise from its use as a focal point for discussion with employees, about the relationship between their performance and results, areas and targets for improvement etc. Management must be seen to be **committed** to the principle.

Share schemes

4.17 Some firms choose to reward employees and managers by way of shares, again allowing them to participate in the success of the company as measured by the share price. In effect, the employee is allowed to purchase, at a future date, shares in the firm at the current price or perhaps at a discount. If the share price has risen the employee can sell the shares and make a profit.

(a) This is used often in the remuneration of chief executives; there has been some criticism especially with regard to rewarding executives of privatised utilities.

(b) Many firms have introduced such schemes for all their staff. There have been some tax incentives also.

Chapter roundup

- People have certain innate needs (Maslow: physiological, security, love/social, esteem, self-actualisation. People also have goals, through which they expect their needs to be satisfied.
- Content theories of motivation suggest that the best way to motivate an employee is to find out what his/her needs are and offer him/her rewards that will satisfy those needs.
    - ○ Maslow identified a hierarchy of needs which an individual will be motivated to satisfy, progressing towards higher order satisfactions, such as self-actualisation.
    - ○ Herzberg identified two basic need systems: the need to avoid unpleasantness and the need for personal growth. He suggested factors which could be offered by organisations to satisfy both types of need: hygiene and motivator factors respectively.
- Process theories of motivation help managers to understand the dynamics of employees' decisions about what rewards are worth going for (eg the expectancy model: $F = V \times E$).
- There is little evidence that a satisfied worker actually works harder.
- Pay is the most important of the hygiene factors, but it is ambiguous in its effect on motivation.
- Ways in which managers can improve employees' motivation range from encouraging employees to accept responsibility to careful design of jobs (including job enrichment, job enlargement and job rotation) to performance-related pay and incentive schemes.

Quick quiz

1 What is (a) 'positive reinforcement' and (b) self actualisation?
2 List the five categories in Maslow's Hierarchy of Needs.
3 How do an individual's goals change with age?
4 List three ways in which an organisation can offer motivational satisfaction.
5 What is the difference between a reward and an incentive?
6 List five motivator and five hygiene factors.
7 Explain the formula '$F = V \times E$'.
8 'People will work harder and harder to earn more and more pay.' Do you agree? Why (or why not)?
9 Distinguish between job enrichment and job enlargement.

Answers to quick quiz

1 (a) Encouraging a certain type of behaviour by rewarding it. (b) Personal growth and fulfilment of potential.

2 Physiological, safety, love/social, esteem, self-actualisation.

3 Increasingly they include forming relationships, having children, power and autonomy.

4 Relationships, belonging, challenge, achievement, progress, security, money.

5 A reward is given for some contribution or success. An incentive is an or offer of reward.

6 Motivator - status, advancement, recognition, responsibility, challenging work, achievement, growth. Hygiene - company policy and administration, salary, quality of supervision, relationships, job security, working conditions.

7 Force of motivation - Valence × Expectation

8 See Paragraphs 4.10-4.12.

9 People work to earn enough pay which can then be converted into other satisfactions. If they enjoy a good income, they may become more concerned with increasing leisure time.

Now try the question below from the Exam Question Bank

Question to try	Level	Marks	Time
13	Exam	15	27 mins

BPP PUBLISHING

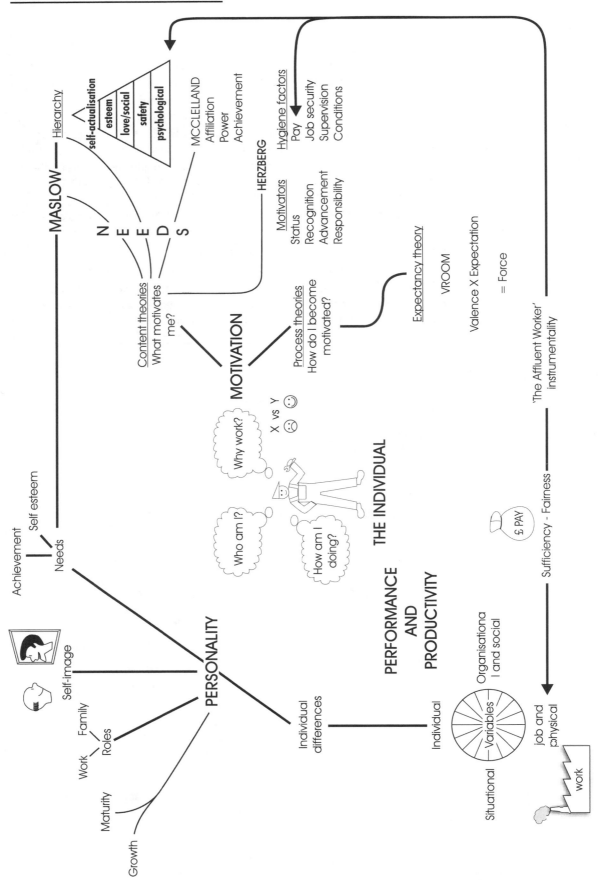

Chapter 14

EFFECTIVE LEADERSHIP

Topic list	Syllabus reference
1 What is leadership?	4(c)
2 Trait theories of leadership	4(c)
3 Style theories of leadership	4(c)
4 Task, team and people	4(c)

Introduction

Leadership is different from management, as our quote in Section 1 makes clear. After all, not every manager exhibits leadership qualities.

Study guide

Section 2.4(b) – Motivation and leadership

- See the front of this Study Text for full contents of this session of the Study Guide

Exam guide

This topic is likely to appear in Section B, perhaps as part of a question.

1   WHAT IS LEADERSHIP?

1.1   There are many different definitions.

> **KEY TERM**
>
> **Leadership** is the process of **influencing others to work willingly** towards goals, to the best of their capabilities, perhaps in a manner different to that which they would otherwise have chosen.
>
> A **leader** perhaps is a group member who exercises **acts of influence** frequently and persistently.

1.2   **Kotter** has made one of the most detailed and helpful distinctions between **leadership** and **management**, and in so doing has further described both. According to Kotter, **management** involves the following activities.

   (a) **Planning and budgeting** - target-setting, establishing procedures for reaching the targets, and allocating the resources necessary to meet the plans.

(b) **Organising and staffing** - designing the organisation structure, hiring the right people and establishing incentives.

(c) **Controlling and problem-solving** - monitoring results against the plan, identifying problems, producing solutions and implementing them.

1.3 Everything here is concerned with logic, structure, analysis and control. If done well, it produces predictable results on time. **Leadership** requires a different set of actions and, indeed, a completely different mind set.

(a) **Creating a sense of direction** - usually borne out of dissatisfaction with the *status quo*. Out of this challenge a vision for something different is created.

(b) **Communicating the vision** - which must meet the realised or unconscious needs of other people and the leader must work to give it credibility.

(c) **Energising, inspiring and motivating** - in order to stimulate others to translate the vision into achievement.

1.4 All of these activities involve dealing with people rather than things. But remember that leadership is a conscious activity. If you yawn and others around you do the same, it is more properly called **behavioural contagion** than leadership.

1.5 Viscount Slim summed up the difference between leadership and management when addressing the Australian Institute of Management in 1957.

'Leadership is of the spirit, compounded of personality and vision: its practice is an art. Management is of the mind, more a matter of accurate calculation of statistics, of methods, time tables, and routine: its practice is a science. Managers are necessary; leaders are essential.

2 TRAIT THEORIES OF LEADERSHIP

2.1 Early theories suggested that there are certain personality characteristics or traits that make a good leader. These might be aggressiveness, self-assurance, intelligence, initiative, a drive for achievement or power, appearance, interpersonal skills, administrative ability, imagination, a certain upbringing and education, or the ability to rise above a situation and analyse it objectively.

2.2 Trait theory, although superficially attractive, is now largely discredited, in favour of other theories which we now discuss. This is because no two lists of leadership traits were the same.

3 STYLE THEORIES OF LEADERSHIP

3.1 Leaders accept responsibility for the outcomes of the groups they lead. While leaders have to exercise authority, the way in which this is done (the *style* of leadership) might vary. It is generally accepted that a leader's style of leading can affect the motivation, efficiency and effectiveness of the leader's followers.

3.2 Management style can be analysed using a spectrum or continuum with **autocratic** and **laissez-faire** styles at the extremes. **Tannenbaum and Schmidt** produced one of the earliest of such analyses by considering the way in which the power and influence of managers and non managers varied.

Dictatorial	Autocratic			Democratic			Laissez-faire
Manager makes decisions and enforces them	Manager makes decisions and announces them	Manager 'sells' his decisions to subordinates	Manager suggests own ideas and asks for comments	Manager suggests his sketched ideas, asks for comments and amends his ideas as a result	Manager presents a problem, asks for ideas, makes a decision from the ideas	Manager presents a problem to his group of subordinates and asks them to solve it	Manager allows his subordinates to act as they wish within specified limits

The Ashridge model

3.3 The Research Unit at Ashridge Management College distinguished four different management styles. They are outlined, with their strengths and weaknesses, in the table on the next page. (Note that the Ashridge model has not included any real equivalent of the laissez-faire style.) Here are their findings.

(a) In an ideal world, subordinates preferred the **consults** style of leadership. Those managed in that way had the most favourable attitude to work, but managers were most commonly thought to be exercising the **tells** or **sells** style.

(b) In practice, consistency was far more important. The least favourable attitudes were found amongst subordinates who were **unable to perceive a consistent style** of leadership in their boss.

Question 1

Suggest an appropriate style of management for each of the following situations. Think about your reasons for choosing each style in terms of the results you are trying to achieve, the need to secure commitment from others, and potential difficulties with both.

(a) Due to outside factors, the personnel budget has been reduced for your department and one-quarter of your staff must be made redundant. Records of each employee's performance are available.

(b) There is a recurring administrative problem which is minor, but irritating to every one in your department. Several solutions have been tried in the past, but without success. You think you have a remedy which will work, but unknown problems may arise, depending on the decisions made.

Answer

Styles of management suggested in the situations described, using the tells-sells-consults-joins model.

(a) You may have to 'tell' here: nobody is gong to like the idea and, since each person will have his or her own interests at heart, you are unlikely to reach consensus. You could attempt to 'sell', if you can see a positive side to the change in particular cases: opportunities for retraining, say.

(b) You could 'consult' here: explain your remedy to staff and see whether they can suggest potential problems. They may be in a position to offer solutions - and since the problem effects them too, the should be committed to solving it.

(c) We prefer a 'joins' style here, since the team's acceptance of the decision is more important than the details of the decision itself.

(d) We would go for 'consult' despite the staff's apparent reluctance to participate. They may prefer you to 'tell' - but may resist decisions they disagree with anyway. Perhaps their reluctance is to do with lack of confidence - or lack of trust that you will take their input seriously, in which case, persistent use of a 'consults' style may encourage them. You could use a 'sells' approach initially, to get them used to a less authoritarian style than they seem to expect.

Style	Characteristics	Strengths	Weaknesses
Tells (autocratic)	The manager makes all the decisions, and issues instructions which must be obeyed without question.	(1) Quick decisions can be made when speed is required. (2) It is the most efficient type of leadership for highly-programmed routine work.	(1) It does not encourage the sub-ordinates to give their opinions when these might be useful. (2) Communications between the manager and subordinate will be one-way and the manager will not know until afterwards whether the orders have been properly understood. (3) It does not encourage initiative and commitment from subordinates.
Sells (persuasive)	The manager still makes all the decisions, but believes that subordinates have to be motivated to accept them in order to carry them out properly.	(1) Employees are made aware of the reasons for decisions. (2) Selling decisions to staff might make them more committed. (3) Staff will have a better idea of what to do when unforeseen events arise in their work because the manager will have explained his intentions.	(1) Communications are still largely one-way. Sub-ordinates might not accept the decisions. (2) It does not encourage initiative and commitment from subordinates.
Consults	The manager confers with subordinates and takes their views into account, but has the final say.	(1) Employees are involved in decisions before they are made. This encourages motivation through greater interest and involvement. (2) An agreed consensus of opinion can be reached and for some decisions consensus can be an advantage rather than a weak compromise. (3) Employees can contribute their knowledge and experience to help in solving more complex problems.	(1) It might take much longer to reach decisions. (2) Subordinates might be too inexperienced to formulate mature opinions and give practical advice. (3) Consultation can too easily turn into a façade concealing, basically, a sells style.
Joins (democratic)	Leader and followers make the decision on the basis of consensus.	(1) It can provide high motivation and commitment from employees. (2) It shares the other advantages of the consultative style (especially where subordinates have expert power).	(1) The authority of the manager might be undermined. (2) Decision-making might become a very long process, and clear decisions might be difficult to reach. (3) Subordinates might lack enough experience.

Style and effectiveness: Likert

3.4 Rensis Likert also described a range of four management systems.

- System 1 - Exploitative authoritative
- System 2 - Benevolent authoritative
- System 3 - Consultative
- System 4 - Participative

Likert's research showed that **effective managers** display each of the four characteristics below, in relation to leadership skills. Such managers:

(a) **They expect high levels of performance** from subordinates, other departments and themselves.

(b) **They are employee-centred.** They spend time getting to know their workers and develop a situation of trust whereby their employees feel able to bring their problems to them. Such managers face unpleasant facts in a constructive manner and help their staff to do the same.

(c) **They do not practise close supervision.** The truly effective manager knows performance levels that can be expected from each individual and has helped them to define their own targets. The manager judges results and does not closely supervise the actions of subordinates.

(d) **They operate the participative style of management as a natural style.** If a job problem arises they do not impose a favoured solution. Instead, they pose the problem and ask the staff member involved to find the best solution. Having then agreed their solution the participative manager would assist his staff in implementing it. Leadership involves trust and confidence in subordinates; motivation is based on rewards for achievement of agreed goals.

Leadership, motivation and productivity: Lewin, Lippitt and White

3.5 With his colleagues Lippitt and White, Lewin established clubs for boys to study leadership.

3.6 Club **leaders** were **trained** to act as **autocratic, democratic** or **laissez-faire** leaders, and the purpose of the experiments was to learn how **the children reacted** to different styles of leadership. The leaders were moved from one club to another every six weeks and by means of rotation each club (consisting of ten year old boys) experienced three different styles of leadership, under the three different leaders.

(a) The **autocratic** leader tended to give orders, and to interrupt the activities of the boys by giving commands to do something else. Criticism and praise were given out non-objectively, ie at the **whim** of the leader.

(b) The **democratic** leader suggested what the boys should do, showed concern for each boy's individual welfare, participated in the activities of the group, but left the decisions about what to do to the boys themselves.

(c) The **laissez-faire** leader also made suggestions, but was more 'stand-offish' and did not involve himself with the boy's welfare, nor did he join in the group activities, so that the boys were effectively left to do what they wanted by themselves.

3.7 Lewin, Lippitt and White were particularly interested in aggressive social behaviour, either within the group or shown to outsiders.

BPP PUBLISHING

(a) In one experiment, aggressive behaviour was very much more common among the autocratic group than the democratic group, but none of the aggression or hostility was directed at the leader himself.

(b) In a subsequent experiment, boys in four out of five autocratic groups showed 'apathetic' behaviour and lack of aggression. This apathy was attributed by the experimenters to the repressive style of the club leader.

(c) Aggression is only **partly** caused by leadership style. Other factors arousing hostile behaviour are tension, restriction of physical space and the cultural background of the boys in the group. Nevertheless, leadership style contributes towards such behaviour.

(d) 95 per cent of boys preferred a democratic to an autocratic leader, and 70 per cent preferred a laissex-faire leader to an autocratic one.

3.8 In a subsequent publication many years later (1960) **Lippitt and White** investigated the effect of **leadership on productivity** in different groups. They concluded the following.

(a) **Work-orientated conversation was greatest in a democratic group**, less in an autocratic group and, interestingly, least in a laissez-faire group.

(b) The amount of **work actually done was greatest in an autocratic group** and least in a **laissez-group**.

(c) **Motivation was strongest in a democratic group where boys often carried on working even when a leader left the room**. Interestingly, however, motivation was not sufficient to increase output above the level of the autocratic group.

(d) Hostility and discontent were greatest in an autocratic group. Four dropped out of the experiment, and all belonged to an autocratic group at the time. Boys in an autocratic group were more dependent on their leader, and submissive; their hostility was towards each other.

(e) In contrast, **originality, group-mindedness and friendly playfulness were greatest in a democratic group**.

4 TASK, TEAM AND PEOPLE

Blake and Mouton's managerial grid

4.1 **Robert Blake** and **Jane Mouton** carried out research (The Ohio State Leadership Studies) into managerial behaviour and observed two basic dimensions of leadership: **concern for production** (or task performance) and **concern for people**.

4.2 Along each of these two dimensions, managers could be located at any point on a **continuum** from very low to very high concern. Blake and Mouton observed that the two concerns did not seem to correlate, positively or negatively: a high concern in one dimension, for example, did not seem to imply a high or low concern in the other dimension. Individual managers could therefore reflect various permutations of task/people concern.

4.3 Blake and Mouton modelled these permutations as a grid. One axis represented concern for people, and the other concern for production. Blake and Mouton allotted nine points on each axis, from 1 (low) to 9 (high).

4.4 A questionnaire was designed to enable users to analyse and plot the positions of individual respondents on the grid. This was to be used as a means of analysing individuals'

managerial styles and areas of weakness or 'unbalance', for the purposes of management development.

The managerial grid

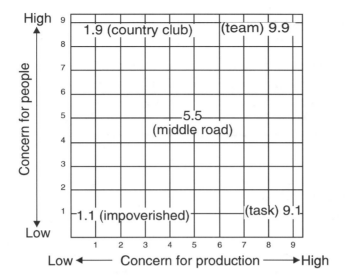

4.5 The extreme cases shown on the grid are these:

(a) 1.1 **impoverished:** the manager is lazy, showing little interest in either staff or work.

(b) 1.9 **country club:** the manager is attentive to staff needs and has developed satisfying relationships. However, there is little attention paid to achieving results.

(c) 9.1 **task management:** almost total concentration on achieving results. People's needs are virtually ignored.

(d) 5.5 **middle of the road** or the **dampened pendulum:** adequate performance through balancing the necessity to get out work while maintaining morale of people at a satisfactory level.

(e) 9.9 **team:** high performance manager who achieves high work accomplishment through 'leading' committed people who identify themselves with the organisational aims.

The usefulness of the managerial grid

4.6 The managerial grid was intended as an **appraisal and management development tool.** It recognises that a balance is required between concern for task and concern for people, and that a high degree of both is possible (and highly effective) at the same time.

4.7 The grid thus offers a number of useful insights for the identification of management **training and development** needs. It shows in an easily assimilated form where the behaviour and assumptions of a manager may exhibit a lack of balance between the dimensions and/or a low degree of concern in either dimension or both. It may also be used in team member selection, so that a 1.9 team leader is balance by a 9.1 co-leader, for example.

4.8 However, the grid is a **simplified** model, and as such has **practical limitations.**

(a) It assumes that 9.9 is the desirable model for effective leadership. In some managerial contexts, this may not be so. Concern for people, for example, would not be necessary in a context of comprehensive automation: compliance is all that would be required.

(b) It is open to oversimplification. Scores can appear polarised, with judgements attached about individual managers' suitability or performance. The Grid is intended as a simplified 'snapshot' of a manager's preferred style, not a comprehensive description of his or her performance.

(c) Organisational context and culture, technology and other 'givens' (Handy) influence the manager's style of leadership, not just the two dimensions described by the Grid.

(d) Any managerial theory is only useful in so far as it is useable in practice by managers: if the grid is used only to inform managers that they 'must acquire greater concern for people', it may result in stress, uncertainty and inconsistent behaviour.

Question 2

Here are some statements about a manager's approach to meetings. Which position on Blake's Grid do you think each might represent?

(a) I attend because it is expected. I either go along with the majority position or avoid expressing my views.

(b) I try to come up with good ideas and push for a decision as soon as I can get a majority behind me. I don't mind stepping on people if it helps a sound decision.

(c) I like to be able to support what my boss wants and to recognise the merits of individual effort. When conflict rises, I do a good job or restoring harmony.

Answer

Blake's Grid positioning of the given managerial approaches are:

(a) 1.1: low task, low people
(b) 9.1: High task, low people
(c) 1.9: high people, low task

Contingency approaches to leadership

4.9 John Adair was not concerned so much with leadership *style* as with **what leaders actually do.** this led to a **functional** approach to leadership. His **action-centred leadership** model sees the leadership process in a context made up of three interrelated variables, task needs, the individual needs of group members, and the needs of the group as a whole.

(a) The total situation dictates the relative priority that must be given to each of the three sets of needs.

(b) Effective leadership is identifying and acting on that priority.

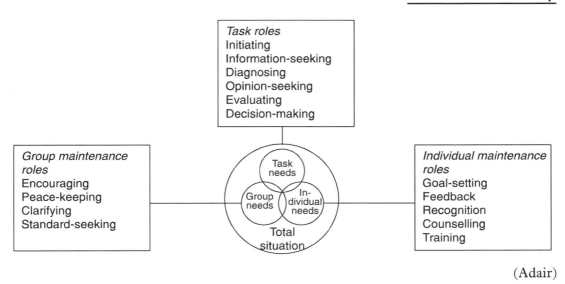

(Adair)

Question 3

In your career so far, you might have worked for a number of managers. Jot down the following features of each situation on a scale of 1-5 for comparative purposes.

(a) The degree to which you had autonomy over your own work.
(b) The degree to which you were consulted on decisions which affected you.
(c) The degree to which your advice was sought about decisions affecting your section.

If you worked for managers who had different approaches to these issues, do you think these approaches influenced **your** effectiveness? What score to questions (a), (b) and (c) would you give your **ideal boss**? and your **current boss**?

Handy

4.10 Handy argues that the ability of a manager to lead and to influence his work group will vary according to three contingencies.

(a) The **leader's** personality, character and preferred style of operating.

(b) The **subordinates**. their individual and collective personalities, and their preference for a particular style of leadership.

(c) The **task**. If the tasks of a work group are simple, few in number and repetitive, the best style of leadership will be different from a situation in which tasks are varied and difficult.

(d) The **context**

(i) The position of **power** held by the leader in the organisation and the group. A person with power is better able to choose a personal style and leadership, select subordinates and re-define the task of the work group.

(ii) Organisational **norms** and the structure and technology of the organisation. No manager can act in a manner which is contrary to the customs and standards of the organisation.

4.11 For each of the three factors, a spectrum can be drawn ranging from 'tight' to 'flexible'. Handy argues that the most effective style of leadership in any particular situation is one which brings the first three factors - a leader, subordinates and task - into a 'best fit'.

	The leader	*The subordinates*	*The task*
Tight ↑	Preference for autocratic style, high estimation of his own capabilities and a low estimation of his subordinates. Dislikes uncertainty.	Low opinion of own abilities, do not like uncertainty in their work and like to be ordered. They regard their work as trivial; past experience in work leads to acceptance of orders, cultural factors lean them towards autocratic/dictatorial leaders.	Job requires no initiative, is routine and repetitive or has a certain outcome; short time scale for completion. Trivial tasks.
The Spectrum ↓	Preference for democratic style, confidence in his subordinates, dislikes stress, accepts reasonable risk and uncertainty.	High opinion of own abilities; likes challenging important work; prepared to accept uncertainty and longer time scales for results; cultural factors favour independence.	Important tasks with a longer timescale; problem-solving or decision-making involved, complex work.
Flexible			

4.12　(a)　A **best fit** occurs when all factors are on the same level in the spectrum.

(b)　In practice, there is likely to be a misfit. Confronted with a lack of fit, **the leader must decide which factor(s) should be changed** to bring all three into line. In the short-term, the **easiest is to change the leadership style**. There are often long-term benefits to be achieved from re-defining the task (eg job enlargement) or from developing the work group.

Question 4

List four ways in which an organisation, by dealing with 'environmental constraints' can help its managers to adopt an appropriate management style.

Answer

The 'environment' can be improved for leaders if senior management ensure that:

(a)　Managers are given a clear role and the power (over resources and information) to back it up.

(b)　Organisational 'norms' can be broken without fear of punishment - ie the organisation culture is adaptive, and managers can change things if required.

(c)　The organisational structure is not rigid and inflexible: managers can redesign task and team arrangements.

(d)　Team members are selected or developed so that they are, as far as possible, of the same 'type' in terms of their attitudes to work and supervision.

(e)　Labour turnover is reduced as far as possible (by having acceptable work conditions and terms, for example), so that the team does not constantly have to adjust to new members, or leaders

Fiedler: Contingency theories of leadership

4.13　Perhaps the leading advocate of contingency theory is Fiedler. He studied the relationship between style of leadership and the effectiveness of the work group are identified two types of leader.

(a)　**Psychologically distant managers** (PDMs) maintain distance from their subordinates.

(i)　They formalise the roles and relationships between themselves and their superiors and subordinates.

(ii) Therefore withdrawn and reserved in their inter-personal relationships within the organisation (despite having good inter-personal skills).

(iii) They prefer formal consultation methods rather than seeking opinions of their staff informally.

PDMs judge subordinates on the basis of performance, and are primarily task-oriented: Fiedler found that leaders of the most effective work groups tend to be PDMs.

(b) **Psychologically close managers** (PCMs) are closer to their subordinates.

(i) They do not seek to formalise roles and relationships with superiors and subordinates.

(ii) They are more concerned to maintain good human relationships at work than to ensure that tasks are carried out efficiently.

(iii) They prefer informal contacts to regular formal staff meetings

4.14 Fiedler suggested that the **effectiveness of a work group depended on the situation**, made up of three variables.

(a) The **relationship between the leader and the group**: that is, the amount of trust and respect the group feels

(b) The extent to which the task is defined and structured

(c) The **power of the leader in relation** to the group (authority, and power to reward and punish)

4.15 A situation is favourable to the leader when three conditions apply.

- The leader is liked and trusted by the group
- The tasks of the group are clearly defined
- The power of the leader to reward and punish with organisation backing is high

4.16 Fiedler reached two conclusions.

(a) A structured (or psychologically distant) style works best when the situation is either very favourable, or very unfavourable to the leader

(b) A supportive (or psychologically close) style works best when the situation is moderately favourable to the leader.

> 'Group performance will be contingent upon the appropriate matching of leadership styles and the degree of favourableness of the group situation for the leader, that is, the degree to which the situation provides the leader with influence over his group members.' *Fiedler*

Hersey and Blanchard: follower maturity

4.17 *Hersey and Blanchard* developed a model of **situational leadership** which appears to map style theories on to the grid suggested by Blake and Mouton. They identify two axes of behaviour, similar to Blake and Mouton's concern for tasks and people

(a) **Task behaviour** is concerned with getting the job done.

(b) **Relationship behaviour** is equivalent to concern for people, and their involvement.

The four quadrants of the upper part of the diagram identify the different leadership styles. Each is appropriate under different conditions of subordinate **maturity**.

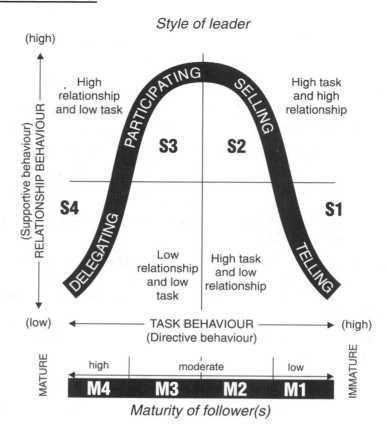

4.18   '**Maturity**' depends on job ability, willingness and confidence.

- M4: able and willing or confident
- M3: able but unwilling or insecure
- M2: unable but willing or confident
- M1: unable and unwilling or insecure

Hersey and Blanchard suggest that the leadership styles are appropriate for the similarly numbered subordinate maturity states.

Chapter roundup

- **Leadership** is the proves of influencing others to work willingly towards the achievement of organisational goals.

- **Theories of leadership** have been based on the following aspects.

  (a) Traits which appear to be common to successful leaders.

  (b) Styles which can be adopted. These are often expressed as a range or continuum, reflecting either the manager's approach to control or the manager's priorities.

  Tells ⟵——————— sells ——————— consults ——————⟶ joins

  Tight ⟵———————————————————————————⟶ loose

  Wholly task oriented ⟵———————————————————⟶ Wholly people oriented

- A **contingency approach** to leadership suggests that a style may be appropriate or inappropriate (and therefore effective or ineffective) depending on variables including:

  (a) the structure and demands of the task

  (b) the characteristics and needs of the team and its individual members

  (c) the characteristics and needs of the leader

  (d) the organisational development

Quick quiz

1   How do people become leaders in a group or situation?

2   What is the difference between a 'sells' and 'consults' style of management?

3   What might be the disadvantages of a 'tells' style of management?

4   What type of task makes tight control a suitable style?

5   What factors in the environment influence the choice of a tight or loose style?

6   What is the most effective style suggested by Blake's managerial grid and why is it so effective in theory? Why might it not be effective in practice?

7   Do teams need to have a leader? Would they be as effective without one?

8   Why is consistency of management style important - and why might this be a problem?

Answers to quick quiz

1   Through different forms of influence such a vision, inspiration and motivation.

2   'Sells' - the manager still makes all decisions but explains them to subordinates to get them to carry them out willingly. 'Consults' - the manager confers with subordinates, takes their views and feelings into account, but retains the right to make the final decision.

3   'Telling' is one-way, there is no feedback. It does not encourage contributions or initiative.

4   Those which lack initiative, are routine, trivial or have a short time scale.

5   The position of power held by the leader, organisational norms, structure and technology, the variety of tasks and subordinates.

6   9.9. It is effective if there is sufficient time and resources to attend fully to people needs, if the manager is good at dealing with people and if the people respond. It is ineffective when a task **has** to be completed in a certain way or by a certain deadline even if people don't like it.

7   Someone has to ensure the objective is achieved, make decisions and share out resources. If everyone on the team is equally able and willing to do these things (unlikely in practice) a good information system is probably all that is needed, not a leader.

8   Inconsistency results in subordinate feeling unsure and distrusting the manager.

Now try the question below from the Exam Question Bank

Question to try	Level	Marks	Time
14	Exam	15	27 mins

Part E
Effective communication practices

Chapter 15

INTERPERSONAL AND COMMUNICATION SKILLS

Topic list	Syllabus reference
1 Interpersonal skills and working relationships	5(a)
2 Assertiveness	5(a), 5(b)
3 Communication in the organisation	5(b)
4 Face-to-face and oral communication	5(b), 5(c)
5 Textual communications	5(b), 5(c)
6 Counselling	5(d)

Introduction

Communication is fundamental to all human activity involving more than one person. Good communications are essential within organisations if they are to prosper. Assertiveness and counselling are specialised aspects of communication with which managers must be familiar.

Study guide

This chapter covers the content of Study Guide Sections

25(a) – Working with people - interpersonal skills

26(b) – Communication

27(c) – The role of counselling

The detailed contents of these sections can be found in the front of this Study Text.

Exam guide

Section B of the pilot paper included a fifteen mark question on the fundamentals of communication. However, this is a topic that could appear in either section A or section B and as a stand-along question, or as an aspect of a wider question.

1 INTERPERSONAL SKILLS AND WORKING RELATIONSHIPS

KEY TERM

Interpersonal behaviour is behaviour between people. It includes:

(a) Interaction between people, a two way process such as communication, delegating, negotiating, resolving conflict, persuading, selling, using and responding to authority.

(b) An individual's behaviour in relationship to other people.

1.1 The way you behave in response to other people includes:

- How you **perceive** other people

- **Listening to** and **understanding** other people

- **Behaving** in a way which builds on this understanding

- Being **sensitive** to the impression you give, in the light of the roles you are expected to play.

Interpersonal skills

1.2 **Interpersonal skills a**re needed by an individual in order to:

(a) Understand and manager the roles, relationships, attitudes and perceptions operating in any situation in which two or more people are involved

(b) Communicate clearly and effectively

(c) Achieve his or her aims from an interpersonal encounter (ideally, allowing the other parties to emerge satisfied too)

1.3 **Issues to consider in interpersonal communication and work relationships**

Issue	Comment
Goal	What does the other person want from the process? What do you want from the process? What will both parties need and be trying to do to achieve their aims? Can both parties emerge satisfied?
Perceptions	What, if any, are likely to be the factors causing 'distortion' of the way both parties see the issues and each other? (Attitudes, personal feelings, expectations?)
Roles	What 'roles' are the parties playing? (Superior/subordinate, customer/server, complainer/soother?) What expectations does this create of the way they will behave?
Resistances	What may the other person be 'afraid' of? What may he or she be trying to protect? (His or her ego/self-image, attitudes?) Sensitivity will be needed in this area.
Attitudes	What sources of difference, conflict or lack of understanding might there be, arising from attitudes and other factors which shape them (sex, race, specialism, hierarchy)?

Issue	Comment
Relationships	What are the relative positions of the parties and the nature of the relationship between them? (Superior/subordinate? Formal/ informal? Work/non-work)? What 'style' is appropriate to it?
Environment	What factors in the immediate and situational environment might affect the issues and the people? (eg competitive environment customer care; pressures of disciplinary situation nervousness; physical surroundings formality/ informality)

1.4 In addition, a range of **communication skills** will be deployed.

1.5 **Skills in the selected medium of communication.** (Use this as a checklist.)

Oral	Written	Visual/non verbal
Clear pronunciation	Correct spelling	Understanding of control
Suitable vocabulary	Suitable vocabulary	over 'body language' and
Correct grammar/syntax	Correct grammar/syntax	facial expressions
Fluency	Good writing or typing	Drawing ability
Expressive delivery	Suitable style	

1.6 **General skills in sending messages**

(a) **Selecting and organising your material:** marshalling your thoughts and constructing your sentences, arguments and so on

(b) **Judging the effect of your message** on the particular recipient in the particular situation

(c) **Choosing language and media** accordingly

(d) **Adapting your communication style** accordingly: putting people at their ease, smoothing over difficulties (tact), or being comforting/challenging/informal/formal as the situation and relationship demand

(e) **Using non-verbal signals** to reinforce (or at least not to undermine) your spoken message

(f) **Seeking and interpreting feedback**

1.7 **Skills in receiving messages**

(a) **Reading** attentively and actively: making sure you understand the content, looking up unfamiliar words and doubtful facts if necessary; evaluating the information given: is it logical? correct? objective?

(b) **Extracting relevant information** from the message, and filtering out inessentials

(c) **Listening** attentively and actively; concentrating on the message - not on what you are going to say next, or other matters; questioning and evaluating what you are hearing

(d) **Interpreting the message's underlying meaning**, if any, and evaluating your own reactions: are your reading into the message more or less than what is really there?

(e) **Asking questions** in a way that will elicit the information you wish to obtain. This will usually involve **open** questions

(f) **Interpreting non-verbal signals**, and how they confirm or contradict the spoken message

(g) **Giving helpful feedback**, if the medium is inappropriate (eg a bad telephone line) or the message is unclear, insufficient or whatever

The importance of good working relationships and good interpersonal skills

1.8 Good interpersonal relationships assist in the following areas of the manager or supervisor's position.

Area	Comment
Motivation	Work can satisfy people's social needs, according to Maslow, because it provides relationships.
Communication	Bad interpersonal relationships can form a barrier to communicating effectively - messages will be misinterpreted
Teamworking and team building	In Chapter 4 we discussed team building and the importance of developing a climate in which people can communicate openly and honestly.
Customer care	Good interpersonal skills are recognised as being increasingly important when dealing with customers.
Career development	Good interpersonal skills are increasingly necessary to get promotion
Managerial roles	Chapter 3 listed some management roles. Many of these - such as the liaison role - require interpersonal skills
Power: persuade, not command	Interpersonal skills can be a source of personal power in an organisation. The supervisor may not be in a position to command or coerce individuals for information or favours – interpersonal skills may help make the supervisor more effective.
Team management	The manager's tasks of appraisal, interviewing etc require good interpersonal skills if they are to be performed effectively.

2 ASSERTIVENESS

KEY TERM

Assertiveness may be described as clear, honest and direct communication. It is not to be confused with 'bossiness' or aggression.

Aggressive behaviour is competitive and directed at 'beating' someone else.

Assertion is based on equality and co-operation. Assertion is simple affirmation that every individual has certain rights and can stand by them in the face of pressures from other people.

2.1 The psychologist and assertiveness trainer Anne Dickson identifies eleven 'human rights' which form the basis of any approach to assertiveness.

1	'I have the right to state my own needs and set my own priorities as a person; independent of any roles that I may assume in my life.' (eg as employee, or wife and mother).
2	'I have the right to be treated with respect as an intelligent, capable and equal human being.'
3	'I have the right to express my feelings.'
4	'I have the right to express my opinions and values.'
5	'I have the right to say "yes" or "no" for myself' (ie not to have other people's expectations say it for me)
6	'I have the right to make mistakes.'
7	'I have the right to change my mind.'
8	'I have the right to say I don't understand.'
9	'I have the right to ask for what I want.'
10	'I have the right to decline responsibility for other people's problems.'
11	'I have the right to deal with others without being dependent on them for approval.'

Techniques of assertion

2.2 **Asking for what you want: essential skills**

(a) **Decide what it is you want or feel, and express it directly and specifically.** Don't assume that others will know, or work out from hints, what it is that you really want.

(b) **Stick to your statement.** If you are ignored, refused or responded to in some other negative way, don't back down, 'fly off the handle', or enter into arguments designed to deflect you from your purpose. Stick to your position, and repeat it calmly, as often as necessary: repetition projects an image of determination and reinforces your own confidence and conviction.

(c) **Deflect responses from the other person.** Show that you have heard and understood the other person's response, but are not going to be sidetracked.

2.3 **Saying no without upsetting yourself or your colleagues**

Saying 'no' can be very difficult for people: they feel it is selfish, or will cause offence.

(a) **Don't be pushed.** If you are at all hesitant about whether to say 'yes' or 'no' try asking for time to decide, to think or obtain more information. Why should you make an instant decision? Acknowledge your doubts: ask your questions. Feel free to change your mind.

(b) **Say 'no' clearly and calmly, if that is your answer.** Explain why, if you think it appropriate - not because you are anxious to excuse yourself, as if it were not your right to say 'no'. Don't express regret unless you feel regretful. Remember that when you say 'no', you are refusing a request, not rejecting a person.

(c) **Acknowledge your feelings.** If you feel awkward about refusing, or under pressure to accept, say so: the other person will be reassured that you are giving him or her due consideration.

(d) **Watch your body language.** If you have said 'yes' when you wanted to say 'no', don't start giving 'no' signals by sulking. If you are saying 'no', don't give contradictory signals by smiling ingratiatingly, lingering as if waiting to be talked out of it etc.

2.4 Receiving criticism and feedback

Distinguish between **valid criticism** (which you know to be legitimate), **invalid criticism** (which you now to be untrue) and a **put down** (intended to be hurtful or humiliating).

(a) **Invalid criticism and put-downs** should be handled simply and assertively with a straightforward denial: 'I don't accept that at all'.

(b) **Valid criticism** should be regarded positively as a potentially helpful experience.

(i) **Negative assertions:** learning how to agree with a criticism if it does in fact apply to you, without growing defensive or abjectly apologetic. You simply acknowledge the truth in what the critic is saying, together with your response to the situation.

(ii) **Negative enquiry:** learning how to take the initiative, to **prompt** specific criticism, in order to use the information if it is constructive **or** expose an attempt to put you down or be negative.

2.5 Giving criticism

Expressing negative feelings to others so that they hear what you are saying but do not feel personally attacked or rejected is not easy. Effective communication will be impossible if you make the other person defensive or aggressive, or if you let your own feelings get in the way. Guidelines are as follows.

(a) **Describe the behaviour and express your feelings about the behaviour - to the individual personally.**

(b) **Ask for a specific change of behaviour.** Being specified separates constructive criticism (which involves give and take) from attack or complaint.

(c) **End on a positive note.** This does not mean backing off your criticism ('it's not that important, really: I just thought I'd mention it'), but stating something positive that you feel. For example: 'I'm glad I've had a chance to say this', or 'In all other areas, you're doing fine, so I hope we can get this sorted out'.

Question 3

Look at 'right' number 3 in paragraph 2.1: 'I have the right to express my feelings'. Why do you need to be assertive about this: in what sort of situations is this right denied you (even by yourself)? For example: suppose a colleague - or even your boss - asks you to come in to work early to discuss something. You turn up - but he or she does not. You are reluctant to say how angry and aggrieved you feel, because you might appear to be petty or irrational - or you fear that the other person was prevented by some genuine problems and you might offend or upset him/her - or you want the other person to like and approve of you because you are so understanding and forgiving. You are denying yourself the right to say what you felt. The appropriate assertive response would be: 'I was annoyed that you didn't turn up, especially after I had come in early at your request. [I would like you to show more consideration in future.]'

For each of the other 'rights' listed:

(a) Think of the way or situation in which you would tend to deny yourself that right.

(b) Give the appropriate assertive response for that situation - including some of the techniques discussed in this section.

Assertiveness and the role of women at work

2.6 Assertiveness training is popularly seen as a prime means of remedying underachievement in women, or of helping women to avoid exploitation at work. It is likely to be a part of a 'Women Into Management' or similar training and education programme. The techniques and insights involved are likely to be of benefit to men as well, but it has been recognised that it is primarily women who are disadvantaged in western society by the failure to distinguish between assertion and aggression, submission and conflict-avoidance.

3 COMMUNICATION IN THE ORGANISATION

3.1 In any organisation, the communication of information is necessary for:

(a) **Management decision-making**

(b) **Interdepartmental co-ordination.** All the interdependent systems for purchasing, production, marketing and administration can be synchronised to perform the right actions at the right times to co-operate in accomplishing the organisation's aims.

(c) **Individual motivation and effectiveness,** so people know what they have to do and why.

3.2 Communication in the organisation may take the following forms.
- Giving instructions
- Giving or receiving information
- Exchanging ideas
- Announcing plans or strategies
- Comparing actual results against a plan
- Rules or procedures
- Communication about the organisation structure and job descriptions

The communication process

3.3 The process of communication can be shown as follows.

The communication process

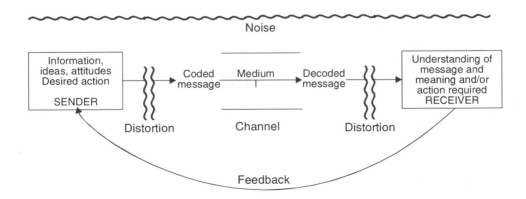

Process	Comment
Coding of a message	The code or 'language' of a message may be verbal (spoken or written) or it may be non-verbal, in pictures, diagrams, numbers or body language.
Medium for the message	There are a number of channels for communication, such as a conversation, a letter, a notice board or via computer. The choice of medium used in communication depends on a number of factors such as urgency, permanency, complexity, sensitivity and cost.
Feedback	The sender of a message needs feedback on the receiver's reaction. This is partly to test the receiver's understanding of it and partly to gauge the receiver's reaction.
Distortion	The meaning of a message can be lost in coding and decoding stages. Usually the problem is one of language and the medium used; it is easier to 'get the wrong end of the stick' in a telephone call than from a letter.
Noise	Distractions and interference in the environment in which communication is taking place may be physical noise (passing traffic), technical noise (a bad telephone line), social noise (differences in the personalities of the parties) or psychological noise (anger, frustration, tiredness).

Direction of communication flows

3.4 Communication flows can go in three directions.

(a) **Vertical** ie up and down the scalar chain (from superior to subordinate and back). This is mainly used for reporting and feedback, and sometimes also suggestions and problem-solving input.

(b) **Horizontal or lateral:** between people of the same rank, in the same section or department, or in different sections or departments. Horizontal communication between 'peer groups' is usually easier and more direct then vertical communication, being less inhibited by considerations of rank.

  (i) **Formally:** to co-ordinate the work of several people, and perhaps departments, who have to co-operate to carry out a certain operation.

  (ii) **Informally:** to furnish emotional and social support to an individual.

(c) **Diagonal**. This is interdepartmental communication by people of different ranks. Departments in the technostructure which serve the organisation in general, such as Human Resources or Information Systems, have no clear 'line authority' linking them to managers in other departments who need their involvement. Diagonal communication aids co-ordination, and also innovation and problem-solving, since it puts together the ideas and information of people in different functions and levels. It also helps to by-pass longer, less direct channels, avoiding blockages and speeding up decision-making.

Communication patterns (or networks)

3.5 A **communication pattern** channels communication between people. One of the purposes of a **formal organisation structure** is the design of a communications pattern for the organisation.

3.6 **Leavitt**, in a series of experiments, examined the effectiveness of four communication networks for **written** communication between members of a small group. The five network patterns were these.

(a) The **circle.** Each member of the group could communicate with only two others in the group, as shown.

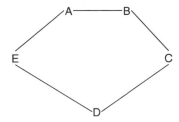

(b) The **chain**

A — B — C — D — E

Similar to the circle, except that A and E cannot communicate with each other and are therefore at both ends of a communication chain.

(c) The **'Y'**

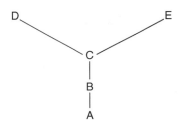

(d) The **wheel**

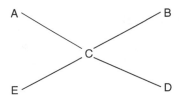

In both the 'Y' and the 'wheel' patterns, C occupies a more central position in the network.

(e) The **'all channel'** pattern

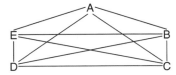

3.7 **Comparing the All-channel system, the Wheel and the Circle**

(a) **Simple problem-solving.** The **Wheel system solves problems quickest**, and the Circle is the slowest, with the All-channel system in between.

BPP PUBLISHING

(b) **Complex problem-solving.** The **All-channel system is best,** with its participatory style, and more open communication system, generally provides the best solutions to complex problems. The efficiency of the Wheel depends on the ability of the leader, or central figure. In the Circle, there is a lack of co-ordination and solutions to problems are poor.

(c) The All-channel system tends to disintegrate under pressure (eg time pressure to get results) into a Wheel pattern.

Question 4

What do you think the relevance of Leavitt's experiment to your earlier learning of leadership?

Answer

The central figure on the communications network has emerged as 'leader' in the example. Or is it only **position power**? The results of the all-channel system, comparing its effectiveness in solving simple and complex problems, might indicate a sort of contingency approach to leadership. In other words, effective communications and problem solving is affected by leadership style and formal design.

Barriers to communication

3.8 **Desirable qualities of a communication system in an organisation**

(a) **Clarity.** The coder of a message must bear in mind the potential recipient. **Jargon can be used** - and will even be most appropriate - **where the recipient shares the same expertise.** It should be avoided for those who do not.

(b) **Recipient.** The recipient should be clearly identified, and the right medium should be chosen, to minimise distortion and noise.

(c) **Medium.** The channel or medium should be chosen to ensure it reaches the target audience. Messages of general application (eg Health and Safety signs) should be displayed prominently.

(d) **Timing.** Information has to be timely to be useful.

3.9 **General faults in the communication process**

- **Distortion** or omission of information by the sender
- **Misunderstanding** due to lack of clarity or technical jargon
- **Non-verbal signs** (gesture, facial expression) contradicting the verbal message
- **'Overload'** - a person being given too much information to digest in the time available
- **People** hearing **only what they want** to hear in a message
- **Differences** in social, racial or educational **background**

3.10 **Communication difficulties at work**

(a) **Status** (of the sender and receiver of information).

  (i) A senior manager's words are listened to closely and a colleague's perhaps discounted.

  (ii) A subordinate might mistrust his or her superior and might look for 'hidden meanings' in a message.

(b) **Jargon.** People from different job or specialist backgrounds (eg accountants, personnel managers, IT experts) can have difficulty in talking on a non-specialist's wavelength.

(c) **Suspicion.** People discount information from those not recognised as having expert power.

(d) **Priorities.** People or departments have different priorities or perspectives so that one person places more or less emphasis on a situation than another.

(e) **Selective reporting.** Subordinates giving superiors incorrect or incomplete information (eg to protect a colleague, to avoid 'bothering' the superior); also a senior manager may only be able to handle edited information because he does not have time to sift through details.

(f) **Use.** Managers who are prepared to make decisions on a 'hunch' without proper regard to the communications they may or may not have received.

(g) **Timing.** Information which has **no immediate** use tending to be forgotten.

(h) **Opportunity.** No opportunity, formal or informal, for people to say what they think may be lacking.

(i) **Conflict.** Where there is conflict between individuals or departments, communications will be withdrawn and information withheld.

(j) **Personal differences,** such as age, educational/social background or personality mean that people have different views as to what is important or different ways of expressing. sometimes views may be discounted because of who they are, not what they say.

(k) **Culture**

   (i) **Secrecy.** Information might be given on a need-to-know basis, rather than be considered as a potential resource for everyone to use.

   (ii) **Can't handle bad news.** The culture of some organisations may prevent the communication of certain messages. Organisations with a 'can-do' philosophy may not want to hear that certain tasks are impossible.

Improving the communications system

3.11 Depending on the problem, the solution may be as follows.

(a) **Establish better communication links** in all directions.

   (i) **Standing instructions** should be recorded in easily accessible manuals which are kept fully up-to-date.

   (ii) Management **decisions** should be sent to all people affected by them, preferably in writing.

   (iii) Regular **staff meetings**, or formal consultation with trade union representatives should be held.

   (iv) **A house journal** should be issued regularly.

   (v) **'Appraisal' interviews** between a manager and his subordinates, to discuss the job performance and career prospects of the subordinates.

   (vi) Use **new technology** such as e-mail - but not so as to overload everybody in the financial messages of no importance.

(b) Use the **informal organisation** to supplement this increased freedom of communication.

3.12 **Clearing up misunderstandings** about message content.

BPP PUBLISHING

(a) **Redundancy** - issuing a message in more than one form (eg by word of mouth at a meeting, confirmed later in minutes)

(b) **Reporting by exception** should operate to prevent **information overload** on managers.

(c) **Train** managers who do not express themselves clearly and concisely. Necessary jargon should be taught in some degree to people new to the organisation or unfamiliar with the terminology of the specialists.

Case example

Procter and Gamble have a rule that no memo should be longer than one side of paper.

3.13 Communication between superiors and subordinates will be improved when **interpersonal trust** exists. Exactly how this is achieved will depend on the management style of the manager, the attitudes and personality of the individuals involved, and other environmental variables. Peters and Waterman advocate 'management by walking around' (MBWA), and **informality in superior/subordinate relationships** as a means of establishing closer links.

4 FACE-TO-FACE AND ORAL COMMUNICATION

Oral communication

4.1 Face-to-face communication (meetings etc) plays an important part in the life of any organisation, whether it is required by government legislation or the Articles of a company, or is held informally for information exchange, problem-solving and decision-making.

4.2 Face-to-face communication is good for:

- **Generating new ideas**
- **'On the spot' feedback**, constructive criticism and exchange of views
- **Co-operation** and sensitivity to personal factors
- **Spreading information quickly** through a group of people

4.3 However, such communication can be non or counter productive unless:

(a) People **know the reason** for the group discussion.

(b) Participants are **willing and effective communicators** and are concise and clear in what they have to say.

(c) There is sufficient **guidance** or leadership to control proceedings.

(d) People maintain standards of **courtesy**.

Listening

4.4 Listening is about **decoding and receiving** information and carries much of the burden of communication. Listening is more than just a natural instinct, and listening skills can be taught and developed. Effective listening helps:

- The **sender** to listen effectively in return to the receiver 's reply
- **Reduce** the effect of '**noise**'
- **Resolve problems by encouraging understanding** from someone else's viewpoint

4.5 **Good listening checklist**

(a) **Be prepared to listen**. Put yourself in the right frame of mind (ie a readiness to maintain attention). In meetings, be prepared to grasp the main concepts.

(b) **Try to be interested**. Make an effort to analyse the message for its relevance.

(c) **Keep an open mind**. Your own beliefs and prejudices can get in the way of what the other person is actually saying.

(d) **Keep an ear open for the main ideas**. Learn to distinguish between the 'gist' of the argument and supporting evidence.

(e) **Listen critically**. Assess what the other person is saying by identifying any **assumptions, omissions and biases**.

(f) **Avoid distraction**. People have a natural attention curve, high at the beginning and end of an oral message, but sloping off in the middle.

(g) **Take notes,** although note taking can be distracting at times.

(h) **Wait** before interrupting.

Non-verbal interpersonal communication

4.6 Non-verbal communication (often called **body language**) consists of facial expression, posture, proximity, gestures and non-verbal noises (grunts, yawns etc).

(a) Consciously or unconsciously, we send messages through body language during every face to face encounter.

(b) We can use it deliberately to confirm our verbal message - for example, by nodding and smiling as we tell someone we are happy to help them - or to contradict it, if we want to be sarcastic (saying 'How interesting!' with a yawn, for example).

(c) More often, however, our body language **contradicts** our verbal message without our being aware of it, giving a 'mixed message' like your saying you understand an instruction while looking extremely perplexed.

(d) Body language can also 'give away' messages that we would - for social or business reasons - rather not send, such as lack of interest, hostility or whatever.

4.7 **Control and use of body language** is needed to:

- Provide an appropriate 'physical' **feedback** to the sender of a message
- Create a desired **impression**
- Establish a desired **atmosphere** or conditions (friendly smile)
- **Reinforce our spoken messages** with appropriate indications

4.8 **Reading other people's body language** helps you to:

- Receive **feedback** from a listener and modify the message accordingly.
- Recognise people's **real feelings** when their words are constrained by formalities.
- Recognise **existing or potential personal problems**.
- '**Read**' situations in order to modify our own communication and response strategy.

4.9 **Improved performance**. This can be achieved in the following ways.

(a) Become more aware of what your body language is 'saying' to people.

(b) **Control your body language**. If you are bored or irritated when talking to a customer, in particular, suppress the signals. On the other hand, you can use positive body language to reinforce the message you want to give - of professionalism, confidence etc.

(c) **Seek feedback** when communicating: you will then discover when a recipient is getting a 'mixed message' from you.

(d) Ask colleagues and friends to be honest with you about when your body language is confusing or off-putting, to help you become more aware.

Committees

4.10 A committee is a group of people who meet for a particular purpose, often on a permanent basis. Uses of committees are these.

(a) **Making decisions**

(b) **Delaying** decisions (for more information)

(c) The **relaying of decisions** and instructions (eg briefings)

(d) The **dissemination of information** and the collection of feedback.

(e) **Problem solving**, by consultation with people in different departments or fields (eg a task force or working party).

(f) **Brainstorming**: free exchanges with a view to generating new approaches and ideas.

(g) **Co-ordination** of the efforts of a large number of people representing department or interest groups.

(h) Formal **recommendations** that others follow a course of action.

(i) **Representation** of a number of people from divergent disciplines.

4.11 **Disadvantages of committees**

(a) **Size.** They are apt to be too large for constructive action, since the time taken by a committee to resolve a problem tends to be in direct proportion to its size.

(b) **Time-consuming and expensive.** In addition to the cost of highly paid executives' time, secretarial costs will be incurred in the preparation of agendas, recording of proceedings and the production and distribution of minutes.

(c) **Delays** may occur in the production cycle if matters of a routine nature are entrusted to committees.

(d) **Distraction.** Operations of the enterprise may be jeopardised by the frequent attendance of executives at meetings, and by distracting them from their real duties.

(e) **Superficiality.** Incorrect or ineffective decisions may be made, owing to the fact that members of a committee are unfamiliar with the deeper aspects of issues under discussion.

(f) **Weakened individual responsibility** throughout the organisation.

(g) **Dominance.** Proceedings may be dominated by outspoken or aggressive members, thus unduly influencing decisions and subsequent action, perhaps adversely; there may be 'tyranny' by a minority.

4.12 **Potential misuses of committees**

(a) **Replace managers.** A committee cannot do all the tasks of management (eg leadership) and therefore cannot replace managers entirely.

(b) **Carry out research work.** A committee may be used to create new ideas, but work on those ideas cannot be done effectively by a committee itself.

(c) **Make unimportant decisions**. This would be expensive and time-consuming.

(d) **Discuss decisions beyond the authority of its participants**. This might occur, for example, when an international committee of government ministers is created, but ministers send deputies in their place to meetings, without giving the deputy sufficient authority to enable the committee to make important decisions.

(e) Committees '**paper over the cracks**' in a badly designed organisation structure.

Using committees successfully

4.13 Here are some guidelines.

(a) **Well defined areas** of authority, time scales of operations and purpose must be specified in writing.

(b) The **chairman must have the qualities** of leadership to co-ordinate and motivate the other committee members.

(c) **Size**. The committee should not be so large as to be unmanageable.

(d) **Membership**. The members of the committee must have the necessary skills and experience to do the committee's work. Where the committee is expected to liaise with functional departments, the members must also have sufficient status and influence with those departments.

(e) **Minutes**. Minutes of the meetings should be taken and circulated, with any action points arising out of the meetings notified to the members responsible for doing the work (see below).

Other group communication methods

4.14 **Brainstorming sessions** are problem-solving conferences of six to twelve people who produce spontaneous 'free-wheeling' ideas to solve a particular problem. Ideas are produced but not evaluated at these meetings, so that originality is not stifled in fear of criticism. Brainstorming sessions rely on the ability of conference members to feed off each other's ideas. They have been used in many organisations and might typically occur, for example, in advertising agencies to produce ideas for a forthcoming campaign.

4.15 **Quality circles** emerged first in the United States, but it was in Japan that they were adopted most enthusiastically. They are still used, but some commentators suggest they are outmoded and are being superseded by other team-based working methods.

> **KEY TERM**
>
> A **quality circle** consists of a group of employees which meets regularly to discuss problems of quality and quality control in their area of work, and perhaps to suggest ways of improving quality. The quality circle has a leader or supervisor who directs discussions and possibly also helps to train other members of the circle.

4.16 A **team briefing** is a means of communicating at team level, not in the more impersonal or abstract level of the house journal or noticeboard. It is given by a **team leader**, who should have been thoroughly trained and briefed, or, occasionally, a more senior member of management.

KEY TERM

Team briefings are a form of face-to-face communication mechanism which are designed to increase the commitment and understanding of the workforce.

4.17 The **purpose of a team briefing** is to communicate and explain management decisions in the hope that this will reduce any disruption, dispel any rumours, and enhance employees' commitment. Subjects include:

- Policies (new or changed, and why)
- Plans
- Progress
- Personnel issues

4.18 **Reasons for failure**
- Lack of senior management commitment
- Interference
- A lack of enthusiasm shown by middle managers
- The reluctance of management to allow the discussion of matters of real importance.

4.19 Team briefings can be seen as a tool which tries to **motivate** by **communicating**. However, it is **not** clear whether, using Herzberg's model, information has a role in motivation.

(a) If lack of information (as a result of management secrecy) is a **hygiene** factor, you would expect little **long-term** change in the level of motivation from a more open management approach.

(b) If providing more information and being more open is a **motivator** factor, you would expect greater enthusiasm.

Interviews

4.20 The interview informal or otherwise is an excellent internal system for handling the problems or queries of individuals, allowing **confidentiality** and flexible response to personal factors. Interviews are, however, costly in terms of managerial time. Some interviews are built into the **formal** communication system.

(a) **Grievance** interviews are where employees voice their complaints.

(b) **Disciplinary** interviews are where the organisation can air its complaints.

(c) **Appraisal** interviews are used to discuss the employee's performance, progress and possible need for improvement.

(d) **Counselling** interviews will be discussed below.

Telephone calls and voice mail

4.21 The **telephone** provides all the interactive and feedback advantages of face to face communication, while saving the travel time. It is, however, more 'distant' and impersonal than an interview for the discussion of sensitive personal matters, and it does not **by itself** provide the concreteness of written media.

4.22 **Voice mail** is a means of leaving spoken memos, for someone to listen to later. It can be useful as an extension of **paging**, so that a person can leave detailed messages for someone who is absent without the inconvenience of having to write a memorandum or the hazard of leaving a message.

4.23 **Video conferencing** has grown in popularity since the Gulf War and with the decreasing cost of technology compared to the cost and inconvenience of flying. It is a meeting conducted over long distance. Each participant shares a room, and interacts with a video broadcast image of the other participants.

5   TEXTUAL COMMUNICATIONS

Forms

5.1   Routine information flow is largely achieved through the use of **forms**. A well designed form can be filled quickly and easily with brief, relevant and specifically identified details of a request or instruction. They are simple to file, and information is quickly retrieved and confirmed. Examples include: expense forms, timesheets, insurance forms, stock request forms etc.

Notice board

5.2   **A notice board** is a channel through which various written media can be cheaply transmitted to a large number of people. It allows the organisation to present a variety of information to any or all employees: items may have a limited time span of relevance but will at least be available for verification and recollection for a while. The drawbacks to notice boards are that:

(a)   They can easily fall into **neglect**, and become untidy or irrelevant (or be sabotaged by graffiti).

(b)   They are wholly **dependent** on the intended recipient's **curiosity** or desire to receive information.

House journal

5.3   Larger companies frequently run an **internal magazine** or newspaper to inform employees about:

- Staff appointments and retirements
- Meetings, sports and social events
- Results and successes; customer feedback
- New products or machinery
- Motivating competitions eg for suggestions, office maintenance, safety

Organisation manual or handbook

5.4   An organisation (or office) manual is useful for drawing together and **keeping up to date** all relevant information for the guidance of individuals and groups as to:
- The structure of the organisation (perhaps an organisation chart)
- Background: the organisation's history and geography
- The organisation's products, services and customers
- Rules and regulations
- Conditions of employment: pay structure, hours, holidays, notice etc
- Standards and procedures for health and safety
- Procedures for grievance, discipline, salary review
- Policy on trade union membership
- Facilities for employees

Letters and faxes

5.5 **The letter** is flexible in a wide variety of situations, and useful in providing a written record and confirmation of the matters discussed.

(a) It is widely used for external communication, via the **external mailing system** (Post Office) or taxi or courier.

(b) A direct letter may be used internally in certain situations where a confidential written record is necessary or personal handling required.

5.6 **Fax** achieves the same object as a letter, but is more immediate. Most faxes are followed up with a letter.

Memoranda

5.7 **A memorandum** is the equivalent of the letter in internal communication. It is sent via the **internal mail system** (eg in special envelopes) of an organisation. Memoranda are useful for exchanging many sorts of message and particularly for confirming telephone conversations: sometimes, however, they are used instead of telephone conversations, where the call would have been quicker, cheaper and just as effective. Many memoranda are unnecessarily typed where a short hand-written note would be adequate.

E-mail

5.8 As an alternative to paper-based media such as letters and memos, people are increasingly using **e-mail**, especially in firms with a high penetration of **networked PCs.**

(a) Each PC on the network is connected to a **central server.**

(b) Messages are sent to the central server. At regular intervals (eg every 30 minutes) these are distributed to each PC on the network.

5.9 E-mail addresses are accessible to those **inside** the organisation and to **outsiders,** if they too have e-mail facilities and are signed up with a service provider (such as Compuserve or Demon). The facilities of e-mail can also be supplemented by promotional media such as **internet web-sites.** Many firms have **intra-nets.**

5.10 **Problems with e-mail**

(a) **Information overload** - it is easier to send an e-mail than to distribute a memo, so people perhaps send unnecessary messages.

(b) **E-mails,** unlike other forms of communication, are **not private**, and can be cited in legal actions for libel etc.

(c) They are an excuse for not communicating face-to-face.

Report writing

5.11 A formal **report** enables a number of people to review the complex facts and arguments relating to an issue on which they have to base a plan or make a decision. This is primarily an **internal medium** used by management, but can be used externally for the information of shareholders, the general public, government agencies etc (eg the company's Annual Report).

5.12 The written report does not allow for effective discussion or immediate feedback, as does a meeting, and can be a time-consuming and expensive document to produce. However, as a medium for putting across a body of ideas to a group of people, it has several **advantages.**

(a) People can **study the material in their own time,** rather than arranging to be present at one place and time

(b) **No time need be wasted on irrelevancies** and the formulation of arguments, such as may occur in meetings

(c) The report should be **presented objectively and impartially,** in a formal and impersonal style: emotional reactions or conflicts will be avoided.

5.13 **Stylistic requirements in the writing of reports**

(a) A report must first **identify** the recipient, the preparer, the date and subject matter.

(b) **Bias and over-emotive language** can undermine the credibility of the report and its recommendations.

(c) Avoid **colloquialisms** and abbreviated forms.

(d) **Ease of understanding.**

(i) Write for the **user:** jargon is perfectly suitable for some readers, but intimidating to others.

(ii) Organise material logically, especially if it is leading up to a conclusion or recommendation. Aim for clarity.

(iii) Signal relevant themes by appropriate headings or highlighting.

(iv) The **layout** of the report should display data clearly and attractively. Figures and diagrams should be used with discretion, and it might be helpful to highlight key figures which appear within large tables of numbers.

5.14 Here is an example of a report.

To: [Name(s)/position(s) of recipient(s)]
From: [Sender]
Date:
Subject: [Title of report, such as *Communication Media in A Ltd*]

Contents:

1 Terms of reference and work undertaken
2 Executive summary
3 Organisational problems
4 Operational issues
5 Conclusion and recommendation

1 **Terms of reference and work undertaken**

1.1 [Here is laid out the scope and purpose of the report: what is to be investigated, what information is required, whether recommendations should be made.

1.2 The scope of work done, how data was collected etc

2 **Executive summary** [Many reports have a brief description of their key points at the top.]

BPP
PUBLISHING

---

3   **Organisation issues**

3.1   [Reports could use numbered paragraphs like this. This makes it easier for the user to refer to them.]

3.2   [The content in this and the following sections should be complete but concise and clearly structured in chronological order, order of importance or any other logical relationship.]

4   **Operational problems**

5   **Conclusion and recommendations**

5.1   [This section allows for a summary of main findings and their implications. Recommendations could come here, referenced, if necessary, to the findings of the earlier section. The recommendations will allow the recipient to make a decision if necessary.]

Question 6

Indicate the most effective way in which the following situations should be communicated.

(a)   Spare parts needed urgently.

(b)   A message from the managing director to all staff.

(c)   Fred Bloggs has been absent five times in the past month and his managers intends taking action.

(d)   You need information quickly from another department.

(e)   You have to explain a complicated operation to a group.

Answer

Communicating the situations given might best be done as follows.

(a)   Telephone, confirmed in writing (order form, letter)

(b)   Noticeboard, general meeting or email.

(c)   Face-to-face conversation. It would be a good idea to confirm the outcome of the meeting in writing so that records can be maintained.

(d)   Either telephone or face to face.

(e)   Team briefing

---

6   **COUNSELLING**

KEY TERM

'**Counselling** can be defined as 'a purposeful relationship in which one person helps another to help himself. It is a way of relating and responding to another person so that that person is helped to explore his thoughts, feelings and behaviour with the aim of reaching a clearer understanding. The clearer understanding may be of himself or of a problem, or of the one in relation to the other.'   (Rees)

6.1   The need for workplace counselling can arise in many different situations.
   • During appraisal
   • In grievance or disciplinary situations
   • Following change, such as promotion or relocation

- On redundancy or dismissal
- As a result of domestic or personal difficulties
- In cases of sexual harassment or violence at work

6.2 Effective counselling is not merely a matter of pastoral care for individuals, but is very much in the **organisation's** interests. Counselling:

(a) **Prevents underperformance**, reduces labour turnover and absenteeism and increase commitment from employees.

(b) Demonstrates an organisation's **commitment** to and concern for its employees.

(c) Give employees the confidence and encouragement necessary to take responsibility for self and career development.

(d) Recognises that the organisation may be contributing to the **employees' problems** and therefore it provides an opportunity to reassess organisational policy and practice.

6.3 Most of what follows is derived from the IPD's 1992 *Statement on Counselling in the Workplace*.

The counselling process

6.4 The counselling process has three stages.

Step 1. **Recognition and understanding**. Often it is the employee who takes the initiative, but managers should be aware that the problem raised initially may be just the tip of the iceberg. (*Personnel Management Plus*, February 1993, cites a case where an employee came forward with a problem about pension contributions, and mentioned, as he was about to leave 'By the way - my wife wants a divorce'.)

Step 2. **Empowering**. This means enabling the employee to recognise their own problem or situation and encouraging them to express it.

Step 3. **Resourcing**. The problem must then be managed, and this includes the decision as to who is best able to act as counsellor. A specialist or outside resource may be better than the employee's manager.

Counselling skills

6.5 Remember that the aim of counselling is to help the employee to help himself. Counsellors need to be **observant** enough to note behaviour which may be symptomatic of a problem, be **sensitive** to beliefs and values which may be different from their own (for example religious beliefs), be **empathetic** to the extent that they appreciate that the problem may seem overwhelming to the individual, and yet remain **impartial** and refrain from giving advice. Counsellors must have the belief that the individual has the resources to solve their own problems, albeit with passive or active help.

6.6 Interviewing skills are particularly relevant. Open questioning, listening actively (probing, evaluating, interpreting and supporting), seeing the problem from the individual's point of view, and above all being genuinely and sincerely interested are skills identified in the IPD Statement.

Confidentiality

6.7 There will be situations when an employee cannot be completely open unless he is sure that his comments will be treated confidentially. However, certain information, once obtained by the organisation (for example about fraud or sexual harassment) calls for action. In spite of the drawbacks, therefore, the IPD statement is clear that employees must be made aware when their comments will be passed on to the relevant authority, and when they will be treated completely confidentially.

The interview

6.8 The checklist below contains much useful advice for meeting and interviewing people generally, not merely in counselling situations.

Counselling checklist

Preparation

- Choose a place to talk which is quiet, free from interruption and not open to view

- Research as much as you can before the meeting and have any necessary papers readily available

- Make sure you know whether the need for counselling has been properly identified or whether you will have to carefully probe to establish if a problem exists

- Allow sufficient time for the session. (If you know you must end at a particular time, inform the individual of this)

- Decide if it is necessary for the individual's department head to be aware of the counselling and its purpose

- Give the individual the option of being accompanied by a supportive colleague

- If you are approaching the individual following information received from a colleague, decide in advance the extent to which you can reveal your source

- Consider how you are going to introduce and discuss your perceptions of the situation

- Be prepared for the individual to have different expectations of the discussion, eg the individual may expect you to solve the problem - rather than come to terms with it himself/herself

- Understand that the individual's view of the facts of the situation will be more important than the facts themselves and that their behaviour may not reflect their true feelings

Format of discussion

- Welcome the individual and clarify the general purpose of the meeting

- Assure the individual that matters of confidentiality will be treated as such

- The individual may be reticent through fear of being considered somewhat of a risk in future and you will need to give appropriate reassurances in this regard

- Be ready to prompt or encourage the individual to move into areas he/she might be hesitant about

- Encourage the individual to look more deeply into statements

- Ask the individual to clarify statements you do not quite understand the individual and which you both might prefer to avoid

- Recognise that some issues may be so important to the individual that they will have to be discussed over and over again, even though this may seem repetitious to you

---

- If you sense that the individual is becoming defensive, try to identify the reason and relax the pressure by changing your approach

- Occasionally summarise the conversation as it goes along, reflecting back in your own words (not parrot phrasing) what you understand the individual to say

- Try to take the initiative in probing important areas which may be embarrassing/emotional to the interviewee

- Sometimes emotions may be more important than the words being spoken, so it may be necessary to reflect back what you see the individual feeling

- At the close of the meeting, clarify any decisions reached and agree what follow-up support would be helpful

Overcoming dangers

- If you take notes at an inappropriate moment, you may set up a barrier between yourself and the individual

- Realise you may not like the individual and be on guard against this

- Recognise that repeating problems does not solve them

- Be careful to avoid taking sides

- Overcome internal and external distractions. Concentrate on the individual and try to understand the situation with him/her

- The greater the perceived level of listening, the more likely the individual will be to accept comments and contributions from you

- Resist the temptation to talk about your own problems, even though these may seem similar to those of the individual

Source: IPD Statement on Counselling in the Workplace

BPP PUBLISHING

Chapter roundup

- **Interpersonal behaviour** is behaviour between one or more individuals and the behaviour of one individual in relation to others.

- Individuals assume **roles** in relation to each other and to the situation: these are the 'hats' that people wear.

- **Communication** is a two-way process involving the transmission or exchange of information, and the provision of feedback. Individual differences, poor communication skills and situational factors may create barriers to effective communication which must be overcome.

- The way in which the communication **process** is structured can influence the effectiveness with which tasks are handled.

- Any communication can be mapped on a simple model. The sender codes the message and transmits it through a medium to the receiver who decodes it into information.

- **Barriers to communication** are 'noise' (from the environment), poorly constructed or coded/decoded messages (distortion) and failures in understanding caused by the relative positions of senders and receivers.

- A variety of communication **media** exist, written and oral. **Electronic communication** has some of the features of both written and oral communication. Electronic communications facilitate homeworking.

- **Informal communication** supplements the formal system. The grapevine can act very fast in spreading rumours. Networking is a technique whereby an 'informal' communications network is created. It can be recognised as such by the management hierarchy.

- **Counselling** is an interpersonal interview, the aim of which is to facilitate another person's identification and working through a problem.

Quick quiz

1   What are (a) role signs and (b) role ambiguity?

2   Draw a simple diagram of the communication process using dotted or broken lines where 'distortion' may be a problem.

3   Give five examples of non-verbal communication, and suggest what they might be used to indicate.

4   What is the difference between aggression and assertiveness?

5   What is meant by communication which is:

   (a)   Upward?
   (b)   Downward?
   (c)   Horizontal?

6   What are the advantages and disadvantages of giving orders or briefings by telephone?

7   What might be covered in regular 'team briefings'?

8   What are the main purposes of upward communication in organisations?

9   What are the stages of the counselling process?

Answers to quick quiz

1   (a)   How someone dresses and behaves to match the role.

    (b)   If an individual is unsure of what his/her role is in a certain situation.

2   Refer to Section 4.9. The dotted lines would run alongside all the arrows.

3   A nod of agreement, a smile to encourage, a frown to disapprove, a yawn to show boredom, turning away to discourage.

4   Aggressive behaviour is competitive; assertion means that every individual has certain rights, and is entitled to stand by them.

5   (a)   From subordinate to superior

    (b)   From superior to subordinate

    (c)   Between individuals, teams, departments on the same level of the organisation chart

6   Advantages are that it cuts down on time and physical movement. Disadvantages are that only one person is reached at a time, there are no non-verbal signals and it is more difficult to persuade and to respond to physical factors.

7   Organisational policy and changes, plans, progress, results.

8   To give feedback, to inform and to make suggestions.

9   Recognition and understanding; empowerment; resourcing.

Now try the question below from the Exam Question Bank

Question to try	Level	Marks	Time
15	Exam	15	27 mins

BPP
PUBLISHING

Chapter 16

CONFLICT, GRIEVANCE AND DISCIPLINE

Topic list	Syllabus reference
1 Conflict in organisations	5(e)
2 Causes, symptoms and tactics of conflict	5(e)
3 Managerial response to conflict	5(e)
4 Discipline	5(f)
5 Grievance	5(f)

Introduction

Conflict of various kinds seems as inescapable feature of the human condition and therefore of organisations. Managers must know how to deal with conflict, both in its everyday form and when a more structured response is required. Grievances and disciplinary problems can be sources of major unrest, so extensive procedures exist for handling them.

Study guide

Section 4 – Effective communication practices

- Controlling conflict
- Grievance and discipline

Exam guide

Conflict is a major topic in organisational studies and could form the basis for a question in either Section A or Section B. Grievance and discipline are rather more specialised aspects of human resource management and it is unlikely that either would justify a complete question. They are perhaps most likely to appear as aspects of Section B questions.

1   CONFLICT IN ORGANISATIONS

1.1   The existence of **conflict** in organisations might be considered inevitable or unnatural, depending on your viewpoint.

The happy family view: conflict is unnatural

1.2   The happy family view presents organisations as:

(a) **Co-operative structures**, designed to achieve agreed common objectives, with no systematic conflict of interest.

(b) **Harmonious environments**, where conflicts are **exceptional** and arise from:
- Misunderstandings
- Personality factors

- The expectations of inflexible employees
- Factors outside the organisation and its control

1.3 Conflict is thus **blamed** on bad management, lack of leadership, poor communication, or 'bloody-mindedness' on the part of individuals or interest groups that impinge on the organisation. The theory is that a strong culture, good two-way communication, co-operation and motivational leadership will eliminate conflict.

Question 1

How accurate is the happy family perspective when applied to your own organisation, or to any organisation with which you are sufficiently familiar?

To what extent would you subscribe to the claim that the 'happy family' view is publicised by managers within their own organisations, not so much as an accurate description of reality, but rather because adoption of the 'happy family' perspective itself helps to reduce the level of articulated conflict?

Answer

The happy family perspective rarely fits most organisations, even those pursuing a common ideological goal, like a political party. Such organisations regularly face. Cynics argue that managers promote the 'happy family' view to suppress conflict.

The conflict view

1.4 In contrast, some see organisations as **arenas** for conflict on individual and group levels.

(a) Members battle for limited resources, status, rewards and professional values.

(b) **Organisational politics** involve constant struggles for control, and choices of structure, technology and organisational goals are part of this process. Individual and organisational interests will not always coincide.

The evolutionary view

1.5 This view regards conflict as a means of **maintaining the status quo**, as a useful basis for **evolutionary change**.

- **Conflict** keeps the organisation **sensitive to the need to change**, while reinforcing its essential framework of control.

- The **legitimate pursuit of competing interests** can balance and preserve social and organisational arrangements.

1.6 This **constructive conflict** view may perhaps be the most useful for managers and administrators of organisations, for two reasons.

(a) It does not attempt to dodge the issues of conflict, which is an observable fact of life in most organisations.

(b) Neither does it seek to pull down existing organisational structures altogether.

1.7 Conflict can be highly desirable. Conflict is constructive, when its effect is to:

- Introduce different **solutions** to problems
- **Define power relationships** more clearly
- Encourage **creativity**, the testing of ideas

- **Focus attention** on individual contributions
- **Bring emotions** out into the open
- **Release of hostile feelings** that have been, or may be, repressed otherwise

1.8 **Conflict can also be destructive.** It may:

- **Distract attention** from the task
- **Polarise** views and 'dislocate' the group
- Subvert **objectives** in favour of secondary goals
- Encourage **defensive** or 'spoiling' behaviour
- Force the group to **disintegrate**
- Stimulate emotional, **win-lose conflicts,** ie hostility

1.9 **Role playing**

Case example

Tjosvold and Deerner researched conflict in different contexts. They allocated to 66 student volunteers the roles of foremen and workers at an assembly plant, with a scenario of conflict over job rotation schemes. Foremen were against, workers for.

One group was told that the organisational norm was to 'avoid controversy'; another was told that the norm was 'co-operative controversy', *trying* to agree; a third was told that groups were out to win any arguments that arose, 'competitive controversy'. The students were offered rewards for complying with their given norms. Their decisions, and attitudes to the discussions, were then monitored.

(a) Where controversy was avoided, the foremen's views dominated.

(b) Competitive controversy brought no agreement - but brought out feelings of hostility and suspicion.

(c) Co-operative controversy brought out differences in an atmosphere of curiosity, trust and openness: the decisions reached seemed to integrate the views of both parties.

But can real managers and workers be motivated to comply with useful organisational norms in this way?

Conflict between groups

1.10 **Conflicts of interest** may exist throughout the organisation - or even for a single individual. There may be conflicts of interest between local management of a branch or subsidiary and the organisation as a whole.

- Sales and production departments in a manufacturing firm (over scheduling, product variation)
- Trade unions and management.

1.11 **Interest groups** such as trade unions tend to wield greater power in conflict situations than their members as individuals. Trade Unions are organisations whose purpose it is to promote their members' interests. (Strike action has to be preceded by a ballot.)

Question 2

What other examples of 'conflicts of interest' can you identify within an organisation? Having selected some instances, can you detect any common patterns in such conflicts?

Answer

Conflicts occur anywhere in an organisation. Individuals, groups, departments or subsidiaries compete for scarce (financial/human/physical) resources.

1.12 Co-operation and competition

Conflict can also operate **within** groups.

Case example

In an experiment reported by *Deutsch* (1949), psychology students were given puzzles and human relation problems to work at in discussion groups. Some groups ('co-operative' ones) were told that the grade each individual got at the end of the course would depend on the performance of his group. Other groups ('competitive' ones) were told that each student would receive a grade according to his own contributions.

No significant differences were found between the two kinds of group in the amount of interest and involvement in the tasks, or in the amount of learning. But the co-operative groups, compared with the competitive ones, had greater productivity per unit time, better quality of product and discussion, greater co-ordination of effort and sub-division of activity, more diversity in amount of contribution per member, more attentiveness to fellow members and more friendliness during discussion.

Conflict and competition

1.13 *Sherif and Sherif* conducted a number of experiments into groups and competing groups.

(a) People tend to **identify with a group**.

(b) **New members** of a group **quickly learn the norms** and attitudes of the others, no matter whether these are positive or negative, friendly or hostile.

(c) When a **group competes**, this is what happens to it **within the group**.

    (i) Members close ranks, and submerge their differences; loyalty and conformity are demanded.

    (ii) The 'climate' changes from informal and sociable to work and task-oriented; individual needs are subordinated to achievement.

    (iii) Leadership moves from democratic to autocratic, with the group's acceptance.

    (iv) The group tends to become more structured and organised.

    (v) The opposing group begins to be perceived as 'the enemy'.

    (vi) Perception is distorted, presenting an idealised picture of 'us' and a negative stereotype of 'them'.

    (vii) Communication between groups decreases.

1.14 In a 'win-lose' situation, competition is not perceived to result in benefits for both sides.

(a) The **winning** group will:

- Retain its cohesion
- Relax into a complacent, playful state
- Return to group maintenance and concern for members' needs
- Be confirmed in its group self-concept with little re-evaluation

(b) The **losing** group might behave as follows.

- Deny defeat if possible, or place the blame on the arbitrator, or the system

- Lose its cohesion and splinter into conflict, as 'blame' is apportioned

- Be keyed-up, fighting mad

- Turn towards work-orientation to regroup, rather than members' needs or group maintenance

- Tend to learn by re-evaluating its perceptions of itself and the other group.

1.15 Members of a group will act in unison if the group's existence or patterns of behaviour are threatened from outside. Cohesion is naturally assumed to be the result of positive factors such as communication, agreement and mutual trust - but in the face of a 'common enemy' (competition, crisis or emergency) cohesion and productivity benefit.

Question 3

How applicable are Sherif's 1965 research findings to the cause, symptoms and treatment of conflict in a modern organisation? In what ways, if at all, could Sherif's findings be used as a means of improving employee performance within an organisation?

Answer

Sherif's work applies to conflict in organisations. To improve employee performance, win-lose conflict can be turned towards competitors, who become 'the enemy'.

2 CAUSES, SYMPTOMS AND TACTICS OF CONFLICT

2.1 Causes of conflict

(a) **Differences in the objectives** of different groups or individuals.

(b) **Scarcity of resources**.

(c) **Interdependence of two departments** on a task. They have to work together but may do so ineffectively.

(d) **Disputes about the boundaries of authority.**

 (i) The technostructure may attempt to encroach on the roles or territory of line managers and usurp some of their authority.

 (ii) One department might start **'empire building'** and try to take over the work previously done by another department.

(e) **Personal differences,** as regards goals, attitudes and feelings, are also bound to crop up. This is especially true in **differentiated organisations**, where people employed in the different sub-units are very different.

2.2 Symptoms of conflict

- Poor communications, in all directions
- Interpersonal friction
- Inter-group rivalry and jealousy
- Low morale and frustration
- Widespread use of arbitration, appeals to higher authority, and inflexible attitudes

2.3 **The tactics of conflict**

(a) **Withholding information** from one another

(b) **Distorting information**. This will enable the group or manager presenting the information to get their own way more easily.

(c) **Empire building**. A group (especially a specialist group such as accounting) which considers its influence to be neglected might seek to **impose rules, procedures,** restrictions or official requirements on other groups, in order to bolster up their own importance.

(d) **Informal organisation**. A manager might seek to by-pass formal channels of communication and decision-making by establishing informal contacts and friendships with people in a position of importance.

(e) **Fault-finding** in the work of other departments: department X might duplicate the work of department Y - hoping to prove department Y wrong - and then report the fact to senior management.

3 MANAGERIAL RESPONSE TO CONFLICT

3.1 **Management responses to the handling of conflict** (not all of which are effective).

Response	Comment
Denial/withdrawal	'Sweeping it under the carpet'. If the conflict is very trivial, it may indeed blow over without an issue being made of it, but if the causes are not identified, the conflict may grow to unmanageable proportions.
Suppression	'Smoothing over', to preserve working relationships despite minor conflicts. As Hunt remarks, however: 'Some cracks cannot be papered over'.
Dominance	The application of power or influence to settle the conflict. The disadvantage of this is that it creates all the lingering resentment and hostility of 'win-lose' situations.
Compromise	Bargaining, negotiating, conciliating. To some extent, this will be inevitable in any organisation made up of different individuals. However, individuals tend to exaggerate their positions to allow for compromise, and compromise itself is seen to weaken the value of the decision, perhaps reducing commitment. **Negotiation** is: 'a process of interaction by which two or more parties who consider they need to be jointly involved in an outcome, but who initially have different objectives seek by the use of argument and persuasion to resolve their differences in order to achieve a mutually acceptable solution'.
Integration/ collaboration	Emphasis must be put on the task, individuals must accept the need to modify their views for its sake, and group effort must be seen to be superior to individual effort.
Encourage co-operative behaviour	Joint problem-solving team, goals set for all teams/departments to follow.

Question 4

In the light of the above consider how conflict could arise, what form it would take and how it might be resolved in the following situations.

(a)   Two managers who share a secretary have documents to be typed.

(b)   One worker finds out that another worker who does the same job as he does is paid a higher wage.

(c)   A company's electricians find out that a group of engineers have been receiving training in electrical work.

(d)   Department A stops for lunch at 12.30 while Department B stops at 1 o'clock. Occasionally the canteen runs out of puddings for Department B workers.

(e)   The Northern Region and Southern Region sales teams are continually trying to better each others results, and the capacity of production to cope with the increase in sales is becoming overstretched.

Answer

(a)   Both might need work done at the same time. Compromise and co-ordinated planning can help them manage their secretary's time.

(b)   Differential pay might result in conflict with management - even an accusation of discrimination. There may be good reasons for the difference (eg length of service). To prevent conflict such information should be kept confidential. Where it is public, it should be seen to be **not arbitrary.**

(c)   The electricians are worried about their jobs, and may take industrial action. Yet if the engineers' training is unrelated to the electricians' work, management can allay fears by giving information. The electricians cannot be given a veto over management decisions: a 'win-lose' situation is inevitable, but both sides can negotiate.

(d)   The kitchen should plan its meals better - or people from both departments can be asked in advance whether they want puddings.

(e)   Competition **between** sales regions is healthy as it increases sales. the conflict lies between sales regions and the production department. In the long-term, an increase in production capacity is the only solution. Where this is to possible, proper co-ordination methods should be instituted.

The win-win model

3.2   One useful model of conflict resolution is the **win-win model**. This states that there are three basic ways in which a conflict or disagreement can be worked out.

Method	Frequency	Explanation
Win-lose	This is quite common.	**One party gets what (s)he wants at the expense of the other party:** for example, Department A gets the new photocopier, while Department B keeps the old one (since there were insufficient resources to buy two new ones). However well-justified such a solution is (Department A needed the facilities on the new photocopier more than Department B), there is often lingering resentment on the part of the 'losing' party, which may begin to damage work relations.

Method	Frequency	Explanation
Lose-lose	This sounds like a senseless outcome, but actually **compromise** comes into this category. It is thus very common.	**Neither party gets what (s)he really wanted**: for example, since Department A and B cannot both have a new photocopier, it is decided that neither department should have one. However 'logical' such a solution is, there is often resentment and dissatisfaction on *both* sides. (Personal arguments where neither party gives ground and both end up storming off or not talking are also lose-lose: the parties may not have lost the argument, but they lose the relationship …) Even positive compromises only result in half-satisfied needs.
Win-win	This may not be common, but working towards it often brings out the best solution.	**Both parties get as close as possible to what they really want**. How can this be achieved?

3.3 It is critical to the **win-win approach** to discover **what both parties really want** - as opposed to:

- What they think they want (because they have not considered any other options)
- What they think they can get away with
- What they think they need in order to avoid an outcome they fear

For example, Department B may want the new photocopier because they have never found out how to use all the features (which do the same things) on the old photocopier; because they just want to have the same equipment as Department A; or because they fear that if they do not have the new photocopier, their work will be slower and less professionally presented, and they may be reprimanded (or worse) by management.

3.4 The important questions in working towards win-win are:

- What do you want this for?
- What do you think will happen if you don't get it?

These questions get to the heart of what people really need and want.

3.5 In our photocopier example, Department A says it needs the new photocopier to make colour copies (which the old copier does not do), while Department B says it needs the new copier to make clearer copies (because the copies on the old machine are a bit blurred). Now there are **options to explore**. It may be that the old copier just needs fixing, in order for Department B to get what it really wants. Department A will still end up getting the new copier - but Department B has in the process been consulted and had its needs met.

3.6 EXAMPLE: THE WIN-WIN APPROACH

Two men are fighting over an orange. There is only one orange, and both men want it.

(a) If one man gets the orange and the other does not, this is a **win-lose** solution.

(b) If they cut the orange in half and share it (or agree that neither will have the orange), this is a **lose-lose** solution - despite the compromise.

(c) If they talk about what they each need the orange for, and one says 'I want to make orange juice' and the other says 'I want the skin of the orange to make candied peel', there are further options to explore (like peeling the orange) and the potential for both men to get exactly what they wanted. This is a **win-win** approach.

3.7 **Win-win** is not always possible: It is **working towards it** that counts. The result can be mutual respect and co-operation, enhanced communication, more creative problem-solving and - at best - **satisfied needs all round.**

Question 5

Suggest a (i) win-lose, (ii) compromise and (iii) win-win solution in the following scenarios.

(a) Two of your team members are arguing over who gets the desk by the window: they both want it.

(b) You and a colleague both need access to the same file at the same time. You both need it to compile reports for your managers, for the following morning. It is now 3.00pm, and each of you will need it for two hours to do the work.

(c) Manager A is insisting on buying new computers for her department before the budgetary period ends. Manager B cannot understand why - since the old computers are quite adequate - and will moreover be severely inconvenienced by such a move, since her own systems will have to be upgraded as well, in order to remain compatible with department A. (The two departments constantly share data files.) Manager B protests, and conflict erupts.

Answer

(a) (i) **Win-lose**: one team member gets the window desk, and the other does not. (Result: broken relationships within the team.)

(ii) **Compromise**: the team members get the window desk on alternate days or weeks. (Result: half satisfied needs.)

(iii) **Win-win**: what do they want the window desk for? One may want the view, the other better lighting conditions. This offers options to be explored: how else could the lighting be improved, so that both team members get what they really want? (Result: at least, the positive intention to respect everyone's wishes equally, with benefits for team communication and creative problem-solving.)

(b) (i) **Win-lose**: one of you gets the file and the other doesn't.

(ii) **Compromise**: one of you gets the file now, and the other gets it later (although this has an element of win-lose, since the other has to work late or take it home).

(iii) **Win-win**: you photocopy the file and **both** take it, or one of your consults his or her boss and gets an extension of the deadline (since getting the job done in time is the real aim - not just getting the file). These kind of solutions are more likely to emerge if the parties believe they **can** both get what they want.

(c) (i) **Win-lose**: Manager A gets the computers, and Manager B has to upgrade her systems.

(ii) **Compromise**: Manager A will get some new computers, but keep the same old ones for continued data-sharing with Department B. Department B will also need to get some new computers, as a back-up measure.

(iii) **Win-win**: what does Manager A want the computers for, or to avoid? Quite possibly, she needs to use up her budget allocation for buying equipment before the end of the budgetary period: if not, she fears she will lose that budget allocation. Now, that may not be the case, or there may be other equipment that could be more usefully purchased - in which case, there is no losing party.

4   DISCIPLINE

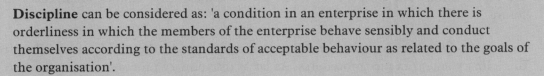

KEY TERM

Discipline can be considered as: 'a condition in an enterprise in which there is orderliness in which the members of the enterprise behave sensibly and conduct themselves according to the standards of acceptable behaviour as related to the goals of the organisation'.

4.1   Another definition of 'positive' and 'negative' discipline makes the distinction between methods of maintaining sensible conduct and orderliness which are technically co-operative, and those based on warnings, threats and punishments.

(a)   Positive (or constructive) discipline relates to procedures, systems and equipment in the work place which have been designed specifically so that the employee has **no option** but to act in the desired manner to complete a task safely and successfully. A machine may, for example, shut off automatically if its safety guard is not in place.

(b)   **Negative discipline** is then the promise of **sanctions** designed to make people choose to behave in a desirable way. Disciplinary action may be punitive (punishing an offence), deterrent (warning people not to behave in that way) or reformative (calling attention to the nature of the offence, so that it will not happen again).

4.2   The best discipline is **self discipline**. Even before they start to work, most mature people accept the idea that following instructions and fair rules of conduct are normal responsibilities that are part of any job. Most team members can therefore be counted on to exercise self discipline.

Types of disciplinary situations

4.3   There are many types of disciplinary situations which require attention by the manager. Internally, the most frequently occurring are these.

- Excessive absenteeism
- Poor timekeeping
- Defective and/or inadequate work performance
- Poor attitudes which influence the work of others or reflect on the image of the firm
- Breaking rules regarding rest periods and other time schedules
- Improper personal appearance
- Breaking safety rules
- Other violations of rules, regulations and procedures
- Open insubordination such as the refusal to carry out a work assignment.

4.4   Managers might be confronted with disciplinary problems stemming from employee behaviour *off* the job. These may be an excessive drinking problem, the use of drugs or some form of narcotics, or involvement in some form of law breaking activity. In such circumstances, whenever an employee's off-the-job conduct has an impact upon performance on the job, the manager must be prepared to deal with such a problem within the scope of the disciplinary process.

Disciplinary action

4.5   The purpose of discipline is not punishment or retribution. Disciplinary action must have as its goal the improvement of the future behaviour of the employee and other members of the organisation. The purpose obviously is the avoidance of similar occurrences in the future.

4.6   In the UK, discipline in civilian organisations is governed by the ACAS Code of Practice on disciplinary and grievance procedures. As far as disciplinary procedures are concerned, the code of practice lays down certain essential features.

...good disciplinary procedures should:

- be in writing

- specify to whom they apply

- be non-discriminatory

- provide for matters to be dealt with without undue delay

- provide for proceedings, witness statements and records to be kept confidential

- indicate the disciplinary actions which may be taken

- specify the levels of management which have the authority to take the various forms of disciplinary action

- provide for workers to be informed of the complaints against them and where possible all relevant evidence before any hearing

- provide workers with an opportunity to state their case before decisions are reached

- provide workers with the right to be accompanied

- ensure that, except for gross misconduct, no worker is dismissed for a first breach of discipline

- ensure that disciplinary action is not taken until the case has been carefully investigated

- ensure that workers are given an explanation for any penalty imposed

- provide a right of appeal – normally to a more senior manager – and specify the procedure to be followed

---

4.7   The Code goes on to discuss how disciplinary matters should be dealt with. All disciplinary incidents should be thoroughly investigated and a written record made by the appropriate manager. It will then be necessary to decide how to proceed. Many minor cases of poor performance or misconduct are best dealt with by informal advice, coaching or counselling. An informal oral warning may be issued. None of this forms part of the formal disciplinary procedure, but workers should be informed clearly what is expected and what action will be taken if they fail to improve.

4.8   In cases involving gross misconduct, breakdowns in relationships or risk to persons or property, a brief suspension on pay may be ordered while the case is investigated. Such a suspension is not in itself a disciplinary sanction.

4.9   Any **disciplinary action** must be preceded by a **disciplinary hearing** at which the worker must be told of the allegations made and allowed to answer them. Any rights under the organisation's own disciplinary procedure should be explained at this stage.

4.10   When the facts of the case have been established, it may be decided that formal disciplinary action is needed. The Code of Practice divides this into three stages. These are usually thought of as consecutive, reflecting a progressive response. However, it may be appropriate to miss out one of the earlier stages when there have been serious infringements.

4.11 **First warning**. A first warning could be either oral or written depending on the seriousness of the case.

(a) An **oral warning** should include the reason for issuing it, notice that it constitutes the first step of the disciplinary procedure and details of the right of appeal. A note of the warning should be kept on file but disregarded after a specified period, such as 6 months.

(b) A **first written warning** is appropriate in more serious cases. It should inform the worker of the improvement required and state that a final written warning may be considered if there is no satisfactory improvement. A copy of the first written warning should be kept on file but disregarded after a specified period such as 12 months.

A first written warning may also be appropriate if there has not been satisfactory improvement after an oral warning has been issued.

4.12 **Final written warning.** If an earlier warning is still current and there is no satisfactory improvement, a final written warning may be appropriate. Also, sufficiently serious infringements may lead directly to the issue of a final written warning.

4.13 A final written warning should give details of the offence, state that failure to improve may lead to dismissal or a lesser sanction and explain the appeals procedure. Despite its name, a final written warning is not necessarily final, since the ACAS Code of Practice requires that it should be disregarded for disciplinary purposes after a specified period such as 12 months.

4.14 Note that, depending on the offence, it is not necessary to progress through all of these levels of warning. One could go straight to the final written warning. This is thus a very flexible system, capable of dealing with disciplinary problems in a measured and proportionate way. It is however **always** necessary to investigate the allegations and to give the worker opportunity to reply to them.

Disciplinary sanctions

4.15 The final stage in the disciplinary process is the imposition of sanctions.

(a) **Suspension without pay**

This course of action would be next in order if the employee has committed repeated offences and previous steps were of no avail. Disciplinary lay-offs usually extend over several days or weeks. Some employees may not be very impressed with oral or written warnings, but they will find a disciplinary lay-off without pay a rude awakening. This penalty is only available if it is provided for in the contract of employment

(b) **Demotion**

This course of action is likely to bring about dissatisfaction and discouragement, since losing pay and status over an extended period of time is a form of constant punishment. This dissatisfaction of the demoted employee may easily spread to co-workers, so most enterprises avoid downgrading as a disciplinary measure like suspension without pay, this sanction may only be imposed if it is provided for in the contract of employment.

(c) **Discharge**

Discharge is a drastic form of disciplinary action, and should be reserved for the most serious offences. For the organisation, it involves waste of a labour resource, the expense of training a new employee, and disruption caused by changing the make-up of the work team. There also may be damage to the morale of the group.

Question 6

How (a) accessible and (b) clear are the rules and policies of your organisation/office: do people really know what they are and are not supposed to do? Have a look at the rule book or procedures manual in your office. How easy is it to see - or did you get referred elsewhere? is the rule book well-indexed and cross-referenced, and in language that all employees will understand?

How (a) accessible and (b) clear are the disciplinary procedures in your office? Are the employees' rights of investigation and appeal clearly set out, with ACAS guidelines? Who is responsible for discipline?

Relationship management in disciplinary situations

4.16 Even if the manager uses sensitivity and judgement, imposing disciplinary action tends to generate **resentment** because it is an unpleasant experience. The challenge is to apply the necessary disciplinary action so that it will be least resented.

(a) **Immediacy**

Immediacy means that after noticing the offence, the manager proceeds to take disciplinary action as *speedily* as possible, subject to investigations while at the same time avoiding haste and on-the-spot emotions which might lead to unwarranted actions.

(b) **Advance warning**

Employees should know in advance (eg in a Staff Handbook) what is expected of them and what the rules and regulations are.

(c) **Consistency**

Consistency of discipline means that each time an infraction occurs appropriate disciplinary action is taken. Inconsistency in application of discipline lowers the morale of employees and diminishes their respect for the manager.

(d) **Impersonality**

Penalties should be connected with the act and not based upon the personality involved, and once disciplinary action has been taken, no grudges should be borne.

(e) **Privacy**

As a general rule (unless the manager's authority is challenged directly and in public) disciplinary action should be taken in private, to avoid the spread of conflict and the humiliation or martyrdom of the employee concerned.

Disciplinary interviews

4.17 **Preparation for the disciplinary interview**

(a) **Gathering the facts** about the alleged infringement

(b) **Determination of the organisation's position:** how valuable is the employee, potentially? How serious are his offences/lack of progress? How far is the organisation prepared to go to help him improve or discipline him further?

(c) **Identification of the aims of the interview**: punishment? deterrent to others? improvement? Specific standards of future behaviour/performance required need to be determined.

(d) **Ensure that the organisation's disciplinary procedures have been followed**

    (i)   Informal oral warnings (at least) have been given.

    (ii)   The employee has been given adequate notice of the interview for his own preparation.

    (iii)   The employee has been informed of the complaint against his right to be accompanied by a colleague or representative and so on.

4.18   **The content of the disciplinary interview**

Step 1.   The manager will explain the purpose of the interview.

Step 2.   The charges against the employee will be delivered, clearly, unambiguously and without personal emotion.

Step 3.   The manager will explain the organisation's position with regard to the issues involved: disappointment, concern, need for improvement, impact on others. This can be done frankly - but tactfully, with as positive an emphasis as possible on the employee's capacity and responsibility to improve.

Step 4.   The organisation's expectations with regard to future behaviour/performance should be made clear.

Step 5.   The employee should be given the opportunity to comment, explain, justify or deny. If he is to approach the following stage of the interview in a positive way, he must not be made to feel 'hounded' or hard done by.

Step 6.   The organisation's expectations should be reiterated, or new standards of behaviour set for the employee.

    (i)   They should be specific and quantifiable, performance related and realistic.

    (ii)   They should be related to a practical but reasonably short time period. A date should be set to review his progress.

    (iii)   The manager agrees on measures to help the employee should that be necessary. It would demonstrate a positive approach if, for example, a mentor were appointed from his work group to help him check his work. If his poor performance is genuinely the result of some difficulty or distress outside work, other help (temporary leave, counselling or financial aid) may be appropriate.

Step 7.   The manager should explain the reasons behind any penalties imposed on the employee, including the entry in his personnel record of the formal warning. He should also explain how the warning can be removed from the record, and what standards must be achieved within a specified timescale. There should be a clear warning of the consequences of failure to meet improvement targets.

Step 8.   The manager should explain the organisation's appeals procedures: if the employee feels he has been unfairly treated, there should be a right of appeal to a higher manager.

Step 9.   Once it has been established that the employee understands all the above, the manager should summarise the proceedings briefly.

Records of the interview will be kept for the employee's personnel file, and for the formal follow-up review and any further action necessary.

Question 7

Outline the steps involved in a formal disciplinary procedure (for an organisation with unionised employees) and show how the procedure would operate in a case of:

(a) Persistent absenteeism

(b) Theft of envelopes from the organisation's offices

Answer

Apart from the outline of the steps involved - which can be drawn from the chapter, this question raises an interesting point about the nature of different offences, and the flexibility required in the handling of complex disciplinary matters.

There is clearly a difference in kind and scale between

o   unsatisfactory conduct (eg absenteeism)

o   misconduct (eg insulting behaviour, persistent absenteeism, insubordination) and

o   'gross misconduct' (eg theft or assault).

The attitude of the organisation towards the purpose of disciplinary action will to a large extent dictate the severity of the punishment.

o   If it is punitive it will 'fit the crime'.

o   If it is reformative, it may be a warning only, and less severe than the offence warrants.

o   If it is deterrent, it may be more severe than is warranted (ie to 'make an example').

The absenteeism question assumes that counselling etc. has failed, and that some sanction has to be applied, to preserve credibility. The theft technically deserves summary dismissal (as gross misconduct), but it depends on the scale and value of the theft, the attitude of the organisation to use of stationery for personal purposes (ie is it theft?) etc. Communicating the situations given might best be done as follows.

(a) Telephone, confirmed in writing (order form, letter)

(b) Noticeboard or general meeting

(c) Fact-to-face conversation. it would be a good idea to confirm the outcome of the meeting in writing so that records can be maintained.

(d) Either telephone or face-to-face.

5   GRIEVANCE

> **KEY TERM**
>
> A **grievance** occurs when an individual thinks that he is being wrongly treated by his colleagues or supervisor; perhaps he or she is being picked on, unfairly appraised in his annual report, unfairly blocked for promotion or discriminated against on grounds of race or sex.

5.1   When an individual has a grievance he should be able to pursue it and ask to have the problem resolved. Some grievances should be capable of solution informally by the individual's manager. However, if an informal solution is not possible, there should be a formal grievance procedure.

5.2   The **ACAS Code of Practice** also deal with grievance procedures and describes essential features of such procedures.

(a)   Procedures should be simple, set down in writing and rapid in operation.

(b)   Grievance proceedings and records should be kept confidential.

(c)   It is good practice for individuals to be accompanied at grievance hearings

(d)   In order for grievance procedures to be effective, all workers are should be made aware of them and understand them and if necessary that supervisors, managers and worker representatives are trained in their use.

5.3   **Formal grievance procedures** should accomplish the following.

(a)   State the **rights** of the employee for each type of grievance. For example, an employee who is not invited to attend a promotion/selection panel might claim that he has been unfairly passed over. The grievance procedure must state what the individual would be entitled to claim. In our example, the employee who is overlooked for promotion might be entitled to a review of his annual appraisal report, or to attend a special appeals promotion/ selection board if he has been in his current grade for at least a certain number of years.

(b)   State what the **procedures** for pursuing a grievance should be.

   Step 1.   The individual should **discuss the grievance** with a staff/union representative (or a colleague). If his case seems a good one, he should take the grievance to his immediate boss. The grievance should ideally, be stated in writing.

   Step 2.   The **first interview** will be between the immediate manager (unless he is the subject of the complaint, in which case it will be the next level up) and the employee, who has the right to be accompanied by a colleague or representative.

   Step 3.   If the immediate manager cannot resolve the matter, or the employee is otherwise dissatisfied with the first interview, the case should be referred to his superior (and if necessary in some cases, to an even higher authority).

   Step 4.   Cases referred to a **higher manager** should also be reported to the personnel department. Line management might decide at some stage to ask for the assistance/advice of a personnel manager in resolving the problem.

(c)   Distinguish between **individual** grievances and **collective** grievances.

(d)   **Allow for the involvement of an individual's or group's trade union or staff association representative**. Indeed, many individuals and groups might prefer to initiate some grievance procedures through their union or association rather than through official grievance procedures.

(e)   State **time limits** for initiating certain grievance procedures and subsequent stages of them. For example, a person who is passed over for promotion should be required to make his appeal within a certain time period of his review, and his appeal to higher authority (if any) within a given period after the first grievance interview. There should also be timescales for management to determine and communicate the outcome of the complaint to the employee.

(f)   Require **written records** of all meetings concerned with the case to be made and distributed to all the participants.

BPP PUBLISHING

Grievance interviews

5.4 The dynamics of a grievance interview are broadly similar to a disciplinary interview, except that it is the subordinate who primarily wants a positive result from it. Prior to the interview, the manager should have some idea of the complaint and its possible source. The meeting itself can then proceed through three phases.

Step 1. **Exploration**. What is the problem: the background, the facts, the causes (manifest and hidden)? At this stage, the manager should simply try to gather as much information as possible, without attempting to suggest solutions or interpretations: the situation must be seen to be open.

Step 2. **Consideration**. The manager should:

- Check the facts

- Analyse the causes - the problem of which the complaint may be only a symptom

- Evaluate options for responding to the complaint, and the implication of any response made

It may be that information can be given to clear up a misunderstanding, or the employee will - having 'got it off his chest' - withdraw his complaint. However, the meeting may have to be adjourned (say, for 48 hours) while the manager gets extra information and considers extra options.

Step 3. **Reply**. The manager, having reached and reviewed his conclusions, reconvenes the meeting to convey (and justify, if required) his decision, hear counter-arguments and appeals. The outcome (agreed or disagreed) should be recorded in writing.

5.5 Grievance procedures should be seen as an employee's right. To this end, managers should be given formal training in the grievance procedures of their organisation, and the reasons for having them. Management should be persuaded that the grievance procedures are beneficial for the organisation and are not a threat to themselves (since many grievances arise out of disputes between subordinates and their boss).

Question 8

Find your organisation's grievance procedures in the office manual, or ask your union or staff association representative. Study the procedures carefully. Think of a complaint or grievance you have (or have had) at work. Have you taken it to grievance procedures? If so, what happened: were you satisfied with the process and outcome? If not, why not?

Chapter roundup

- **Conflict** can be viewed as:

  - Inevitable owing to the class system
  - A continuation of organisation politics by other means
  - Something to be welcomed as it avoids complacency
  - Something resulting from poor management
  - Something which should be avoided at all costs

- Conflict is possible owing to the different degrees of **power**, **influence** and **authority** that different groups have. Negative power, for example, is the power to disrupt.

- Conflict can be **constructive**, if it introduced new information into a problem, if it denies a problem or if it encourages creativity. It can be destructive if it distracts attention from the task or inhibits communication.

- One constructive response to conflict is the **'win-win' model**.

- **Discipline** has the same end as **motivation** - ie to secure a range of desired behaviour from members of the organisation.

  - Motivation may even be called a kind of **self discipline** - because motivated individuals exercise choice to behave in the way that the organisation wishes.

  - Discipline however, is more often related to **negative motivation**, an appeal to the individual's need to avoid punishment, sanctions or unpleasantness.

- Progressive **discipline** includes the following **stages**.

  - Informal talk
  - Oral warning
  - Written/official warning
  - Lay-off or suspension
  - Dismissal

- **Grievance procedures** embody the employee's right to appeal against unfair or otherwise prejudicial conduct or conditions that affect him and his work.

- **Grievance interviews** follow: exploration, consideration, reply.

Quick quiz

1   What are the features of the 'happy family view' of the organisation?

2   Give an alternative to the happy family view.

3   When can conflict be constructive?

4   What happens when two groups are put in competition with each other?

5   What are the possible outcomes of conflict, according to the 'win-win' model?

6   What causes conflict?

7   What is discipline?

8   What is progressive discipline?

9   What factors should a manager bear in mind in trying to control the disciplinary situation?

10   Outline typical grievance procedures, or the grievance procedures of your own firm.

Answers to quick quiz

1   Organisations are co-operative and harmonious. Conflict arises when something goes wrong.

2   Conflict is inevitable, being in the very nature of the organisation. Conflict can be constructive.

3   It can introduce solutions, define power relations, bring emotions, hostile or otherwise, out into the open.

4   They become more cohesive internally and more achievement-orientated.

5   Win-lose, lose-lose, win-win.

6   Different objectives, scarcity of responses, personal differences, interdependence of departments.

7   People behave according to the standard the organisation has set.

8   A system whereby the disciplinary action gets more severe with repeated 'offence'.

9   Immediacy, advance warning, consistency, impersonality, privacy.

10 Grievance procedures should state employees' rights, the procedures distinguish between individual and collective grievances state time limits. The interview should explore the facts, consider the issues and provide a resolution.

Now try the question below from the Exam Question Bank

Question to try	Level	Marks	Time
16	Exam	12	22 mins

Question bank

1   **MECHANISTIC AND ORGANIC APPROACHES**   *27 mins*

Contrast the **mechanistic** and **organic** approaches to management.   **(15 marks)**

2   **PROPOSALS**   *27 mins*

Contrast the proposals of TWO of the following writers regarding the role/functions of the Manager.

(5 marks each)

(a)   Fayol
(b)   Drucker
(c)   Handy
(d)   Mintzberg   **(15 marks)**

3   **ORGANISATIONAL CULTURE**   *27 mins*

(a)   Define organisational culture and describe the most important factors in its development.(5 marks)

(b)   Explain the meaning of **two** of role culture, task culture, power culture and person culture. Illustrate your choices with examples.   (10 marks)
(15 marks)

4   **TEAM SUCCESS (Pilot paper)**   *27 mins*

A team differs from an informal work group.

Required

(a)   Explain the way in which a team differs from an informal work group.   (5 marks)
(b)   Describe any five factors required to ensure team success.   (10 marks)
(15 Marks)

5   **DELEGATION**

Professional accountants often need to delegate duties to others in the organisation.

Required

(a)   Explain what is meant by delegation   (5 marks)
(b)   Explain how effective delegation might be achieved   (10 marks)
(15 Marks)

6   **GOOD BUSINESS SENSE**   *18 mins*

Explain the arguments for and against the claim that the exercise of social responsibility makes good business sense.   **(10 Marks)**

7   **JOB ANALYSIS (Pilot paper)**   *27 mins*

The manager of the finance department has asked you to carry out a job analysis of the other employees in your department.

Required

(a)   Briefly explain what is meant by the term 'job analysis'.   (3 marks)

(b)   Briefly explain the four stages involved in carrying out a job analysis.   (4 marks)

(c)   Identify and briefly explain the information you would expect to collect during the job analysis investigation.   (8 marks)
(15 marks)

BPP
PUBLISHING

8   SELECTION INTERVIEWS   27 *mins*

'The one-to-one selection interview is irredeemably flawed because it offers too much scope for the exercise of prejudice and favouritism.'

(a)   To what extent do you agree with this statement?   (8 marks)
(b)   Discuss alternatives to the one-to-one selection process.   (7 marks)
                                                                        (15 Marks)

9   EQUAL OPPORTUNITY   27 *mins*

A recent report from the International Labour Organisation, collating research from around the world, shows that women continue to be excluded from senior executive positions and are clustered in occupations that are segregated by gender, such as cleaning, catering and the health service. Worldwide, the average female participation in management jobs is just 20 per cent.

(a)   What are the causes of this state of affairs?   (8 marks)
(b)   Why should it be a cause for concern?   (7 marks)
                                                                        (15 marks)

10   LEARNING STYLE (Pilot paper)   27 *mins*

Different learning styles and approaches suit different individuals.

(a)   Identify and explain Honey & Mumfords theory on learning styles.   (10 marks)
(b)   Explain the experiential learning cycle.   (5 marks)
                                                                        (15 Marks)

11   PERFORMANCE MANAGEMENT   27 *mins*

(a)   What in practice are the differences between 'performance appraisal' and 'performance management'?   (10 marks)

(b)   Why has there been a shift towards 'performance management' and away from 'performance appraisal'?   (5 marks)
                                                                        (15 marks)

12   OFFICE RISKS

List the likely risks of personal injury and ill-health **in the office.**   **(15 marks)**

13   REWARDS   27 *mins*

Financial rewards are not appropriate in all circumstances.

Required

(a)   Briefly explain what is meant by **intrinsic** rewards.   (3 marks)
(b)   Briefly explain what is meant by **extrinsic** rewards.   (3 marks)
(c)   List any six types of extrinsic reward.   (9 marks)
                                                                        (15 marks)

14   LEADERSHIP STYLES   27 *mins*

'Choosing a leadership style which is entirely appropriate to any given situation is one of the most important skills that an effective manager can possess.'

Describe the range of leadership styles which it is possible for managers to display.

15   COMMUNICATION (Pilot paper)   *27 mins*

Much of the work of professional accountants involves communicating information for others to use.

Required

(a)   Explain the importance of clear communication.   (5 marks)
(b)   Explain two main communication methods.   (5 marks)
(c)   Describe two barriers to communication.   (5 marks)
                                                                            (15 marks)

16   DISCIPLINE MISTAKES   *27 mins*

(a)   What are the common mistakes made by managers when conducting disciplinary interviews?
                                                                                  (7 marks)

(b)   What are the fundamental criteria which should be met by an organisation's disciplinary
      procedure?   (8 marks)
                                                                            (15 Marks)

17   SCENARIO: ACCOUNTS CLERK (Pilot paper)   *72 mins*

Deborah Williams, the Finance Director of SMG Ltd, thinks that the staff in the accounts department
are overworked and has asked the Human Resource Department for an additional accounts clerk,
preferably two.

SMG has no formal procedures or processes to ensure that appropriate and qualified staff are
appointed. In the past SMG Ltd has relied on agencies and informal contacts to recruit new employees.

SMG Ltd has recently appointed you as assistant Human Resource Manager. You have been asked to
take charge of the situation, to see if Ms Williams has a case and then to manage the new
appointments process if the vacancy is approved.

Required

(a)   Explain how you would establish whether Deborah Williams has a legitimate case for a new
      member of staff.   (8 marks)

(b)   Given that the vacancy is approved, discuss the procedure you would take to appoint a qualified
      accounts clerk.   (7 marks)

(c)   Describe the contents of a job description and person specification for the new accounts clerk.
                                                                                  (10 marks)

(d)   Explain how you would carry out the recruitment and selection of the new clerk.
                                                                                  (10 marks)

(e)   What might be the benefits of ongoing training and development to the clerk and the business?
                                                                                  (5 marks)
                                                                            (40 marks)

> **BPP Note**. Parts (b) and (d) of this question appear similarly worded. One possible approach -
> adopted by BPP - is to view section (b) as the **resourcing** process looking at **all** options and
> section (d) as the process recruitment, after the decision as been taken that the resource
> shortage should be met in this way.

Index

1 MECHANISTIC AND ORGANIC APPROACHES

Contrast between mechanistic and organic approaches

The distinction between mechanistic and organic organisations was highlighted by Burns and Stalker, who coined the terms.

Characteristics of a mechanistic organisation

(a) **Hierarchy**: each lower office is under the control and supervision of a higher one.

(b) **Specialisation and training**: there is a high degree of specialisation of labour. Employment is based on ability, not personal loyalty.

(c) **Impersonal nature**: employees work full time within the impersonal rules and regulations and act according to formal, impersonal procedures.

(d) **Professional nature of employment**: an organisation exists before it is filled with people. Officials are full-time employees, promotion is according to seniority and achievement; pay scales are prescribed according to the position or office held in the organisation structure.

(e) **Rationality**: the 'jurisdictional areas' of the organisation are determined rationally. The hierarchy of authority and office structure is clearly defined. Duties are established and measures of performance set.

(f) **Uniformity:** in the performance of tasks is expected, regardless of whoever is engaged in carrying them out.

(g) **Technical competence** in officials is rarely questioned within the area of their expertise.

(h) **Stability**.

Mechanistic systems are **unsuitable in conditions of change** because they tend to deal with change by cumbersome methods.

Organic structures

(a) There is a **contributive nature** where specialised knowledge and experience are contributed to the common task of the organisation.

(b) Each individual has a realistic task which can be understood **in terms of the common task of the organisation.**

(c) **Flexible job descriptions**. There is a continual re-definition of an individual's task, through interaction between the individual and others.

(d) There is a spread of **commitment** to the concern and its tasks.

(e) There is a **network** structure of authority and communication.

(f) Communication tends to be *lateral* rather than vertical (ie gangplanks, rather than up and down the scalar chain).

(g) Communication takes the form of **information and advice** rather than instructions and decisions.

In contrast to mechanistic structures, Burns and Stalker identified the organic structure. Organic structures are better suited to conditions of change than mechanistic structures. The organic structure has the following characteristics.

2 PROPOSALS

> **Tutor's note.** You are asked to discuss **two** of the writers named in the question. We have covered all four for completeness.

(a) **Fayol**

Henri Fayol, an early management theorist working in nineteenth century France, proposed that certain functions were common to the management of all types of organisations.

- **Planning**. This is selecting objectives, and the strategies, policies, programmes and procedures for achieving the objectives either for the organisation as a whole or for a part of it.

- **Organising**. This is the establishment of a structure of tasks that support the organisation's goals; grouping these tasks into individual jobs; creating groups of jobs within sections and departments; delegating authority to carry out the jobs; and providing systems of information and communication.

- **Commanding**. This is giving instructions to subordinates to carry out tasks over which the manager has authority for decisions and responsibility for performance.

- **Co-ordinating**. This is the task of harmonising individual activities and reconciling differences in approach, effort, interest and timing. This is best achieved by showing how individual efforts contribute to the overall goals of the organisation.

- **Controlling**. This is the task of measuring and correcting the activities of individuals and groups, to ensure that their performance is in accordance with plans.

Fayol was writing at a time when large organisations were fairly uncommon and tended to be concerned with fairly stable activities, such as the operation of railways. There is a link between his ideas and scientific management in that both were concerned with efficiency of operation. Fayol was aware of the importance of the human factor, but the functions outlined above do not include any specifically concerned with the human resource, such as training or leadership.

(b) **Drucker**

Drucker grouped the operations of management into five categories.

- **Setting objectives for the organisation**. Managers decide what the objectives of the organisation should be and quantify the targets of achievement for each objective. They must then communicate these targets to other people in the organisation.

- **Organising the work**. The work to be done must be divided into manageable activities and manageable jobs. The jobs must be integrated into a formal organisation structure, and people must be selected to do the jobs.

- **Motivation**. Managers must motivate employees and communicate information to them to enable them to do their work.

- **The job of measurement**. Management must establish yardsticks of performance, measure actual performance, appraise it against the yardsticks, and communicate the findings both to subordinate employees and to superiors.

- **Developing people**. The manager 'brings out what is in them or he stifles them. He strengthens their integrity or he corrupts them'.

It is clear from this analysis that Drucker was much more concerned than Fayol with the human resource aspects of management. He also differed from Fayol in suggesting that management of commercial enterprises was fundamentally different from managing other types of organisation. Management can only justify its existence and authority by the economic results it produces. He suggested there were three aspects.

- **Managing a business**. This revolves around marketing and innovation.

- **Managing managers**. Drucker was the first to use the phrase 'management by objectives'.

- **Managing worker and work**.

(c) Handy

Charles Handy suggested that a definition of a manager or a manager's role is likely to be so broad as to be fairly meaningless. His own analysis of being a manager was divided into three aspects.

The manager as a general practitioner. Managers are the first recipients of the organisation's problems. They must identify the symptoms (such as falling sales); diagnose the cause of the trouble (such as increased competition); decide how it might be dealt with (for instance by increasing promotional spending); and start the treatment. Handy suggested that typical strategies for health would involve changing **people**, either literally or figuratively, restructuring **work** or making changes to **systems and procedures**.

The managerial dilemmas. Managers are regularly faced with dilemmas which have to be resolved.

- **The dilemma of the cultures**. Management must guide the development of an appropriate culture. As managers rise in seniority, they will find it necessary to behave in a

culturally diverse manner to satisfy the requirements of both work and the expectations of employees.

- **The dilemma of time horizons**. The manager must reconcile the frequent conflict between short and long term priorities.

- **The trust-control dilemma**. Management must delegate, but this inevitably reduces immediacy of control.

- **The commando leader's dilemma**. Junior managers often prefer working in project teams, to working within the bureaucratic structure of a large organisation. Unfortunately, having too many ad hoc groups leads to confusion.

The manager as a person. Management is increasingly seen as a profession and managers accorded appropriate status. However, at the same time the manager is coming under more pressure from customers to deliver and from employees and society to exercise social responsibility.

Handy's analysis contrasts with both Fayol's and Drucker's in its lack of prescription. Instead of specifying a list of functions, Handy discusses some of the types of problems the manager may have to solve.

(d) **Mintzberg**

Handy's rather vague approach is much improved upon by Henry Mintzberg's empirical research into how managers in fact do their work. He contends 'The classical view says that the manager organises, co-ordinates, plans and controls; the facts suggest otherwise.'

Mintzberg instead identifies three types of role which a manager must play.

- **Interpersonal roles**. Senior manager spend much of their time in figurehead or ceremonial roles. The leader role involves hiring, firing and training staff, motivating employees and reconciling individual needs with the requirements of the organisation. The liaison role is performed when managers make contacts outside the vertical chain of command.

- **Informational roles**. As a leader, a manager has access to every member of staff, and is likely to have more external contacts than any of them. Managers are a channels of information from inside the department to outside and vice versa. The manager monitors the environment, and receives information from subordinates or peers, much of it informally. The manager disseminates information both formally and informally to subordinates. As a spokesman the manager provides information to interested parties.

- **Decisional roles**. The manager takes decisions of several types relating to the work of the department. A manager acts as a sort of **entrepreneur** by initiating projects to improve the department or to help it react to a changed environment. A manager responds to pressures and is therefore a disturbance handler taking decisions in unusual situations which are impossible to predict. A manager takes decisions relating to the allocation of **scarce resources**. **Negotiation** inside and outside the organisation is a vital component of managerial work.

Mintzberg drew a number of conclusions about managerial work which contrast strongly with Fayol's prescriptions and even Drucker's more pragmatic approach.

- Managerial work is disjointed and planning is conducted on a day to day basis, in between more urgent tasks.

- Managers perform a number of routine duties, particularly of a ceremonial nature, such as receiving important guests.

- Managers prefer *verbal* communication. Information conveyed in an informal way is likely to be more current and concrete than that produced by a formal management information system.

- General management is, in practice, a matter of judgement and intuition, gained from experience in particular situations rather than from abstract principles. 'The manager is . . . forced to do many tasks superficially. Brevity, fragmentation and verbal communication characterise his work.'

3 ORGANISATIONAL CULTURE

(a) **Culture** is the pattern of beliefs, attitudes and behaviour which distinguishes a society. **Organisation culture is the particular type of culture which prevails within a given organisation**. Not all organisations have the same culture. There are a number of influences on the development of an organisation's culture.

(i) The **wider cultural background of society** influences basic assumptions and sets limits upon what is appropriate within the culture of the organisation.

(ii) Within that setting, the **industry itself may have strong cultural norms**, as for instance in mining or the film industry.

(iii) A major **influence** can be exerted by the organisation's **founder**, in both commercial and not-for-profit organisations. This is particularly apparent when charismatic individuals establish new methods and approaches.

(iv) The organisation's history and the way the organisation has developed. Many business organisations originate with successful sole traders or partnerships but grow, sometimes rapidly, to many times their original size. **Success reinforces the methods and attitudes** prevailing in such organisations and increasing size brings its own imperatives.

(v) **Management style** both reflects organisation culture and helps to form it. An organisation with a strong culture, of whatever type, will tend to recruit managers who will conform to its norms. A more anonymous organisation may find recruits shaping its culture in their own image.

(b) The analysis of organisational culture into four types called role, task, power and person was popularised by Charles Handy in his book *The Gods of Management.*

(i) The **role culture** is typical of the large organisation operating in a stable environment. Generally, this cultural type will have the following characteristics.

- Its structure is likely to be formal and static, with functional departmentation and clear lines of authority and responsibility.

- It will be process oriented, with considerable prescriptiveness about communication, procedure and behaviour. Individuals will be appointed to discharge defined responsibilities in accordance with the rules. Initiative may not be welcomed. Efficient discharge of duty is the priority.

- The culture is not entrepreneurial and will be slow to change. It takes its environment for granted but is very effective when not faced with sudden change.

This type of culture is found in military services, central and local government, nationalised monopolies and conservative businesses such as banks and insurance companies.

(ii) The **task culture** is more dynamic and responsive. It is based on a team work approach to changing circumstances. An organisation with this culture will have the following characteristics.

- Structure will be flexible and fluid, with project teams formed and adjusted as required. There will be little hierarchy or formal leadership responsibility since members will tend to be specialists and experts in their own fields.

- The main concern will be results rather than procedures and expertise will be employed wherever it can be found.

- There will be an expectation of high personal satisfaction. Technical challenge and an opportunity to make a contribution will be valued highly.

This type of culture is common in some professional practices, such as architects and engineers, in advertising agencies and in creative work such as film and television production.

(iii) The **power culture** is found in highly centralised organisations, typically those run by an entrepreneurial owner-manager.

- All decisions are taken at the centre and all the strings are in the owner's hands. Like the task culture, this culture enhances the ability to respond to a rapidly changing environment, but authority is exercised much more clearly.

- Subordinates will have little freedom to manoeuvre or develop. They must accept their role as supporting the leader.

Successful start-up businesses often develop this culture; it is also seen in smaller military units and voluntary bodies which employ talented individuals to administer them.

(iv) The **person culture** grows up where the organisation exists to serve its members.

- An **example** is a barristers' chambers, where professionals come together to share expenses and employ staff collectively to organise the facilities they need.

- Power is shared among the principal members and the managers may be of lower status, often no more than administrators.

- The members of such an organisation value independence and achievement and may work more or less in isolation from their colleagues.

4 TEAM SUCCESS

(a) While different from one another, informal work groups and teams are both **groups** and have shared attributes.

- Purpose and leadership
- A sense of identity
- Loyalty to the group

The differences between teams and informal work groups lie within these shared attributes and exist primarily because of the sharp distinction in **reason for existence**.

- **Teams** are established by an organisation to perform organisational tasks, often with an official leader.

- **Informal groups** come into existence in response to the social and personal needs of the members. This difference is reflected in the nature of the leadership exercised within the two types of group.

In an informal group, leadership is likely to be exercised in a more **fluid** way, possibly with several members sharing the leadership role. Satisfaction of group and individual needs will depend on individual initiatives by the more perceptive and influential members of the group. Loyalty and identification with the group may be very strong, but this is likely to result from commonality of personal interest rather than effective leadership.

(b) **A variety of factors will contribute to team success**

(i) **Leadership** is probably the most important single factor and the one most often lacking. Good leadership will promote co-operation between team members, motivate the individuals towards the task and ensure that work is properly organised.

A team is likely to have a **leader** appointed by the organisation and it is one of the tasks of leadership to promote the coherence of the group. This will include motivating, organising and controlling the efforts of individuals in pursuit of the team's work objectives; these are what *Adair* calls **task needs**.

Adair suggests that the leader should also pursue **individual needs** and **group needs**. The process of motivation is also an individual need, as are the requirements for recognition and counselling. Group needs include peacekeeping and standard setting. Successful leadership is likely to produce a sense of identity and loyalty to the team almost as by-products of the satisfaction of other group and individual needs.

(ii) The **task** or **role** of the team must be defined. This can be seen in terms of the objectives set for the leader, since the leader must take responsibility for the team's work.

(iii) The members of the team must possess the **skills** required for them to perform their roles. To some extent, these can be learned on the job, under the supervision of the leader.

(iv) A proper level of **resources** must be provided, though motivation can overcome many resource deficiencies.

(v) The efforts of the team must be **co-ordinated** with those of the rest of the organisation. To some extent this is a task for the leader, but there must be mechanisms in place to allow sideways communication between team members and other parts of the organisation and to permit proper response to changed circumstances.

5   **DELEGATION**

(a) **Delegation** occurs in an organisation when a superior grants to a subordinate the **authority to take decisions within specified terms of reference**. The authority granted must lie within the superior's own area of responsibility. The subordinate becomes responsible to the superior for the proper use of the authority granted, but the superior remains responsible to the next higher echelon for the overall performance level achieved.

Delegation enables formal organisations to **make use of the efforts and abilities of large** numbers of people while retaining direction and control.

(b) A **number of features contribute to effective delegation**.

The **subordinate must possess the personal qualities, ability, training and experience** required to discharge the allotted duties.

The **superior must maintain a proper degree of supervision**. This will vary from case to case and there is a difficult balance to strike between control and interference. Management by objectives (MBO) can be used at more senior levels, where proper use of discretion may be relied upon. The essence of MBO is that the subordinate's tasks or targets are agreed in discussion with the superior and objective performance measures are established.

Authority and responsibility must be commensurate. Authority without responsibility leads to arbitrary decisions and careless behaviour, while responsibility without authority leads to stagnation and stress for the subordinate. The allocation of a proper level of resources is an important aspect of this balance.

The subordinate's responsibility and authority must be **clearly specified and understood by all those affected**. This ensures that the subordinate can exercise authority and obtain the co-operation required from other managers. MBO can form a basis for the establishment and promulgation of written authority, though a less detailed specification is probably more appropriate. With more senior managers a brief statement of overall responsibility is probably most appropriate, so that initiative is encouraged.

6   **GOOD BUSINESS SENSE**

Economists such as Milton Friedman suggest that so **long as a company obeys the law, it discharges any social responsibility it may have by maximising its profits**. This is because the profits depend on economic efficiency and effectiveness and the company that makes **high profits is by definition making the best use of its resources**. It is providing **customer satisfaction**, paying its **work force, paying taxes** and paying its **providers of capital**. The last category are increasingly pension funds whose incomes benefit large sections of society.

An alternative view is that business and society are interdependent and if business ignores society's concerns, society will find a way to punish it. This is almost a marketing approach, emphasising the wholeness of a business's relationship with society. It can be seen cynically as emphasising the PR aspect of business and the importance of image.

A synthesis of these two views is possible.

- Most companies behave to some extent as though ordinary business motivations like profitability and market share are their main concerns, but with social responsibility as a subsidiary concern.

- This means that socially responsible actions are evaluated in terms of costs and benefits to the company before they are undertaken.

Examples include:

- Sponsorship of the arts, which can raise publicity among key audiences

- Secondments of management and staff can be good for motivation and morale

- Charitable giving, which can also be publicised

- Companies with high standards can shape the political debate more easily than those seen dragging their feet, and may also enjoy a competitive advantage if others have to catch up with them

7   JOB ANALYSIS

(a)   **Job analysis** is the process of examining a job to determine its essential characteristics, including its component tasks and the circumstances and constraints under which it is performed. It provides the basis for the preparation of a job description and may also contribute to a scheme of **job evaluation**.

(b)   There are four main sources of information about a job. It would be sensible to approach them in the order given below.

   (i)   There may be **documentation** such as written procedures, organisation charts, quality manuals and even earlier job descriptions. These can be consulted at leisure.

   (ii)   An early approach to the relevant **supervisor** is advisable. This person is likely to have clear ideas about what the job includes and may be able to resolve subsequent queries.

   (iii) The **job-holder** should be consulted. What the person concerned thinks the job consists of is likely to differ noticeably both from what the supervisor thinks is done and from what the documentation says should be done.

   (iv)   A possible final stage is **observation** of what the job-holder **actually does**. Once again, this may differ from what the job-holder has described.

   (v)   A full picture of the job will emerge from these four sources. An important task for the analyst is to establish what adjustments need to be made to the documentation and whether extra activities that have developed should be done elsewhere.

(c)   **Job analysis should produce information that relates to both the job and, in general terms, to the person doing it.**

   Job-related information should start with the overall **purpose and scope** of the job. This sets the job in its organisational context and should be stated briefly. For example, the scope of an accounts clerk's job might be to maintain ledgers on a computerised system. Direct accountability may be included at this stage by stating the supervisor to whom the job-holder reports

   It will then be appropriate to list the specific **duties and responsibilities** of the job, setting them out in logical groups. For instance, it would be sensible to list all the duties relating to the purchase ledger separately from those relating to the sales ledger. **Performance** criteria should be included.

   Duties and **responsibilities** may be discussed together or separately, depending on the nature of the job. However, it is important to include information on the levels of responsibility held for staff, money, equipment and other resources.

   The **environment** and **conditions** of the job should be investigated. This includes such factors such as pay and benefits, shift work and holidays. Particular attention should be paid to the physical environment and to potential hazards.

   The **social factors** relating to the job should be stated. This will include whether it is done in isolation or as part of a team; the level in the organisation at which the job-holder interacts; and whether there is external contact, as with customers, for instance.

8   SELECTION INTERVIEWS

(a)   **Flaws in the one-to-one selection interview?**

   While not 'irredeemably' flawed (as will be suggested below), the one-to-one selection interview undoubtedly has limitations. It is barely better than pure chance at predicting a candidate's success in the job.

   The statement attributes this to the scope given to prejudice and favouritism. This is supported by the following observations.

   (i)   **Candidates can disguise their lack of knowledge**, in areas of which the interviewer also knows little and is therefore unable to challenge the candidate. Conversely, a candidate's knowledge may go untested or unrecognised by an interviewer who does not ask the right questions or appreciate the answers.

   (ii)   The **interviewer's perception may be selective or distorted**, due to stereotyping, personal prejudice or inadequate information, and this lack of objectivity may go unchallenged, since (s) he is the sole arbiter.

(iii)   The **greater opportunity to establish personal rapport** with the candidate may cause a **weakening of the interviewer's objective judgement**: (s)he may favour someone (s)he 'got on with', over someone who was better-qualified, but perceived as unresponsive. Again, there will be no counter- balancing view.

However, this is also an opportunity to observe and experience the candidate's **personality, rapport-building, image-projecting, influencing and communication skills** and self-concept and expression in action. The flaws of prejudice and favouritism are arguably in some interviewers - not in the interpersonal dynamic of the one-to-one interview itself, which can be an advantage.

(b)   **Alternatives to the one-to-one selection process**

Panel and selection-board interviews are designed to overcome the dangers of bias by providing a multiple (and therefore balanced) assessment. They have the additional advantage of allowing information gathering and provision by different stakeholders in the selection decision, at the same time. On the other hand, they are **more daunting for the candidate than a one-to-one interview**, offering less opportunity to assess the candidate's rapport- building skills, and potentially some performance distortion from nervous tension. The situation is **more formal and artificial**, and therefore potentially less relevant to job performance. The pressures favour individuals who are confident and extraverted - which may not be relevant to all positions for which they are being assessed.

Group selections, using role-play exercises, case studies and simulations, can offer more **extensive, 'live' opportunities to observe candidates' interpersonal skills** (and their reception by others in a team situation), problem-solving abilities and leadership potential, as well as their demonstrated knowledge/expertise and expressed attitudes. They may therefore be more relevant to the competency requirements of the job, as well as offering direct comparability between candidates. As a specialist tool, they are more frequently supported by trained assessors and prepared criteria and standards of assessment than one-to-one interviewing.

Testing of various kinds (psychometric, cognitive, aptitude, proficiency) are also alternatives to the one-to-one approach, and score relatively highly (.40 and above) on the predictive validity scale.

9   **EQUAL OPPORTUNITY**

(a)   **Causes of exclusion/segregation of women in employment**

(ii)   There are **continuing social pressures on women to bear and rear children**, and on the man to be the 'breadwinner'. Employers have assumed that women's paid work would be short-term or interrupted, and that training and development was not sound investment. In practice, child-bearing and family responsibilities do interrupt women's career progressions, or limit them to part-time employment which may restrict prospects for promotion.

(ii)   The 'heavy' nature of earlier industrial work placed legal restrictions on women's employment in areas such as mining, nightwork in factories and so on. This also contributed to the lack of organisation and trade union influence of women (except in segregated industries like textiles) up until the 1970s and '80s.

(iii)   Segregation, once established, tends to be self-perpetuating. Once an occupation becomes dominated by one sex, those of the opposite sex will tend to depart.

(iv)   Segregation is reinforced by stereotypical modelling of gender roles at home and in the education system. For example, lack of encouragement to girls to study maths and sciences has been evident even in the West, and in more traditional cultures, access to educational opportunities and career aspirations for women are severely restricted.

(v)   Career ladders (including, for example, apprenticeships) often fail to fast-track women.

(b)   **Reasons for concern**

Quite apart from any philosophical or humanitarian concerns about the stereotyping of gender roles and inequality of access to educational and career opportunities, there are 'business' reasons to address employment discrimination.

(i)   Stereotypical and discriminatory assumptions may lead organisations into illegal practices through indirect discrimination (as defined by the Sex Discrimination Acts) in which a policy or practice appears fair in form but is discriminatory in operation. This in turn has negative consequences in terms of legal costs and damaged reputation, possibly with knock-on problems in attracting skilled female staff.

(ii)   Women make up a high proportion of the consumer base. In societies where equal opportunity has a high profile, women may exercise protest influence by choosing to purchase from less discriminatory competitors.

(iii)   Women make up a significant proportion of the workforce, if not in managerial grades: by perceived discriminatory policies and practices, the organisation may reduce its ability to attract and retain skilled female employees in the support, HR and other areas in which it relies on their contribution. In other words, it may damage its 'employer brand'.

(iv)   In times of persistent skill and local labour shortages – despite overall decline in the demand for labour – organisations can ill afford to overlook or alienate a significant source of ability and experience, particularly where there is potential for enriching business practice with additional or alternative viewpoints and strengths. A recent report in *Personnel Management*, for example, suggested that women had been instrumental in increasing 'emotional intelligence' in business.

10   LEARNING STYLE

(a)   **Honey and Mumford**

The way in which people learn best will differ according to the type of person. That is, there are learning styles which suit different individuals. Peter Honey and Alan Mumford have drawn up a popular classification of four learning styles.

(i)   **Theorists** seek to understand basic principles and to take an intellectual, 'hands-off' approach based on logical argument. They prefer training to be:

- Programmed and structured
- Designed to allow time for analysis
- Provided by teachers who share his/her preference for concepts and analysis

(ii)   **Reflectors**

- Observe phenomena, think about them and then choose how to act
- Need to work at their own pace
- Find learning difficult if forced into a hurried programme
- Produce carefully thought-out conclusions after research and reflection
- Tend to be fairly slow, non-participative (unless to ask questions) and cautious

(iii)   **Activists**

- Deal with practical, active problems and do not have patience with theory
- Require training based on hands-on experience
- Are excited by participation and pressure, such as new projects
- Flexible and optimistic, but tend to rush at something without due preparation

(iv)   **Pragmatists**

- Only like to study if they can see its direct link to practical problems
- Good at learning new techniques in on-the-job training
- Aim is to implement action plans and/or do the task better
- May discard good ideas which only require some development

Training programmes should ideally be designed to accommodate the preferences of all four styles. This can often be overlooked especially as the majority of training staff are activists.

(b)   **Kolb** suggests that effective learning takes place in a cycle of four phases.

(i)   The first stage is to be involved in a new experience.

(ii)   The second stage is to review and reflect upon the experience.

(iii)   The third stage is to use concepts and theories to integrate the experience and the reflection.

(iv)   The final stage is one of application: to make use of the integrated for planning and decision making in new situations involving new experiences. Kolb felt that some people have a preference for a particular phase and so do not complete the cycle. They thus do not learn as effectively as they might. Honey and Mumford identified four learning styles that correspond to the four phases of Kolb's cycle and can be used to design effective learning events.

11   PERFORMANCE MANAGEMENT

(a)   **The difference between a 'performance appraisal' and a 'performance management approach**

Performance appraisal is traditionally a process whereby the performance of employees, over the past year, is assessed according to various criteria (from personality factors to more effective key results indicators), for a variety of purposes, including reward-setting, identification of training needs and standard- setting.

Performance management is a process of continuous collaborative planning and control, whereby managers and individuals or teams jointly set key accountabilities, objectives, measures and priorities for performance and performance improvement, and review and adjust performance on an on-going basis.

Key differences in these approaches

(i)   The emphasis of **appraisal was primarily retrospective**. Performance management focuses on the following review period, and on progress towards continuous improvement goals, and is therefore more forward-looking, pro-active and stimulating in its orientation.

(ii)   **Appraisals have traditionally been held annually**, especially where they are tied in to pay awards. Performance management is an on-going control system, with in-built feedback and review timescales.

(iii)   Appraisal, at its most positive and solution-focused, can concentrate exclusively on the (personal) development and reward aspirations of the employee, at the expense of the need to **add value to the business**.

(iv)   Performance management is more thoroughly focused on performance, through the integration of employee improvement and reward goals with the strategic objectives of the business.

Further difference in practice will be discussed in section (c).

(b)   **Reasons for the shift towards 'performance management'**

(i)   Competitive pressures make continuous improvement a condition of survival.

(ii)   It is now realised that **strategic objectives** can be more effectively implemented by linking them to individual objectives.

(iii)   The new **focus on quality** has necessitated the feeding through of new quality standards to performance management processes.

(iv)   **Performance-related pay** is being used more widely, necessitating clear objectives, measures and time scales.

Increased employee expectations and increased competitive pressures have led to a recognition that business success requires both attention to employee development and satisfaction and the requirement that employees 'add value' to the business. Performance management focuses on both, by dovetailing employee objectives, problem- solving and developmental goals with the strategic objectives of the organisation.

12   **OFFICE RISKS**   *8 mins*

You perhaps associate risk in the workplace with building sites or factories with heavy machinery or coal mines, but assuming you work in an office of some sort you need only look about you to find many potential **sources of injury** or **ill-health.**

- Slippery or uneven floors
- Frayed carpets
- Trailing electric leads, telephone cables and other wires
- Obstacles (boxes, files, books, open drawers) in gangways
- Standing on chairs (particularly swivel chairs) to each high shelving
- Blocked staircases, for example where they are used for extra storage space
- Lifting heavy items without bending properly
- Removing the safety guard on a machine to free a blockage or to make it run faster
- Using chemicals without protective clothing or adequate ventilation
- Taking inadequate word breaks, allowing excessive exposure or strain

Sometimes none of these things are needed to cause an accident: it is very easy to do it without props. Carelessness or foolishness are major causes of accidents. Practical jokes and cutting corners in work practices can have unforeseen consequences.

13   REWARDS

(a)   **Intrinsic rewards** are those which arise from the performance of the work itself. They are therefore psychological rather than material and relate to the concept of job satisfaction. Intrinsic rewards include the satisfaction that comes from completing a piece of work, the status that certain jobs convey, the feeling of achievement that comes from doing a difficult job well. Intrinsic rewards tend to be associated with **autonomy** in the planning and execution of work.

(b)   **Extrinsic rewards** are separate from the job itself and dependent on the decisions of others. Pay, benefits and working conditions are all examples of extrinsic rewards.

(c)   **Rewards**

- Pay
- Bonuses
- A car
- Medical insurance
- Pension scheme
- Subsidised canteen facilities
- Working clothing such as uniform, but not safety equipment
- Share option schemes
- Subsidised loans and mortgages
- Subsidised transport to and from work
- Assistance with child care
- Holiday entitlement

BPP note. An incredibly easy question: 9 marks for a simple list you could jot down in half the time.

14   LEADERSHIP STYLES

The range of leadership styles

The 'range' of leadership styles a manager may display may be discussed across the body of leadership style theories, taking in, for example, the following different classifications.

(a)   Huneryager and Heckman: dictatorial, autocratic, democratic, laissez-faire

(b)   The Ashridge Studies: tells, sells, consults, joins

(c)   Douglas McGregor: Theory X and Y

(d)   Tannenbaum and Schmidt: a continuum between autocratic and democratic

(e)   Rensis Likert: exploitative-authoritative, benevolent-authoritative, consultative- authoritative and participative

(f)   FE Fiedler: psychologically distant or close

Broadly, the classifications are based on continuums from authoritarian to democratic (or 'tight' to 'loose' control) and from wholly task-focused to wholly people-focused.

We will describe the range of style across one such continuum.

The research unit at Ashridge Management College carried out studies in UK industry in the 1960s and identified four styles.

(a)   The autocratic or 'tells' style. This is characterised by one-way communication between the manager and subordinate, with the manager telling the subordinate what to do. The leader makes all decisions and issues instructions, without consultation, and expecting compliance.

(b)   The persuasive or 'sells' style. The manager still makes all the decisions, but believes that subordinates need to be motivated to accept them before complying. (S)he therefore tries to explain instructions and decisions in an effort to get subordinates' agreement and co-operation.

BPP
PUBLISHING

(c) The 'consults' style. This involves discussion between the leader and the subordinates who will be involved in carrying out a decision, while the leader retains authority to make the decision. By consulting before making the decision, the leader takes account of subordinates' attitudes and feedback. Consultation is a form of limited participation in decision making for team members - but it is easily 'faked', if the leader has already made up his or her mind before 'asking' the group: a facade for a 'sells' style'.

(d) The democratic or 'joins' style. This is an approach whereby the leader empowers the team to make a decision on the basis of consensus or agreement. It is the most democratic style of leadership identified by the study. Subordinates with the greatest understanding of the problem will have most influence over the decision. The joins style is therefore most effective where all members of a team are able to contribute.

15   COMMUNICATION

(a) Communication is the process of **transferring information** from one person to another. In an organisational context, communication may be internal, as when colleagues discuss a problem, or it may be that the participants are representatives of their organisations, as when a credit control manager writes to a named manager in an overdue debtor organisation.

Organisations exist to achieve goals which individuals could not achieve independently. Communication is therefore **fundamental** to their operations. The classic managerial functions of planning, organising, directing and controlling depend on the manager's ability to communicate requirements and information and to obtain reports. Other management responsibilities such as motivating, training and counselling depend equally upon clear communication.

It is in the general area of human behaviour and relations that **manner, tone and body language** become important supplements to the written or spoken word. This applies equally to managers and to members of work groups who must communicate with one another.

If communication is not clear, there will be bias, omission and distortion. Confusion, conflict and stress arise as a result.

(b) The two main methods of communication are **speech** and **writing**. Both may be used between individuals, as in the interview or personal letter, or by an individual to more than one person, as in the lecture or circulated memo.

The two basic methods vary in their effect and usefulness in different situations. Speech is immediate and tone, manner and body language can be used to enhance its impact. Feedback can be instant and a disciplined discussion can cover a lot of ground rapidly. The written word is easier to use with precision, though this takes time, practise and ability. It is inherently capable of repeated reference using the simplest technology; speech requires electronic equipment such as a video system if its full impact is to be recorded.

A wide range of media may be used for both spoken and written communications. Some are listed below.

Speech may be used face-to-face, on the telephone, on video (including video conferencing) on public address and loudspeaker systems and on radio broadcast.

Writing is used in paper communications of all kinds, including letters, memos, procedure manuals, forms and books. It is also used in e-mail, fax and telex systems and in pager systems.

(c) Good communication is essential to getting any job done: co-operation is impossible without it. Difficulties occur because of **general faults** in the communication process:

- Distortion or omission of information by the sender

- Misunderstanding due to lack of clarity or technical jargon

- Non-verbal signs (gesture, posture, facial expression) contradicting the verbal message, so that its meaning is in doubt

- 'Overload' - a person being given too much information to digest in the time available

- Differences in social, racial or educational background, compounded by age and personality differences, creating barriers to understanding and co-operation

- People hearing only what they want to hear in a message

(b) There may also be **particular difficulties** in a work situation

- A general tendency to distrust a message in its re-telling from one person to another, (eg a subordinate mistrusting his superior and looking for 'hidden meanings' in a message)

- The relative status in the hierarchy of the sender and receiver of information (a senior manager's words are listened to more closely and a colleague's perhaps discounted)

- People from different job or specialist backgrounds (accountants, personnel managers, DP experts) having difficulty in talking on a non-specialist's wavelength

- People or departments having different priorities or perspectives so that one person places more or less emphasis on a situation than another

- Conflict in the organisation. Where there is conflict between individuals or departments, communications will be withdrawn and information withheld

16 DISCIPLINE MISTAKES

(a) **Common mistakes**

(i) Not following the right procedure. Most firms have a disciplinary procedure, commencing with verbal warnings, followed by more formal written warnings if the 'offence' is repeated. Failure to follow this procedure can invalidate the process.

(ii) Failure to investigate the problem properly and prejudging the issue. As it is a serious matter, the 'offence' should be properly investigated. Facts are often in dispute. This is especially a problem in the existence of a personality clash between manager and subordinate.

(iii) Confusing disciplinary with appraisal interviews. An appraisal is an ongoing process to review past performance with a view to improving it, even though, if performance is not up to scratch, this can also result in dismissal. A disciplinary interview is generally the result of a specific issue.

(iv) Failure to keep records and to follow-up. To be successful the disciplinary interview must have a result, even if this is only a mild rebuke or an acceptance that there has been a problem disciplinary interview.

(b) **Fundamental criteria of a disciplinary procedure**

(i) Immediacy - disciplinary action needs to be speedy, so that the action and the 'offence' are related to each other. A time lapse can make it harder to take action. However, investigation can take time and in some cases a person might be suspended on full pay pending the results of the enquiry.

(ii) Advance warning. Employees should know what the rules are and managers should make clear that everybody knows what is expected from them. Also, the details of the procedure should be laid down in the staff handbook.

(iii) Consistency. Each time an infraction occurs, disciplinary action should result. Inconsistency leads to charges of favouritism and even discrimination. Also standards will fall to that of the lowest common denominator.

(iv) Impersonality. The disciplinary action should be directed at the offence not the person. Penalties should be based on the offence. However, the offence will remain on file, and any repetition will lead to more serious consequences.

(v) Privacy. As far as possible, discipline should be private affair to avoid excess humiliation and the resentment it causes and the creation of a 'martyr'.

17 SCENARIO: ACCOUNTS CLERK

(a) **Deborah's case for a new staff member**

Staff are a major element of **cost** and headcount should be subject to careful control. In a large, mature organisation with established procedures and methods, the **human resource plan** or establishment document would lay down the staff requirements for the accounts department.

Permission to recruit would depend on either a member of staff having left (staff **turnover**), or the **expansion of the department's task**. The latter might result from organisational growth or, particularly in the case of an accounts department, from the increasing burden of government-imposed work, as with the maintenance of working time records, for instance. Where the task had expanded, the human resource plan would have to be amended.

However, SMG Limited 'has no formal procedures or processes' for recruitment and, therefore, reference to an agreed establishment is not possible. It will be for Deborah Williams to demonstrate just why she thinks that the accounts staff are overworked before recruitment is authorised.

Another way would be to look to see if the accounts department can be run more efficiently. An examination of its procedures would be extremely time consuming and probably beyond the capacity of a human resources specialist. However, it may be possible to carry out a job analysis in broad terms if the department is not too large. This would attempt to measure the volume and nature of the work flowing through the office by collecting information from four sources:

Documentation, such as forms and instructions

Interviews with managers and supervisors

Interviews with job holders

Observation

If it is found that this is not possible, the **fall-back position would be for Deborah Williams to justify the recruitment in concrete terms.** However, because Deborah Williams is a **director** of the company, a recently appointed assistant manager in HR would find it difficult to demand such a justification. A suitable procedure would probably have to be established by agreement among the directors: perhaps Deborah has the authority anyway.

(b) **Procedures to appoint a qualified accounts clerk**

Step 1. Obtain agreement that there is a vacancy – already presupposed from the question.

Step 2. Clearly detail the total mix of tasks to be carried out in the department, including work that is not being done owing to lack of resources.

Step 3. Assess whether current employees have the competences currently to carry out all the tasks, or whether these can be developed.

Step 4. Assess whether the current allocation of work amongst employees genuinely reflects their competences. Could there be greater job specialisation?

Step 5. Assess the future needs of the department in terms of the quality and nature of competences required.

Step 6. Identify the mix of training and resourcing needs necessary to carry out the department's task.

Step 7. Develop or revise job descriptions based on the roles currently performed in the department. Existing members of staff will welcome clear descriptions of what is expected of them if roles are to change.

Step 8. Develop person specification as the basis of the recruitment and selection process, based on the job descriptions and required competences which are going to be met by recruitment.

Step 9. Develop plan for recruitment and selection of new staff, if this is the preferred way of matching the resource and competences of the department with the work expected of it.

Step 10. Implement the plan (see part (d) of this answer).

The process involves **two types of company policy**.

(i) The procedures manual, which deals with the steps gone through, any legal requirements (guaranteeing conformance with equal opportunities legislation)

(ii) The human resources plan, which details the overall requirements for employees, investment in training and so on.

(c) **Job description and person specification**

A **job description** is a statement of the tasks, responsibilities and working relationships making up a job. At lower levels it will concentrate on the specification of duties, but at managerial levels it is likely to be written in broader terms dealing with scope and responsibilities. It forms an important part of the documentation needed by a complex organisation, since, in combination with other job descriptions, it defines how work is done.

A **person specification** details the personal qualities, abilities, qualifications and experience required of the holder of a job. A job description is useful in several human resource management contexts, including recruitment, appraisal and career development. A person specification, on the other hand, is rarely useful for anything other than recruitment.

Since it is rare to find a perfect fit between any job and its holder, the task of recruitment is eased if the job description is divided into core and peripheral elements. This allows the features of the person specification to be divided into those that are essential and those that are merely desirable. This split makes it easier to select the best person for the job when no ideal candidate applies.

(d) **Recruitment and selection of the clerk**

The recruitment and selection process is based on the needs of the department, and the state of the labour market. There are a number of different steps. Once it has been decided that recruiting a new member of staff (rather than redeploying current members) is the right course then the following steps should be taken.

Step 1. Obtain job description, which details job content, responsibilities, and the job's relation to other positions in the department, authorisation limits. It might be phrased in more general terms as an accountability profile.

Step 2. If a person specification has not yet been drawn up, identify the type of candidate suitable for the job, noting essential attributes (eg for an accounts clerk post, the firm may require a candidate with the ACCA's Certified Accounting Technician qualification), desirable attributes (eg experience in a similar **company**) and contra-indications (ie matters that would rule out the candidate, for example no work experience at all).

Step 3. Identify appropriate media for recruitment. To reach the right people, the firm has to find the right medium.

The firm could use a **recruitment agency** to suggest suitable candidates already on their books, to do some preliminary screening and to suggest a shortlist.

The firm may choose to **advertise**. The job advertisement will cover details of the role and the company and should be targeted at the target candidates, with an attractive, but realistic, description of the company and role; salary details may also be included. Most importantly, contact details and the desired manner of application (eg letter and cv, or application form) must be made clear.

Step 4. Place the advertisement in suitable **publications** (such as newspapers, professional journals). The firm might also use **government employment offices** (job centres, in the UK). Moreover, firms are increasingly advertising on the **Internet**, either on their own websites or via recruitment services (often owned or run by newspaper groups) such as workthing.com.

Step 5. Review application forms/cvs received. As a matter of courtesy all applicants should receive a reply; some may be rejected out of hand; others may be told that their application has been received and is being reviewed. Application forms are a standard way of gathering data, for comparison, and also to require candidates to answer specific questions, to collect data about qualifications and experience and to allow the candidate to write about themselves and why the want the position.

Step 6. Shortlist desirable candidates and contact them to arrange interviews. Write to unsuccessful candidates

Step 7. Interviews and tests

Most firms use the interview as the heart of their recruitment procedures even though it is not reliable as a predictor of job performance. It does enable a firm to assess some of the candidate's interpersonal skills. A mixture of open and closed questions should be used. The interview is also an opportunity for the candidate to talk about the role

Step 8. **Tests**

A variety of tests can be employed, often relating to the task to be done. This may be of limited relevance to an accounts position where work experience can be validated.

However, it should be possible to assess basic numeracy. A person with a technician or professional qualification may have a training record which can be used as evidence of competence. More complicated tests (psychometric etc) are not appropriate for this position.

Step 9. **Make offer, subject to references**

References are of limited value, but they can be used to check the candidate's basic honesty (eg in seeing that the candidate's past employment history is truthful, that the candidate worked in a the positions and over the timescales mentioned).

The offer of employment may contain contractual details.

Step 10. **Induction**

When the new employee starts, he/she needs to become familiar with the firm.

(e)   Training and development are usually regarded as two different things.

Training is the process by which workpeople are taught job-related skills.

Development is a more general process by which people are prepared for wider future responsibilities.

(i)   While it will be possible to establish very specific training objectives and to measure progress towards them in some detail, the objectives of development are likely to be more conceptual and progress may take a variety of forms.

(ii)   Both training and development are likely to offer benefits to the individual and to the organisation.

(iii)   Increased job competence makes the organisation more efficient. It also reduces stress on the individual and is a source of pride and competence and hence of motivation. The achievement of a specific qualification or level of competence may entitle the individual to a pay rise.

(iv)   Organisational flexibility is enhanced when staff are well trained, since they can deputise for absent colleagues and adapt rapidly to new procedures and other changing circumstances.

(v)   A programme of personal development contributes to succession and promotion planning.

(vi)   It helps with the identification of people with the potential for promotion.

(vii)   It provides promotees with at least some of the knowledge and skills they will need, so that they can tackle their new responsibilities with confidence.

(viii)   The efficiency of the organisation is thus enhanced, and the individuals concerned are advanced in their careers. Even if they are not promoted, they are likely to be more employable. This improves their job security within the organisation and their prospects elsewhere if they wish to move.

Index

Note: **Key Terms** and their page references are given in **bold**.

BPP
PUBLISHING

BPP PUBLISHING

Psychologically close managers (PCMs), 247
Psychologically distant managers (PDMs), 246
Public sector, 30
Pychometric testing, 139

Quality circle, **267**
Quality, 166
Questions, 135

Race, culture or religion, 59
Rationality, 22
Recruitment, 109
    advertising, 124
    and selection, 154
    consultants, 110
    policy, 113
    practices, 143
    process, 111
Rees, 272
References, 142
Reflectors, 175
Rehabilitation of Offenders, 153
Relationship behaviour, 247
Relationships, 255
Religion, 153
Remuneration, 9
Repetitive Strain Injury (or RSI), 204
Report, 270
Resistances, 254
Resource allocator, 36
Resource power, 75
Resource-investigator, 64
Resources, 40
Response to conflict, 283
Responsibility, 77
    without authority, 78
Results-orientated scheme, 188
Reward, 226
    system, 191
Rewarding teams, 71, 233
Rituals, 46
Rodger, 121
Role ambiguity, 60
Role culture, 47
Role set, 60
Role signs, 60
Role theory, 60
Rules, 22

Safety Representative Regulations, 201
Satisficing, 7
Saying no, 257
Scalar chain, 9, 13
Scheduling, 41
Scientific management, 31

Selection, 109
    boards, 137
    interview, 134
    methods, 134
    process, 129
    test, 139
Selective reporting, 263
Self discipline, 287
Self, 55
Self-appraisals, 188
Self-image, 55
Self-learning, 175
Senge, 176
Sensor/detector, 90
Service industries, 6
Seven Point Plan, 121
Sex Discrimination Act, 152
Sex, 59
Shamrock organisation (Handy's), 19
Shaper, 64
Shared objectives, 67
Sherif and Sherif, 281
Sick Building Syndrome, 211
Simon, 7
Skills, 168
Social responsibility, 91, 94
Social Trends, 148
Society, 50
Socio-technical systems, 25
Span of control, 12
Specialisation, 22
Specialist newspapers or magazines, 126
Specialist, 64
Spokesperson, 35
Staff appraisal system, 183
Staff authority, 76
Stakeholders, 29
Sternberg, Elaine, 94
Standards, 89
Standing aims and objectives, 96
Stewart, 37
Storming, 66
Strategic alliances, 37
Strategic apex, 10
Stress management, 210
Structure, 51
Style theories, 238
Subordination of individual interests, 9
Supervision, 38
Supervisor, 42
    job, 38
Supervisors, managers and training, 178
Support staff, 10
Suppression, 283
Symbols, 46
Synergy, 37

BPP PUBLISHING

REVIEW FORM & FREE PRIZE DRAW

All original review forms from the entire BPP range, completed with genuine comments, will be entered into a draw on 31 January 2002 and 31 July 2002. The names on the first four forms picked out will be sent a cheque for £50.

Name: _____ Address: _____

_____

How have you used this Text?
(Tick one box only)

☐ Home study (book only)

☐ On a course: college _____

☐ With 'correspondence' package

☐ Other _____

Why did you decide to purchase this Text?
(Tick one box only)

☐ Have used complementary Study Text

☐ Have used BPP Texts in the past

☐ Recommendation by friend/colleague

☐ Recommendation by a lecturer at college

☐ Saw advertising

☐ Other _____

During the past six months do you recall seeing/receiving any of the following?
(Tick as many boxes as are relevant)

☐ Our advertisement in *ACCA Students' Newsletter*

☐ Our advertisement in *Pass*

☐ Our brochure with a letter through the post

Which (if any) aspects of our advertising do you find useful?
(Tick as many boxes as are relevant)

☐ Prices and publication dates of new editions

☐ Information on Text content

☐ Facility to order books off-the-page

☐ None of the above

Have you used the companion Kit/Passcard/Video/Tape * for this subject? ☐ Yes ☐ No
(* Please circle)

Your ratings, comments and suggestions would be appreciated on the following areas

	Very useful	Useful	Not useful
Introductory section (Key study steps, personal study)	☐	☐	☐
Chapter introductions	☐	☐	☐
Key terms	☐	☐	☐
Quality of explanations	☐	☐	☐
Case examples and other examples	☐	☐	☐
Questions and answers in each chapter	☐	☐	☐
Chapter roundups	☐	☐	☐
Quick quizzes	☐	☐	☐
Exam focus points	☐	☐	☐
Question bank	☐	☐	☐
Answer bank	☐	☐	☐
List of key terms and index	☐	☐	☐
Icons	☐	☐	☐
Mind maps	☐	☐	☐

	Excellent	Good	Adequate	Poor
Overall opinion of this Text	☐	☐	☐	☐

Do you intend to continue using BPP Products? ☐ Yes ☐ No

Please note any further comments and suggestions/errors on the reverse of this page. The BPP author of this edition can be e-mailed at: glennhaldane@bpp.com

Please return to: Katy Hibbert, ACCA Range Manager, BPP Publishing Ltd, FREEPOST, London, W12 8BR

REVIEW FORM & FREE PRIZE DRAW (continued)

Please note any further comments and suggestions/errors below

FREE PRIZE DRAW RULES

1   Closing date for 31 July 2002 draw is 30 June 2002. Closing date for 31 January 2002 draw is 31 December 2001.

2   No purchase necessary. Entry forms are available upon request from BPP Publishing. No more than one entry per title, per person. Draw restricted to persons aged 16 and over.

3   Winners will be notified by post and receive their cheques not later than 6 weeks after the draw date.

4   The decision of the promoter in all matters is final and binding. No correspondence will be entered into.

See overleaf for information on other
BPP products and how to order

ACCA Order – New Syllabus

To BPP Publishing Ltd, Aldine Place, London W12 8AA

Tel: 020 8740 2211. Fax: 020 8740 1184

Mr/Mrs/Ms (Full name)

Daytime delivery address

Postcode

Daytime Tel

Date of exam (month/year)

	2/01 Texts	9/01 Kits	9/01 Psscrds	MCQ cards	Tapes	Videos
PART 1						
1.1 Preparing Financial Statements	£19.95	£10.95	£5.95	£5.95	£12.95	£25.00
1.2 Financial Information for Management	£19.95	£10.95	£5.95	£5.95	£12.95	£25.00
1.3 Managing People	£19.95	£10.95	£5.95		£12.95	£25.00
PART 2						
2.1 Information Systems	£19.95	£10.95	£5.95		£12.95	£25.00
2.2 Corporate and Business Law (6/01)	£19.95	£10.95	£5.95		£12.95	£25.00
2.3 Business Taxation FA 2000 (for 12/01 exam)	£19.95 (4/01)	£10.95 (4/01)	£5.95 (4/01)		£12.95	£25.00
2.4 Financial Management and Control	£19.95	£10.95	£5.95		£12.95	£25.00
2.5 Financial Reporting (6/01)	£19.95	£10.95	£5.95		£12.95	£25.00
2.6 Audit and Internal Review (6/01)	£19.95	£10.95	£5.95		£12.95	£25.00
PART 3						
3.1 Audit and Assurance Services (6/01)	£20.95	£10.95	£5.95		£12.95	£25.00
3.2 Advanced Taxation FA 2000 (for 12/01 exam)	£20.95 (4/01)	£10.95 (4/01)	£5.95 (4/01)		£12.95	£25.00
3.3 Performance Management	£20.95	£10.95	£5.95		£12.95	£25.00
3.4 Business Information Management	£20.95	£10.95	£5.95		£12.95	£25.00
3.5 Strategic Business Planning and Development	£20.95	£10.95	£5.95		£12.95	£25.00
3.6 Advanced Corporate Reporting (6/01)	£20.95	£10.95	£5.95		£12.95	£25.00
3.7 Strategic Financial Management	£20.95	£10.95	£5.95		£12.95	£25.00
INTERNATIONAL STREAM						
1.1 Preparing Financial Statements	£19.95	£10.95	£5.95	£5.95		
2.5 Financial Reporting (6/01)	£19.95	£10.95	£5.95			
2.6 Audit and Internal Review (6/01)	£19.95	£10.95	£5.95			
3.1 Audit and Assurance services (6/01)	£20.95	£10.95	£5.95			
3.6 Advanced Corporate Reporting (6/01)	£20.95	£10.95	£5.95			
SUCCESS IN YOUR RESEARCH AND ANALYSIS PROJECT						
Tutorial Text (9/00)	£19.95					

SUBTOTAL £

POSTAGE & PACKING

Study Texts

	First	Each extra	
UK	£3.00	£2.00	£
Europe*	£5.00	£4.00	£
Rest of world	£20.00	£10.00	£

Kits/Passcards/Success Tapes/MCQ cards

	First	Each extra	
UK	£2.00	£1.00	£
Europe*	£2.50	£1.00	£
Rest of world	£15.00	£8.00	£

Breakthrough Videos

	First	Each extra	
UK	£2.00	£2.00	£
Europe*	£2.00	£2.00	£
Rest of world	£20.00	£10.00	£

Grand Total (Cheques to *BPP Publishing*) I enclose a cheque for (incl. Postage) **£**

Or charge to Access/Visa/Switch

Card Number

Expiry date   Start Date

Issue Number (Switch Only)

Signature

We aim to deliver to all UK addresses inside 5 working days; a signature will be required. Orders to all EU addresses should be delivered within 6 working days. All other orders to overseas addresses should be delivered within 8 working days. * Europe includes the Republic of Ireland and the Channel Islands.